THE BLESSING AND THE CURSE

The Blessing and The Curse

Trajectories in the Theology
of the Old Testament

JEFF S. ANDERSON

CASCADE *Books* · Eugene, Oregon

THE BLESSING AND THE CURSE
Trajectories in the Theology of the Old Testament

Cascade Books
An Imprint of Wipf and Stock Publishers
199 W. 8th Ave., Suite 3
Eugene, OR 97401

www.wipfandstock.com

ISBN 13: 978-1-62032-821-7

Cataloguing-in-Publication data:

Anderson, Jeff S.

The blessing and the curse : trajectories in the theology of the
Old Testament / Jeff S. Anderson.

xii + 404 pp. ; 23 cm. Includes bibliographical references and indexes.

ISBN 13: 978-1-62032-821-7

1. Bible. Old Testament—Theology. 2. Blessing and cursing in the Bible. 3. Bible. Old Testament—Criticism and interpretation. I. Title.

BS1192.5 A1 A54 2014

Manufactured in the U.S.A.

Permissions

Contents

Contents

Acknowledgments

A PROJECT LIKE THIS is never a unilateral enterprise. I am thankful to Wayland Baptist University for providing the generous time and financial support during a sabbatical in the summer and fall of 2012. This institution has influenced my life in more ways than I can imagine and provided opportunities to me and many others like me, well beyond the geographical confines of Wayland's respective campuses.

During my time in Jerusalem as a Senior Associate Fellow at the W. F. Albright Institute of Archaeological Research, Dr. Sy Gitin and his staff went out of their way to provide an extensive research library, opportunities for lectures and seminars, plus venues to gain some needed hands-on experience in archaeology. The Albright's proximity to major research libraries, its culture of camaraderie, and location at the heart of the land of the Bible benefited this project significantly.

Fr. Pawel Trzopek, OP, and his helpful staff at the École Biblique et Archéologique Française provided the resources of one of the premier biblical and theological research libraries in the world. The beautiful grounds at the École Biblique offered respite between periods of study. The Judaica collection at the National Library of Israel, located on the Givat Ram Campus of the Hebrew University of Jerusalem, along with the Judaica reading room there provided the resources of their vast and varied collection.

I am thankful for several friends and colleagues who assisted in reviewing various chapters of this manuscript: Loren Crow, Kathy Maxwell, Nathan Maxwell, and Carolyn Ratcliffe. While I take full responsibility for the finished product, their input was useful and needed. I am also thankful for my colleague Don Ashley, who covered some of my classes as well as ministry responsibilities in my absence.

Most of all, I'm thankful to my wife, B. J., who kept the home fires burning in my absence.

Abbreviations

ATANT	Abhandlungen zur Theologie des Alten und Neuen Testaments
AnBib	Analecta Biblica
AB	Anchor Bible
ABD	*Anchor Bible Dictionary*. Edited by D. N. Freedman. 6 vols. New York, 1992
AOAT	Alter Orient und Altes Testament
ANET	*Ancient Near Eastern Texts Relating to the Old Testament*. Edited by J. B. Prichard. 3rd ed. Princeton, 1969
AGJU	Arbeiten zur Geschichte des antiken Judentums und des Urchristentums
BZAW	Beihefte zur Zeitschrift für die alttestamentliche Wissenschaft
BZNW	Beihefte zur Zeitschrift für die neutestamentliche Wissenschaft
BRev	*Bible Review*
BHS	*Biblia Hebraica Stuttgartensia*. Edited by K. Elliger and W. Rudolph. Stuttgart, 1983
Bib	*Biblica*
BAR	*Biblical Archaeological Review*
BibInt	*Biblical Interpretation*
BIS	Biblical Interpretation Series
BETL	Bibliotheca Ephemeridum theologicarum Lovaniensium
BJS	Brown Judaic Studies
BDB	F. Brown, S. R. Driver, and C. A. Briggs. *A Hebrew and English Lexicon of the Old Testament*. Oxford, 1907
BBR	*Bulletin for Biblical Research*
BBRSup	Bulletin for Biblical Research Supplements`
BASOR	*Bulletin of the American Schools of Oriental Research*
CTJ	*Calvin Theological Journal*
CBQ	*Catholic Biblical Quarterly*
DSD	*Dead Sea Discoveries*
EAJT	*East Asia Journal of Theology*
EuroJTh	*European Journal of Theology*
ExpTim	*Expository Times*
FAT	Forschungen zum Alten Testament
GBS	Guides to Biblical Scholarship
HR	*Harvard Review*
HSM	Harvard Semitic Monographs

HAR	*Hebrew Annual Review*
HUCA	*Hebrew Union College Annual*
Hen	*Henoch*
Int	*Interpretation*
IBC	Interpretation: A Bible Commentary for Teaching and Preaching
IBS	*Irish Biblical Studies*
IDB	*The Interpreter's Dictionary of the Bible.* Edited by G. A. Buttrick. 4 vols. Nashville, 1962
JBQ	*Jewish Bible Quarterly*
JSJ	*Journal for the Study of Judaism*
JSNT	*Journal for the Study of the New Testament*
JSOT	*Journal for the Study of the Old Testament*
JSOTSup	Journal for the Study of the Old Testament Supplement Series
JAAR	*Journal of the American Academy of Religion*
JAOS	*Journal of the American Oriental Society*
JBL	*Journal of Biblical Literature*
JESHO	*Journal of the Economic and Social History of the Orient*
JHS	*Journal of Hellenic Studies*
JR	*Journal of Religion*
JETS	*Journal of the Evangelical Theological Society*
JTS	*Journal of Theological Studies*
KTU	*Keilalphabetische Texte aus Ugarit*
Levant	*Levant*
NEA	*Near Eastern Archaeology*
NCB	New Century Bible
NICOT	New International Commentary on the Old Testament
NIB	*New Interpreter's Bible*
NTS	*New Testament Studies*
NovT	*Novum Testamentum*
NovTSup	Novum Testamentum Supplements
OTE	*Old Testament Essays*
OTL	Old Testament Library
OBT	Overtures to Biblical Theology
SBL	Society of Biblical Literature
SBLDS	Society of Biblical Literature Dissertation Series
SBLMS	Society of Biblical Literature Monograph Series
SBLSymS	Society of Biblical Literature Symposium Series
Semeia	*Semeia*
SJOT	*Scandinavian Journal of the Old Testament*
SwJT	*Southwestern Journal of Theology*
ST	*Studia theologica*
STDJ	Studies on the Texts of the Desert of Judah
NovTSup	Supplements to Novum Testamentum
VTSup	Supplements to Vetus Testamentum
TDOT	*Theological Dictionary of the Old Testament.* Edited by G. J. Botterweck, H. Ringgren, and H.-J. Fabry. Translated by J. T. Willis, G. W. Bromiley, and D. E. Green. 15 vols. Grand Rapids, 1974–
TS	*Theological Studies*
TynBul	*Tyndale Bulletin*

Abbreviations

1

The Challenges of Old Testament Theology

Five Challenges in Old Testament Theology

THERE IS A NEW pluralism in the discipline of Old Testament theology today, with a fresh set of challenges. These challenges are not, however, because of a dearth of interest in the discipline. This pluralism signals no disaster; in fact, it is good fortune.[1] Interest in Old Testament theology appears to be as active as ever. Yet scholars, for better or worse, have been unable to reach much of a consensus on virtually any subject related to the discipline. Perhaps this is no surprise. The lack of scholarly consensus tends all too often to lead to embattled silence, where the results of one's research seldom produces true dialogue with others in and outside the discipline, and even less often trickles down to the realm of practical theology. One octogenarian minister I knew quipped about dearth of application in biblical scholarship today, "There is plenty of heat generated but not much light by individuals with a lot of degrees but not much temperature."

Giants in the discipline have also lamented this impasse. Brevard Childs used the term "stalemate" to describe the seeming inability to come to virtually any kind of consensus.[2] Leo Perdue likened the myriad

---

1. Gerstenberger, *Theologies in the Old Testament*, 284.
2. Childs, *Biblical Theology in Crisis*.

of diverse voices in biblical theology to a tower of Babel, with articulations that command no consensus, ignore alternative approaches, and draw no overwhelming following.[3] R. N. Whybray described Old Testament theology as a mythical beast whose hunters cannot even agree on the exact nature of that beast. The reason is precisely because this beast, as painful as it might be to admit it, does not exist.[4] There are many disparate voices in the enterprise of biblical theology, and intense theological ferment is the order of the day. The history of the present debate has been rehearsed at length in numerous sources, and I will review only a few of the most vexing questions in this introductory chapter.[5]

Why write an Old Testament theology that traces trajectories of a theme such as blessings and curses through pertinent texts of the Bible? While biblical theology may be in "crisis," it is by no means stagnant. Theological tastes have begun to change. Interest remains high. The biblical-theology movement of the past is dead, and we are now off on a mergent venture. After a lifetime of reflection on the discipline of Old Testament theology, James Barr wrote the following hard-nosed assessment about the contested nature of the discipline,

> If there is any theme that runs through this work, it is the *contested* character of biblical theology, as it has been in this century. Biblical theology has had its enthusiasts, who cannot understand why anyone would question its validity as a subject; it has also had its opponents, some of whom consider it to be impracticable as an area of research, or unacceptable as an academic subject, or useless to the religious community, or all three of these. It is my belief that these elements of opposition have to be faced and understood, and that the understanding of them may paradoxically assist in the continuance and future prosperity of biblical theology, or of something like it.[6]

It is those last few words, "or of something like it," that, to my mind, are most telling. What is biblical theology, or something like it? It is like the story of a sculptor, when asked how he produced such exquisite beauty from a nondescript piece of stone, blithely mused that he simply eliminated

---

3. Perdue, *The Collapse of History*, 7.

4. Whybray, "Old Testament Theology, a Non-Existent Beast?," 168–80.

5. See the helpful reader, Ollenburger, *Old Testament Theology: Flowering and Future*. Also see Perdue, "Old Testament Theology since Barth's *Epistle to the Romans*," 55–136. A brief survey of pertinent issues is present in, Martens, *God's Design*, 292–303.

6. Barr, *The Concept of Biblical Theology*, xiv.

everything in the stone that didn't look like the object he wanted to produce. Like that sculptor viewing the stone, Barr views the definition of biblical theology partly as a contrastive notion.

In some respects, the discipline can essentially be defined by what it is not. Just as the stone cannot be mistaken for the sculpture, certain important theological enterprises are not to be identified as biblical theology. Biblical theology, for example, is not exegesis, which revolves around a systematic analysis of a single passage of Scripture with a goal of reaching an informed understanding of that particular passage. Biblical theology is also not systematic theology, which seeks to understand interrelationships of biblical themes from both testaments through their historical and philosophical explications. Systematic theology, or the older designation, dogmatic theology, typically pursues five traditional thematic categories: God, humanity, salvation, God's people, and eschatology. These categories are imposed on the Bible's more nondescript theological message.

Dogmatic theology is typically not merely a descriptive task but has a normative function for the church or synagogue. Therefore, all virtuous theological reflection is ultimately practical. In many ways, systematic theology is a Western enterprise; it is a contemplative, reflective, systematic way of speaking about God. Biblical theology is also different from the nontheological study of the Bible—it takes a synchronic approach that primarily seeks to apply the Scriptures to one's own life and witness. Finally, biblical theology also differs from the study of the history of religion, a diachronic enterprise that seeks to describe the development of Israel's or the church's religious faith over time in comparison with the development of other cultures, theological movements, and religions.

Yet biblical theology need not be completely defined simply by what it is not. Biblical theology is unique in that it seeks to explore and investigate themes that arise directly from the Bible. Furthermore, it seeks to parse out the interrelationships of those themes. Properly employed, the discipline takes up biblical rather than philosophical categories. Consequently, the rubrics for organizing a biblical theology will be different from other theological methodologies. Rather than the standard categories of God, humanity, salvation, God's people, and eschatology provided by systematic theology, completely new rubrics, like those drawn here from the theme of blessings and curses, may be deployed by the biblical theologian. In some respects, biblical theology adopts a midpoint between exegesis and systematic theology. Old Testament theology, then, is one example of biblical theology; other examples include New Testament theology, the theology of Paul and John, the theology of the Old Testament prophets, and the like.

The Theological Challenge

A myriad of challenges present themselves when we seek to settle on a method for producing theological work on the Old Testament. I would like to pose these challenges in the next several sections below in the form of a handful of crucial questions. The first question is perhaps the most pertinent: Does the Old Testament contain theology at all? The word *theology* comes from two Greek roots: *theos*, which means "God," and *logos*, which means "a word." If theology is "a word about God," or even "God-talk," then from the outset one wonders to what extent the Old Testament is a proper source for the study of theology. To be sure, the Old Testament does speak a great deal about God. The Old Testament writers tell stories, present laws, express prophecies of hope and judgment. They cajole, lament, bless, and curse, but they do not *do* theology as such. These writers did not contemplate God from a theological perspective; they experienced God in personal vitality. Religious expressions or opinions such as those articulated in the Old Testament, even if argued strongly, are not necessarily theology as one considers it today. Today's discipline of theology is an analytical, contemplative, reflective, and therefore a deliberately reformulative way of speaking about God.

By its very nature the discipline of theology is, to be brutally frank, an artificial discipline. Two concepts illustrate this artificiality: categories and coherence.[7] First, to decide on the categories and structure for one's Old Testament theology is to impose something artificial on the literature from outside it. One would certainly hope that those categories and their general structure would accurately reflect the literary evidence found in the Old Testament, but the Old Testament is not organized in tight theological categories . . . or, frankly, in any sustained theological categories. Any attempt at imposing theological categories or organizational structure on this diverse collection of literature will always, at least to some extent, be reductionistic.[8] To those in the discipline I am saying nothing new here. Second, coherence represents the attempt to corral all the diversity of the Old Testament's writings and explain the relationship of these disparate parts to the whole of the Old Testament's message. As you might guess, attempts at providing coherence often lead to oversimplification, given the variety of Old Testament texts.

---

7. Perdue, "Old Testament Theology since Barth's *Epistle to the Romans*," 55–136.

8. Barr, *The Concept of Biblical Theology*, 546.

The Illusion of a Theological Center

Next question . . . Is it appropriate to speak about *the* theology of the Old Testament? In attempting to answer this question for himself, one of the pioneers of the discipline of Old Testament theology, Walther Eichrodt, quoted Adolph von Harnack: "the man who knows the religion of the Old Testament knows many."[9] Emil Brunner, likewise asserted, "There is no theology of the Old Testament."[10] I understand the complexity, but is there categorically no center to the theology of the Old Testament, no way of bringing some sense of order to the disparate texts in the Old Testament canon?

Particularly before the 1980s, and in some cases afterwards, scholars generally sought a way to describe the unity of Old Testament theology by seeking a center or a unifying theme that permeated the entire Old Testament. Some notable examples are covenant (Eichrodt), promise and fulfillment (Kaiser), communion (Vriezen), revelation (Vos), a God who acts (Wright), and election (Pruess). Gerhard von Rad, of course, was a notable exception to this trend. He argues that unlike the New Testament, the Old Testament lacks a coherent theological center. Instead, von Rad suggests that God's self-revelation is grounded in a theology of history founded on specific historical acts that revealed the hand of Yahweh at work.[11]

I often ask my students to distill the overarching theme of the Old Testament down to a few sentences. Initial attempts appear relatively straightforward until scrutinized by others in the class. Suggested themes of Torah, covenant, exodus, promised land, a holy people, and so forth, are all seemingly viable candidates for such an overarching theme. Yet every attempt at developing a central theme leads down a blind alley at some point because of tensions in the biblical text itself as evidenced by thematic variation and theological discontinuity. And the Bible's discontinuity is most impressive. The simple fact is that there are few sustained themes that permeate the entire Old Testament. The maxim "too tidy to be true" certainly fits. From the first page of the Bible's creation story, the two accounts—in Genesis 1 and 2—display both stark and subtle differences. The legal collections in the Torah also vary in content from one legal code to the next. The retribution theology of Deuteronomy, the Deuteronomistic History, and the prophets contrasts with the Wisdom perspective in

---

9. Eichrodt, *Theology of the Old Testament*, 1:25.

10. Brunner, *Revelation and Reason*, 290.

11. Von Rad, *Old Testament Theology*, 1:106.

Job and Ecclesiastes, where good people often receive evils that they do not deserve. Even the historical accounts in Kings and Chronicles vary widely over matters both historical and theological. The theological diversity within the Old Testament presents enormous challenges to one who would search for a center to Old Testament theology or one who would attempt to speak of *the* theology of the Old Testament.[12] Gaping lacunae sabotage efforts to convince others of a thematic center to Old Testament theology.

One attempt at a solution is to broaden the proposed center of the Old Testament's message. Why not just say that the Old Testament is about Yahweh? Fine. Yet to say that Yahweh is the center of the Old Testament's message does not actually help all that much. The real question is, *in what way* is Yahweh that center?[13] And that answer, as you might have guessed by now, is more than a bit complicated.[14]

When all is said and done, we are obviously left with a dilemma. Yet must those interested in biblical theology throw up their hands in desperation? Given that there is no central framework to the Old Testament, is there really no defensible way to distinguish between a central message and its periphery?[15] Are not some concepts more fundamental to the witness of the Old Testament canon than others? It appears to me that one can make convincing arguments that some themes are more central, more pivotal, and more crucial than others without forcing a single theme into every nook and cranny of the literature present in the Old Testament.

The Canonical Challenge

A Roman Catholic colleague of mine once kidded when pressed on the nature and task of Old Testament theology, "Which Old Testament, yours

12. Rolf Knierim observes that the problem is not simply the existence of theological pluralism in the Old Testament but the coexistence of particular theologies due to the juxtaposition of these theologies in a synchronous canon; Knierim, *Task of Old Testament Theology*, 1–7.

13. For Zimmerli, Yahweh's self-introduction formula (*Selbstvorstellungsformel*) assumes a central position in the continuity of thought about God in the Old Testament; Zimmerli, "Zum Problem 'Die Mitte des Alten Testament.'"

14. Paul R. House, for example, chooses one characteristic of God for each major book of the Hebrew Bible. Most chapters have the title, "The God Who . . ." The unwieldy result is some thirty-odd qualities of God's character in nearly 600 pages, *Old Testament Theology*.

15. Barr, *The Concept of Biblical Theology*, 20.

or mine?" This question points out the often unobserved fact that there are serious differences between Protestant, Catholic, and Orthodox Christian canons. This question also raises the more foundational issue of exactly how today's Old Testament relates to the original Hebrew Scriptures. Another way of putting the question is, since the Old Testament canon was a later development than the Hebrew Bible, wouldn't it be better to limit the task only to describing the theology of the Hebrew Scriptures? Some have obviously chosen this course. Admittedly, the designation *Old Testament* is a decidedly Christian one, and as a result, Old Testament theology is, by definition, a Christian discipline. A theology of the Hebrew Bible would end up being a very different kind of enterprise, as the end of the two canons illustrates. For example, the language about the old and new covenants comes from the Hebrew Bible—specifically the promise of a new covenant in Jer 31:31–33; but in Christian theology, the idea of new covenant is based primarily on the subsequent revelation of Jesus the Messiah in the New Testament. In the Second Temple period, Christians were not the only ones who envisioned themselves as inheritors of a new covenant. The community at Qumran's self-perception is a striking example of a movement that also perceived itself as the fulfillment of Jeremiah's new-covenant promise.[16]

There are admitted dangers in the use of dualistic language of *old* and *new* when one is communicating about religious traditions.[17] *New* obviously implies that it replaces or supersedes the *old*. In an effort to be sensitive to other religious traditions, particularly Judaism, some have abandoned the terms *Old Testament* and *New Testament* for more neutral descriptions: *Hebrew Bible, Christian Testament*, and the like. One merit of this use of inclusive language is that it defuses some of the flagrant abuses of past anti-Semitism. Supersessionism—the theological trend in historic Christianity that portrays Judaism as that stale, outdated religion, good only insofar as it exemplifies the embodiment of divine judgment—has hopefully now been repudiated in post-Holocaust Christianity. However, while the term *supersessionism* elicits a visceral response, the fact of the matter is that although Christianity emerged as a sect of Second Temple Judaism, it is very much a different religion from Judaism. And there is nothing wrong with being honest about those differences.

While recognizing and admitting those differences, Christians may, for strong reasons, retain the use of the designations *Old Testament* and

16. See 1Q34 3.ii.5–6; 1QM xvii.3; 1Q28b i.2, ii.25; CD iii.4.
17. See discussion in B. W. Anderson, *Contours of Old Testament Theology*, 6ff.

New Testament, in spite of prejudicial dangers. One reason is historical. For centuries, *the Old Testament* has been the standard designation for the Scriptures passed down from Judaism. But the second reason is theological. The theology of the Old Testament implies a larger literary context than a theology of the Hebrew Bible. This context includes the New Testament: the canonical collection of literature that bears witness to the life and ministry of Jesus.[18] This later collection, by the way, is one canon on which the majority of Christians agree.

For Christians, it is important to reemphasize that the Hebrew Bible does not belong to the Jewish community alone. Protestants, for example, chose none of the following three options that minimalize the Hebrew Bible: they did not simply incorporate the Hebrew Scriptures into the New Testament; nor did they alternatively remove the Hebrew Scriptures from the canon; neither did they dramatically revise the textual content of the books in the Hebrew Scriptures. Even though the Christian church generally adopted the Greek canon of the Hebrew Scriptures, it should never be forgotten that this Septuagint was a Jewish translation, not a Christian one.[19] And Jesus himself states that he does not come to destroy or abolish the Law, but to fulfill it (Matt 5:17). The gospel writers are clearly dependent on the Hebrew Bible for an understanding of why Jesus often did what he did and said what he said. One example in the New Testament illustrates this fact. Immediately after the resurrection, two disciples who walked the road to Emmaus met a stranger who interpreted the events of Jesus's death and resurrection, but he did so in light of Israel's Scriptures. This stranger turned out to be their Messiah. Later, Paul and other New Testament writers relied heavily on the Old Testament, as Paul interpreted Christianity in light of two covenants: old and new.

While the Protestant Old Testament contains identical books to those in the Hebrew canon, depending on which one you read, the order of the canon varies significantly. Some of the theological differences based on the sequencing of books have been sensitively explored by Richard Elliott Friedman.[20] Most important, the two collections end in different ways that are significant theologically. The Hebrew Bible ends with the book of Chronicles. At the close of that book its very last words invite readers to "go up" to Jerusalem, a postexilic invitation to go back to their spiritual home, a summons meaningful to religious Jews and even secular Israelis

18. Hasel, *Old Testament Theology*, 183.

19. Childs, *Old Testament Theology in a Canonical Context*, 7.

20. Friedman, *The Disappearance of God*.

today.[21] The Christian Old Testament, on the other hand, ends with the book of Malachi, which has an invitation of its own. It speaks of one who would come in the spirit and power of Elijah, who would prepare the way for God's messenger (Mal 3:1; 4:5–6). In the New Testament, all four gospels begin with the ministry of a transitional figure, John the Baptizer. Jesus explicitly stated that John was the fulfillment of this Elijah/messenger prophecy (Matt 11:7–15).

So significant theological differences arise because of the variance in the order of books in the Hebrew Bible and Christian Old Testament. Yet oddly, these differences pale in comparison to the differences between the various canons within Christendom. This takes us back to the question of my colleague: "Which Bible, yours or mine?" If Old Testament theology is a Christian discipline, then which Old Testament canon is the proper source for that theology? The various canons go back to the first translation of the Hebrew Scriptures: the (Greek) Septuagint (LXX), which was completed in the third to second centuries BCE. The Septuagint quickly gained popularity and became the authoritative version for the emerging Christian church. It contains Jewish religious literature that never became part of the canon of the Hebrew Scriptures. These books are called the Apocrypha in Protestant circles and the deuterocanonical books in Catholic tradition. Even though these books were part of the Christian canon until the sixteenth century, the reformers removed the apocryphal books for several reasons. The biggest reason was that these documents were never part of the original Hebrew canon.[22] The issue of canon also begs a new question: Should a theology of the Old Testament include or exclude apocryphal or noncanonical texts? Harmut Gese's approach is that the Old and New Testaments form a single, complete, coherent continuum, so he takes up the theology of the apocryphal books in his biblical theology.[23] He felt that the Reformation did the emerging Protestant churches a disservice by separating the Apocrypha from the Old Testament.

Not that this is any solution, historically—the most significant body of literature related to the discipline of biblical theology has been produced

---

21. The *aliyah* in Zionist rhetoric refers to the voluntary immigration to Israel, or at least visiting Israel. Traveling to Jerusalem is an ascent, both geographically and metaphorically.

22. Other reasons included historical inaccuracies—they were written in the closing centuries of the first millennium BCE—and doctrinal differences (such as prayers for the dead) with the Hebrew Bible.

23. Gese, *Essays on Biblical Theology*; and Gese, "Tradition and Biblical Theology."

by Protestants.[24] This fact raises an interesting dilemma for Protestant Old Testament theologians. Most Protestant approaches, including the approach adopted in this volume, pursue a most unusual course. Protestant thinking privileges the same canonical books as the Hebrew Bible but follows the general order of the Septuagint translation; yet Protestant interpretation denies that the additional books in the Septuagint are authoritative for Old Testament theology. Confused? This is odd reasoning that demands an explanation. One would think that the options would be to follow the order and books of the Hebrew Bible, or follow the order and books of the Greek Septuagint. It does not appear to be logical to retain the books of the Hebrew Bible but reject the order in which those books are presented. This is why many have objected to Brevard Childs's and others canonical approaches to biblical theology—especially those that give priority to their own tradition's canon at the expense of the canon of other Christian traditions. While a canon develops diachronically (over time), it is a synchronic collection. Protestants are giving preference to a canon that did not even exist until the sixteenth century, and readers of this volume are generally aware of the arguments Protestants make to justify the exclusion of the deuteronocanonical books. The theological implications are what are relevant here.

Childs was fully aware that canonical shaping directly influences theological interpretation. Perhaps a safe course would be to begin with the narrowest scope of the Christian canon on which Catholics and Protestants agree, with eyes wide open to observe where the apocryphal/ deuterocanonical books build upon theology of that minimalistic canon. While the focal text of this present study is the Protestant Old Testament, we will be incorporating texts from the Greek Septuagint that specifically take up the theme of blessings and curses as well as texts from Second Temple Judaism that may have influenced New Testament readings and interpretations of these blessing-and-curse texts in the Old Testament. Daniel's prayer in Daniel 9, for example, has remarkable parallels to the apocryphal book of Baruch. Covenantal blessing and curse rituals are reflected in *Jubilees, 1 Enoch,* and texts from Qumran.

Once again, many Christians blindly assume that Protestants, Catholics, and Orthodox Christians share a common canon. As biblical literacy among Christians decreases, this naivete has become an even greater problem. It is only relatively recently that the discoveries of the Dead Sea Scrolls and the Gnostic documents of Nag Hammadi have reopened the

24. Brettler, "Biblical History and Jewish Biblical Thought," 564.

question of canon. At the same time, a burgeoning lucrative media market catapults half-cooked arguments that various and sordid conspiracies were behind eliminating the noncanonical books. In part due to the popularity of these kinds of media, people are once again revisiting the theme of the Christian canon. Because the issue of canon is once again on the table, it is notable that a growing number of traditionally Protestant commentary series now include the apocryphal or deuterocanonical books. For instance, in the *New Interpreter's Bible* series, four of the seven volumes on the Old Testament include apocryphal books.[25]

The Cultural Challenge

The task of Old Testament theology is shaped by two profound cultural influences. First, the Bible is obviously a product of the culture in which it was written. This prompts our next question: What is the relationship between the Old Testament and its ancient Near Eastern environment? For example, now for over a century, students of the Bible have noted numerous parallels between the biblical creation story and the Babylonian *Enuma Elish*, between the Bible's flood story and the Gilgamesh Epic, between the Bible's legal collections and the Code of Hammurabi, or even between biblical and ancient Egyptian wisdom. What does it mean for the Old Testament theologian to affirm that other cultures had a literary influence on the Old Testament? This is not merely a historical question. What does it mean *theologically* when some writers of the Old Testament adapt and transform the literature and worldviews of their neighbors in the ancient Near East? To put it negatively, does this in some way diminish the uniqueness of the writings of the Old Testament? Or to put it positively, in what ways does the reworking of these older traditions from Israel's neighbors make the theology of the Old Testament vibrant and unique? Methodological clarity is essential when one is attempting to articulate a theology based on texts of the Old Testament that in turn were grounded in texts or traditions from other cultures of the Levant. Such clarity has never really been attained.[26]

Using a comparative approach that examines the history of the religion of Israel set alongside other religious customs of the Near East yields two methodological questions: When is a parallel truly a parallel?

25. See Keck, ed., *The New Interpreter's Bible*.

26. Childs, *Old Testament Theology*, 5. See also Talmon, *The Comparative Method in Biblical Interpretation*, 320–56.

And, how do we make use of the parallels that present themselves in the literature?[27] There is a big difference, for example, between the direct literary parallels between the Genesis flood story and the Gilgamesh Epic, and more general references to the mythological sea monsters—Rahab and Leviathan—in the Psalms and Isaiah (Pss 87:4; 89:10; 104:26; Isa 27:1; 51:9). It is one thing to say that such references are part of the cultural milieu of the first or second millennium BCE, but quite another to argue for direct literary dependence on a particular tradition. Shemaryahu Talmon imposed rigorous limitations on the comparative method, suggesting that from a methodological standpoint innerbiblical parallels should take precedence over Near Eastern parallels. Biblical texts should be interpreted "from within." Admittedly, parallels often operate on a variety of levels so imposing limitations does not rule out their fundamental importance.[28] Nevertheless, something theologically profound happened when the writers of the Old Testament took various stories, characters, and metaphors and reworked them in a way that conveyed a very different message to their own audiences.

Rainer Albertz has suggested favoring the discipline of the history of Israelite religion over that of Old Testament theology.[29] He suggests this because traditional theologies are far too many, too varied, and too subjective. He does have a point. A history-of-religions approach, he claims, contains more controls and has a more clearly defined methodology than biblical theology. The superiority of a diachronic pattern could also allow for synchronic divergences within the history of Israelite religion.[30] That contention, however, is entirely arguable. Albertz's argument against a theological reading of the Bible does, however, raise a second cultural challenge. Drawing relevant application from these ancient texts to contemporary culture today is a challenge all its own. Can an approach that derives exclusively from the history of Israelite religion be a basis for faith

27. Ringgren, "The Impact of the Ancient Near East on Israelite Tradition." See also the classic article, based on his presidential address to the Society of Biblical Literature, by Samuel Sandmel, "Parallelomania." See also Overholt, "Prophecy: The Problem of Cross-Cultural Comparison."

28. See, e.g., Hallo et al., eds. *More Essays on the Comparative Method*; and C. D. Evans et al, eds., *Scripture in Context*.

29. Albertz, "Religionsgeschichte Israels statt Theologie des Alten Testaments! Plädoyer für eine forschungsgeschichtliche Umorientierung." See also Albertz, *A History of Israelite Religion in the Old Testament Period*, 2 vols. See Perdue, *The Collapse of History*, 49–60, esp. 50n59

30. For an example of a history-of-religions approach to blessing, see Spieckermann, "YHWH Bless You and Keep You," 165–82.

for a believing community—any believing community? It appears to me, anyway, that approaches from the history of Israelite religion alone cannot bear the weight of establishing theology identity in Old Testament texts.

The Challenge for Christian Faith

The designation *Old Testament* obviously assumes that there is something more . . . something new. Three questions define the dilemma of integrating Old Testament theology with Christian faith. First, what is the *theological* relationship between the Old and New Testaments?[31] Next, how can Christians undertake a project in Old Testament theology in a way distinct from New Testament theology and yet still relevant to the Christian community? And last, does one read from the Old Testament looking forward to the New, or does one read the New Testament looking back to the Old, or does one read reciprocally in both directions?[32] Separate disciplines of Old Testament theology, New Testament theology, and systematic theology were unknown to the church prior to the nineteenth century. One could even argue that the Christian church does not really need an Old Testament theology at all but rather a metabiblical theology of sorts. Peter Enns did just that in his review of Paul House's *Old Testament Theology*:

> Perhaps what is needed in Christian theological circles is a theology of the Old Testament that explicitly takes as its starting point what Christians have always confessed and what the New Testament writers were at great pains to demonstrate, that the coming of Christ is not only the completion of Israel's journey, but is also the lens through which the Old Testament story itself should be read.[33]

Yet such a task is not as easy as it might sound. A close examination of the New Testament's interpretation of the Old Testament demonstrates that the New Testament authors read the Old Testament very naively in some respects and with nuanced subtlety in others. First Corinthians 10:4 and Gal 4:22–26 are two notable examples of such reading. In 1 Cor 10:1–5 Paul says,

> For I do not want you to be ignorant of the fact, brothers, that our forefathers were all under the cloud and that they all passed

31. See Silva, "The New Testament Use of the Old Testament."

32. Hasel, *Old Testament Theology,* 145.

33. Enns, "Review of *Old Testament Theology,* by Paul House."

through the sea. They were all baptized into Moses in the cloud and in the sea. They all ate the same spiritual food and drank the same spiritual drink; for they drank from the spiritual rock that accompanied them, and that rock was Christ. Nevertheless, God was not pleased with most of them; their bodies were scattered over the desert.

Here the Apostle Paul allegorizes a portion of the Old Testament wilderness narratives, decontextualizes it, and applies it directly to Jesus the Messiah. In Gal 4:22–26 he applies the same exegetical technique to the narrative of Sarah and Hagar. My point is not to exegete these texts here but to show that even the New Testament's use of the Old raises questions of method. These methodological problems can easily be resolved by ignoring either one or the other Testament, but for Christian biblical theology, this is not a very helpful option. Developing a grand narrative involving both testaments does not eliminate these problems mentioned above. In fact it exacerbates them.

For the task of Old Testament theology, the relationship between the Old and New Testaments must be one of both continuity and discontinuity. The Old Testament is Scripture, but it is the Scripture of the Christian faith. Overemphasis on discontinuity between the two testaments essentially extracts the Old Testament from the Christian canon. On the other hand, lack of emphasis on the discontinuity between the testaments defrauds the Old Testament of its autonomy as a collection and essentially Christianizes the Old Testament, ignoring its original setting and intent. In Christian history as well as in the church today one can find a disturbing tendency to artificially shift the interpretation of the Old Testament to a nonliteral, metaphorical level in order to read the ministry of Jesus Christ back into Old Testament texts.

There is also a sense of unevenness between the testaments. Some issues that are central to one are nearly or completely neglected in the other. For example, the so-called fall of Adam, which is central to Paul's theology relating to the human need for salvation in the New Testament, is rarely even mentioned in the Old Testament outside the opening chapters of Genesis. Without the New Testament, one would probably not think of Genesis 3 as a fall story at all. It is simply a mirrored portrayal of the broader human condition. Another example, messianic expectation, extremely muted in the Old Testament, is a primary theme of the New Testament. No wonder these problems have led some to write a theology of the Old Testament as if the New Testament did not exist![34] Since the original

---

34. See Hasel's discussion of this topic in *Theology of the Old Testament*, 59.

authors of the Old Testament knew nothing about the life and ministry of Jesus, it is certainly appropriate to let the Old Testament speak for itself. Yet if the Old Testament is part of the canon of Christian Scripture, this christological dimension should not be neglected. The Old Testament's voice must somehow resonate with that of the New, but in ways that read the Old Testament in its own right. Perhaps one way to say it is that Old Testament theology reflects only on one portion of the Christian canon, but as Christian Scripture. Therefore, a properly theological view of the Old Testament would also make clear its organic relation with the New.[35]

Perhaps it might be wise to also rethink the problem of application mentioned above. The issue of application relates to the question that has been the concern of the discipline since historical criticism. Is Old Testament theology primarily a descriptive or a normative task? Ever since Johann Philipp Gabler's inaugural lecture at the University of Altdorf in 1787, biblical theology has been perceived as a primarily descriptive enterprise, unencumbered by the ballast of Christian dogma.[36] He erected a sharp distinction between biblical and systematic theology—the former being descriptive, and the latter normative. In the last century, Krister Stendahl applied the distinction between what the text meant vs. what the text means—a practice that also disconnected the descriptive from the normative approach to the biblical text.[37] Stendahl's approach has been criticized on several fronts. Foremost among these criticisms is that this task of biblical theology involves more than just organizing or systemizing various doctrines. A descriptive approach alone fails at the need for a depth of meaning. Here is James Barr again,

> Of too many of the critical commentaries of the turn of the century it was felt that they made no attempt to state the meaning of a passage in any profound way at all: they dealt with the textual questions, provided a complex analysis of sources, discussed the problem of authorship, authenticity and date, touched on the historicity or otherwise of the content, and—on to the next passage![38]

---

35. Barr, *The Concept of Biblical Theology*, 172.

36. Gabler, "About the Correct Distinction between Biblical and Dogmatic Theology," 2:179–98; see the important essay on Gabler by Knierim, "On Gabler," in *The Task of Old Testament Theology*, 495–556.

37. Stendahl, "Biblical Theology, Contemporary."

38. Barr, *The Concept of Biblical Theology*, 20.

Again, numerous problems can be solved by simply jettisoning the troubling complexity of drawing normative application from an ancient text like the Old Testament. Confining oneself to simply describing what the Old Testament teaches without making any judgments on its application to the church today makes life a lot easier. Yet, simply put, the Old Testament is Christian Scripture. Admittedly, the faith of those described in the Old Testament may be akin to our own, but it is not our own.[39] That makes a reading of the Old Testament's story in light of the New Testament such a necessity. The application of the biblical text to the mission of the church is one of the principal roles of theology. So the writers, editors, and interpreters of the Bible privilege their own cultural context, social position, and theological disposition.[40] All this is nothing new. As Lemche observes, there have always been different ways of reading the Bible.[41] A theological reading that strives to derive application for the Christian church from a canonical text comes from a long line of rich interpretive tradition in Christianity.

A Basic Proposal for Reconfiguring an Old Testament Theology

For over forty years, scholars interested in biblical theology have candidly admitted the need for fresh methods that distinguish themselves from the approaches used by the biblical theology movement so popular in the first half of the twentieth century.[42] As a result, the discipline is now in transition. The question is, what are we transitioning to? Moberly expresses the process well.

> There is something intrinsically contextual and provisional about theological use of the biblical text. Theology is not a once-for-all exercise in finding right words and/or deeds, but rather a continuing and ever-repeated attempt to articulate what a

39. Reventlow's discussion of Gunkel in *Problems of Old Testament Theology in the Twentieth Century*, 8ff.

40. Perdue, *The Collapse of History*, 11.

41. Lemche, *The Old Testament between Theology and History*, 258.

42. The biblical-theology movement took place in the first half of the twentieth century and was a reaction against classic liberalism. Its proponents focused on the acts of God in history, the near absolute uniqueness of Israel among her neighbors in the Near East, the unity of the Bible, the uniqueness of Hebraic thought, and an opposition to philosophical theology. The rise and fall of this movement is traced in the classic study by Childs, *Biblical Theology in Crisis*.

faithful understanding and use of the biblical text might look like in the changing circumstances of life.[43]

The approach in this volume is to embrace a dialectic between the historical and theological tasks, and between descriptive and the normative outcomes. The wedge of exclusivity between what the text meant and what the text means must be suspended at points and engaged at others. Both domains of meaning are important.[44] One cannot simply make an interpretive leap to what the text means without considering historical concerns and authorial intent, in spite of the enormous challenges. That's why at least some exploration of blessings and curses in the ancient Near East is important, even for a theological project such as this one. Serious attention to literary, historical, cultural, and canonical context will hopefully avoid neglecting the developmental elements in the composition *of* and the history contained *in* the Old Testament. For example, there is still room today, in spite of the waning consensus in the field, to address source-critical influences on the theology of the Pentateuch. I hope to demonstrate that a source-critical approach to pentateuchal blessings and curses yields some intriguing results. Literary concerns regarding the function of genre, such as the nature of story, also bear upon serious theological reflection. And the kerygmatic function of the canonical shape of the Old Testament cannot be blindly disregarded.[45]

Perhaps such an undertaking is foolish. The fallacies and hardships of determining authorial intent from such ancient, ideologically loaded texts are well known. The groundbreaking work of Walter Brueggemann has chosen another path by emphasizing theology as testimony.[46] Rather than search for theology in history, he searches instead in words alone, raising speech to the center of Israel's life and faith. Brueggemann's work is unique because it was the first modern Old Testament theology from a nonhistorical foundation. The theological consequence of such an approach is that even when God is speaking in the Old Testament, it is the double agency of the human writer from ancient Israel who speaks for God. So what is said is ultimately Israel's testimony about God.[47] Brueggemann's

---

43. Moberly, *The Theology of the Book of Genesis*, 19.

44. Hasel, *Old Testament Theology*, 169.

45. Childs, *Old Testament Theology*, 40, says the worst kind of literalism disregards this kerygmatic intention.

46. Brueggemann, *Old Testament Theology of the Old Testament*.

47. On biblical testimony as a speech-event, see Brueggemann, "Theology of the Old Testament Revisited," 33.

binary approach, based on rhetorical criticism and sociological analysis, exploits the tension between some texts that serve to legitimate existing structures and others that challenge the established order. He adopts the metaphor of a court trial, which includes three elements: a core testimony, countertestimony, and new theological witness. His somewhat Hegelian approach, unfortunately, intentionally brackets out nearly every question about history. James Barr noted this weakness and has rightly criticized the work as a "conglomeration of predicates" with no subject. God never really *does* anything.[48] It is Israel's testimony that is everything. In spite of Barr's criticism of Brueggemann's *Theology of the Old Testament*, Brueggemann's work consistently continues to produce innovative and imaginative theological insights, even if his theology proper may at times limp along as a result.

One can clearly see why Brueggemann chose a nonhistorical approach. Many today would argue that Gabler's project is impossible because of the stark limitations of the historical sources of the Old Testament. The relationship between Israel's story and history is complex and variegated.[49] Postmodernism has accurately observed that the goal of an exact retelling of what took place in Israel's history is largely impossible due to the biases and ideologies of writers: ancient and modern.[50] The history the Bible conveys is quite different from the history we might reconstruct from other kinds of evidence. The Bible's interest in the past had little to do with simple curiosity about the past. The Bible's history is theologically potent. In spite of the complexities, when it comes to historical concerns, one does not have to resort to either extreme and become a harmonist or a nihilist.

Not to sound pedantic, but the theology of the Old Testament should primarily be composed of materials from . . . the Old Testament. Acknowledging that the task of Old Testament theology is a Christian enterprise, the Old Testament should be allowed to speak with its own voice. While the designation *Old Testament* presupposes some relationship to the New Testament, the New Testament should not be arbitrarily imposed on the earlier voice. The persistent challenge of viewing Old Testament theology as a Christian discipline in the context of that faith community is not to Christianize the Old Testament by eliminating the distinction between

48. Barr, *The Concept of Biblical Theology*, 558.

49. Barr, "Story and History in Biblical Theology," 1–17; Nicholson, "Story and History in the Old Testament," 135–50; Brettler, "Biblical History and Jewish Biblical Thought," 563–83; Burkert, *Structure and History in Greek Mythology and Ritual*.

50. Collins, *The Bible after Babel*.

the witness of the New and Old Testaments. Gerhard Von Rad is correct that there is something about the Old Testament that points mysteriously toward the future with ever increasing anticipation.[51] That reading of the Old Testament is well worth pursuing.

Brevard Childs was right that any approach to Old Testament theology should be sensitive to canonical concerns. The assumption of such a statement is that the thirty-nine books in the Old Testament have at least some literary association with one another. Childs again: "The divine revelation of the Old Testament cannot be abstracted or removed from the form of the witness which the historical community of Israel gave it."[52] Additionally, the materials for theological reflection cannot be construed apart from the community of faith.

We have already noted, however, the problem that the canon of the Christian Bible, like any canon, flattens historical differences. A canon is a synchronic statement; every book in it, every chapter, every verse, is contemporaneous with every other one.[53] Historical and canonical approaches are not necessarily mutually exclusive. Here I find Paul House's definition of a canonical approach helpful: "analysis that is God-centered, intertextually oriented, authority-conscious, historically sensitive and devoted to the pursuit of the wholeness of the Old Testament message."[54] The enterprise of embracing descriptive and normative tasks towards Old Testament theology is not just pedagogical fantasy. Much of the literature of the Old Testament purports to be historical, yet that history comes to many readers, particularly those interested in the theological implications of the Bible, via the canon of sacred Scripture. Perhaps it would be wise to be sensitive to the diverse character of theology today. Maybe it would also be wise to give up looking for a consensus and just continue with the exploration. James Barr delivers the invitation, "For the critical scholar, biblical theology is a vital interest because it is an exploratory subject: the true theology of the Bible is not already known, now is the chance to discover it."[55] Such an approach can correct a distorted view of the Old Testament based on a haphazard and uncritical way that the Old Testament is

---

51. Von Rad, *Old Testament Theology*, 2:319–87.

52. Childs, *Old Testament Theology in a Canonical Context*, 12.

53. Levenson, *Sinai and Zion*, 1. On multiple theological frameworks in the Old Testament see Dirksen, "Israelite Religion and Old Testament Theology," 97–98.

54. House, *Old Testament Theology*, 57.

55. Barr, "The Literal, the Allegorical, and Modern Biblical Scholarship," 3–9.

preached in many pulpits.[56] I am drawn to Elmer Martens's definition of biblical theology:

> Biblical theology is to the health of the church what the Center for Disease Control in the USA is to a nation's health. Just as the Center for Disease Control monitors trends and offers directives to the public, so biblical theology serves as a resource whereby the church can do a reality check to ensure that the faith community is not aberrant or one-sided in its beliefs. Norms for belief and behavior are important for the church in whose service the discipline of biblical theology is placed.[57]

BLESSING AND CURSE AS A THEOLOGICAL THEME

The approach followed in this study is essentially a thematic one. The theological tension between blessings and curses is both substantive and pervasive in many of the dominant texts of the Old Testament. The chief concepts and practices of blessings and curses are also deeply rooted in the broad cultural environment of the ancient Near East. Since blessings and curses are speech acts, this study will apply contemporary speech act theory to understand the performative force of these kinds of utterances. In Alaska, where I teach, we have a saying: "one mosquito does not mean that it is summer." My purpose in this thematic study is not to randomly swat at a blessing here or a curse there. Undoubtedly, this theme of the blessing and the curse is not evenly distributed throughout the entire Old Testament, but it is distributed significantly enough to be a dominant motif, not merely in a few isolated texts but in grand metanarrative of the testaments, both Old and New. The Bible begins with a threefold blessing. The Pentateuch (Deuteronomy 27–28), the Old Testament (Malachi 3:9–12), and the New Testament (Rev 22:14–19) all end with this poignant theme of blessings and curses.

The goal here is to trace trajectories of this theme through the disparate genres and collections of the literature of the Old Testament canon, to explore the social function of these speech acts, and to apprehend the theological implications of those themes for the Christian church. I am particularly interested in probing the appearance of blessings and curses in prominent seams of biblical narratives as well as in structural seams

56. McKeown, "A Theological Approach," 50.

57. Martens, "Old Testament Theology since Walter C. Kaiser, Jr.," 681.

within a variety of Old Testament books. I am not advocating blessing and curse as a center around which an entire theology for the Old Testament coalesces but merely as one point of contact. I hope to demonstrate, however, that this point of contact is inescapable and extends throughout the pages of the Old Testament.[58] Note below a few prominent literary seams in which this theme is portrayed in the Old Testament:

- The Torah begins (Genesis 1) and ends (Deuteronomy 33) with a blessing.

- The primeval history in Genesis 1–11 presents the problem of the curse as a central theme.

- The ancestral blessing of Abraham and his family in Genesis 12–50 counters the problem of curse in Genesis 1–11. Abraham's blessing is universal, extending to all the peoples of the earth. In the New Testament, Paul takes up Abraham's blessing and the curse of the law in Romans 4; Romans 10; and Galatians 3.

- The entire Pentateuch takes up the promise of the blessing and the challenge of the curse as a recurring refrain.

- The four hypothetical sources of the Documentary Hypothesis handle blessing-and-curse themes uniquely.

- Jacob/Israel blesses Pharaoh, Esau, Joseph's sons, and Jacob's own sons. The pharaoh of the exodus asks his nemesis, Moses, for a blessing.

- All three major legal codes depict that the sacred boundaries of biblical law are enforced by divine blessings and curses.

- Blessing and curse rituals make up the climax of the book of Deuteronomy (Deuteronomy 27–30). The working out of that blessing and curse pervades the Deuteronomistic History and dominates covenant-renewal rituals.

- The reigns of the kings of the united monarchy (Saul, David, and Solomon) all follow the same pattern: first blessing, then curse.

- Abraham's descendants are to be a blessing to all the peoples of the earth. In the writings of the prophets, Israel ironically becomes a curse and a horror among all the peoples of the earth.

58. Barr rightly states that "no one thinks their theology encompasses everything" in the Old Testament anyway (*The Concept of Biblical Theology*, 335).

- Blessings and curses are vital components of Israel's public worship. Blessing is a prominent part of the structure of the five anthologies that form the book of Psalms.

- The entire book of Job revolves around a single question: will Job curse God?

- The two-way instruction of Proverbs is reminiscent of the choice of blessing and curse specified to Israel in Moab in Deuteronomy 30.

- Old Testament apocalyptic literature (the Little Apocalypse of Isaiah 24–27; Zechariah 14; and Daniel 9) employs the theme of blessings and curses.

- Judah's exile is portrayed as living under the curse.

- The Old Testament ends with a promise of blessing and a threat of curse.

From these examples, one can see that the theme of blessings and curses is pervasive in the Old Testament. More important, the theme appears at some important seams in the biblical narrative, such as at the beginning of the Pentateuch, the Old Testament, and the Christian Bible, as well as at the end of the Pentateuch, the Old Testament, and the Christian Bible. Blessings and curses dominate crucial narratives such as the creation stories, the Eden story, the call of Abraham, the blessing and birthright of Abraham's grandsons, the exodus story, all three legal codes, the end of the wilderness narrative, the covenant with David, the dedication of the Jerusalem temple, and the destruction of the Northern Kingdom. The book of Ruth is structured by the theme of blessing. The theme of blessings and curses is prominent in Jeremiah's and Ezekiel's warnings of doom for Judah. After the restoration, Jeremiah's prophecy about the good and bad figs denotes which returning communities are blessed . . . and cursed. The book of Nehemiah ends with a curse that involves physical violence against those who marry outside the Judean community. Daniel frankly admits to living under the curse, and Zechariah promises blessing to the postexilic restoration community and ends by promising that there will be no more oaths of destruction of Jerusalem. Finally, Malachi's threat of turning blessing into curse closes out the Old Testament.

Admittedly, in places the theme is conspicuously absent. Blessings and curses are prominent in all kinds of genres—from narratives to poetry; from laws to sermons; in prayers, testaments, prophecies, and apocalyptic visions. They are represented in some of the earliest biblical texts, such as the Song of Deborah and Barak, and in later, postexilic texts of Zechariah and Malachi. Yet they are also fitfully observed elsewhere. For example, while the motif is prominent among the stories about the ancestors of Israel, it is never mentioned in relationship to the birth or the commission of Moses. Wisdom literature, for example, has proved nearly impossible to integrate into the artificial categories of most Old Testament theologies. I will attempt to provide a few examples where two-way theology dominates the early chapters of Proverbs. I will also explore whether Job steps over the line regarding the question of whether he will curse God. These examples from Proverbs and Job do not, however, mean that the theme permeates every facet of biblical Wisdom literature.

As a Christian theology of the Old Testament this binary theme may improve upon supersessionist tendencies of some Christian theologies of the Old Testament. Theologically, blessing-and-curse is preferable to simplistic *replacement* dichotomies of old/new, promise/fulfillment, and law/grace that have been applied to the study of Old Testament theology, which have tended to depict the Old Testament as only minimally important and entirely superseded by the New. In regard to the blessing and the curse, it is not an either/or scenario. What is advocated here is a tension lying at the heart of the relationship between Yahweh and believing humanity, as well as between humans. Blessings and curses lurk as open and lasting alternatives for the community of faith of *any* generation. To say it another way, there is no defensible theology in which *curse* in the Old Testament followed by *blessing* in the New Testament.

Finally, let us return to the two problems mentioned above: categorization and coherence. Rather than imposing a schema upon the Bible, tracing trajectories, in my view, is a better approach to the daunting problem of categorization in biblical theology. Rather than imposing artificial categories that force the entire Old Testament into somewhat arbitrary classifications, or forcing diverse texts into some kind of center, tracing a thematic trajectory permits one to follow that theme where it is present without forcing that theme upon texts where it is not. Brevard Childs concluded his *Old Testament Theology in a Canonical Context* by drawing attention to these two theologically rich categories in two brief concluding chapters titled "Life under Threat" and "Life under Promise."[59] Childs concludes:

> It does justice to the theological witness of the Old Testament to treat the subject of life under threat by itself. This chapter is not the end of the story, nor the full message to Israel. Certainly one

---

59. Childs, *Old Testament Theology in a Canonical Context*, 222ff.

needs also to hear the message of life under promise. Nevertheless, these two biblical testimonies are not automatically linked. Threat does not flow naturally into promise of its own accord. To pass all too quickly from threat to promise can jeopardize the overpowering reality of life under divine judgment. From the biblical perspective, the threat was not a momentary phase or an introductory stage, but a recurring danger of catastrophic proportions, always present and continuously to be faced. Indeed because of its awesome and terrifying dimensions, the note of redemption, of promise and of a future life broke upon Israel as an overwhelming surprise and incomprehensible wonder.

As far as the second problem, coherence is the task of relating disparate and at times competing theologies to the larger message of the entire Old Testament. Admittedly, all interpretation is selective. Historically, modern interpreters have been much more comfortable with the topic of blessing than curse, for obvious reasons. This project is going to have to grapple with the sticky issue of how curses relate to the nature and character of God, and in particular, the doctrines of divine providence and election.

Life in the believing community is lived between threat and promise, curse and blessing, but not in an evolutionary "first comes curse, then comes blessing" way—or even worse . . . curse in the Old Testament followed by blessing in the New. Blessing and curse, old and new, promise and fulfillment, are always in tension. This tension refuses to trivialize life: a person's choices are not simply subsumed into God's sovereign purposes. One's choices are genuinely real and give birth to life-impacting consequences. The Old Testament is no mere straw man that serves as a preliminary evolutionary stage toward a fulfilled revelation in Christ, because there are many elements in tension in the New Testament as well. The end of the New Testament provides an example of this tension-filled dichotomy in its concluding blessing, invitation, and threat:

> Blessed are those who wash their robes, so that they may have the right to the tree of life and that they may enter the city by the gates. Outside are the dogs and sorcerers and the sexually immoral and murderers and idolaters, and everyone who loves and practices falsehood. "I, Jesus, have sent my angel to testify to you about these things for the churches. I am the root and the descendant of David, the bright morning star. "The Spirit and the Bride say, "Come." And let the one who hears say, "Come." And let the one who is thirsty come; let the one who desires take

the water of life without price. I warn everyone who hears the words of the prophecy of this book: if anyone adds to them, God will add to him the plagues described in this book, and if anyone takes away from the words of the book of this prophecy, God will take away his share in the tree of life and in the holy city, which are described in this book. (Rev 22:14–19, ESV)

2

Considering Blessings and Curses Theologically

Blessing and Curse Terminology and Formulae

Definitions matter. What, then, does it mean to bless, to be a blessing, or to pronounce a blessing? First, blessings and curses are activities of pronouncement, or "performative" utterances. They are wishes but are much more than wishes. They may also be prayers but are more than prayers. A blessing is a potent way to invoke, distribute, or celebrate the well-being that comes from divine favor. In the Old Testament, blessings primarily invoked fertility, authority and dominion, wholeness, peace, and rest.[1] Therefore these blessings might proceed from God to humans, from humans to other humans, and even from humans towards God. But almost never does the Old Testament show someone blessing an inanimate object.[2] Theologically, with God as the subject, a blessing is God's enhancement of a life of fullness. In the Psalms, God is often extolled as holy by means of a blessing (Pss 26:12; 34:1; 63:4; 66:8; 68:26; 96:2; 100:4; 103:1ff.; 104:1, 35; 134:1ff.; 135:19ff.; 145:10, 21). English translations often completely miss this, as they usually render the translation, "Praise the Lord."

---

1. Pedersen's classic, *Israel, Its Life and Culture,* cites four characteristics of blessing: power to multiply; establishing a home or a house; fertility of animals, crops, family; and strength of life (1:204–12).

2. One possible exception might be in 1 Sam 9:13, where Samuel blesses the sacrifice before the people eat.

Other important Old Testament texts also reveal blessings towards God as well (Gen 9:26, 24:48; Deut 8:8; Josh 22:33). Blessing God returns praise to the deity who initially graciously exercised God's providential enhancement of life. Last, by metonymy, an individual or group who had received blessings could themselves be considered a blessing to others. This can be seen in the blessing of Abraham in Gen 12:3 and in Balaam's blessing of Israel in Num 24:9.

There are various ways blessings can be exchanged between people.[3] To bless is to convey some kind of benefit, and the focus is less on the benefit itself and more on the life or relationship thus enhanced by the blessing. A blessing may serve as a short greeting (Ruth 2:4) or a brief expression to acknowledge kindness done (Ruth 2:20; 3:10; 1 Sam 23:21; 25:33). More often, however, blessings are effective utterances when invoked by subjects with proper authority. For example, when parents bless children (Gen 27:27–40; 49:1–27), they have the authority similar to prophetic testaments (*Jub.* 20:10–30, 26:22–25, 31:13–20). Testaments of blessing may also be uttered by leaders in behalf of their people (Deuteronomy 33) or by priests (Num 6:23–26). Blessings are also common when people are gathered for festive occasions (Ps 115:12–14; 134:1–3). Just as in prayers so in blessings it is often customary to mention God's name in this benevolent utterance (Gen 27:28; Ruth 3:10; Num 6:27; Deut 21:5).

Conversely, curses are expressions of misfortune, calamity, and evil.[4] They, like blessings, are not mere wishes but are powerful and effective performatives that have potency when uttered, but only in appropriate contexts by appropriate individuals. A curse is an illocution. It is intended to do something by its invocation. As with blessings, so the focus is less on the utterance itself and more (in the case of a curse) on the relationship severed or at least marginalized by the curse. Although curses occur less often in the Old Testament than blessings, the Bible expresses some of the same social relationships in cursing as in blessing, such as parents toward children (Gen 9:25; 49:7), priests toward people (Num 5:21–22), and other religious leaders toward the community of God's people (Deuteronomy 27–28). Therefore curses can refer to the divine bestowal of these misfortunes and calamities. A curse can also simply denote the use of insolent language against individuals or groups. For example, it was

---

3. Nitzan, *Qumran Prayer and Religious Poetry*, 119–22. Nitzan has an excellent treatment of blessings and curses in this work; as does Grüneberg. *Abraham's Blessing and the Nations*, 90–122.

4. A helpful review on curses can be found in Kitz, "Curses and Cursing in the Ancient Near East," 615–27.

expressly forbidden to curse one's parents (Exod 21:17; Lev 20:9). These curses were so powerful that if uttered improperly or undeservedly against guarantors of the social order (such as against God, a king, or a parent), then cursing became a blasphemous act and even a capital offense. Covenantal ceremonies also regularly counterpoised blessings and curses.

Theologically, both blessings and curses grow out of two important biblical doctrines: divine providence and election. Divine providence is the idea that God can influence the life and destiny of individuals or peoples. Understood narrowly, election is the concept that God chooses particular individuals and peoples for covenant blessing or for curse. Understandably, the concept that God can bless has been more readily accepted than its counterpart. The notion that God can either advance or oppose a life of fullness is at the heart of these two doctrines. If the potency of a blessing or curse is influenced by the power and authority of the subject behind it, then God, who controls all good and evil (Isa 45:6), is the ultimate source of power behind these utterances. Thus, humans can invoke God as the source of curses as well as blessings. While less customary, individuals can indeed be cursed before Yahweh (*ārûr lipnê yhwh*) as in Josh 6:26 and 1 Sam 26:19, or can be cursed in the name of Yahweh (*wayqallēm bĕšēm yhwh*) as in 2 Kgs 2:24 and Deut 28:22, 25. These texts, understandably, make today's readers of the Old Testament uncomfortable. The fact that God is the subject of the blessing or curse mitigates notions of the magical power of words alone, as God is able to revoke both blessing and curse after they are uttered. This raises an important theological dilemma that will be addressed throughout this study as to what constitutes divine backing of blessings and curses. God certainly is the subject of some curses, but instead of God's saying, "I curse you," significant reticence is employed in the biblical language of curse used by God.

Several theological questions lie at the heart of notions of blessing and cursing. If the relationship between subject and object of the blessings or curses is central to understanding their operation, how is that relationship described? How can God curse? To what extent are blessings and curses primarily driven by human initiation (anthropocentric) or by divine prerogative (theocentric)? If God utters a curse or blessing, is it unconditional or conditional? If blessings and curses are rooted in the doctrine of divine providence, how to these themes interplay with the doctrines of redemption and creation? Such matters are worth exploring, and we will face them in the chapters that follow. But first . . . an analysis of the language that the Old Testament employs for these illocutions.

The Language of Blessing

The Hebrew root *brk* produces the verb "to bless," and the noun "blessing" as well as the verb, "to kneel" and the noun "knee" (Gen 24:11; Isa 45:23). The etymological connection to the idea of a person's kneeling to receive a blessing is tempting, but such a connection is not clearly sustained in the literary context of the Old Testament itself, so we need to exercise caution. The verbal and nominal forms of this root occur over 400 times in the Old Testament. Genesis and Psalms alone account for nearly half of these occurrences, and Deuteronomy adds an additional 51 examples. The root *brk* occurs 160 times in the Torah, 88 times in the Prophets, and 148 times in the Writings.[5] Most of the verbal forms are present in the Piel passive participle, as in the formula, *bārûk ătâ* ("blessed are you"). The Old Testament commonly deploys this blessing formula and distributes the formula nearly evenly between God's blessing humans, humans' blessing other humans, and humans' blessing God. The feminine plural noun often pairs up with its linguistic and theological counterpart, "blessings and curses" (*bārûkôt wĕqālĕlôt*). The language of blessing is varied, including additional specific terminology as well as idioms. Christopher Mitchell sites twenty-nine lively synonyms that broaden the semantic field of the root *brk*.[6] Most sources agree that the closest synonym to *brk* is *šry* (Jer 17:7–8; Ps 1:1–3), which is typically translated "happy." However, K. C. Hanson posits that *brk* is a word of power, while *šry* instead entails a value judgment that imputes honor. These two words are thematically related but linguistically and contextually distinct. Thus *šry* should not be translated "blessed" or even "happy," but instead, "how honored is/are . . ."[7] Mark Biddle has put it succinctly: blessing means three things: prosperity, protection, and prominence.[8]

These blessings of prosperity, protection, and prominence can also be freely composed without using any specific vocabulary words that mean "to bless." Note the freely composed blessings in Gen 24:60 and 27:27b–29:

> Our sister, may you become
> thousands of ten thousands,

---

5. Mitchell, *The Meaning of BRK 'to Bless' in the Old Testament*, 185.

6. Ibid., 201. In addition to the work of Mitchell, see Hempel, "Die israelitischen Anschauungen von Segen und Fluch." See also Wehmeier, *Der Segen im Alten Testament*, 140.

7. K. C. Hanson, "'How Honorable!' 'How Shameful!'"

8. Biddle, *Deuteronomy*, 413.

and may your offspring possess
the gate of those who hate him. (Gen 24:60, ESV)

See, the smell of my son
is as the smell of a field that the LORD has blessed!
May God give you the dew of heaven
and of the fatness of the earth
and plenty of grain and wine.
Let peoples serve you,
and nations bow down to you.
Be lord over your brothers,
and may your mother's sons bow down to you.
Cursed be everyone who curses you,
and blessed be everyone who blesses you!
(Gen 27:27b–29, ESV)

Or in Balaam's blessing of Israel:
From the rocky peaks I see them,
from the heights I view them.
I see a people who live apart
and do not consider themselves one of the nations.
Who can count the dust of Jacob
or number the fourth part of Israel?
Let me die the death of the righteous,
and may my end be like theirs! (Num 23:9–10)

The language of blessing is intended to promote a strengthening of solidarity. Could a blessing be revoked? In the story of Jacob's filching of the blessing from Esau, it seems like once the blessing is uttered according to social convention, it cannot be retracted (Gen 27:33, 37). Balaam's comment in Num 23:20 also affirms the lasting power of blessings or curses. But it appears that later curses may actually reverse the course of blessing, and (as in the case of Saul's foolish curse) divine will trumps an uttered curse. The theology of the history of Israel subsequent to Jacob's and Moses's tribal blessings of Genesis 49 and Deuteronomy 33 appears to support this case. In Old Testament law, volatile curses were used as a deterrent to theft, receiving stolen goods, embezzlement, and to guarantee a witness to an oath. Yet there is no such parallel of blessing, no promise that if one refrains from thievery and fraud, a person's life will be enhanced and made strong. So the lopsided sanctions of curses are used as a club, a form of social control, more often than blessings.[9] A blessing is also a means of expressing gratitude to humans or God.[10]

The Language of Cursing

The Old Testament also reveals a rather wide semantic range of terminology to express the concept of cursing. The roots *'rr*, *'lh*, and *qll* are by far the most common, but half a dozen other terms may also be translated as "curse" or "oath," depending on context. Additionally, like blessings, many curses are freely composed using none of the terms just mentioned. The blessings and curses of Leviticus 26, for example, draw upon none of the specific vocabulary words meaning "to bless" or "to curse." Also, the line between curses and other types of malevolent speech acts in biblical literature is often thin. Prayers for the defeat of an enemy, prophetic proclamation of doom to Israel and Judah, prophecies against foreign kingdoms, proclamations during water ordeals,[11] military bans against taking the spoil, and oaths all vividly express some affinities with curses. If a blessing is intended to invoke fertility, authority and dominion, wholeness, peace, and rest, and so advance a life of fullness, then a curse can summon a startling reversal of fortune, opposing that life of *shalom*. Any adequate definition of curses must consider three elements: literary and grammatical characteristics, propositional content, and appropriate use according to social convention of the day. A curse can also refer to divinely imposed misfortune.

The root *'rr* is generally recognized as the strongest example of curse language in the Old Testament.[12] The root occurs 63 times in the Old Testament as a verb, usually in the Qal stem (54 times), most frequently in Deuteronomy 27–28 (19 times). The derivate noun occurs on five occasions. This is much less than the roughly 400 times that the root *brk* is used. The *'ārûr* formula, formed with the Qal passive participle of *'rr*, is unique in the Old Testament.[13] It begins with a predicate participle followed by the sub-

9. J. S. Anderson, "The Social Function of Curses in the Hebrew Bible."

10. Scharbert, "*brk*."

11. A water ordeal was an ancient Near Eastern way of determining guilt, either by throwing someone into flowing water or by forcing someone to drink water that might be contaminated (e.g., Num 5:11–22).

12. Schottroff, *Der altisraelitische Fluchspruch*, 61–70; and Pedersen, *Der Eid bei den Semiten*, 68.

13. Schottroff, *Der altisraelitische Fluchspruch*, 231; Scharbert, "*'rr*," 408.

ject, which can be a personal pronoun, a specific individual or group, or an unidentified subject. Consider these examples: "Cursed is the ground because of you" (Gen 3:17); "Cursed be Canaan! The lowest of slaves will he be to his brothers" (Gen 9:25); and "Cursed be anyone who eats food before evening comes" (1 Sam 14:24). An inscription at Khirbet Beit Lei excavated in 1961 includes this 'rr curse formula. Khirbet Beit Lei is a sixth-century-BCE burial complex with three chambers. Along the walls are seven inscriptions, including one which reads, "Cursed be . . . who/he will sing in time to come . . ."[14] This particular curse is probably intended to prevent opportunistic thieves from desecrating or robbing the tomb. A similar curse was discovered over an eighth- to ninth-century-BCE tomb across the Kidron from the City of David: "This is [the tomb of XY]yahu, who is over the house. [He]re is no silver or gold; [on]ly [his bones] and the bones of his slave-girl with him. Cursed (is) the man who opens this.[15]

Nearly all commentators agree that the English equivalent, "curse," does not do justice to the meaning of 'rr and its Akkadian cognates.[16] Opinions regarding the basic sense of the term vary but fall roughly into two camps: some argue a curse is a separation or ban from community, an act of public shaming or humiliation (Pedersen, Scharbert). Others (Speiser and Bricho) interpret a curse to be a magical spell, a metaphorically sticky substance that attaches itself to the evildoer, bringing all sorts of negative consequences to that individual or group. Willy Schottroff and others take a middle course, arguing that the root encompasses both ideas. Most authorities agree that 'rr entails a twofold separation: a severance of the one who uttered the curse from its object, and a severance of the object from the community. It is a form of shunning. Scharbert depicts the ārûr curse formula as the most severe means of separating the community from the evildoer and points to a host of texts in which the purpose of the curse is to define social and ethnic boundaries by the exclusion or humiliation of the individual or group under the curse.[17] Scharbert attests that 'rr is never used in private situations but only by persons in positions of authority.[18] Thus, the ārûr formula is basically a decree of excommunication uttered publicly as an act of humiliation by those in authority. The

14. Zevit, *The Religions of Ancient Israel*, 429–32.

15. Albertz and Schmitt, *Family and Household Religion*, 413.

16. Brichto, *The Problem of Curse in the Hebrew Bible*, 82; Speiser, "The Angelic Curse: Exodus 14:20," 198.

17. Scharbert, "'rr," 409.

18. Ibid., 1:411.

only individuals who utter this formula are God, those in authority (like the king), and the gathered community of the people in a ritual setting. For example, In Genesis 4, Cain is driven away because of a curse, and in Joshua 9 the Gibeonites are marginalized due to a curse. Significantly the word *'rr* never has God as its object. As a noun, *hamměěrâ*, which comes from the same root, is translated "sudden ruin" (Deut 28:20). A virtual catalogue of these calamities appears in Deut 28:20ff.

Ritually enacted blessings and curses are also present at Qumran in two broad public contexts with highly stylized rituals: rites of initiation and expulsion (1QS 2:1–18; 4Q280, CD vii 4–10; 4Q266) and battle liturgies (1QM xiii 2–13; 4Q510–11). Additionally, like the biblical blessings and curses in Leviticus and Deuteronomy that follow immediately after legal collections, 4QMMT, the Damascus Document, and the Temple Scroll contain examples of blessings and curses immediately following legislation that were likely to have been repeatedly performed in public contexts (4Q266 also follows halakhic material). Associating blessings and curses with these three social contexts is not unusual when compared with other cultures in the ancient Near East and with Israel's own culture in the biblical tradition. Yet the community's own adaptation and modification of blessings and curses is consistent with the community of the renewed covenant.[19] In cultures of the ancient Near East, curses were often a private law of the vulnerable when the enforcing arm of the law was limited. Boundary inscriptions were a common ancient Near Eastern example of this use of curses, a metaphor alluded to often in the scrolls, not only here, but also in the War Scroll and Damascus Document. Therefore curses were a last resort of the weak based on a transcendental principle of justice that covered the limited arm of the legal system. As Weber retorts, "the curse of the poor is the weapon of democracy."[20] Such denouncement rhetoric promoted egalitarianism or a leveling effect to broader society.

Of all curse terminology, the root *qll* exhibits the widest semantic range. In the Piel stem it is rendered "curse," "abuse," "scorn," "derogate," "denigrate," "repudiate," and the like. The Piel verb occurs 40 times in the Old Testament and the noun an additional 33 times with Deuteronomy (12 times) and Jeremiah (10 times) having the most instances of the root.[21] The basic denotation of the verb is "to be light" or "small." Pedersen argued that *qll* is an antonym to *kbd*, which means "to be heavy" or

19. J. S. Anderson, "Curses and Blessings."
20. Weber, *Ancient Judaism*, 256–57.
21. Keller, "*qll*"; Scharbert, "*qll*," 38.

"to honor/glorify." Today in English we often use these same ideas metaphorically when we say that someone is a lightweight or a heavyweight in
terms of their public popularity, academic prowess, or athletic ability. In
the Piel stem, the verb takes on a declarative function, as in the Abrahamic blessing: "I will bless those who bless you and curse those who curse
(*ûmĕqallekâ*) you (Gen 12:3). In 2 Sam 19:21, David's military leaders
wanted to kill Shimei because he "cursed the LORD's anointed." Earlier,
when David had to flee the city, Shimei had thrown stones and hurled insults. Later David instructs Solomon to kill Shimei because he called down
bitter curses (*qilĕlanî qĕlālâ*); literally, he "cursed a curse" against David (1
Kgs 2:8). Psalm 37:22 (ESV) states, "for those blessed (*mĕbōrākāyw*) by the
LORD will inherit the land, but those cursed (*ûmĕqūlālāyw*) by him shall
be cut off." Note the powerful effect of marginalization and exclusion due
to curse.

As a noun, *qĕlālâ* is often contrasted with blessing (Gen 27:12–13;
Deut 11:26–29; Josh 8:34). Just as *blessing* is used for those who have seen
prosperity, so the noun *qĕlālâ* is also used metonymically for those who
have suffered such a calamity that their very existence could be defined
as cursed. This usage becomes patently formulaic in Jeremiah (Jer 24:9;
25:18; 26:6; 42:18; 44:8, 12, 22; 49:13), and it is also present in 2 Kgs 22:19.
Finally, Ps 109:17 reads, "He loved to pronounce a curse [*qĕlālâ*]—may it
come on him; he found no pleasure in blessing [*bibĕrākâ*]—may it be far
from him." And see Deut 21:23 (my translation): "cursed of God is one
who is hanged" (*qilĕlat ĕlōhîm tālûy*).

The root 'lh has been translated with a number of different English
equivalents, typically "curse" or "oath." The Old Testament employs the
verb only six times and the noun occurs 37 times. Virtually all sources
agree that the root 'lh, a synonym of *šbwʿ*, entails a penalty-laden oath or
self-curse. Ancient Near Eastern literature expresses oaths regularly and
with great diversity.[22] Herbert Brichto has argued successfully that the
curse motivates and fuels the oath.[23] Either implicitly or explicitly every
oath, including behind covenant relationship, involves a conditional self-
curse.[24] The term 'rr can also be used as an adjuration or conditional curse

22. Lehmann catalogues twenty-two different ways of expressing oaths in the Old
Testament ("Biblical Oaths," 89–90). See also Gehman, "The Oath in the Old Testament"; and Parker, "The Vow in Ugaritic and Israelite Narrative Literature."

23. Brichto, *The Problem of Curse*, 40–76.

24. Cartlege has drawn clear distinctions between promises, oaths, and vows.
An oath consists of a promise that is attached to a curse, with an appeal to divinity
or king to carry out the curse. Oaths begin with human action and move to God's

to another party in the second or third person to motivate them toward a desired action (1 Sam 14:24; Neh 10:29). For example, oath-curses protect tombs from desecration, and boundary markers protect property lines from being moved. Oaths can also be used to ascertain guilt, either of an unknown offender or of a person suspected of an offense (Judg 17:2; 1 Kgs 8:31). One particularly telling example is found in Numbers 5. The woman suspected of adultery must drink holy water mixed with dust from the tabernacle floor. She must swear an oath of fidelity. If she is innocent, then nothing negative will happen. If she is guilty, then her "womb [will] miscarry and . . . abdomen swell." The evil consequences of oaths like this will fall on individuals if they are indeed guilty.

At other times, *'lh* can refer metonymically as a noun to persons who have experienced the calamities resulting from having a curse pronounced on them. The person under consideration is placed in such a dreadful situation that if someone wanted to curse another individual, they would simply refer to the fate of the person whose present existence was so miserable that they could be considered a curse themselves.[25] Saul's oath-curse in 1 Sam 14:24 has no magical element, because even though Jonathan violates the oath, no immediate misfortune overtakes him. Johannes Pedersen's comments reveal the horrors of the *'lh*:

> . . . this poisonous substance which spreads about is in Hebrew called *'lh*. It consumes the earth, which loses its power of germination; the plants fade, towns collapse, the inhabitants wail and disappear from the surface of the earth (Isa 24:6–12), the whole of the country decays, all pastures are dried up (Jer 23:10). A woman is penetrated with *'lh* and her belly is made to swell and her thigh to rot (Num 5:21, 27); children she cannot bear, and she becomes a curse among her people.[26]

Other terms such as *qbb*, *z'm*, and *šbw'* are often translated "curse" or "oath." Even the word "to bless," (*brk*) is employed as a euphemism for *qll* when God is the object of a supposed curse (Job 1:11, 2:5, 9; Ps 10:3).

Sheldon Blank has distinguished three different forms of curses in the Hebrew Bible.[27] The simple curse formula includes the Qal passive participle of *'rr* plus a subject. This kind of curse is often followed by the

---

potential response. Vows move in the opposite direction and can only be uttered to God (Cartlege, *Vows in the Hebrew Bible*).

25. Scharbert, "*'lh*," 265.

26. Pedersen, *Israel, Its Life and Culture*, 2:437.

27. Blank, "The Curse, Blasphemy, the Spell, the Oath," 73–83.

reason for the malediction. Blank calls the second form a "composite" curse. This form contains the formula above plus a freely composed curse as an addition (for example, "Cursed be Canaan," followed by, "he shall be an abject slave to his brothers" [Gen 9:25]). The third form, a freely composed curse, may be wholly independent from the other two forms. God is the agent in these curses and the imprecatory Psalms are the most common examples. Note a few examples:

> Let death take my enemies by surprise;
>> let them go down alive to the grave,
>> for evil finds lodging among them. (Ps 55:15)

> May his days be few;
>> may another take his place of leadership.
> May his children be fatherless
>> and his wife a widow.
> May his children be wandering beggars;
>> may they be driven from their ruined homes.
> May a creditor seize all he has;
>> may strangers plunder the fruits of his labor.
> May no one extend kindness to him
>> or take pity on his fatherless children.
> May his descendants be cut off,
>> their names blotted out from the next generation.
> May the iniquity of his fathers be remembered before the Lord;
>> may the sin of his mother never be blotted out.
> May their sins always remain before the LORD,
>> that he may blot out their names from the earth.
>> (Ps 109:8–15)

There is no real pattern to freely composed curses. They may be uttered in the second or third person, in conditional constructions, as jussives, or even in the indicative. They can be in prose or poetry, and the objects can be individuals or groups. Often employing vivid imagery from treaty-curses from the ancient Near East, these curses utilize ritual actions (such as the woman drinking the water with dirt from the tabernacle floor) accompanying the curse. Other examples of freely composed curses include Isaac's malevolent "blessing" of Esau in Gen 27:39–40, Balaam's curse on Moab and prophecies against the kingdoms in Num 24:15–24, and Jotham's curse on Abimelech and the Shechemites in Judges 9. Note the backhanded blessing of Esau, the derogative language against Moab in the Psalms, and the powerful Ugaritic curse in the three examples below:

Behold, away from the fatness of the earth shall your dwelling
be;
    and away from the dew of heaven on high.
By your sword you shall live, and you shall serve your brother;
But when you grow restless you shall break his yoke from his
neck. (Gen 27:39–40, ESV)

Moab is my sink. I throw my sandal at Edom. I will triumph
over Philistia. (Ps 108:9, my translation)

The loss of honor in freely composed curses is also reflected in curse
texts from Ugaritic literature.

May Horon smash, O my son,
    may Horon smash your head,
Athtart-the-name-of-Baal your crown!
May you fall down in the prime of life,
    empty handed and humiliated! (*KTU* 1.16)[28]

The writers of the Old Testament used vivid and varied language to
denote blessing and cursing. Over the last century, scholars have attempted to come to grips with the lexical meaning of blessings and curses, the
power behind these utterances, parallels to ancient Near Eastern cultures,
and their social function in Israelite society. A few questions tended to
fuel the discussion. Are blessings and curses potent utterances because
of the magical power of words, or does power rest in the social authority of the individual or community that utters these performatives? What
can be learned about blessings and curses in the Bible from the ancient
Near Eastern milieu in which it was written? How did the writers of the
Bible understand the operation of blessings and curses as religious utterances? We now turn to a review of some of the dominant thinkers who
have shaped this field and four paradigms for understanding blessings and
curses.

Blessings and Curses and Critical Scholarship

A Historical Paradigm

Johannes Pedersen led the pioneering work in blessings and curses as they
relate to the Old Testament. Two of his important works, *Der Eid bei den*

---

28. Watson and Wyatt, eds., *Handbook of Ugaritic Studies*, 571.

Semiten[29] and *Israel, Its Life and Culture,* reflected on what Pedersen perceived to be the peculiar character and psychology of Israel over against other societies of the ancient Near East. One of Pedersen's most well-known contributions lay in his discussion of the notion of the power of the soul. Pedersen defined the soul as the source of power for an individual to grow and to thrive, encompassing virtually every aspect of life. Life was no mere empty idea of existence but included "everything that fills the soul, making it wide and full of matter."[30] The human soul is both visible and invisible. A momentary impression, based on only the visible elements of personhood and personality, can only be complete when that impression also finds its place in the invisible whole of the person. The blessing enhanced the power that filled the soul, allowing it to thrive, while the curse poisoned, consumed, and emptied the soul of its vitality. The cursed one was the individual for whom everything in life failed; essentially the negation of life via the power of the soul. Since these blessings and curses affected all of life, they had wide implications for the fertility of land, produce, and even family. For Pedersen, the power behind the blessings and curses did not lie in the wish or the word necessarily, but in the power of one soul to act upon another. As the blessing transferred power from one individual to the next, the curse could effectively be put into the soul from outside, robbing it of its vitality. Since the power of the curse resided in the power of the soul, Pedersen contended that persons of strong souls speak stronger blessings and curses than ordinary people. Thus both blessings and curses were considered by Pedersen to be *self-fulfilling utterances.* The curse undermined the vitality of the soul, and the "ties which connect it with an organism from which it sucks strength and nourishment are irreparably broken: peace, honor, and blessing are lost."[31] The curse gnaws at the substance of the soul, making it light, which conveys the basic meaning of the Hebrew root *qll.* Pedersen concluded that the content of the curse entailed three elements: loss of honor, ban, and excommunication.

A blessed person could therefore become a blessing for society, and a cursed person could be a curse for society, affecting the collective soul of that community. This social function of blessings and curses was of particular interest to Pedersen. He argued that Israel, far more than its neighbors, employed the blessing to enhance communal status, and also uttered the curse to exclude individuals from community and reduce one's

29. Pedersen, *Der Eid bei den Semiten.*

30. Pedersen, *Israel, Its Life and Culture* 1:451.

31. Ibid.

social standing.[32] Pedersen's influential work was been criticized on several fronts, now for nearly a century.[33] The two most glaring weaknesses are the strong contrast between primitive and modern mindsets, as well as a naïve overemphasis on parallels between disparate cultures. Pedersen's eloquent but mistaken notions of soul power have also been effectively refuted.[34] Pedersen's uncritical parallels between Arabic, Assyrian, and Israelite literature were often overly analogical; like many comparative studies done around the turn of the twentieth century. The most telling weakness, however, was Pedersen's tendency to argue that the psychology of the Hebrew people could be directly derived from the structure of Hebrew language. James Barr's classic, *The Semantics of Biblical Language,* refuted Pedersen's affirmation that Semitic languages are a perfect reflection of Semitic thought and that any statement identified with European ideas must be rejected out of hand from applications to Semitic phenomena.[35] Yet Barr also points to the rich theological nature of much of Pedersen's work, which is therefore important for this present study. Barr regards Pedersen's *Israel* as one of the great and seminal works of the twentieth century, as both epochmaking in itself and groundbreaking for many trends toward contemporary Old Testament theology.[36]

Although Johannes Pedersen's studies had limitations that were shared with similar studies of his day, his work has had lasting influence on several individuals, most notably Sigmund Mowinckel, Johannes Hempel, and Claus Westermann. Mowinckel's primary interests lay in the influence of blessings and curses in a cultic setting.[37] Mowinckel's work will be particularly important for the examination of ritual blessings and curses in this present study. He, more than Pedersen, stressed the idea that the effectual word creates a thing out of nothing simply by being spoken. Mowinckel uniquely perceived that the operative base for blessings and curses existed, not in the power of one soul upon another, but in the cult. A few examples will suffice. In the case of Numbers 5, for example, the curse is conditional upon the guilt of the woman. Before war, Israel's

32. Pedersen, *Der Eid*, 68–79.

33. A helpful evaluation of the contributions and criticisms of Pedersen's *Israel* is presented by Porter, "Biblical Classics III."

34. Throughout Mitchell's, *The Meaning of BRK.*

35. Barr, *The Semantics of Biblical Language*, 41.

36. Barr, *The Concept of Biblical Theology*, 55.

37. Sigmund Mowinckel has written a chapter, "Der Fluch in Kult und Psalmdichtung," in his *Psalmenstudien*, 5:61–96. See also Mowinckel, "Psalms of Blessing and Cursing," in his *The Psalms in Israel's Worship*, 44–52.

military leaders would curse enemies or even one of their own towns that did not take part in a mandatory battle. When one swore upon the altar of the temple, the self-curse operated much like a mine that detonates when the cultic oath is broken.[38] Additionally, the priests and Levites publicly broadcast the blessings and curses of Deuteronomy 27 in a cultic setting. Even the prophets presented woe prophecies in what Mowinckel considered cultic contexts. Along with the social anthropologists of his day, Mowinckel argued that behind the blessings and curses lay the power of the community through the cult. This power could exclude individuals or groups from community, prevent illicit activity, or act as judge to point out unknown offenders to the community.

Much of Mowinckel's analysis of blessings and curses came out of his excellent exegetical work on the book of Psalms. In the Psalter, speakers utter blessings toward God and humans, and proclaim curses in prayers for revenge and punishment of enemies. In these imprecatory prayers, the psalmist replaced the ancient magical curse with the prayer for Yahweh to crush the enemy. The evolutionary elements of Mowinckel's cult-historical approach greatly impacted future studies. Mowinckel's placement of cultic blessing and cursing at the center of his discussion was perhaps his greatest contribution yet was also the target of the strongest criticism against him.

About the same time, Johannes Hempel also addressed the phenomenon of blessing and cursing in the Old Testament.[39] While acknowledging his indebtedness to Mowinckel, Hempel argued that his predecessor had given too much emphasis to the role of blessings and curses in cultic contexts. Hempel examined four issues related to the history of Israelite religion: roots of blessing/curse in magic, the content of the blessing/curse, prayers for intercession and revenge, and the blessing and curse as the activity of Yahweh. Drawing widely from the literature of Mesopotamia, Hellas, Rome, India, the Far East, the New Testament, and even the Talmud, Hempel identified the roots of blessing and cursing almost exclusively in the realm of magic. The contagious, self-fulfilling nature of the curse, the union of word and deed, the formulation of curses by incantations, and the physical aspects associated with blessings and curses all point to magical qualities.[40] He, rather arbitrarily, divided ancient Israel's history into three evolutionary periods: the period of folk religion, where

38. Mowinckel, "Der Fluch," 64–65.
39. Hempel, "Die israelitischen Anschauungen von Segen und Fluch," 58–61.
40. Ibid., 53–54.

the blessings and curses were magical and self-fulfilling; a period dependent on the cultic ritual, where a ceremony was required for blessings and
curses to be effective; and a final period of ethical monotheism, where
blessings and curses are completely independent of the realm of magic.
In this final stage, magic gave way to religion, and magical notions were
suppressed under the sovereign activity of Yahweh, the originator of both
blessings and curses. Hempel's work, like other scholarship of his time, has
been criticized for relying too heavily on an evolutionary argument from
folk magic to religion, and for its uncritical comparisons to other cultures.

Claus Westermann placed his discussion of the blessing squarely in
the context of the work of the three scholars just mentioned.[41] Westermann's monograph *Blessing in the Bible and the Life of the Church* represents a unique approach to the study of the blessing.[42] He agreed with
Mowinckel and Hempel that both blessing and curse had roots in primitive magic, but he argued that the blessing and curse followed completely
different lines of development. The blessing lost its magical elements and
Yahweh became the subject and initiator of the blessing, but Yahweh never
initiates the curse. The biblical writers brought the blessing early on under
the activity of Yahweh while cursing retained its primitive magical roots.[43]

This distinction allowed Westermann to submit two basic ways
that God deals with humans: deliverance and blessing. This distinction
is particularly important for this study because Westermann's work is the
most explicitly theological reviewed so far. Humans experience deliverance through events that represent God's direct intervention in history,
but they experience blessing as the continuing activity of God that is either
present or absent in day-to-day life. The blessing is not a well-constructed
theological tenet but still merges with the redemptive actions of God at the
heart of the Old Testament revelation. The Yahwist, according to Westermann, united blessing with history by connecting blessing and promise.
While this continuous activity of providence is characteristic of the blessing, Westermann posited that there is no biblical notion of a continuous
malevolent counterpart that alternatively corresponds to the blessing. He
preferred, instead, to speak of acts of disobedience and transgression.
Thus, Westermann's case was strongly dependent on the view that blessing

41. An excellent survey of Westermann's blessing theology is in Perdue, "Old Testament Theology since Barth's *Epistle to the Romans*, 102–9.

42. Westermann, *Blessing in the Bible*. See also Westermann, *Elements of Old Testament Theology*, 102–17.

43. Westermann, *Blessing in the Bible*, 23.

and curse followed two divergent evolutionary lines of development. This, perhaps, is more wishful thinking than sustained argument, as he does not attempt to demonstrate exactly how these two lines evolved. It is doubtful whether such evolutionary lines are demonstrable anyway, given the paucity of evidence in the biblical text.[44] Westermann pressed the stark distinction between God's salvation and blessing too far.

What can be said about these twentieth-century contributions to the study of blessings and curses from the history of Israelite religion? First, these studies laid the groundwork for virtually all future studies on blessings and curses.[45] There are valid criticisms of naïve comparisons of numerous disparate cultures to Israel, criticisms of the orientalistic bias against Arab cultures, and criticisms of the tendency to make unguarded pronouncements about primitive thinking. That these studies all tended to rely heavily on nineteenth-century evolutionary concepts that sought to trace the development of Israelite religion from a primitive, magical practice to advanced religious faith has also been rightly criticized.[46] Yet these studies formulated the basic questions, provided philological insights, accumulated massive amounts of comparative data, and continue to inform current scholarship.[47]

Two recent twenty-first-century studies are worthy of note in that they demonstrate the influences of earlier work; plus they extend thinking about blessings and curses in new directions: these are works by Martin Leuenberger and Hermann Spieckermann. Martin Leuenberger completed an extensive doctoral dissertation: *Blessing and the Theology of Blessing in Ancient Israel*.[48] The work is foremost a religiohistorical approach to the topic, but Leuenberger is also interested in theological implications as well. The work begins with a careful lexical review of the use of the word *brk*, the strength of Leuenberger's study. In the heart of his study he examines

---

44. Scharbert takes issue with Westermann on this point. He argues that the Yahwist interprets the history of Israel and indeed of all humanity from the viewpoint of both blessing and curse. He also questions the distinction between saving deeds and blessings, "*brk*," 306

45. Lyder Brun, for example, applied the insights of Pedersen, Mowinckel, and Hempel to the New Testament as well as noncanonical literature of early Christianity, in *Segen und Fluch im Urchristentum*.

46. A helpful discussion of these issues can be found in Rogerson, *Anthropology of the Old Testament*, 22–65.

47. Westermann limits the contribution of Pedersen's work to the accumulation of raw materials (Westermann, *Blessing in the Bible*, 20).

48. Leuenberger, *Segen und Segenstheologien im alten Israel*.

epigraphic examples of blessing texts discovered in the twentieth century from Kuntillet Ajrud, Khirbet el-Qom, and Ketef Hinnom. Consistent with a history-of-religions approach, he considers the epigraphic evidence as the primary witness to Israelite religion and the biblical witness as secondary. In regards to the biblical witness, he chooses four primary blessing texts: the ancestral narratives, Deuteronomy, P, and Job. In accordance with religiohistorical treatments discussed above, Leuenberger's traces a linear development between primary and secondary religion. This is surprising, considering the criticisms of similar studies in the last several decades. For example, he observes the following developmental changes in Israelite religion: a change from localized to universal religious practices, a change from earlier naturalistic foundations of blessing to an increased focus on Yahweh as source of blessing, a shift from a magical to more abstract understanding of blessing, plus a decrease in fertility as a means of blessing. Like Pedersen and others, Leuenberger does not completely deny the magical transfer of blessing power, nor does he neglect performative aspects of blessing utterances. The more primitive, elaborate magical workings led to a more advanced, Christian theology of blessing.[49] His work, like the studies above, contains a wealth of philological insights along with sensitive treatments of comparative epigraphic data. Sadly, as with many evolutionary approaches, his case for the development of the blessing is questionable, especially considering how little evidence there is, both epigraphic and textual. In spite of the title of the book, Leuenberger's interests are primarily religiohistorical, not theological. He claims to be interested in the theological implications for a postmodern context but really doesn't explore those implications in depth.

As I already noted, recent trends have led to the separation of the disciplines of the history of the religion of Israel from Old Testament theology.[50] Hermann Spieckermann has taken up a case study on blessing as a means of pointing out the convergences and differences of religiohistorical and theological approaches to Israelite religion.[51] He admits that the discipline of Old Testament theology is a canon-related discipline with normative outcomes, while approaches from the history of religions often directly conflict with the dominant theological ideology of the biblical text. After a review of the historical relationship of the two disciplines,

49. Ibid., 485.

50. See Smith, *The Early History of God*; see Smith, *The Origins of Biblical Monotheism*; Zevit, *The Religions of Ancient Israel*.

51. Spieckermann, "YHWH Bless You and Keep You."

Spieckermann moves on to current trends in research on Israelite religion, which he says is characterized by the undeniable fact that preexilic Israelite religion can only be characterized as a "multi-faceted monolatry" which—especially in its early stages—is hardly distinguishable from a moderate polytheism.[52] Yahweh is indeed God but a chief among equals. In spite of what the Bible teaches Israel should do, the Israelites were, in reality, no monotheists. Spieckermann cites examples in extrabiblical evidence of composite names with Baal, examples of Yahweh and his spouse, and the iconographic images of the bull borrowed from Baal worship. In all these cases, external evidence challenges the supposed absolute monotheism of the Old Testament.

In his case study of blessing, he begins with the topic of amulets, something popular for centuries in Israel but looked on with disdain in the biblical text. He places these amulets in the sphere of magic, which he argues was an intentionally theologically reflective practice. As he amusingly expresses it, "magic is the mother of educated theology."[53] He cites the example of the silver amulet found at Ketef Hinnom, containing the Aaronite blessing. Here he stresses the need to distinguish between the actual magical use of the amulet and what the text of the amulet says, which is a simple quotation from Aaron's blessing in Numbers. Moving on to textual examples of blessing, Spieckermann cites a tomb inscription found in Khirbet el-Qom, dated to the last quarter of the eighth century BCE, which reads,

> Uriyahu the rich commissioned it.
> Blessed was/is/be Uriyahu by YHWH,
> and from his enemies by his Asherah he has delivered him.
> (Written?) by Oniyahu
> . . .
> . . . by his Asherah . . .
> . . . and by his Asherah . . .[54]

As a historian of religion, Spieckermann is interested in why Asherah is mentioned three times and YHWH only once. Of course, he is primarily

52. Ibid., 171

53. Ibid., 175.

54. Ibid., 176. An alternative translation, "I blessed Uryahu to YHWH," has some interesting parallels from ostraca found at Arad and Edom. See Zevit, *The Religions of Ancient Israel*, 361–62. Also note similar blessings to Baal and El from Kuntillet 'Ajrud in Zevit, *The Religions of Ancient Israel*, 372–74.

interested in defining the relationship between YHWH and Asherah.[55] But there is simply not that much to go on. In addition, he points to the over nine hundred pillar figurines found in Judah dating from the eighth to the sixth centuries BCE. He suggests that a historian of religion will try to explain how something that appears so commonly would eventually fall out of use altogether in Judah.[56] The historian of religion will look for explanations outside the Old Testament, which was written later than the artifacts that have been found. He suggests that the religiohistorical approach can assist Old Testament theology to look in the right direction for the theological thrust behind these artifacts, while Old Testament theology can assist the history-of-religions approach to be aware of the theological implications signified by the presence of such artifacts.

As far as his target topic, Spieckermann thinks the Aaronic blessing in Num 6:22–27 is a postexilic, not a preexilic, reflection on the protective power of the blessing, reflected in texts like the one found at Ketef Hinnom, a mere hundred meters from the Temple Mount. This blessing is drawn into a theological context in Numbers 6, where God is certain to be the source of blessing. Thus the interrelation of private piety and public religion is illustrated by the interaction of both disciplines. The work of the biblical theologian and the historian of religion overlaps, but each pursues a different goal. Similarly, Mark S. Smith cites Near Eastern texts that invoke the gods to bring about blessing. Divine blessing also apparently included deceased royal ancestors. Some deities may undertake the destruction of others. What he calls monstrous forces can threaten human life, a view expressed with equal conviction by the Israelite sources.[57]

A Comparative Paradigm

In 1955, George Mendenhall published his influential *Law and Covenant in Israel and the Ancient Near East*.[58] Here he delineated similarities between Hittite suzerainty treaties and the biblical covenant-renewal ceremony of

---

55. Kuntillet ʿAjrud has provided nine blessing formulas, five with the root *brk*. Three contain the expression "Yahweh and his asherah," and one parallels Aaron's blessing, "may he bless you and keep you, and may he be with my lord [forever?]" (Meshel, *Kuntillet ʿAjrud*, 127).

56. Kletter, "Between Archaeology and Theology."

57. Smith, *The Origins of Biblical Monotheism*, 30–32.

58. Mendenhall, *Law and Covenant in Israel*. Victor Korošec actually introduced this topic in his work on Hittite treaties in 1931, "Hethitische Staatsverträge."

Joshua 24. Most of these treaties included blessings and curses. He argued that the influence of the Hittite treaty patterns must have been introduced to Israel early in its history. This thesis struck a devastating blow to the Wellhausenian view that covenant was a late creation of the prophets. Mendenhall's work influenced numerous scholars who were interested in comparing blessing-and-curse texts from ancient Near Eastern treaties to that of the Old Testament. One such scholar was F. Charles Fensham, who concluded that the covenant form of the Old Testament, which promises blessing for obedience and cursing for disobedience, follows patterns to similar treaties.[59] He speculated that the blessing-and-curse form might be the background behind theological concepts of salvation and damnation, a thesis that has never found much support. Klaus Baltzer reached similar conclusions. Baltzer argued that the most far-reaching transformations made to the ancient treaties by the biblical writers occurred in the blessings and curses. He maintained that the alternatives of blessing and curse were originally presented as two equal possibilities, historicized over time in antiquity. Early on in Israel's history, the blessing constituted present experience and the curse threatened the future. After the destruction of Jerusalem, the blessing represented the promise of the future and the curse constituted the present experience of Israel. Baltzer also contended that the texts of covenant renewal at Qumran portrayed curses and blessings eschatologically.[60] Another of Fensham's studies focused on parallels between curses in prophetic literature and curses of these ancient treaties.[61] Fensham proposed a link between curses in vassal-treaties and prophetic maledictions. However, the mechanical magical execution of the broken treaty-curse stands in "glaring contrast to the ego-theological approach of the prophetic writers."[62] In the Old Testament, the sole subject of the curse is Yahweh, and only in the Old Testament can a curse be changed into a blessing. This potential for change contrasts with Pedersen's magical notion of a self-fulfilling curse and with Westermann's notion that curses underwent a completely different evolutionary development from blessings in ancient Israel's religious literature.

Delbert Hillers reached similar conclusions to Mendenhall's in an independent study published about the same time.[63] He specified similarities

59. Fensham, "Malediction and Benediction."
60. Baltzer, *The Covenant Formulary*, 180.
61. Fensham, "Common Trends in Curses."
62. Ibid., 173.
63. Hillers, *Treaty-Curses and the Old Testament Prophets.*

between the covenant curses in Deuteronomy 28 and Leviticus 26 with treaty curses of the ancient Near East. He also argued that the prophets used these curse threats as means to pronounce doom upon the people of Israel. He cautiously did not make too much of this, aware that these coincidences between treaties and prophecies of judgment do not demonstrate unequivocally that the prophets borrowed from the treaty style. Hillers followed Mendenhall, proposing that the covenant blessings and curses are older than the prophets. He further contended that there is an increase in the proportion of expressions with parallels in treaty curses among the prophecies against foreign kingdoms, possibly implying that these kingdoms might have broken certain political treaties with Israel.

Writing roughly a decade after the studies of Hillers and Fensham, Moshe Weinfeld published his influential and controversial study of Deuteronomy.[64] Building on these earlier studies, Weinfeld argued that the book of Deuteronomy, the Deuteronomistic History, and the prose sermons of Jeremiah were all strongly influenced by these treaties of the Near East. He pointed out that the evils listed in Deut 28:26–30 are listed in exactly the same order as in the Esarhaddon treaties. Going against the cautions of Hillers, Weinfeld argued that there must be a literary connection, not merely a connection of milieu, between the biblical texts and Near Eastern treaties.[65]

A Linguistic Paradigm

Blessings and curses are often defined as magical phenomena, but the relationship between magic and religion has historically been notoriously slippery to pin down. Raz Kletter provides a mercifully brief synopsis of various approaches to the relationship of magic, religion, and archaeology.[66] In some respects, one could argue that the dichotomy between magic and religion is a product of Western monotheism, the Enlightenment, or both. James Frazer famously drove a wedge between magic and religion. In his 1890 classic *The Golden Bough*, Frazer defined magic as that which emerged from a *primitive* worldview—something driven by completely natural forces.[67] Religion, on the other hand, emerges from

64. Weinfeld, *Deuteronomy and the Deuteronomic School*.

65. Ibid., 116–57.

66. Kletter, "Between Archaeology and Theology: The Pillar Figurines from Judah and the Asherah."

67. Frazier, *The Golden Bough*.

the *supernatural* world of faith. Today's readers can immediately detect problems with this simplistic dichotomy. Max Weber reduced somewhat the absolute separation of magic and religion but still held to the belief that magic and religion were opposites.[68] Marcel Mauss proposed a social definition of magic.[69] Any rite that is not a part of an organized cult is considered folk religion derived from the realm of magic. Religion, according to Mauss, trends towards metaphysics, while magic migrates towards the concrete. Keith Thomas's *Religion and the Decline of Magic* argues that the Protestant revolution attempted to take magic out of religion, and that science and rationalism introduced new ways of thinking that led to the collapse of magic in England.[70]

But in the 1970s scholars began to back off of the dichotomy between magic and religion; yet they struggled with a viable alternative to that dichotomy. John Skorups's solution was similar to Weber's: magic runs counter to the conceptual way people interpret the world.[71] The trend toward softening the boundaries between magic and religion continued through the end of the twentieth century. R. K. Ritner defined *magic* in a less sophisticated way: "the religious practices by one group held in disdain by another." Thus, your religion is my magic.[72] Gideon Bohak's recent *Ancient Jewish Magic* surveys the history of Jewish magical practices from the Second Temple to the rabbinic period.[73]

Over the course of time, a few constants did indeed emerge from these studies on the relationship between magic and religion. Magic is not typically concerned with causality, only repeatability, whereas religion is all about causality. For magic, it is more about proper mechanics. There are two basic kinds of magic: sympathetic or imitative magic and contagion magic. A biblical example of sympathetic blessing might be sexual participation in temple prostitution banned by Old Testament law and prophets. By a person's enacting a fertility rite with a sacred prostitute, the fruitfulness of the person's fields, flocks, and family is ensured.[74] An example of contagion magic associated with a curse is the water ordeal in Numbers 5. The curse adheres to the evildoer like some sticky substance.

68. Weber, *The Sociology of Religion.*
69. Mauss, *A General Theory of Magic.*
70. Thomas, *Religion and the Decline of Magic.*
71. Skorupsk, *Symbol and Theory.*
72. Ritner, *The Mechanics of Ancient Egyptian Magical Practice.*
73. Bohak, *Ancient Jewish Magic.*
74. Yamauchi, "Magic in the Biblical World."

All this is to say that while there is no completely acceptable solution to the relationship of magic and religion, there is one promising methodology that helps to lessen the divide between magic and religion. We now turn to a particular view of language that will be the basis for the methodology followed in this study; a view about how words relate to things and how words can be effective, without notions of magic.[75]

Nearly fifty years ago, J. L. Austin's, *How to Do Things with Words* developed the notion of performative utterances that do not merely describe or report things but are simultaneously a verbal utterance and a deed performed.[76] With these illocutions, to say something is literally to do something. Thus, there is power in language to constitute reality, not just describe it; not for any magical reason, but because such speech is uttered in accordance with recognized social conventions. Performative speech can only be effective in a social setting where a constative or informational utterance remains unaffected by context. For Austin, performatives become effective to the extent that they are uttered in appropriate ways and in appropriate social circumstances. For example, I cannot catch a fish simply by uttering, "I now catch a fish," but I can say, "I promise to invite you next time I go fishing." The second phrase draws on social conventions that the first simply does not. Austin posits four conditions for effective performatives. First, there must be an accepted conventional procedure having a certain conventional effect. Second, the particular personas and circumstances in a given case must be appropriate for the invocation of the particular procedure. Third, the procedure must be executed by all participants, both correctly and completely. Finally, if a procedure is designed for use by persons having certain thoughts and feelings, then the person participating in so invoking the procedure must in fact have those thoughts and feelings.[77]

As it pertains to ritual speech acts of blessings and curses, Austin's work has tended to shift the discussion away from a Frazierian dichotomy between magic and religion, as well as away from the magical power of words or notions of power of the soul. Social anthropologists have widely applied Austin's theory of performative utterances and illocutionary speech acts (although significantly modified over time) to functional

75. Thiselton, "The Supposed Power of Words in Biblical Writings," 286.

76. Austin, *How to Do Things with Words*. Austin's distinction between words that describe things and words that do something proved insufficient, and the theory was modified by John Searle, *Speech Acts*.

77. Austin, *How to Do Things with Words*, 14–15.

models of societal social control and self-definition.[78] Performative language thus enables one to approach ritual words from the fundamental linguistic level to see how words actually can accomplish certain ends, apart from magical or symbolic notions alone.[79] Austin dissected speech acts into three constitutive dimensions: the utterance itself (locution), the force of that utterance (illocution), and the effect of that utterance (perlocution). An illocutionary utterance entails a social action. Illocutionary utterances are the performance of an act *in* saying something opposed to the performance of an act *of* saying something. The pervasive power of words in performative utterances has little or nothing to do with a natural cause and effect. It's all about accepted social conventional procedures in which appropriate persons take part. It is less about mechanics and more about convention. One does not have to resort to the notion of word magic to claim that words actually do things.

Biblical scholars have applied the notion of speech acts to blessings and curses, viewing them as illocutionary utterances whose power lies in the nature of human language uttered under appropriate circumstances by appropriate individuals.[80] The words of blessing and curse are not magically self-fulfilling yet are nevertheless incredibly potent in proper social contexts. These performatives can at once both maintain and challenge social structures, serving as social propagandists and iconoclasts alike. When associated with legal collections, these illocutions can coerce the community to conform to a rigid set of social norms at the same time as they maintain the distinct social solidarity and identity of that community. Blessings and curses often employ stereotypical language combined with vividly enacted intramural rituals that evoke the powers of the blessing or curse. For example, Moshe Weinfeld mentions a number of dramatic acts that typically accompany curses in ancient treaties, including burning wax figurines, breaking bows and arrows, scattering salt, cutting up animals,

78. See Finnegan, "How to Do Things with Words"; Ray, "Performative Utterances in African Rituals"; Onibere, "Potent Utterance"; Tambiah, "Form and Meaning of Magical Acts"; Kratz, "Genres of Power."

79. Austin discusses three categories of fallacies that render speech-acts impotent: misinvocations, misapplications, and misexecutions (*How to Do Things with Words,* 14–15).

80. Thiselton, "The Supposed Power of Words in Biblical Writings"; Hillers, "Some Performative Utterances in the Bible." Mitchell, *The Meaning of BRK "to Bless" in the Old Testament*; J. S. Anderson, "The Social Function of Curses in the Hebrew Bible." Anthony Thiselton has applied speech-act theory to the study of hermeneutics in *New Horizons in Hermeneutics,* 283–307, as has Patrick, *The Rhetoric of Revelation in the Hebrew Bible.*

and offering covenantal sacrifices.[81] While no destructive ritual acts typically accompanied these biblical utterances, they were nonetheless powerful. When paired together with blessings, the typically lopsided sanctions of the curses evoke effective social functions of these rituals.

Austin's theory is no mere imposition of twentieth-century philosophy onto a written text. Speech-act theory brings a convincing challenge to the traditional view about the dynamic power of the word or the older idea of the power of the soul. Words produce effects because of the societal understanding of the function of speech acts, not because of some magical power of the spoken word alone. This theory allows for genuine power in uttered speech *without* resorting to taking a hard line on the distinction between magic and religion. Indeed, words uttered in the wrong circumstances may even have the opposite effect from what was intended,

> If anyone loudly blesses their neighbor early in the morning,
>   it will be taken as a curse. (Prov 27:14)

> Like a fluttering sparrow or a darting swallow,
>   an undeserved curse does not come to rest. (Prov 26:2)

When God is the subject of the blessing or curse, divine sovereignty trumps social convention, power of the spoken word, and power of the soul, "'If you do not listen, and if you do not set your heart to honor my name,' says YHWH of hosts, 'I will send a curse upon you, and I will curse your blessings. Yes, I have already cursed them, because you have not set your heart to honor me'" (Mal 2:2b).[82] Theologically, the power of the spoken word yields itself to the power of divine authority.

This present study is like a number of promising applications of speech-act theory to biblical texts. One recent example is David McCabe's playful reworking of Austin's original title, *How to Kill Things with Words: Ananias and Sapphira under the Prophetic Speech-Act of Divine Judgment (Acts 4:32–5:1)*.[83] Yet, the broader application of the theory to matters of a general theory of hermeneutics we will leave to other specialists in the discipline.[84]

81. Weinfeld, "The Loyalty Oath in the Ancient Near East," 400–402. See also Faraone, "Molten Wax, Spilt Wine, and Mutilated Animals."

82. See also Deut 23:5; Neh 13:2.

83. McCabe, *How to Kill Things with Words*. Some other examples are Upton, *Hearing Mark's Endings*, 88–102; Adams, *The Performative Nature and Function of Isaiah 40–55*, 18–63. Botha, *Jesus and the Samaritan Woman*.

84. Vanhoozer, "The Semantics of Biblical Literature"; Vanhoozer, *Is There a*

The Blessing and the Curse

A Theological Paradigm

We have learned from the history of scholarship presented above that much of the interest in blessings and curses has been historically driven. This review of scholarship has also highlighted the divide between biblical theology and the history of religion. Biblical theologians may charge that historico-religious approaches are too developmental to be supported by the data. The biblical evidence, which tends to be hit-and-miss, is not a convincing foundation for the idea that blessings and curses underwent clear developmental change in Israelite society. Historians of religion, on the other hand, may charge that the theological approach of adopting canonical categories flattens all historical dimensions, making it nearly impossible to determine from the biblical text how blessings and curses may have actually functioned in Israelite society. The Bible's perspective represents the writer's or editor's outlook regarding the way things should be rather than the way things actually were. While these two disciplines are headed in opposite directions, this does not mean that one cannot enlighten the other.[85] The wide variety of projects in both disciplines demonstrates that both enterprises still hold promise.[86]

But we now turn to blessings and curses as theological concepts. The notion of blessings and curses is theologically linked to two important theological doctrines: the doctrine of divine providence and the doctrine of election.[87] Both these doctrines are rooted in the character of God. Not surprisingly, the idea that God can actively bless, thus enhancing the well-being of humans, is celebrated in theology as well as in daily life. The view that God can oppose such well-being trips up traditional thinking about these two doctrines. Theologically, scholars have chosen one of several options when it comes to the divine backing of various biblical curses. The first is to simply ignore the theological implications of Old Testament

Meaning in This Text?; Vanhoozer, *First Theology*; Wolterstorff, *Divine Discourse*; Watson, *Text and Truth*.

85. An excellent integration of the advantages and disadvantages of the use of both archeology and texts for unpacking religious belief, particularly related to the cult of the dead in Israel, has been written by Theodore J. Lewis, "How Far Can Text Take Us."

86. Robert Miller's excellent study examines how biblical writers applied Neo-Assyrian royal propaganda to describe a relationship with God. His historio-religious insights are summarized in a chapter entitled "Election and Grace in Israelite Religion," and his concluding applications to Roman Catholic biblical theology are included in a loosly-autonomous chapter titled "The Triumph of Grace" (*Covenant and Grace in the Old Testament*).

87. Rogerson, "Can a Doctrine of Providence be Based on the Old Testament?"

curse texts. This is perhaps the option chosen by most who have worked in Old Testament theology. Even a perfunctory look at an index of any Old Testament theology will reveal this. One can usually observe a number of citations about blessing and next to nothing on the curse. John Goldingay explicitly follows this approach: blessings and curses are correlative but are not expressed as exact antonyms. God actively blesses but does not actively curse.[88] This is a simple solution but not a very satisfying one. David Gunn argued that it is tempting for Christians to read the Old Testament in terms of the "optimistic God of Christian theology."[89] Evil is always something of an embarrassment in this tradition. Another proposed solution is to argue for two different evolutionary lines of development, as Westermann has done. This approach all too conveniently allows an easy way out—for the blessing to come under the doctrine of God's providence and the curse to be something of the past, a remnant of ancient folk religion. A third solution, one followed here, is blatantly to admit that the texts of the Old Testament routinely portray God as the subject of both blessing and curse, and to come to grips with exactly what it means that God not only chooses to enhance a life of fullness but also oppose it.

Pedersen's treatment of blessing and curse is particularly rich, even given his propensity to go overboard on the power of the soul. Theologically, Pedersen links righteousness to blessing and sin to curse. The sinner is one who counteracts the positive forces of blessing that uphold community, and since this community is a divine community, those sins violate God's nature. Note Pedersen's comments on the curses of Leviticus 26:

> The cursed is the man for whom everything fails. The paralysis is in him: whatever he puts his hand to; illness, drought, crop failure, defeat is the result. He is so dissolved and confused in his soul that he staggers on blindly. If he takes a wife, she is taken away by another, if he builds a house or plants a vineyard, others will reap the benefit of his efforts, provided there be any fruits. The power to create posterity fails, his people shrink in insignificance. It is shattered about the world, but nowhere it finds peace. All love disappears. When besieged by the enemy the cursed eats his own children. A greater perversity can hardly be imagined; the picture cannot become much blacker . . .

Hans Walter Wolff and George Goats applied sensitive theological analysis to the message of the Yahwist, which, according to their

---

88. Goldingay, *Old Testament Theology*, 1:139.

89. Gunn, *The Fate of King Saul*, 131.

contention, is the basic supporting stratum in the Pentateuch.[90] Wolff focused on bridge passages, or what I am calling seams in the narrative of the Tetrateuch, beginning with the blessing passage in Gen 12:1–3 and ending with the Balaam prophecies of Numbers 22–25. Wolff's method is kerygmatic; that is, these narratives present a theological message set in a saving matrix. The book of Genesis places the foundational promise of people, land, and blessing given to Abraham immediately after the promise of becoming a people. The ultimate kerygmatic message of that strategic placement is Israel's mediation of blessing to other peoples. Consequently, *blessing* becomes the interpretive word—from Abraham's departure from Haran to David's kingdom in Jerusalem. Sensitive readers know why people need this blessing. The word *'rr* ("curse") appears five times in the primeval history (Gen 3:14, 17; 4:11; 5:29; and 9:25). Consequently the promise in Genesis 12 is the answer to the tragic dilemma of Genesis 1–11. As we will see in the next chapter, Wolff traces this theme of blessing to other peoples through the Mamre-Sodom narrative, the ancestral narratives, the exodus, the giving the law, and the Balaam prophecies. Blessing to the foreign peoples occurs only through Israel's unrelenting intercession, not through acts of power and aggression.

Walter Brueggemann's *Theology of the Old Testament* reveals a great deal of influence from Wolff.[91] Brueggemann explores the topic of blessings in several places. Under the heading "Yahweh: The One Who Makes Promises," he examines verbs of promise, particularly "give" and "bless." In many ways he sounds very much like Pedersen, in that the blessing is the bestowal of life-force relative to generativity, leading to energy, prosperity, abundance, and well-being.[92] The blessing is much more than a friendly wish. Brueggemann traces this blessing to Abraham, then to Isaac, to Jacob, and to Joseph's sons, Ephraim and Manasseh. As a blessed people, Israel is to be the blessing bearer to other peoples. Brueggemann describes in Genesis and Exodus how Jacob and Moses are called to bestow God's blessings on none other than Pharaoh (Exod 12:32). The blessing to Abraham is God's antidote to the sorry state of foreign peoples in Genesis 3–11.[93] Brueggemann also deals with the topic of blessing in his section on creation. Under the heading "The World, Blessed and Fruitful,"

90. Wolff, "The Kerygma of the Yahwist"; Coats, "The Curse in God's Blessing," 31–41.

91. Brueggemann, *Theology of the Old Testament*.

92. Ibid., 165–66, 188.

93. Ibid., 498.

creation is depicted as Yahweh's partner. Blessing is the very outcome of creation.[94] One insightful observation that is vintage Brueggemann points out that what Yahweh does in the wilderness tradition is also what Yahweh does in creation. He transforms nothingness to productivity, well-being, and fruitfulness. He transfers scenes of hopelessness to occasions of life, possibility, and joy.

But this blessing is an open-ended dynamic. In a section titled "Creation in Jeopardy," Brueggemann recognizes the possibility that disobedience to Yahweh can put the entire creation in jeopardy. When discussing the violations of the curses in Leviticus 26, he speaks of "historical-military" assaults disrupting the process of food production. He delineates no distinction between historical and natural threats. The canonical shape of Israel's witness includes threat, Yahweh's capacity to turn the processes of the blessing into the dead end of the curses. The curse comes to focus in the exile, which is no mere geographic displacement alone but the cessation of life's possibilities, a withdrawal of fruitfulness. He cites Zeph 1:2–3; Amos 4:6–11; and Jer 4:23–26 to support this equation of exile and curse. What Yahweh has formed in generosity as a position of blessing can revert, with Yahweh's indignation, to a status of curse. The world Yahweh created in freedom can be terminated, nullified, and abandoned in like freedom. Israel's countertestimony is a response to covenantal sanctions. Their countertestimony arises because Israel experiences the negativity of Yahweh in great disproportion to their disobedience. They protest this disproportion in laments, as curses progressively intensified over Israel's long history.

Brevard Childs closed his *Old Testament Theology in a Canonical Context* with two chapters: "Life under Threat" and "Life under Promise."[95] Israel lived life under countless threats. For example, the primeval threat in Genesis 1–11 is that the world might return to its primordial state of chaos. The problem of evil and a world filled with violence allows for the likelihood of divine judgment through a return to chaos. In the covenantal texts of Leviticus 26 and Deuteronomy 28, the covenant curse is a historical principle that explains the destruction of the people. The prophets and apocalyptic literature also portray the working out of this divine threat. Even the Psalms and Wisdom literature observe that death is the ultimate threat, and rejection of the covenant means forfeiture of life. Even though the world was created by God, humans cannot seem to know this God,

94. Ibid., 529.
95. Childs, *Old Testament Theology*, 222–47.

who has seemingly withdrawn, "Man's calamity is that he cannot make contact with this divine action. The world remains dumb in the face of this quest for salvation."[96] While threat is not the last word, Childs warns against moving too quickly from threat to promise; otherwise one jeopardizes the reality of life under divine judgment. Childs discusses patterns of canonical shaping that retain elements of promise. The polarity between promise and fulfillment is not in a linear, temporal sequence but in the existential tension between threat and promise, disobedience and obedience. Forms of this promise are present in prophetic salvation prophecies and in promises regarding possession of the land. The land functions as a cipher for divine blessing, which could be lost, ironically, even while living in that land.

These examples demonstrate that taking up the theme of blessing and curse is a theologically potent avenue of exploration. The Bible itself is persistently and seriously concerned with the many and various things that can be done with words.[97] New insights from speech-act theory allow the interpreter some fresh ways to reflect on how God enhances or opposes a life of fullness without viewing blessings and curses as some primitive, magical notion that has no place in twenty-first-century reflection about God.

96. Ibid., 232.
97. Briggs, "Speech-Act Theory," 75.

3

Blessings and Curses
in the Pentateuch

Ancient Sources and Narrative Form

THIS CHAPTER BEGINS WITH an important methodological question:
Can historical source criticism and modern literary criticism coexist; or
even more, can they coexist in the same chapter? *Older* and *newer* literary
criticisms actually do share a few commonalities. Both disciplines begin
at the same place (with the final text of the Bible), but from there they
head in entirely opposite directions. Source critics are primarily interested
in understanding how the current text came into being: that is, with the
compositional history of the Bible; while literary critics are interested in
the canonical text—the intricacies and challenges of the text as it stands.
Joel Baden nicely distinguished the two disciplines: "Modern literary criticism is a method meant to help us appreciate the Bible as literature; that
is, *a priori* as a unity. Source criticism is meant to explain why, historically,
such a reading is so difficult."[1] Source criticism has certainly revealed the
limitations of taking the canonical text as it stands. Reading the Pentateuch as a unified whole is a difficult task. Yet, source criticism has come
up against many of its own challengers in the last fifty years, not only
from traditional conservative scholarship, which has always opposed the
Documentary Hypothesis, but from historical critics within its own camp.
More and more, scholars are denying the very existence of the traditional

---

1. Baden, "The Tower of Babel."

sources of Wellhausen's Documentary Hypothesis, particularly in light of studies in the 1970s and 1980s by Hans Heinrich Schmid, John Van Seters, Rolf Rendtorff, and a growing number of other scholars.[2] Simultaneously, the nature and date of these hypothetical sources has varied widely, leaving plenty of room for the hermeneutics of suspicion. Regardless of present uncertainty regarding the sources of the Pentateuch, one thing is clear: the authors of the Pentateuch did what all good authors do; they drew from the cultural memory of their own society and brought together disparate traditions and motifs into a narrative structure.

As foolish as it might appear, I would like to forge ahead in this chapter by adopting an eclectic methodology that involves both disciplines. The first task will be to explore how the theme of blessing and curse might appear, given the critically assured minimum from Wellhausen's traditional Yahwistic (J or JE amalgam), Deuteronomic, and Priestly sources.[3] This is not just an academic exercise. The theological rewards of such an enterprise are surprising, and clearly worth the effort. This is because the theological thrust of these sources is not at all uniform with respect to the theme of blessings and curses. Then a modern literary approach will be employed to examine the narrative integrity of this theme as presented in the entire Pentateuch. By applying these two very different methodologies to the theme of blessings and curses, more can hopefully be said about the content of these performatives, how they are employed, and the subsequent theological message woven into the fabric of the Pentateuch.

First here a few brief general comments. Any reading of the Pentateuch immediately confronts the recurring theme of blessings and curses. Examples of this theme are present from the first chapter in the Pentateuch to Moses's final blessing to the people of Israel in Deuteronomy 33, including in every book in the Torah. The theme is introduced in the primeval history of Genesis 1–11 and reintroduced in the ancestral narratives of Genesis 12–50. With each of the successive ancestors of Israel, the theme resurfaces. In places where the theme is not as prominent, such as in the Joseph story and in the exodus story, it often emerges in surprising places. This blessing/curse theme is present in the context of the plagues in the exodus narrative (Exod 12:32), in the Sinai material (Exod 20:11, 24; Leviticus 26; Num 6:22–27), in the wilderness narratives (Numbers 22–24),

2. Stern, "Recent Trends in Biblical Source Criticism"; Whybray, *The Making of the Pentateuch*.

3. I am following Campbell and O'Brien, *Sources of the Pentateuch*. Campbell and O'Brien present one example of a source-critical model based on Noth, *A History of Pentateuchal Traditions*.

and in Moses's summons to Israel on the plains of Moab (Deut 11:27–30). The theme is reflected in the traditional sources of the Documentary Hypothesis: the Yahwist (J or JE Amalgam), the Deuteronomist (Dtr), and the Priestly (P) source, as well as in all of Martin Noth's major themes of the traditions of the Pentateuch.[4] Each of these traditional sources of the Documentary Hypothesis exhibits the theme of blessings and curses consistent with its own individual theological, kerygmatic, and literary intent. The regularity of this theme urges one to explore the literary and theological phenomenon of blessings and curses in the hypothetical sources of the Pentateuch.

THE YAHWIST: CURSE FIRST, THEN BLESSING

The J source traditionally begins in Genesis 2:4 and probably ends near the incident of Baal Peor in the book of Numbers, although the end of J has always been ambiguous.[5] Given these parameters, both the beginning and the end of J deal with the blessing/curse theme, forming an envelope structure. H. H. Wolff's exegetically meticulous and theologically insightful essay pursued the essential message, or as he called it, the kerygma of the Yahwist. He followed von Rad's presupposition that the Yahwist's work is the basic supporting stratum of the Tetrateuch.[6] By focusing on what he called the "bridge passages," which connect the major elements of the J narrative, Wolff argued that the blessing of Abraham in Genesis 12 lays down the framework for J's narrative structure as it is presented from the curse in the garden to the incident at Baal Peor.

Prior to Genesis 12, the blessing is not even mentioned in the J material of Genesis 1–11, yet the curse is cited multiple times. The primeval history of J begins essentially with the curse and is for all practical purposes an account of a series of transgressions. Adam and Eve have made a

---

4. Martin Noth delineated several major themes in the Pentateuch: guidance out of Egypt, guidance into arable land, the promise to the patriarchs, guidance in the wilderness, and the revelation at Sinai (*A History of the Pentateuchal Traditions*, 46–62).

5. There is considerable debate regarding the very existence of J material. Schmid, *Der sogennante Jahwist*; Van Seters, *Abraham in History and Tradition* have called into question the traditional dating of J to the tenth century BCE, while Rendtorff, *The Problem of the Process of Transmission in the Pentateuch*, argues that a continuous J source never existed at all. See Dozeman and Schmid, *A Farewell to the Yahwist?* The end of J has been elusive. Suggestions have been Num 14:8; 25:9; Joshua 11, 24; Judg 1:26; 1 Kings 2; 12; 14:25. The present argument follows Wolff.

6. Wolff, "The Kerygma of the Yahwist."

muddled mess of things. The intent of the various episodes in the primeval history is to explain why humans desperately need God's blessing. The root for "curse," '*rr*, appears here five times (Gen 3:14, 17; 4:11; 5:28; 9:25). The curse falls on the serpent, the ground, Cain, and Canaan. Wolff states,

> The curse destroys freedom, expels man from a fruitful life, and thrusts him into aimless wandering in fear of death . . . it brings bondage to the dust and exclusion from the community of the free; it yields the land to thorns and thistles, widens infertility, and forces man to vain and agonizing labor.[7]

The curses of Genesis 1–11 are linked together to demonstrate exactly why all the families of the earth need that blessing. The curse has brought about "complete degradation—bondage to the dust and exclusion from the community of the free (Gen 3:14)."[8] Again, J mentions blessing for the first time in Genesis 12. Thus, the Yahwist proclaims the kerygma that only through Abraham's descendants can all humanity find blessing.

Wolff's thesis was revised by George Coats, who argued that Wolff had not given adequate treatment to the relationship between the blessing and curse in J outside the primeval history.[9] Coats demonstrated that the blessing cannot be separated from the curse in Yahwistic theology. By examining the strife stories of Sarah/Hagar and Abraham/Lot, Coats demonstrated that those who hold Abraham in disdain are excluded in some way from God's blessing and put under the repressive thumb of those who are blessed. Thus, the blessing moves from the theological to the political. Coats maintained a strong ethnic content to the Yahwist's theme of blessing and cursing. He cites a relatively large number of specific ethnic groups that are the objects of the curse in J. In the primeval history, the descendants of Cain and the Canaanites (Gen 9:25–26) are excluded by curses while later in J the Edomites (Gen 27:39–40), the Moabites, Amalekites, and Kenites are cursed (Num 24:15–24). Marginal tribes within Israel such as Simeon, who lost its identity as a tribe and was absorbed into Judah; Levi, who became a subordinate priestly class; and Reuben are all disenfranchised via curses:

> Reuben, you are my firstborn,
>   my might, the first sign of my strength,
>   excelling in honor, excelling in power.

7. Ibid., 54.

8. Ibid., 54.

9. Coats, "The Curse in God's Blessing."

Turbulent as the waters, you will no longer excel,
    for you went up onto your father's bed,
    onto my couch and defiled it.

Simeon and Levi are brothers—
    their swords are weapons of violence.
Let me not enter their council,
    let me not join their assembly,
for they have killed men in their anger
    and hamstrung oxen as they pleased.
Cursed be their anger, so fierce,
    and their fury, so cruel!
I will scatter them in Jacob,
    and disperse them in Israel. (Gen 49:3–7)

These curses provided the storytellers of each generation the ammunition to depict these marginal groups in a negative light. Each time the stories were retold they reenacted the subordinate relationship that these marginalized groups had to Israel, thus keeping them under the repressive thumb of those possessing the blessing. Therefore, these stories all have a performative effect. Josef Scharbert echoed the same sentiment: "The Yahwist interpreted not only the history of the tribes and of the people of Israel, but also the history of all mankind, from the viewpoint of blessing and curse."[10]

Wolff pursues the kerygma of the Yahwist into the exodus and wilderness narratives. In the midst of the plagues of the exodus tradition, at a most crucial point, the Yahwist puts on the lips of Pharaoh a surprising request for a blessing. Pharaoh asks Moses to pray to Yahweh on his behalf and asks Moses to bless him. For Wolff, this request for a blessing is tantamount to a request for the removal of the curse of judgment.[11] At the climax of the deliverance from Egypt, the Yahwist employs this motif of blessing in the midst of the curses of the plagues.

Beginning with the journey to Sinai and extending through Israel's experiences there, and continuing in the period of wilderness wandering culminating in the blessing of Balaam, the Yahwist sets up test after test to challenge the promise of blessing. After crossing the Red Sea, the people of Israel almost immediately begin to complain and express dissatisfaction. Would their rebellion negate the promise? They could become a blessing only as Yahweh's people. God gave the law at Sinai to define the nature

10. Scharbert, "*brk*," 306.

11. Wolff, "The Kerygma of the Yahwist," 55.

of that community. While at Sinai, however, the people reject the leadership of Yahweh and his servant Moses by fashioning a golden calf and
desiring to return to, of all places, Egypt. This rebellion continues after
the people leave Sinai, and the Yahwist reaches the narrative climax in
the pronouncements of Balaam.[12] Antony Campbell argues that a curse
is expected, if the behavior of the people is any indication of what might
happen; but in actuality, the people are blessed.

> If the hypothesis survives the testing, what a remarkably pow-
> erful insight into human life the Yahwist narrative provides. It
> opens with the portrayal of the first human representatives in
> the garden, presented with the challenge of life. They are de-
> picted as evading it, seeking to escape the human condition by
> a shortcut to the knowledge of good and evil, taking control of
> their destiny contrary to the creator's dispensation. Mankind
> has been offered the fullness of life and refused it, and this is the
> burden of Genesis 2–11.
>
> Then in Abraham a fresh offer is made, that through Israel
> blessing will be available to all the families of the earth. And
> the promise and a tantalizing taste of its possibilities extend
> through the patriarchal stories. Yet, wandering in the desert,
> Israel declines the challenge of life, hankers to run to Egypt;
> portraying in murmuring rebellion, she is hardly experienc-
> ing blessing, much less able to mediate it to others. But in the
> Balaam story, where curse is expected, blessing is spoken. This
> is Yahweh's doing.[13]

As far as Yahweh is concerned, the blessing will never be revoked, but
it can be negated by the persistent refusal of the people to be faithful to
God. The Yahwist ends the epic story with the sin of Baal Peor. The people,
blessed by God, disappointedly turns their blessing into curse.[14]

The Yahwist's concept of blessing stresses the theocentricity of blessing and curse. Regardless of what external threat to the promise might
appear, or what God's own people might do to negate the promise, that
promise of blessing still endures. Yet the curse remains a potential reality
for the Yahwist. The odd closing of the Yahwist by the juxtaposition of the

---

12. The Balaam prophecies have traditionally been ascribed to the E source; Gnuse,
"Redefining the Elohist."

13. Campbell, "The Yahwist Revisited," Australian Biblical Review 27 (1979) 14.

14. For a delightful discussion of this theme, see Mann, *The Book of the Torah*,
169–74.

Balaam narrative and Baal Peor raises the question, will a people blessed by God turn their blessing into a curse?

THE DEUTERONOMIST: BLESSING OR CURSE AS OPEN POSSIBILITIES

If the blessing/curse theme is theocentric for the Yahwist, then it is predominantly anthropocentric for the Deuteronomist. One might put it this way: in Deuteronomy divine gift leads to human choice. The Deuteronomist presupposes that divine deliverance out of Egypt has already taken place, and that the land will indeed be taken as a possession by God's people in the near future. This source does not say anything explicit about a blessing of the tribal fathers, but Deut 2:7 does begin by affirming the past blessings from God while in the wilderness, and Deuteronomy 23 affirms that it was because of the love of God that Balaam blessed Israel instead of cursing it.

> The LORD your God has blessed you in all the work of your hands. He has watched over your journey through this vast desert. These forty years the LORD your God has been with you, and you have not lacked anything. (Deut 2:7)

> No Ammonite or Moabite may enter the assembly of the LORD. Even to the tenth generation, none of them may enter the assembly of the LORD forever, because they did not meet you with bread and with water on the way, when you came out of Egypt, and because they hired against you Balaam the son of Beor from Pethor of Mesopotamia, to curse you. But the LORD your God would not listen to Balaam; instead the LORD your God turned the curse into a blessing for you, because the LORD your God loved you. You shall not seek their peace or their prosperity all your days forever. (Deut 23:3–6, ESV)

Blessings and curses for the Deuteronomistic tradition become conditional upon the actions of the community. Walter Brueggemann states, "The kerygma of this theology is not only about Yahweh's past action, nor it is only an imperative to Israel. It is an affirmation about the present and future with Yahweh, who invites Israel to make fresh decisions about the covenant."[15] Deuteronomy 7:12–16 indicates that future blessing is conditional upon the obedience of the people to the ordinances of God. The

15. Brueggemann, "The Kerygma of the Deuteronomistic Historian," 393.

Deuteronomistic tradition bluntly states the open possibility of blessing and curse: "Behold I set before you this day a blessing and a curse: the blessing if you obey the commandment of the LORD your God and the curse if you do not obey" (Deut 11:26–27). That choice, along with its consequences, is theirs. Obedience produces the blessing and disobedience yields a curse. Deuteronomy 27–30 is the climax of the work of the Deuteronomist where the renewal of the covenant is foreseen, and the people are challenged to choose between the blessing and the curse. After the blessings and curses of Deuteronomy 27–28 Moses utters a pointed warning regarding the infectious nature of the curse in Deuteronomy 29:

> One who, when he hears the words of this sworn covenant, blesses himself in his heart, saying, "I shall be safe, though I walk in the stubbornness of my heart." This will lead to the sweeping away of moist and dry alike. The LORD will not be willing to forgive him, but rather the anger of the LORD and his jealousy will smoke against that man, and the curses written in this book will settle upon him, and the LORD will blot out his name from under heaven. And the LORD will single him out from all the tribes of Israel for calamity, in accordance with all the curses of the covenant written in this Book of the Law. (Deut 29:19–21, ESV)

The outcome is already in the hands of the one who acts in accordance with or against the law of God. Yet the horrible consequences of curse need not be final. Deuteronomy 30 presents the hopeful possibility that these curses can be canceled and blessing reinstated after repentance.

> And when all these things come upon you, the blessing and the curse, which I have set before you, and you call them to mind among all the nations where the LORD your God has driven you, and return to the LORD your God, you and your children, and obey his voice in all that I command you today, with all your heart and with all your soul, then the LORD your God will restore your fortunes and have compassion on you, and he will gather you again from all the peoples where the LORD your God has scattered you. If your outcasts are in the uttermost parts of heaven, from there the Lord your God will gather you, and from there he will take you. (Deut 30:1–4, ESV)

This perspective also surfaces at key points in the Deuteronomistic History such as covenant renewal, the transition to kingship, and the dedication of the new temple.

Thus, for the Deuteronomist, blessing and curse are conditional upon the choice of the community. However, Deuteronomy, like the Yahwist, ends with a questionable note. Deuteronomy 30:15–20 is essentially an ultimatum to Israel: they have the power of self-determination, they can choose blessing or curse.

> See, I set before you today life and prosperity, death and destruction. For I command you today to love the LORD your God, to walk in his ways, and to keep his commands, decrees and laws; then you will live and increase, and the LORD your God will bless you in the land you are entering to possess. But if your heart turns away and you are not obedient, and if you are drawn away to bow down to other gods and worship them, I declare to you this day that you will certainly be destroyed. You will not live long in the land you are crossing the Jordan to enter and possess. This day I call heaven and earth as witnesses against you that I have set before you life and death, blessings and curses. Now choose life, so that you and your children may live and that you may love the LORD your God, listen to his voice, and hold fast to him. For the LORD is your life, and he will give you many years in the land he swore to give to your fathers, Abraham, Isaac and Jacob. (Deut 30:15–20)

Immediately before his death, Moses blesses the tribes of Israel prior to their entry into the land. These are his final recorded words. The blessing in Deuteronomy 33, which source critics argue is most likely an independent insertion into the Deuteronomic source, serves as a prophecy of what the community can become. Is there a sense that this blessing might be larger than merely something they bring upon themselves?

THE PRIESTLY SOURCE: BLESSING ALONE, NO CURSE

If the J source stresses curse before blessing, and the D source emphasizes the open possibility of either blessing or curse, then the Priestly writer or editor could be said to stress the unconditional nature of God's blessing.[16] The Priestly source has disassociated the tradition with any type of curse. Where J knows of no blessing until Abraham, the primeval history of P knows of virtually no curse . . . at all. Alternatively, the Priestly source places the promise of blessing at crucial points where the Yahwist

16. For a defense of P as a coherent source, see Emerton, "The Priestly Writer in Genesis"; Nicholson, "P as an Originally Independent Source in the Pentateuch."

has pronounced a curse or where no blessing exists. The ratio of curses to blessings in Deuteronomy is nearly 3 to 1, while the opposite ratio of blessings to curses in P is also nearly 3 to 1.

If there were no Priestly tradition, the creation story would begin with a created order that is "not good" (Gen 2:18) and would, in fact, begin with a curse (Gen 3:14, 17). The Priestly writer, however, makes the climax of creation the threefold blessing of the animal life (Gen 1:11), the human community (Gen 1:28), and the Sabbath (Gen 2:3). There is no account of revolt or a fall. In a companion article to Wolff's thesis on the Yahwist, Walter Brueggemann describes the fivefold blessing of the Priestly source: to be fruitful, multiply, fill the earth, subdue the earth, and have dominion over it (Gen 9:7; 17:2; 17:20; 28:1–4; 35:11; 47:27; 48:3–4; Exod 1:7).[17] Immediately after the Yahwist's "fall," the Priestly genealogy of Genesis 5 reaffirms the blessing of the humans: "When God created man, he made him in the likeness of God. He created them male and female and blessed them. And he named them 'Mankind' when they were created" (Gen 5:2). The reference to the curse in Gen 5:29 is no more than a throwback to J's curse in Genesis 3: "He named him Noah and said, 'He will comfort us in the labor and painful toil of our hands caused by the ground the LORD has cursed.'"

After the flood, Noah is blessed and given the charge to "be fruitful and multiply." In the Priestly account of Yahweh's covenant with Abraham, it is surprisingly not Abraham who is specifically blessed but his wife, Sarah—blessed to be a mother of peoples (Gen 17:16). Whereas Ishmael is a "wild donkey of a man" in the Yahwistic source (Gen 16:12), he is given a blessing in the Priestly tradition (Gen 17:20). In the Priestly source the word *brk* applies widely to humankind (Gen 1:22, 28), the Sabbath (2:3), Sarah, Ishmael, Isaac (25:11), Jacob (28:1; 35:9), each of the twelve tribes (49:28), and even Pharaoh (47:10). Oddly, it is not employed in reference to Abraham.

The parallels between Leviticus 26 and Deuteronomy 28 are well known, yet the explicit lexical formulations of blessing and cursing are omitted by the Priestly writer in Leviticus 26. The Priestly source does not ignore the consequences of human actions but does not refer to those consequences as curse.[18] Perhaps this is because the Priestly stratum has

17. Brueggemann affirms that the entire kerygma of the Priestly writer can be summed up in the blessing to be fruitful and multiply, "The Kerygma of the Priestly Writers."

18. See the discussion Hillers, *Treaty-Curses and the Old Testament Prophets*, 30–42.

built into its theology a means of eliminating the curse. The Israelite cult, including a proper tabernacle, proper priesthood, proper calendar, and proper sacrificial system all allow for Israel to be the blessing of God in spite of the shortcomings of the community.

It is somewhat a surprise that in the context of the cult the Priestly tradition has its only mention of the curse. In the jealousy ordeal of Numbers 5, curses were written in a book by the priest and subsequently washed off into the water. The priest gave the water to the woman suspected of adultery to drink. As she drank the water, the curse entered her to perform its juridical action. If she was indeed guilty of adultery, her body would swell and her thigh fall away and she would become a curse among her people. In this way the curse had the power to pursue the guilty party relentlessly until justice was secured. The nature of cultic life in P is such that it can remove the curse and ultimately secure the blessing. At another crucial juncture, Yahwistic theology is enhanced by its juxtaposition to Priestly narrative. After the pathetic ending of the Yahwist at Baal-Peor, the Priestly writer continues with a census of the new obedient community followed by the commandments for the offerings for the appointed feasts and rules about an almost certain land inheritance.

Admittedly, there are innumerable problems with the Wellhausenian version of source criticism. In spite of the limitations of source criticism, the theological implications of applying source-critical methodology to a theological topic such as blessings and curses are revealing. The Yahwist begins with the problem of curse and utilizes the promise to Abraham in Genesis 12 as the backbone for the entire narrative ending with the incident at Baal Peor. No outsider can contravene God's blessing on Israel, yet God's own people can turn the blessing into curse. The Deuteronomist affirms the grace and blessing of God's providence of land and inheritance, but realistically concludes that the preservation of that blessing is in the hands of God's people. While the Deuteronomist is skeptical that Israel has what it takes to keep the covenant, the choice is theirs. The Priestly writer affirms the blessing of God, which continues, not because of Israel's obedience, but in spite of their repeated acts of disobedience.

BLESSING, CURSE, AND THE NARRATIVE FORM OF THE PENTATEUCH

The ancient Greeks used lightly colored stones to decorate jewelry and small household items. Following Alexander's conquests around 330 BCE,

artists created more colorful mosaics using specially made tiles called tesserae. This innovation enabled the mosaic artists to create exquisitely in-
tricate scenes with the colorful tesserae. While the finely worked details of
Greek and Roman mosaics are perhaps more interesting when examined
up close, the beauty of the mosaic can only be comprehended from a little
farther away. By analogy, this truth also applies to the sources and final
narrative form of the Torah. While it is an interesting academic exercise to
contemplate how smaller literary units were incorporated into the larger
whole, the final narrative form of the Pentateuch has a beauty all its own
that cannot be appreciated when one only scrutinizes its smallest units.

The theme of blessings and curses is clearly a dominant force in that
larger, comprehensive Torah story. This theme is present in a wide variety
of literary genres, including narratives, poetry, laws, sermons, prayers,
testaments, and speeches. Additionally, both blessing and curse performatives can be uttered by using traditional blessing and curse formulae and
vocabulary, or they may be freely composed. So we now turn to a brief
exploration of how this theme is present in the structure and message of
the final narrative form of the Pentateuch.

First, we will outline a brief synopsis of the plot, plus delineate a bit
of structure to the Torah narrative.[19] The storyteller introduces the plot
of the Torah in Genesis 1–11, where God blesses all creation, endows
humankind with certain responsibilities, and demands obedience to one
simple command. The humans in the garden spurn this directive, which
unleashes a chain of negative consequences, as God pronounces a curse on
portions of this created order. Essentially, the core of this primeval plot is
that something has gone drastically wrong in a world originally declared
by God to be good. We will explore the specific plot details of Genesis
1–11 in the next chapter. The ensuing primeval history is not entirely
pessimistic, but it does present the case that humans desperately need to
return to God's enhancement of life/fullness so beautifully described by
the Eden imagery. This blessing is reintroduced in Gen 12:1–3 through
the promise to Abram, perhaps demonstrating the hopeful potential that
things might return to the way they once were, or at least to the way things
should be. A series of internal and external forces test the vitality of that
blessing in the remainder of the Pentateuch. The storyteller introduces
numerous challenges to the blessing that threaten its vitality, and the curse
looms threateningly at each stage of the narrative. Each of these challenges
rises to a climax, where a crisis ensues, and God renews the promise to

---

19. I am indebted here to Mann, *The Book of the Torah*, 196–201.

Abraham and his descendants. The potential for curse is every bit as real as the potential for blessing. These crises provide a loose framework for the structure of the blessing/curse as pentateuchal theme. Calamities of drought, infertility, family rivalry, warfare, and enslavement (just to name a few) threaten to extinguish that primordial promise of blessing. Yet the blessing prevails throughout this tumultuous story.

The structure of the Torah story includes an introductory setting, followed by two narrative movements and a legal interlude, and then concludes with two final narrative movements. Genesis 1–11 creates the narrative setting. The first movement occurs in the ancestral narratives of Genesis 12–50, the second in the exodus story of Exodus 1–18. The events and laws at Sinai provide an interlude that slows the pace of the narrative (Exod 19:1—Num 10:10). The third movement begins as the narrative resumes (Num 10:11—36:13). Israel leaves Sinai, sends the spies into Canaan, yet stubbornly refuses to enter the promised land. The exodus generation unceremoniously perishes in the wilderness, and a new generation takes up the hopeful journey where the old generation left off. The climax of the wilderness narrative occurs in the Balaam story. The final movement (Deut 1–34) follows on the plains of Moab, and the blessings and curses of Deuteronomy 27–30 provide the transition to the denouement of the plot. Moses's last words are words of blessing in Deuteronomy 33,

> Blessed are you, O Israel!
> Who is like you,
>> a people saved by the LORD?
> He is your shield and helper
>> and your glorious sword.
> Your enemies will cower before you,
>> and you will tread on their heights. (Deut 33:29)

The Setting: Primeval History (Genesis 1–11)

The Bible introduces God's blessing three times in its first chapter. God creates heaven and earth, blesses animals and humans, and announces that everything that has been created is "very good." Thus, the primeval history begins with a created order that is benevolently related to God. After God finishes this work of creation, God rests on the seventh day, and blesses the Sabbath. But blessing comes with a price. Humans in relationship with God must forsake their own autonomy and yield to the commands of God. Adam and Eve reject this divine order, choose their own autonomy, and get just what they deserve: a life of separation from God. Because of the disobedience of the two humans, the curse falls upon the animal kingdom (Gen 3:14), the ground from which all life arises (Gen 3:17), and ultimately, albeit indirectly at first, upon the larger human community (Gen 4:11). The remainder of the primeval history describes the working out of that curse in a progressively negative way. In the garden, Eve is coerced into eating the forbidden fruit. Later, Cain cannot be talked out of murder by Yahweh, and finally the human condition at the time of the flood is so vile that "every intention of the thoughts of his heart was only evil continually" (Gen 6:5, ESV). Whereas Eve is indirectly cursed, Cain's malediction is explicit. Ironically, the only words spoken by Noah, the hero of the flood narrative, are a curse on his grandson Canaan. He never utters a single word prior to this curse. The primeval history ends on a pessimistic note with the Babel episode, which bears no mention of the vitality of blessing.

Yet, in spite of the spreading curse, the blessing skulks in the background, subtly foreshadowing for readers that it cannot be negated forever. Genesis 5:2 briefly reaffirms that humanity is still ultimately created for a blessing. The alternating themes of judgment and grace are skillfully woven through the fabric of the primeval history. God banishes Adam and Eve from the garden but gives them protective clothing for their departure. Cain is anathema but is given a protective mark against his enemies. After the flood, God remembers the covenant: never again to curse the ground because of human degradation. The only instance when the theme of grace is absent is the Babel episode, which rhetorically creates anticipation for the blessing, which appears later in the ancestral narratives of Genesis 12–50.

The First Episode: The Ancestral Narratives (Genesis 12–50)

Genesis 1–11 asks the question, what has gone wrong with a world initially declared to be good? Genesis 12 responds with an answer that continues through both Old and New Testaments: what is God going to do about it? Yahweh makes a fresh offer of the blessing in Genesis 12. The double theme of blessing and curse is presented to Abram: "I will bless you and make your name great, so that you will be a blessing. I will bless those who bless you, and the one who curses you, I will curse, and by you all the families of the earth will bless themselves" (Gen 12:2–3, my translation). God will renew a blessing for humanity, for everyone on earth, through

Abraham. A benevolent relationship with God is dependent on a relationship with the people of Abraham.[20]

Like the recurring phrase in the blessings of Gen 1:29 where God announces, "I have given you . . . ," Genesis 12 includes three verbs in staccato succession: "I will show you," "I will make of you," and "I will bless you." Throughout the ancestral narratives, the vitality of the blessing is challenged by natural phenomena, struggles with foreign leaders, internal family dissent, barrenness in the ancestral families, and numerous other contenders that threaten to change the blessing into curse. Surprisingly, in spite of trickery, misfortune, and the frailty of the human condition, the blessing prevails. This is God's doing. The theme recurs in the blessing of Melchizedek:

> Then Melchizedek king of Salem brought out bread and wine.
> He was priest of God Most High, and he blessed Abram, saying,
> Blessed be Abram by God Most High,
>> Creator of heaven and earth.
> And blessed be God Most High,
>> who delivered your enemies into your hand."
> Then Abram gave him a tenth of everything. (Gen 14:18–20)

God's blessing continues to Abraham's descendants. The narrative of the search for a wife for Isaac (Gen 24:27, 31, 35, 48,) culminates in the explicit blessing of Rebekah:

> And they blessed Rebekah and said to her,
> "Our sister, may you increase
>> to thousands upon thousands;
>> may your offspring possess
>> the gates of their enemies." (Gen 24:60)

Plus, God's renewal of the promise to Isaac (Gen 26:4), Jacob's theft of the blessing (Gen 27:1–45), God's blessing given to Rachel and Leah (Gen 31:55), Jacob's demand of blessing from the angel (Gen 32:26), Jacob's blessing of Esau (Gen 33:11), and Jacob's blessing of Pharaoh (Gen 47–50) all play roles in the development of the blessing theme.

The Joseph novella plays a unique role, serving both as a climax to the first movement of the Torah, and a fitting transition to the exodus account—the next major movement. In the case of the first three ancestors, God utters the blessing overtly. In the Joseph account, however, the blessing

---

20. A wonderful sermon on the irony of this passage is presented by Elizabeth Achtemeier in *The Old Testament and the Proclamation of the Gospel*.

goes underground. Yahweh never directly promises blessing to Joseph, and Joseph never encounters God face-to-face, so the storyteller raises the reader's anticipation over whether the ancestral blessing, so prominent in the Abraham, Isaac, and Jacob narratives, still thrives. It is not until Joseph rises to power and is secure in Egypt that the motif reemerges, assuring the reader of that the ancestral promise still flourishes. When Jacob appears for the first time in the presence of Pharaoh, in surprising irony, it is Jacob who blesses Pharaoh, not the other way around (Gen 47:10). After a long and arduous life, Joseph receives an overt, superlative-laced blessing, yet not from God, but from his own father Jacob:

> Joseph is a fruitful vine,
>> a fruitful vine near a spring,
>> whose branches climb over a wall.
> With bitterness archers attacked him;
>> they shot at him with hostility.
> But his bow remained steady,
>> his strong arms stayed limber,
>> because of the hand of the Mighty One of Jacob,
>> because of the Shepherd, the Rock of Israel,
>> because of your father's God, who helps you,
>> because of the Almighty, who blesses you
>> with blessings of the heavens above,
>> blessings of the deep that lies below,
>> blessings of the breast and womb.
> Your father's blessings are greater
>> than the blessings of the ancient mountains,
>> than the bounty of the age-old hills.
> Let all these rest on the head of Joseph,
>> on the brow of the prince among his brothers.
> (Gen 49:22–26)

Yet Jacob's blessing on his twelve sons is not without a few curses. Simeon and Levi, who vengefully lashed out against the men of Shechem for the rape of Dinah, are destined to be scattered among the other tribes of Israel. Jacob curses their anger, and the performative force of this curse marginalizes these two tribes. Likewise, Reuben loses the prominent status of the firstborn son because he secretly had sex with his father's concubine, Bilhah, defiling his father's bed. None of this, however, takes away from the fact that Jacob's final act is a blessing: "All these are the twelve tribes of Israel, and this is what their father said to them when he blessed them, giving each the blessing appropriate to him" (Gen 49:28). Before he dies,

Jacob binds Joseph with an oath that his family will bury his body in the field of Machpelah next to his grandfather and grandmother, Abraham and Sarah, and next to his father and mother, Isaac and Rebekah. Prior to his own death, Joseph binds the children of Israel with a similar oath to inter him some day alongside his ancestors (Gen 50:24).

The Second Episode: The Exodus Narrative (Exodus 1–18)

With only one exception, the exodus narrative is completely void of any mention of blessing or curse. When the Lord appears to Moses at the mountain of God, Yahweh acknowledges Abraham, Isaac, and Jacob, and acknowledges awareness of the affliction of God's people in Egypt. But nowhere does God explicitly mention the promise of blessing or threat of curse in regards to the ancestors of Israel. With the submersion of the blessing theme, the reader again wonders whether the blessing to Abraham is still a potentiality. The narrator never mentions the theme in relation to the birth or the commission of Moses. Yet there is one glaring exception in the exodus narrative deployed at a crucial point.

In the ninth plague (Exod 10:28–29) Pharaoh refuses Moses one last time and warns him that if he ever sees Moses's face again, he will have Moses executed. Moses's reply is blunt: "You will not see my face again." This leaves the reader completely unprepared for Moses's unanticipated final encounter with Pharaoh, an encounter on which everything in the narrative depends. As far as Moses is concerned, he is through with Pharaoh. But in the context of the final plague leading to the death of the firstborn in Egyptian households, it is Pharaoh who summons Moses to appear before him one last time. Pharaoh commands, "Take your flocks and your herds, as you have said, and be gone; and bless me (*ûbēraktem*) also" (Exod 12:32).[21] Reminiscent of Jacob's blessing of an earlier pharaoh, with biting sarcasm and artistic mastery, Pharaoh himself concedes that the blessing comes through Israel.

The Pentateuch later reflects on the victory over Egypt as nothing less than a victory against the gods of the Egyptians,

> The Israelites set out from Rameses on the fifteenth day of the
> first month, the day after the Passover. They marched out boldly
> in full view of all the Egyptians, who were burying all their

21. Wolff's discussion of this passage is exceptional (Wolff, "The Kerygma of the Yahwist," 60–61).

firstborn, whom the LORD had struck down among them; for
the LORD had brought judgment on their gods. (Num 33:3–4)

Pharaoh's stubborn denial of Moses's initial requests brought about
the devastating plagues mentioned in Exodus 7–15. The book of Exodus
portrays God's victory as a cosmic victory over all the forces of chaos that
served as a threat to God's creation. God accomplished this cosmic victory through the miraculous plagues described in the narrative. In this
reading, Moses entered the very territory of the Egyptian gods to bring
about the deliverance promised by Yahweh. The finely crafted narrative presents these plagues against Egypt in three cycles, culminating in
the final, tenth plague that leads to the exodus event. This 3+1 cyclical
structure is evidence that, at least to some extent, the plague narratives
were carefully constructed and may have even been developed to be used
liturgically in worship. Theologically, many readers of the exodus narrative are troubled by God's actions in the plague stories—particularly that
Yahweh would harden Pharaoh's heart on several occasions. These acts
are tantamount to turning Pharaoh into a victim rather than an oppressor. A careful reading of the plague narrative, however, indicates a much
more nuanced situation. At times in the narrative, it is God who hardens
Pharaoh's heart, but at other times Pharaoh is the one who hardens his
own heart (Exod 8:15; 9:34). Some have interpreted this mutual harden-
ing: "God becomes the hardener of Pharaoh's heart as an intensification
of Pharaoh's own character."[22] Consequently, Pharaoh's resistance against
Moses intensifies to the point that God ultimately delivers him over to his
own hard-heartedness. The interaction of Yahweh and Pharaoh illustrates
well the enigmatic doctrine of confluence, where human actions and divine actions meet to accomplish divine will.

A new motif is introduced during Israel's approach to Sinai, a motif
of communal dissatisfaction. The same motif reemerges after the congregation leaves Sinai: complaints, rebellion, and outright insurrection erupt
(Num 11–14, 16, 20). This new motif reopens the possibility that the people of God can, of their own selfish initiative, convert blessing into curse.
As in the garden of Eden, so here God does not strong-arm people into
submission. God's desire for human freedom is even greater than a desire
for their redemption. Consequently, humans are responsible moral agents.

---

22 Birch, *A Theological Introduction to the Old Testament*, 112.

Interlude: Events at Sinai (Exodus 19:1—Numbers 10:10)

The Sinai material provides an interlude that marks a distinct shift in the theme of blessing/curse. This interlude interrupts the continuity of the main narrative but relates directly to its theme. The pace of the narrative slows dramatically at Sinai. Portions of three books—Exodus, Leviticus, and Numbers—introduce legal requirements related to Israel's relationship with God; portions of all three books take place at Sinai. Up to this point in the Bible, blessings and curses have been understood looking forward to the existence of the people Israel as an event in the future. Now Israel's existence as a people, while tenuous, is already a historical reality. Yahweh has blessed Abraham, has made him a mighty people, and has brought that people out of Egyptian slavery to become God's own people in God's own land: the land of Canaan. In the Sinai narrative, God specifically blesses Israel: "Make an altar of earth for me and sacrifice on it your burnt offerings and fellowship offerings, your sheep and goats and your cattle. Wherever I cause my name to be honored, I will come to you and bless you" (Exod 20:24). This blessing is also part of God's covenant with the people: "Worship the LORD your God, and his blessing will be on your food and water. I will take away sickness from among you, and none will miscarry or be barren in your land. I will give you a full life span" (Exod 23:25–26).

But this interlude draws a new tension between what God wants the redeemed community to be and what they actually are. What type of community does God require to be the redemptive vehicle through which all the peoples of the earth will bless themselves? Will the people themselves rise up to meet this challenge, or will they settle for the curse, the divine opposition to a life of fullness? In the interlude at Sinai the blessing and curse are no longer dependent merely on a benevolent relation with Abraham but on the people's faithful obedience to the covenant of Yahweh. Can it be that the people themselves can turn the conditional blessing of God into a curse by disobedience toward this covenant? This internal threat is illustrated clearly by one of the few narratives amid the legal materials of the Pentateuch: Exodus 32–34. In this narrative, ironically at the precise moment Moses is receiving the law whereby the community can continue to be the people by whom the foreigners will bless themselves, God's people defy their deity by worshiping a bull-calf made of gold. The timing of this exercise in idolatry is no editorial slipup. The editor places the story of the golden calf in the very heart of the legal materials in the book of Exodus.

It is in this setting that the legal materials of the Pentateuch play an enormous role theologically. It is this context that the foundations of the community of God are laid. God gives the laws that determine the viability of the community, and spells out the penalties for ignoring that law. Simultaneously the congregation rebels while Moses faithfully receives the Torah. The interlude of Sinai effectively raises another threat to the vitality of the blessing. Yet this threat is not from an external power, natural disaster, or lack of an heir, but is an insidious threat from *within* the community itself. It is in this context of the legal materials that one answer to the dilemma of human craving for autonomy is introduced. Indeed, blessing can be found in spite of human frailty. Through a proper tabernacle (Exodus 25–30, 35–40), a proper sacrificial system (Leviticus 1–7), a proper priesthood (Leviticus 8–10), proper cultic observances (Leviticus 11–25, 27), and a proper liturgical calendar (Exod 23:10–19; Lev 16, 23, 25; Num 28–30; Deut 15–16) the covenant relationship with God can be sustained, in spite of the shortcomings of the community. The promise of blessing is the carrot, and the threat of curse is the stick that enhances the covenant relationship. Leviticus ends its legal code with its own list of promises for obedience and the punishment for disobedience of these commands (Leviticus 26).

The Third Episode: In the Wilderness (Num 10:11—36:13)

The story's action, which slowed at Sinai, resumes again in the book of Numbers. The wilderness narratives continue the same theme of the communal discontent and disobedience of God's people. The wilderness period is depicted as an ordeal in which the exodus generation is found wanting. Rebellion thrives. The decision by the tribes to remain in the wilderness instead of entering Canaan costs them their entire generation. The exodus generation, with only a few exceptions, perishes in the Negev desert. Discontent leads to disobedience, which subsequently leads to defeat when they abandon the promise of God and enter the hill country, against the advice of Moses and without the holy ark. The future of the people will be in the hands of a new generation, a generation not born in Egypt but in the arid wilderness. This theme of discontent would spread even to the greatest of their prophets, Moses, who strikes the rock at the waters of Meribah in a fit of anger over Israel's persistent disgruntlement. Even he is not allowed to enter the land with this new generation.

The Balaam story (Num 22–24) provides the climax to this third narrative movement. In this episode, the storyteller pulls together colorful poetry and vivid prose to place Balaam's pronouncements of blessing upon Israel in the midst a narrative in which a Moabite king named Balak attempts to place a battle curse on Israel. Such battle curses were common in the ancient Near East and are even practiced today within cultures of the Middle East.[23] Balak fully expects Balaam's curse to soften up Israel's defenses before the big battle. God uses a rather unlikely figure, a greedy diviner, to bless this new generation as they journey toward Canaan. Balak hires Balaam and directs him to three prominent locations where he can view all or portions of the armies of Israel from a strategic vantage point. These three strategic locations are not for any modern notion of military strategy but for the rhetorical function of providing a proper illocutionary setting for curse pronouncement. But, much to Balak's disbelief, in each of the three instances, Balaam utters a blessing instead of a curse. After Balaam's first blessing/prophecy, Balak is beside himself: "I took you to curse my enemies, and behold, you have done nothing but bless them!" (Num 23:11, ESV). After the second prophecy in which Balak's desired curse is again subversively transformed to blessing, Balak negotiates a measure of rhetorical détente with the recalcitrant Balaam, desperately needing a little breathing room, "Do not curse them at all, and do not bless them at all" (Num 23:25, ESV). But as the reader now suspects, in the third prophecy, Balaam blesses Israel for a third, crucial time. This particular blessing, however, directly—and most significantly for the narrative integrity of the Pentateuch—parallels the blessing of Abraham in Genesis 12, which brings the narrative full circle back to the original ancestral blessing,

> How beautiful are your tents, O Jacob,
>   your dwelling places, O Israel!
> Like valleys they spread out,
>   like gardens beside a river,
>   like aloes planted by the Lord,
>   like cedars beside the waters.

23. During the 1991 Gulf War, traditional Bedouin curse poetry became a weapon in the arsenal of Arabs confronting each other. For hours on end on prime-time television, Saudis and Iraqis battled one another by broadcasting readings by poets. Like Balaam, they were summoned to curse, and the opposing Arab camps traded insults over the airwaves in archaic language, following strict rules, and in proper rhyme. The Saudis actually had to hire Yemenese cursers to compete with the exquisite Iraqi execration poetry (Ya'ari and Friedman, "Curses in Verses").

Water will flow from their buckets;
    their seed will have abundant water.
Their king will be greater than Agag;
    their kingdom will be exalted.
God brought them out of Egypt;
    they have the strength of a wild ox.
They devour hostile nations
    and break their bones in pieces;
    with their arrows they pierce them.

Like a lion they crouch and lie down,
    like a lioness—who dares to rouse them?
May those who bless you be blessed (*mĕbārăkêkā bārûk*)
    and those who curse you be cursed! (*wĕʾōrreykā ʾārûr*)
    (Num 24:5–9)

    May those who bless you be blessed and those who curse you be cursed . . . Such is the case for peoples who would relate to Israel. Balak's own people of Moab receives exactly what this promise entails. Moses had been instructed by God not to harass Moab or contend with them in battle, because none of their land was to be an inheritance to Israel (Deut 2:9). God had already given this land to the descendants of Lot. Yet Balak, king of Moab, opposes even the peaceful movement of God's people through his land. He will get more than he bargained for. After he had contracted these three aborted curses, Balaam finally utters what he was hired to proclaim, a curse. But it is Balaam, not Balak, who has the last word. Balaam utters one final curse/propehcy, but that prophecy is against Moab, Edom, and a small handful of other kingdoms:

Now I am going back to my people, but come, let me warn you
of what this people will do to your people in days to come."
Then he uttered his oracle:

The oracle of Balaam son of Beor,
    the oracle of one whose eye sees clearly,
    the oracle of one who hears the words of God,
    who has knowledge from the Most High,
    who sees a vision from the Almighty,
    who falls prostrate, and whose eyes are opened:
I see him, but not now;
    I behold him, but not near.
A star will come out of Jacob;
    a scepter will rise out of Israel.

He will crush the foreheads of Moab,
>   the skulls of all the sons of Sheth.
Edom will be conquered;
>   Seir, his enemy, will be conquered,
>   but Israel will grow strong.
A ruler will come out of Jacob
>   and destroy the survivors of the city. (Num 24:14–19)

After Balaam, it sounds like there is absolutely no getting around God's unconditional election/blessing upon this new generation of Israelites. Yet, the incident at Baal Peor, which follows on the heels of Balaam's blessing, demonstrates the conditional nature of God's blessing (Num 25:1–9). Immediately after being blessed by Balaam, this new generation that carried with it so much promise brings what is in essence a curse on itself and its descendents. While passing through Moabite territory, Israelite men have sex with Moabite women, and the people offer sacrifices to the gods of Moab. In this direct parallel to the golden-calf incident, the message is upheld that God's promise is both theocentric and anthropocentric.[24] From Yahweh's point of view, God unconditionally extends the blessing to the community, but the community can reject that blessing and turn it into a curse. There can be golden calves in the midst of the blessing of Sinai, and Baal Peors in the midst of the blessings of Balaam.

It is this dialectic of divine sovereignty and free human will that continues well into the book of Deuteronomy. God's blessing is unaltered, undiminished, and available. But it is up to the community of God's people to fulfill the conditions of that blessing, or to reject those conditions and bring the curse upon themselves. Thus, the two censuses (Numbers 1–4 and Numbers 26) serve as paradigms for two potential responses of the human community. The first census delineates a prototype of the disobedience community, while the second census introduces a new community, that at the very least has potential for obedience.[25] If Yahweh distributes the blessing for all peoples through the descendants of Abraham, it must be those descendants who display the same spiritual characteristics that Abraham exemplified: obedience and faith.

Later biblical recollections of Balaam clearly associate him with false prophecy. In two critical covenant-renewal texts, Balaam's infamy is remembered. On the plains of Moab when Moses preaches the law to the new generation, he states that God would not listen to Balaam but

24. Goldingay, *Old Testament Theology,* 3:505.

25. Olson, *The Death of the Old and the Birth of the New.*

turned curse into blessing (Deut 23:4–5). The biblical writers use the same language at the covenant-renewal ceremony in Josh 24:9. In the New Testament, Balaam becomes the stereotypical false prophet, a diviner who would do anything for money (2 Pet 2:15; Rev 2:14). Balaam fares even worse in rabbinic and later Christian tradition.[26]

After the incident at Baal Peor, the narrative looks toward the future. Numbers 26 recounts the census of the new generation, and Moses installs Joshua as a new leader who will replace Moses (Num 27:12–23). For the much of the rest of the book, the narrative assumes this next generation will faithfully take possession of the land. Chapters 27 and 36 form an inclusio related to the theme of the Daughters of Zelophehad. This theme demonstrates how Israelite daughters can legally receive the land inheritance if their father dies with no male heir. In between these bookends are laws related to the sacred calendar, a description of the general boundaries of the land of Israel, laws pertaining to Levitical cities, cities of refuge, and other themes directly related to matters of inheritance. It is important not to miss the weight of these seemingly disparate legal texts. For the most part, they all assume that the land has been occupied, even though Israel still resides outside Canaan. In a sense, they are a statement of faith; Israel will possess the land. Roughly in the middle of this section is the charge "'But if you do not drive out the inhabitants of the land, those you allow to remain will become barbs in your eyes and thorns in your sides. They will give you trouble in the land where you will live. And then I will do to you what I plan to do to them'" (Num 33:55–56). God has given the land, but it must be taken, and it must be kept.

The Fourth Episode: On the Plains of Moab (Deuteronomy 1–34)

The book of Deuteronomy provides an open-ended resolution to the blessing/curse theme of the Pentateuch. But it is only a resolution of sorts. The book opens as Moses reviews the acts of God's guidance from Horeb to Israel's present camp just east of the Jordan in the land of Moab. The Jordan River symbolizes a point of no return. God has chosen and blessed this people by delivering them out of Egypt and by providing for them in the wilderness. The language echoes the blessing of creation as well as the covenant blessing to Abraham: "The LORD your God has increased your numbers so that today you are as many as the stars in the sky. May the LORD, the God of your ancestors, increase you a thousand times and

---

26. Baskin, *Pharaoh's Counsellors*.

bless you as he has promised!" (Deut 1:10–12). Although the nature of this election is unconditional, there still remains a genuine choice for the community. They can either live according to the conditions of the blessing or reject those conditions and face divine opposition to a life of fullness.

Moses is skeptical that things will work out well. He seems to foresee the inevitable. Israel will fail the test and be scattered among the very peoples they were originally intended to bless; but in the distant future, the will once again return to the land of promise. He warns them repeatedly not to forget the covenant that they are making with God, a covenant not to create carved images and worship the gods of the ousted inhabitants of the land.

> I call heaven and earth to witness against you today, that you will soon utterly perish from the land that you are going over the Jordan to possess. You will not live long in it, but will be utterly destroyed. And the LORD will scatter you among the peoples, and you will be left few in number among the nations where the LORD will drive you. And there you will serve gods of wood and stone, the work of human hands, that neither see, nor hear, nor eat, nor smell. But from there you will seek the LORD your God and you will find him, if you search after him with all your heart and with all your soul. When you are in tribulation, and all these things come upon you in the latter days, you will return to the LORD your God and obey his voice. For the LORD your God is a merciful God. He will not leave you or destroy you or forget the covenant with your fathers that he swore to them. (Deut 4:26–31, ESV)

Moses repeats these warnings elsewhere in the three addresses that compose the book of Deuteronomy (Deut 6:12; 8:11; 9:7; 16:12; 24:18; 30:19).

The position of Deuteronomy 27–30 is essential to the Torah's theme of the blessing and the curse. Israel is poised, ready to enter the land. All prior action in the narrative leads up to this crucial point. Moses encourages the people to realize that the blessing of God is upon them should they choose to accept its rather restrictive conditions. Moses also warns that the rejection of these conditions can result in a self-inflicted curse:

> And all these blessings shall come upon you and overtake you, if you obey the voice of the LORD your God. Blessed shall you be in the city, and blessed shall you be in the field. Blessed shall be the fruit of your womb and the fruit of your ground and the fruit of your cattle, the increase of your herds and the young of your flock. Blessed shall be your basket and your kneading bowl.

> Blessed shall you be when you come in, and blessed shall you be when you go out. (Deut 28:2–6, ESV)

> But if you will not obey the voice of the Lord your God or be careful to do all his commandments and his statutes that I command you today, then all these curses shall come upon you and overtake you. Cursed shall you be in the city, and cursed shall you be in the field. Cursed shall be your basket and your kneading bowl. Cursed shall be the fruit of your womb and the fruit of your ground, the increase of your herds and the young of your flock. Cursed shall you be when you come in, and cursed shall you be when you go out. (Deut 28:15–19, ESV)

Moses's final blessing in Deuteronomy 33 is a challenge to the community to receive the blessing. This brings the narrative to its fitting end, providing some resolution to the persistent problem of why the Pentateuch ends as it does. The Pentateuch closes in the same way that it opens in Genesis 1, with the blessing clearly extended to the human community. It is this inconclusiveness at the end of Deuteronomy that is theologically potent. This inconclusiveness is the Torah's resolution to the plot of the narrative. The blessed new world and the covenant community that inhabits it are indeed a reality. However, the writer leaves the ultimate resolution of the plot up to the audience, a message which is timeless for any generation. Thomas Mann's concluding remarks are appropriate and insightful.[27]

> Here again the Pentateuch is at once complete and open-ended. Although it renders the new world created by God—the work God has finished, the covenant community that is "very good"—it ends with the death of Moses, and with the challenge of his testimony. The Torah ends with a charge, and thus with a question: will Israel be the new community God has created, or not? The way of Torah lies open, but it is a straight and narrow path.

---

27. Mann, *The Book of the Torah*, 201.

4

"Cursed Is the Ground Because of You"

A Theology of Genesis 1–11

CREATION AND BLESSING

THE PENTATEUCH BEGINS AND ends with a blessing. Genesis 1 is instrumental theologically, not only because it describes the origin of heaven and earth, but because some of the most foundational aspects of divine character and human nature are first introduced here. God's character and personality depicted in the primeval history not only dominate the creation accounts but permeate much of the rest of the Old Testament—yet not in an analytical, deliberately reformulative way of speaking about God. Surprisingly, many of the specific individuals mentioned in Genesis 1–11 are never mentioned again in the Old Testament. Adam, Eve, Cain Abel, and the serpent are only a few examples. Regardless, Genesis 1 sets the course, not merely for the narratives in the primeval history, but for the rest of the Bible's story,

In Genesis 1, the word of God and the Spirit of God work in tandem to bring creation into order and blessing. The opening chapter of the Bible presents a threefold pattern: God creates, God blesses, and God addresses the cosmos and its inhabitants. Two divine addresses in Genesis 1 contain performative blessings: "Be fruitful and increase in number and fill the waters in the seas, and let birds increase on the earth" (v. 22). "Be fruitful and increase in number; fill the earth and subdue it" (v. 28). The illocutionary force and sobriety of tone depict divine authority that is unchallenged and uninfluenced. The seven-day structure of Genesis 1 is without parallel in other creation accounts of the ancient Near East.[1]

The concept of blessing dominates the book of Genesis more than any other book in the Old Testament. The root *brk*, "to bless," occurs nearly ninety times in Genesis, just over a fifth of the total number of occurrences in the Old Testament. God explicitly declares a threefold blessing in the first creation account (Gen 1:22, 28; 2:3). In succession, animals, humans, and the seventh day all receive divine blessing. The blessing on the fish and the birds was for them to reproduce and increase. God pronounces a similar blessing on the humans, but with the added command to control and subdue the earth. The absence of divine blessing upon the rest of the animal kingdom is noteworthy, and most likely intentional. It is only indirectly, through human stewardship, that these animals can be blessed. Even the language that humans are made in the image of God is linked closely with the divine blessing. This opening panorama of God's activity in the cosmos contains not even a hint of curse. God explicitly repeats the blessing on the seventh day as a rationale for Sabbath rest in the Ten Commandments: "For in six days the LORD made the heavens and the earth, the sea, and all that is in them, but he rested on the seventh day. Therefore the LORD blessed the Sabbath day and made it holy" (Exod 20:11). The Sabbath simply cannot be abrogated by humans, as God has set it apart as holy. Thus the pattern of God's gift (blessing) and God's claim (set apart as holy) are inherent in the Sabbath command of the first creation account, of Genesis 1. One of the documents of rabbinic Judaism amusingly exploits this connection. The *Genesis Rabbah* (1:10) contends that Scripture begins with a *b* not an aleph (') because *b* is the first letter of *brk*, "to bless."[2] Every blessing in Genesis 1 also entails a responsibility. Blessing is a creational category; every created thing to one degree or another experiences God's blessing.

The two creation accounts (Gen 1:1—2:3 and 2:4—2:25) sharply contrast with the famous Babylonian account, the *Enuma Elish*. In the Babylonian account, theogony (theory about the origins of the gods) and cosmogony (theory about the origins of the universe) are essentially linked. Yet the Bible has no interest in divine origins. God simply exists and has always existed. God was "in the beginning." God stands completely outside the realm of nature and has no mythical origins; Genesis 1

---

1. On the seven-day structure see Hall, "The Theology of Genesis 1–11," 59–60.

2. Goldingay, *Old Testament Theology* 1:54.

is devoid of any notion of God's birth or biography.[3] Unlike in the Babylonian account, in Genesis there is no close association between myth and cult. God stands completely unopposed. Also unlike in the Babylonian account, which has the primary purpose of validating Marduk's assumption of divine guardianship over the universe, in Genesis God's ultimate power is unparalleled. This literary unit describes no cosmic battle like that alluded to in the Psalms (Pss 74:11–17; 90:1ff.). The humans are not created from the blood of slain and injured gods but by the performative word of God. In Genesis 2, God creates humans from the clay out of the ground, and the very breath of God gives them life. The sense of order that permeates Genesis 1 contrasts with the cosmogonies of Israel's neighbors. The gods of the ancient Near East were, without qualification, capricious. Because of this, there could be no unwavering sense of morality and no sense of certainty as to God's character. But in the Old Testament, God's expectations for community are based on that divine character.

God operates in an order that people can understand. There is a morality and intentionality to God's world that is no accident. This does not mean that there are no similarities between the creation accounts and the Bible's ancient Near Eastern environment. Jeffrey Niehaus has pointed to parallels between Genesis 1:1—2:3 and the international treaty forms, including the blessings and curses.[4] Elements of similarity include a title/ preamble, a historical prologue, stipulations, witnesses, and blessings and curses. Niehaus contends that the storyteller frames the first creation account similarly to such a treaty. Genesis 1 depicts blessing as fullness and abundance and depicts creation as enjoying rest in harmonious relationship with the Creator. Yet this blessing is not unopposed. "The continual reemergence and reassertion of forces antithetic to the good creation is without a doubt the major theme of Genesis 1–11, and no theology of creation can afford to leave it out of account."[5] Sadly, after Genesis 1, the next time we hear of the blessing is when God launches the new world after the flood.

The linking of creation and blessing is not just limited to the book of Genesis. The book of Isaiah quickly comes to mind. The Hebrew word "to create," *br'*, with God as subject, is found seven times in Genesis 1–2 but sixteen times in Isaiah 40–55. In the book of Isaiah, creation is cited as

---

3. Sarna, *Understanding Genesis*, 7–8.

4. Niehaus, *God at Sinai*, 145.

5. Blenkensopp, *Creation, Un-creation, Re-creation*, 18.

evidence that God nurtures a lasting concern for Israel. God will do a new work with this people, just like the work he began at creation,

> To whom then will you compare me,
>> that I should be like him? says the Holy One.
>> Lift up your eyes on high and see:
>> who created these?
>> He who brings out their host by number,
>> calling them all by name,
>> by the greatness of his might,
>> and because he is strong in power
>> not one is missing. (Isa 40:25–26, ESV)

The Psalmist declared, "by the word of the LORD the heavens were made, and by the breath of his mouth all their host (Ps 33:6, ESV).

CREATION AND THE WORD OF GOD

Genesis 1 affirms that it is the nature of God to speak, a truth absolutely foundational to the Bible. That God speaks everything into existence is not just an indication of how creation happened but a revelation of God's divine nature. The first act in the Bible is a speech act. It is no overstatement to say that this doctrine is foundational to all other doctrines about God.[6] It underlies every other truth about God. The Old Testament witness is that no one would know anything about God if God had never spoken. Revelation or disclosure is only comprehensible within a framework of election.[7] The word of God rings out in the very beginning.[8] The words, "God said" or "God called" occur more than a dozen times in the book of Genesis. "God spoke . . . and it was so" is also repeated in vv. 7, 9, 11, 15, 24, and 30. The first direct divine address to humans is a blessing-command to be fruitful and multiply. Almost all the divine speeches in Genesis include a promise. The fact that God speaks to humans is one thing, but the added dimension that God speaks to humans in a way that they can understand is something else altogether. This is the language of divine revelation. The Lord calls out to Adam and Eve in the garden, God speaks to the ancestors of Israel as well as to Moses and to Israel on the holy mountain: "God spoke all these words, saying, I am the LORD your God, who brought you

---

6. Brueggemann, *Theology of the Old Testament*, 182.

7. Seitz, *Word without End*, 19.

8. On the Word of God as speech-act, see Fretheim, "Word of God," 961–62.

out of the land of Egypt, out of the house of slavery" (Exod 20:1–2). God is sovereign, and God's word is an effective decree, yet divine speech brings about some things immediately and others through a process.

One need not wrongfully polarize the discussion by adopting the old idea of the word as material force, or by blithely assuming that words have no power at all. It is well known that *dbr* can be translated "word" or "thing." This has led to the mistaken notion that words were things, and that ancient Hebrews could not distinguish between thought and action. James Barr and Anthony Thiselton deconstructed this mistaken notion in the last half of the twentieth century.[9] First, Barr declared that one cannot make theological hay out of the history of a word. And Thiselton followed Austin to prove that the power of words does not have all that much to do with natural cause and effect, but everything to do with accepted procedures and conventions in Israelite society. The spoken word clearly does something, but not because of any magical notions. These performatives, like God's divine blessing/command to be fruitful and multiply demonstrate that words have power as speech acts.

Later in the Old Testament God speaks to elite kings and priests, to shepherds and commoners, through ordinary prophets. In regards to the divine voice behind the prophetic voice, Deut 18:18–22 is telling,

> I will raise up for them a prophet like you from among their brothers. And I will put my words in his mouth, and he shall speak to them all that I command him. And whoever will not listen to my words that he shall speak in my name, I myself will require it of him. But the prophet who presumes to speak a word in my name that I have not commanded him to speak, or who speaks in the name of other gods, that same prophet shall die. And if you say in your heart, 'How may we know the word that the LORD has not spoken?'—when a prophet speaks in the name of the LORD, if the word does not come to pass or come true, that is a word that the LORD has not spoken; the prophet has spoken it presumptuously. You need not be afraid of him. (Deut 18:18–22, ESV).

Thus the concept of the word of the Lord in Genesis lays the groundwork for the legal and prophetic traditions of the Old Testament. Divine word and human words merge early and often in the narratives of the Old Testament. From beginning to end, the book of Deuteronomy, for

---

9. Barr, *The Semantics of Biblical Language*, 129–40; Thiselton, "The Supposed Power of Words in Biblical Writings."

example, is presented as the divine word for Israel through the words of Moses. Jeremiah the prophet envisions his own ministry as one that proclaims the Word of God: "Then the LORD put out his hand and touched my mouth. And the LORD said to me, Behold I have put my words in your mouth . . ." (Jer 1:9). And again,

> To whom can I speak and give warning?
>> Who will listen to me?
> Their ears are closed
>> so they cannot hear.
> The word of the LORD is offensive to them;
>> they find no pleasure in it.
> But I am full of the wrath of the LORD,
>> and I cannot hold it in. (Jer 6:10–11)

Likewise, the prophet Amos declares, "The LORD roars from Zion and utters his voice from Jerusalem . . . Thus says the LORD" (Amos 1:2–3a, ESV).

Rolf Rendtorff, speaking about the theological nature of the canon of the Hebrew Bible, describes the three canonical sections as follows: the Law: God Acts, the Prophets: God Speaks, and the Writings: the People Speak. This basically follows von Rad, as he introduced the Writings considered under the heading "Israel's Response."[10] Rendtorff points out that the third section of the Hebrew Bible begins with a blessing, but he argues that this blessing cannot be understood without the Torah.[11] By choosing this structure for his theology of the Old Testament, Rendtorff claims that the speech of God dominates the entire corpus of the Hebrew Bible. Yet often God's people do not recognize God's voice. Why is it so difficult to understand the word of the Lord?

CREATION AND THE SPIRIT OF GOD

In addition to the word of God, one of the vehicles of God's revelation in the Old Testament is the Spirit (*rûaḥ*) of God. Divine word and spirit merge in the creation stories. The "Spirit of God," the "Spirit of Yahweh," and the rather rare "Holy Spirit," are synonyms in the Old Testament for that mysterious, magisterial, and powerful spiritual presence of God. The opening words of the Old Testament introduce the Spirit of God in association with the work of creation in both creation stories (Gen 1:2; 2:7).

---

10. Von Rad, *Old Testament Theology*, vol. 2.

11. Rendtorff, *The Canonical Hebrew Bible*, 6.

In Genesis 1, the Spirit of God "hovers over the face of the deep" as God speaks the world into existence. Thus, from the story of creation to the postexilic prophets, the Spirit of God and the Word of God unite to make something out of nothingness and to call the people of God to be what they are truly created to be. God's Spirit is also that life-force breathed into the first human being by God alone (Gen 2:7) as well as the spirit that will return to God at the time of one's death (Job 12:10; Eccl 12:7). Only context can indicate whether to translate *rûah* as "spirit," "Spirit," "wind," or "breath." The association of the Spirit with creation is also echoed in Wisdom literature (Job 26:13) and the Psalter: "By the word of the LORD the heavens were made and their starry host by the breath (*rûah*) of his mouth" (Ps 33:6; cf. Ps 104:30).

Before moving on, let us look more closely at the understanding of God's Spirit as expressed elsewhere in the Old Testament. The Hebrew word *rûah* refers to those invisible, mysterious, and powerful forces of wind or breath that could just as likely come from the blast of a storm or from a snort of a crocodile's snout (Job 41:18–21). The same word can apply to natural phenomena like a blowing wind (Gen 8:1; Exod 10:13; 19; Num 11:31; 1 Kgs 18:45; Prov 25:23; Jer 10:13; Hos 13:15; Jonah 4:8) and the breath of life (Gen 2:7), as well as to acts of the deity that empower and deliver (Judg 3:10, 6:34, 11:29, 13:25, 14:6, 15:14; 1 Sam 11:6). The Torah even attributes the artistic skills and material craftsmanship of Bezalel and others like him to the activity of the Spirit of God (Exod 28:3, 31:3, 35:31). Obviously then, one should not press the distinction between natural and supernatural phenomena too far, as all these varied expressions of *rûah* are manifestations of divine power. *Rûah* could be a wind that is described poetically as a blast from the nostrils of Yahweh (Exod 15:8), or just as easily that mysterious vital power that came upon prophets and judges alike. A *rûah* from God could bring about evil as well as good (Judg 9:23; 1 Sam 16:14–16; 1 Kgs 22:19–23). The sinister power that drives Saul into depression is called a Spirit of God. "Now the Spirit of the LORD had departed from Saul, and an evil spirit from the LORD tormented him" (1 Sam 16:14). Particularly in the case of the judges, early leadership of the tribal league rested on the authority of men and women who had received a particular manifestation of the Spirit of Yahweh. Samuel and Saul witnessed the manifestation of the Spirit through ecstatic prophets (1 Sam 11:6; 19:20–24).

Strikingly, the early writing prophets were reluctant to attribute their prophecies to the Spirit of Yahweh. With the possible exceptions of Micah

3:8, none of the eighth- or seventh-century writing prophets speak of the Spirit of God as the moving force behind their prophecies but instead refer to the word (Amos 3:8; Jer 20:9) or the hand of God (Isa 8:11; Jer 15:17) being upon them. It is reasonable that this was a reaction against abuses of ecstatic prophecy from the earlier periods of Israel's history, but no one really knows.[12] Regardless, there is a definite shift in the period of the monarchy from the dynamic, charismatic force of ecstatic prophecy to a more permanent manifestation associated with Yahweh's abiding presence. This shift was most dramatic among the postexilic prophets, who willingly embraced the metaphor of the Spirit of Yahweh as source of their inspiration and calling. Isaiah, Ezekiel, and Zechariah alike attribute their prophetic activity and revelation to the prompting of the divine spirit (Isa 59:21; Ezek 2:2; 3:1–14, 22–24; Zech 7:12). Take this example from Ezekiel: "Moreover he said to me, 'Son of man, all my words that I shall speak to you receive in your heart, and hear with your ears. And go, get you to the exiles, to your people, and say to them, 'Thus says the Lord GOD'; whether they hear or refuse to hear'" (Ezek 3:10–11, ESV). Additionally, the prophetic preachers so broadened the metaphor that the Spirit of Yahweh could potentially fall on the entire people of God. Ezekiel most richly describes this in his book (Ezek 11:19; 18:31; 36:26–27; 37:14; 39:29). Isaiah and other postexilic prophets also take up this theme (Isa 32:15; 44:3; Hag 2:5; Zech 4:6). Joel describes the last days as a time when the Spirit of Yahweh will be poured out upon the earth. According to the book of Acts, the Apostle Peter credited this prophecy with the Spirit's empowerment of new believers at Pentecost (Acts 2:16–21).

Theologically, the Spirit of the Lord also marks God's divine presence (Ps 51:11; 143:10; Hag 2:5) and continuing providence (Job 33:4; Ps 104:30) over the created order—and over humans in particular. The writers of the Old Testament use verbs such as "put on/clothed" (Judg 6:34), "fell/rushed upon" (Judg 14:6, 19), "poured out" (Joel 2:28), and "settled/ rested" (Num 11:25) to describe the transcendental nature of this activity of God toward humans. Another transcendental expression, "Holy Spirit," catches the dynamic and static qualities of the nature of God (Ps 51:11; Isa 63:10–11, 14). The messianic king bears the Spirit (Isa 11:12), as does the servant of Yahweh (Isa 42:1).

Finally, there is also some correlation between the Spirit of the Lord and the blessing. The pouring forth of the Spirit of God upon humans is tantamount to receiving the blessing. Note the parallelism of Isa 44:3b:

---

12. See Mowinckel, "The Spirit and the Word in the Prophets."

"I will put out my Spirit on your offspring
and my blessing on your descendants."

Alternatively, the removal of God's Spirit is tantamount to curse. When the Spirit is transferred from Saul to David, the blessing of God comes upon David (1 Sam 18:12–14). Simultaneously, the Spirit of Yahweh departs from Saul, resulting devastating calamity in his life (1 Sam 16:14). Samson faces humiliation and defeat after the Spirit of Yahweh departs from him (Judg 16:20).

This brings us back to the first mention of the Spirit of God in Genesis. As God's Spirit and word unite in creation, God breathes the breath of life into the humans as spiritual beings. God blesses these beings above all the rest of creation, yet ironically and tragically they turn that blessing into curse. Genesis 6:3 taken with Gen 3:22 clearly displays that God's restraining judgment is aimed at a blatant attempt to prolong life. "*My Spirit* shall not abide in man forever, for he is flesh, but his days shall be a hundred and twenty years" (Gen 6:3, ESV).

Three Theological Perspectives on the Primeval History

What is the overarching message of the various episodes that make up the primeval history, and how does the primeval history relate to the rest of the book of Genesis, the Pentateuch, and the Old Testament? There are generally three ways of viewing the opening eleven chapters of the Bible. One reading is that these chapters depict the escalation of sin and degradation among the human community. Another is to note the cyclical pattern of sin, punishment/exile, and grace. A third reading is to interpret these eleven chapters in light of creation and flood stories: creation, uncreation, re-creation. Each of these three perspectives in their own way depict blessing and curse trajectories uniquely.

An Escalation of Sin and Degradation

Even a naïve reader of the primeval history notices the stark contrast between the picture of order, unity, and blessing of Genesis 1–2 and what transpires afterwards. Yahweh places the couple in the garden to care for it. The author is deliberately vague about the location of Eden, just as the author of Exodus was about which pharaoh was the adversary of Israel.

The Eden metaphor depicts a place of blissful innocence, and the pharaoh metaphor portrays human institutions that harshly oppose God's people. In the heart of this primeval garden are two trees: the tree of life and the tree of knowledge (the Hebrew literally reads, "the tree of knowledge . . . good and evil"). The notion of a tree of life has many parallels in cultures of the ancient Near East, but the tree of knowledge is unique to the Old Testament. The human couple in the garden is pictured in innocence. Harmony exists between God and the humans, as Yahweh prepares a woman from the rib of the man; between the man and the woman, as portrayed by the male leaving his family to be united with his wife; between the humans and the soil, as the man is appointed to care for the produce of the ground; and between the humans and the created order, as both the humans and animals were made from the ground and given names by Adam. This harmony is best characterized by the statement that the first human couple was naked (*ărûmmîm*) and not ashamed. Such freedom is not, however, without responsibility. God commands that they not eat of the tree of knowledge. Eating fruit from any other tree in the garden is permissible, but from this specific tree they could not eat. "Both man and woman were created with the capacity for moral deviation."[13] The tree of life and the tree of knowledge represent two possible futures for the human couple. Eating the tree of life led to receiving a special blessing from God, perhaps not immortality in the sense that we think of it, but the ongoing life of fullness. The tree of life and the breath of life symbolize this life of fullness.

> The LORD God formed the man from the dust of the ground and breathed into his nostrils the breath of life, and the man became a living being. Now the LORD God had planted a garden in the east, in Eden; and there he put the man he had formed. And the Lord God made all kinds of trees grow out of the ground—trees that were pleasing to the eye and good for food. In the middle of the garden were the tree of life and the tree of the knowledge of good and evil. (Gen 2:7–9)

It was not long before the serpent disturbed the goodness of the created order. Up until that time the couple in the garden was innocent; they had never been tested. The unfortunate chapter division between chapters 2 and 3 softens the play on words between the couple described as naked (*ărûmmîm*) and the serpent, who was crafty (*ārûm*). Taking Genesis alone, this snake is one of the animals in the garden, not a fallen angel or superhuman being. It is not until the book of Revelation that there is an

---

13. Blenkensopp, *Creation, Un-creation, Re-creation*, 10.

explicit identification between the snake and Satan. Such innocence would not stand against the tempter, and both the Adam and Eve soon violate the command that Yahweh had given. The first of five intensifying curses (Gen 3:14, 17; 4:11; 5:28; 9:25) in Genesis 1–11 appears below:

> So the LORD God said to the serpent, "Because you have done this,
> Cursed (*ārûr*) are you above all the livestock
>> and all the wild animals!
> You will crawl on your belly
>> and you will eat dust
>> all the days of your life.
> And I will put enmity
>> between you and the woman,
>> and between your offspring and hers;
> he will crush your head,
>> and you will strike his heel."
>
> To the woman he said,
> "I will greatly increase your pains in child bearing;
>> with pain you will give birth to children.
> Your desire will be for your husband,
>> and he will rule over you."
>
> To Adam he said, "Because you listened to your wife and ate from the tree about which I commanded you, 'You must not eat of it,'
>
> Cursed (*ārûr*) is the ground because of you;
>> through painful toil you will eat of it
>> all the days of your life.
> It will produce thorns and thistles for you,
>> and you will eat the plants of the field.
> By the sweat of your brow
>> you will eat your food
> until you return to the ground,
>> since from it you were taken;
> for dust you are
>> and to dust you will return." (Gen 3:14–19)

The traditional Christian understanding of this passage is heavily dependent on early Christian theologians, who emphasized the entrance of sin into an innocent cosmos. Jewish interpreters in particular have emphasized that a fall is not of primary importance here. The author is simply observing the way things are in daily life: people seem to be separated from God, they have to work the ground laboriously, women have pain in childbirth yet still desire their husbands. Regardless, in the traditions of Judaism and Christianity alike, Adam and Eve both succumb to the wiles of the serpent, who leads them to reject the command of Yahweh to refrain from eating from the tree of knowledge. God had promised that if this first couple violated this command, death would certainly be the consequence. Literally, the text reads, "in the day you eat of it, dying you shall die" (Gen 2:17). For the first time in the Genesis narrative, the ominous threat of death is introduced.

Adam and Eve get exactly what they want: a life of their own creation. Genesis 3 is fraught with consequences of the disobedient pair, which includes the following binary opposites to the harmony mentioned above between God and the humans, between the man and the woman, between the man and the ground, and between the humans and the animals. Therefore, Genesis 3 highlights estrangement from God, from other humans, from the animals, and even from the soil from which Adam had been formed. Even Eve's fruitfulness of being able to conceive seems like a curse.[14] There is enough blame to go around for everyone concerned. Eve blames the serpent while Adam blames his wife as well as God ("the woman you gave me"). Consequently the couple is pushed out of this pristine garden of innocence and is cast out into a harsh world. Self-autonomy leads to despair.

One reading of Genesis 1–11 traces a deliberate deterioration from the original created order that had been evaluated as "very good" in the first creation account. Genesis 3–5 amounts to an etiology of death. Death reigns in these chapters that follow the actions of the disobedient couple. First, some*thing* must die to provide the clothing for the couple which flees the garden (Gen 3:21). Then, some*one* dies as Genesis 4 traces the murder of Abel, who is murdered by his own brother (Gen 4:8). The first directly explicit curse on a human is against Cain:

> The LORD said, "What have you done? Listen! Your brother's blood cries out to me from the ground. Now you are under a curse (*ārûr*) and driven from the ground, which opened its mouth to receive your brother's blood from your hand. When you work the ground, it will no longer yield its crops for you. You will be a restless wanderer on the earth." (Gen 4:10–12)

14. Goldingay, *Old Testament Theology*, 1:142.

Cain replies that this is more than he can bear. In spite of God's protective mark on Cain, things get worse, not better.[15] The episode of Lamech describes sin's infectious spread from murder to unremitting lust for blood revenge,

> Lamech said to his wives:
> Adah and Zillah, hear my voice;
>> you wives of Lamech, listen to what I say:
> I have killed a man for wounding me,
>> a young man for striking me.
> If Cain's revenge is sevenfold,
>> then Lamech's is seventy-sevenfold. (Gen 4:23–24, ESV)

The genealogy of Genesis 5 that follows is virtually a walk through the cemetery. It underscores that death did indeed come into the world as God has promised. The phrase, "and he died," recurs like the beat of a drum . . . nine times. Ultimately, in Genesis 6 God promises to destroy the world by flood because, "every intent of a man's heart is only evil all the time." The expression in Gen 6:11, "Now the earth was corrupt in God's sight and was full of violence," is placed in tragic juxtaposition with Genesis 1:31, "and God saw all that he had made, and behold it was very good." With the exception of a mere handful, the entire human race dies in the flood. Yahweh's promise that death would follow disobedience is fulfilled . . . with a vengeance. The biblical flood story divides humanity between the old order and the new. Yet nothing really changes. There is a new covenant with Noah full of the promise of blessing. But the unsavory story of Noah's vineyard shows that little has changed.

The story of the tower of Babel is the final episode of the primeval history. While death is not a major theme of the narrative, chaos and confusion certainly is. The primeval history ends with profound disappointment. The human community, which sprang from a common origin and once enjoyed the unity of one language, now is spread throughout the world, and the chaos of variegated speech reigns. Consequently, this community cannot contribute to God's purpose for the world, at least in the way its members were originally intended to contribute. In many ways, the Babel story actually intensifies the problems that brought about the flood. It certainly is no solution. According to the story, flood that envelops the whole earth. The short story Babel story mentions the whole earth five times (Gen 11:1, 4, 8, 9 [twice]). Arrogance and insecurity prompt foolish decisions and lead to a disenchanted view of progress. The people of Babel

15. Schwartz, *The Curse of Cain.*

want to make a name for themselves but do not want to be scattered over the face of the earth.[16] Indeed, the people of Babel do make a name for themselves, but it is a name of infamy. Who will pay the price for Adam's rebellion? How can we get Eden back? The message of the Babel story is that history demands a new beginning. God adopts a new strategy with a narrower perspective, one people: Israel.[17]

Theologically, this first of the three readings of Genesis 1–11 contains a harsh realism. The world as it exists now is certainly not what God intended it to be. Only the one most blinded to the reality of evil would argue that things are getting better. Yet even though creation is now badly flawed, the divine project of filling the earth is still moving forward. The theme of the natural expansion of the peoples after the flood is mentioned three times after the flood (Gen 9:19; 10:18, 32).

The Recurring Cycle of Sin/Exile/Grace

But there is another reading of Genesis 1–11, one which questions the excessive negativity of this first view.[18] From these opening chapters of Genesis one could also easily observe a recurring cycle of sin, punishment/exile, and grace. This threefold cycle has always been a part of the human condition. The narratives of the primeval history simply emphasize the recurrence of human moral failure, its consequences, and a new opportunity to begin again. While both readings accentuate the role of sin and punishment, the first reading perhaps lacks sensitivity to the multiple signs of Yahweh's grace in the primeval history. These markers of grace are obvious in nearly every episode. Adam and Eve are given clothing by God (Gen 3:21) after their willful disobedience, Cain is given a recognizable mark that protects him against his enemies (Gen 4:15) after he murders his own flesh and blood, and the survivors of the flood are shown a rainbow and given the promise that God will never again destroy the world by water (Gen 9:15). It is only the Babel story that exhibits no note of grace. In this reading, the hopeful transition from Babel to Abraham's blessing becomes that note of grace.

In the story of Adam and Eve's disobedience, the sin of the human couple results in all kinds of horrible consequences. These consequences are described as a world no longer characterized by innocence. But most

16. Wright, *The Mission of God*, 196.

17. Lemche, *The Old Testament between Theology and History*, 71, 187, 206.

18. Clines, *The Theme of the Pentateuch*, 64–73.

noteworthy is the couple's banishment from the garden. The language is harsh. The Lord God "drove out" the couple, and placed an angelic guard east of the garden to prevent them from eating of the tree of eternal life. The first reading presented above interprets the clothing of the couple as something negative. Something must die in order for Adam and Eve's nakedness to be covered. But this second reading sees the clothing of the couple as a note of God's grace and protection,

> The LORD God made garments of skin for Adam and his wife and clothed them. And the LORD God said, "The man has now become like one of us, knowing good and evil. He must not be allowed to reach out his hand and take also from the tree of life and eat, and live forever." So the LORD God banished him from the Garden of Eden to work the ground from which he had been taken. After he drove the man out, he placed on the east side of the Garden of Eden cherubim and a flaming sword flashing back and forth to guard the way to the tree of life. (Gen 3:21–24)

The story of Cain continues the theme of sin, punishment, and grace. It is true that sin appears to be worsening as God himself cannot seem persuade Cain not to murder his own brother. The theological truth of humanity's inability to do the right thing even when they know to do it should not be missed here. Instead of being duped into sin like his parents in the garden, he executes his own brother . . . intentionally and willfully. The broken harmony with the ground is a key theme in this narrative and leads to the divine curse. Abel's blood cries to Yahweh from the ground, so the fitting punishment is for Cain to be cursed from the ground. Again the language is stark: "My punishment is greater than I can bear. Behold, you have driven me this day away from the ground; and from they face I shall be hidden; and I shall be a fugitive and a wanderer on the earth" (Gen 4:13–14, ESV). The note of grace is God's protective mark that he places on Cain to prevent others from coming upon him and killing him.

The flood story also describes the theme of sin and punishment in unflinching detail. The entire population of the earth is wiped out by the flood. Literally no one is spared except those few who seek refuge in the ark. Yet, in spite of the harsh dose of reality in this episode, the story ends with a promise. This promise comes from the Lord's own mouth and describes the covenant sign of the rainbow, which assures the people of the earth that it will never be destroyed by flood again. The rainbow becomes a sign of the eternal covenant between God and the human community. The fact that the flood fails to improve the human capacity to obey God is no stumbling block to the sin/punishment/grace reading of Genesis 1–11. The flood episode is merely another in a long line of examples of human failure, divine retribution, and divine grace to begin again. The postflood era ushers in a new epoch of patience, where God decides to simply let things be. As Westermann puts it, "Not every expression of evil is reason for a fixed succession of events: sin/discovery/punishment or forgiveness."[19] God does not simply intervene with punishment on every occasion of sin. The final episode, the Babel story, is the only one in the primeval history that does not have a note of grace. Interpreters have argued that the promise to Abraham in Genesis 12 is exactly that—a new note of grace. In spite of all of humanity's failed efforts, God will make from one obedient man a people through which the entire cosmos will be blessed, or for that matter, cursed.

Theologically, the view that Genesis 1–11 portrays a recurring cycle has much to commend it. One could easily argue that it is a major theme in the entire Bible. The model of sin, punishment, and grace can be traced through the later history of Israel and through the message of the Old Testament prophets. It is this innocence that must be represented through a proper sacrificial victim, because innocence has certainly been lost.

A Story of Creation/Un-creation/Re-creation

Finally, it is possible to read the primeval history from the perspective of the opening chapters of the Bible, as a story of creation/un-creation/re-creation.[20] Indeed, the parallels between the creation and flood stories are rather remarkable. Before (creation) and after the flood (re-creation), the parallel expression of blessing to "be fruitful and increase" is explicit (Gen 1:28; 9:1). Yet in the actual flood story itself God promises to "blot out humanity from the face of the earth (un-creation). Another remarkable parallel is that the original creation account describes the boundary of the firmament that separates the waters from the waters (Gen 1:6). In the creation account this boundary is one of protection and blessing. But in the flood story, water pours down from heaven, and also bursts forth from the ground, creating chaos and destruction. In the creation story,

19. Westermann, *Genesis 1–11*, 456.

20. Blenkinsopp, *Creation, Un-creation, Re-creation*, 186. His commentary is "based on the assumption that the initial act of creation cannot be detached from the sequence of events leading to the deluge as an act of un-creation followed by a renewal of creation under changed circumstances."

God breathes life into the humans and they become living beings. In the flood story, however, God uses the same language to "destroy all flesh in which is the breath of life" (Gen 6:17, ESV). After the flood, Noah's descendents live on to carry on the purpose of God by building a new generation. References to humans being created in the image of God are present in both the creation and flood accounts (Gen 1:27; 9:6). Finally, at the onset of creation, the Bible states that the Spirit of God hovered over the waters. The same word is used in the flood story to describe the abatement of the waters after the flood as a wind of God passed over the earth and dried it up.

Two words dominate the primeval history in Genesis 1–11: "earth" (*'āreṣ*) and "ground" (*'ădāmâ*). According to source criticism, the Priestly source typically adopts the first term and the Yahwist uses the second, but at times both words are present together at points in the Yahwist's source (Gen 2:5; 4:12; 6:6–7; 8:21–22). The word *'āreṣ* is used multiple times in the first creation account. God creates the heavens and gives the dry land the name *earth*. It yields vegetation, including plants and trees. Light appears on the earth, as do the birds and all living creatures, including the humans. The humans are given dominion over the earth and commanded to subdue it. In God's blessing to the humans, God has given every beast on the earth to the humans. The beginning (Gen 1:1) and end (Gen 2:1) of the first creation account mention that God created and finished the heavens and the earth.

But it is the parallel theme of *'ădāmâ* ("ground") that is perhaps more noteworthy and creates a leitmotif for the primeval story. The first expression that stands out is the one typically translated, "to till the earth," or better, "to work the earth" (*la 'ăbōd 'et ha'ădāmâ*) in Gen 2:5. The creation story begins by stating that there was no one to work the earth. Adam (note the parallel to *'ădāmâ*), is created from the ground itself in order to work the ground. Even after the disobedience in the garden, in the midst of stark punishment described in the primeval history, the human couple are expelled from the garden to work the ground from which they were sent (*la 'ăbōd 'et ha'ădāmâ*). Cain is noted for being a worker of the ground (Gen 4:2), and after the flood when all humans have perished, Noah, the first in a new generation is described as the "first to work the ground" (Gen 9:20).

What can one make of this important theological connection with earth and ground in the primeval story? How does that connection relate to the third way of reading Genesis 1–11 via the theme of creation/

un-creation/re-creation? First and foremost, both blessing and curse derive from the ground. The blessing of creation is for the humans to be fruitful and multiply and fill the earth. They are to have dominion over it and to subdue it. Humans are inextricably linked to the ground, not in some absolute monism where there is no distinction between the Creator and the created, but as partners, as created entities. Human origins and human demise are linked to the ground. People come from the ground and will return there after death. The disobedience of the human couple has direct implications on the ground. Blessing is thereby turned into curse: "Cursed is the ground because of you" (Gen 3:17). Working the ground is a part of the very order of things, not just a consequence of the couple's disobedience in the garden, but the working of the soil and the responsibility for all creatures associated with the soil is part of human responsibility and blessing from the beginning. Therefore, work and productivity are good things and are a part of what it means to be truly human. Productivity is a sign of blessing. The two trees in the heart of the garden—the tree of life and the tree of knowledge—derive from the ground: "The LORD God made all kinds of trees grow out of the ground—trees that were pleasing to the eye and good for food. In the middle of the garden were the tree of life and the tree of the knowledge of good and evil" (Gen 2:9). The fates of humans and the ground are intertwined. There is a kind of derivative benefit and derivative misery upon the creation due to humanity's faithful care or unfaithful selfishness. In the Old Testament, the land mourns at the disobedience of God's people (Joel 1). In the New Testament, creation groans, waiting for the children of God to be revealed (Rom 8). Ultimately, the New Testament expects a new created order, a new heaven and a new earth.

The flood story also takes up this theme of earth and ground. The flood story begins by saying that God regretted placing humans on the earth, "Now the earth was corrupt in God's sight, and the earth was filled with violence. And God saw the earth, and behold, it was corrupt; for all flesh had corrupted their way upon the earth (Gen 6:12–13). Source critics argue that these two verses come from J and P respectively. The flood came as punishment for this corruption, as "all flesh on the earth died" (Gen 7:21). The Yahwist's account of the flood ends with this promise:

> I will never again curse (lĕqallēl) the ground because of man, for
> the imagination of man's heart is evil from his youth; neither will
> I ever again destroy every living creature as I have done. While
> the earth remains, seedtime and harvest, cold and heat, summer
> and winter, day and night, shall not cease. (Gen 8:21b–22, ESV)

There is a direct parallel between the language of the original curse and its use of the Hebrew root *qll*. The blessing of fertility is repeated in Gen 9:1 but with a sharp contrast. There will be no peaceful coexistence with the living creatures.[21] Is this a promise of a new dispensation, one that is no longer dominated by curse but instead by God's blessing? In one sense, Noah is a new Adam, whose function is to cultivate the ground and take care of it. It would be ideal if that were the case, but sadly, the flood does not reverse the human sprint toward depravity. Humans certainly do not change. Noah, the first human of the new generation, goes out, plants a vineyard, gets drunk, exposes himself, passes out and is humiliated by his son's callous disregard. Instead of an expected blessing, Noah's first recorded words unleash a horrible curse against Canaan, his grandson. This curse is the only humanly imposed curse in the Torah.[22]

> Cursed (*ārûr*) be Canaan;
>> a servant of servants shall he be to his brothers."
> He also said,
> "Blessed be the LORD, the God of Shem;
>> and let Canaan be his servant.
> May God enlarge Japheth,
>> and let him dwell in the tents of Shem,
>> and let Canaan be his servant." (Gen 9:25–27, ESV)

Note clear parallels between the promise that God will never curse the ground and the original curse of Gen 3:17. Yet, if this is somehow a new dispensation of blessing, how does one explain that the circumstance of the curse are still potent? Has anything really changed? Humans still work the ground with the sweat of their brow, the ground brings forth both thorns and thistles, women still have pain in childbirth and yet desire their husbands. The promise of Gen 8:21–22 must be interpreted in light of Gen 6:5 as well as 3:17. Theologically, the flood does very little to change the heart of humanity.

Some reflection needs to be given to another expression: "the face of the ground" or "the face of the earth." The flood story begins with an expression of the multiplication of the humans over the face of the ground (Gen 6:1). In an inclusio that serves as a parenthesis around the unenviable relationship between the sons of God and daughters of men, God promises that he will blot humans off of the face of the ground (Gen 6:7). At the height of the flood, "all flesh died that moved on the earth" (Gen

21. Rendtorff, *The Canonical Hebrew Bible*, 18.
22. Goldingay, *Old Testament Theology* 1:184.

7:21, ESV). The final story in the primeval history is the infamous story of the tower of Babel. The expression "the face of the earth" is present twice in that account (Gen 11:4, 8, ESV). The residents construct a tower, "lest we be dispersed over the face of the whole earth." God comes down, confuses their languages, and, "dispersed them from there over the face of all the earth." Thus, the Babel story serves as a pathetic ending to the possibility that the flood might introduce a new dispensation—one of blessing, where the curse is no longer a potentiality. This kind of thinking is wishful thinking.

The language of un-creation is also employed by the prophets.

> I looked at the earth, and it was formless and empty;
>   and at the heavens, and their light was gone.
> I looked at the mountains, and they were quaking;
>   all the hills were swaying.
> I looked, and there were no people;
>   every bird in the sky had flown away.
> I looked, and the fruitful land was a desert;
>   all its towns lay in ruins
>   before the LORD, before his fierce anger. (Jer 4:23–26)

GOD'S BLESSING AND THE IMAGE OF GOD

Humans constitute a paradox for a theology of the Old Testament. They are full of contradictions: made in God's image yet bent on living their lives without God; infused with the very breath of God yet finite, with limited existence; endowed with a clear purpose that comes from interaction with God, humans, and the created order, yet they experience one ruptured relationship after another. Humans are blessed and cursed. A theological reading of the Old Testament must grapple with these contradictions.

Genesis 1–11 is the only place in the Old Testament that observes that humans are made in the image of God. In this context the image of God is mentioned three times, each clearly in the larger context of God's blessing (Gen 1:26–28; 5:1–3; 9:1–7). Despite its absence from the rest of the Old Testament, the notion of the image of God has been of great interest for generations of Bible enthusiasts. Some have simply suggested that the expression denotes the physical body. In this reading, God has a physical body like humans. Those who hold this position take up a literal reading of texts that speak of God's hands, heart, arms, and so forth but depart from a literal reading when it comes to texts that refer to God's wings (Pss 17:8; 61:4). This glaring inconsistency renders a literal reading highly problematic, and these expressions of physical characteristics of God are clearly anthropomorphic. Thomas Aquinas sought an understanding of the image of God as the human intellectual capacity for reason. For Aquinas, only humans are capable of such rational thought. It is because of the capacity for reason that humans truly have a free will and the genuine ability to choose from among moral alternatives. Augustine suggested that the capacity of relationship with God is at the heart of what it means to be made in God's image. He spoke of a God-shaped vacuum in the human heart. Such hunger for a relationship with God is based on human freedom of choice and yearning after God. Perhaps the most prominent theologian of the twentieth century, Karl Barth, pointed to the poetic parallelism in Gen 1:26 to suggest that it is the male and femaleness that is behind the expression.[23] According to Barth, something in the character of God transcends gender yet encompasses it. These are only a few among the varied theological viewpoints regarding what it means for humans to be made in God's image.

The term "image" (*ṣlm*) is used sixteen times in the Old Testament and can refer to all kinds images. For example, the Philistines fashioned images of tumors and mice to avert the plague introduced by the capture of their ark of the covenant. Numbers 33:52 requires the destruction of all graven images, and the prophets condemn the use of idolatrous images (Amos 5:26; Ezek 7:20; 23:14). Perhaps the most sarcastic polemic against idol worship is from Isaiah:

> All who make idols are nothing,
> and the things they treasure are worthless.
> Those who would speak up for them are blind;
> they are ignorant, to their own shame.
> Who shapes a god and casts an idol,
> which can profit him nothing?
> He and his kind will be put to shame;
> craftsmen are nothing but men.
> Let them all come together and take their stand;
> they will be brought down to terror and infamy.
> The blacksmith takes a tool
> and works with it in the coals;
> he shapes an idol with hammers,
> he forges it with the might of his arm.

23. Jewett, *Man as Male and Female.*

> He gets hungry and loses his strength;
>> he drinks no water and grows faint.
> The carpenter measures with a line
>> and makes an outline with a marker;
>> he roughs it out with chisels
>> and marks it with compasses.
> He shapes it in the form of man,
>> of man in all his glory,
>> that it may dwell in a shrine.
> He cut down cedars,
>> or perhaps took a cypress or oak.
> He let it grow among the trees of the forest,
>> or planted a pine, and the rain made it grow.
> It is man's fuel for burning;
>> some of it he takes and warms himself,
>> he kindles a fire and bakes bread.
> But he also fashions a god and worships it;
>> he makes an idol and bows down to it.
> Half of the wood he burns in the fire;
>> over it he prepares his meal,
>> he roasts his meat and eats his fill.
> He also warms himself and says,
> "Ah! I am warm; I see the fire."
> From the rest he makes a god, his idol;
>> he bows down to it and worships.
> He prays to it and says,
> "Save me; you are my god."
> They know nothing, they understand nothing;
>> their eyes are plastered over so they cannot see,
>> and their minds closed so they cannot understand.
> No one stops to think,
>> no one has the knowledge or understanding to say,
>> "Half of it I used for fuel;
> I even baked bread over its coals,
> I roasted meat and I ate.
>> Shall I make a detestable thing from what is left?
> He feeds on ashes, a deluded heart misleads him;
>> he cannot save himself, or say,
> "Is not this thing in my right hand a lie?" (Isa 44:9–20)

A reading sensitive to the theme of blessings and curses detects notable similarities in the three occasions in Genesis where the expression image of God, is used.

And God said, Let us make man in our image, after our likeness and let them have dominion over the fish of the sea, and over the birds of the air, and over the cattle, and over all the earth, and over every creeping thing that creeps upon the earth.

> So *God created man in his own image,*
> in the image of God he created him,
> male and female he created them.

And *God blessed them* and said to them, "Be fruitful and multiply and fill the earth and subdue it, and have dominion over the fish of the sea and over the birds of the heavens and over everything that moves on the earth. (Gen 1:26–28, ESV, italics added)

When God created man, he made him in the likeness of God. He created them male and female *and blessed them*. And when they were created, he called them "man." When Adam had lived 130 years, he had a son in his own likeness, *in his own image*; and he named him Seth. (Gen 5:1b–3, ESV, italics added)

And God *blessed Noah and his sons* and said to them, "Be fruitful and multiply and fill the earth. The fear of you and the dread of you shall be upon every beast of the earth and upon every bird of the heavens, upon everything that creeps on the ground and all the fish of the sea. Into your hand they are delivered. Every moving thing that lives shall be food for you. And as I gave you the green plants, I give you everything. But you shall not eat flesh with its life, that is, its blood. And for your lifeblood I will require a reckoning: from every beast I will require it and from man. From his fellow man I will require a reckoning for the life of man.

> Whoever sheds the blood of man,
> by man shall his blood be shed,
> for God made man *in his own image*.
> And you, be fruitful and multiply, teem on the earth and multiply in it" (Gen 9:1–7, ESV, italics added)

In each of these three examples is a link between blessing and the image of God, both rendered above in italics. The blessing of God enhances a life of fullness. Throughout Genesis 1, the expression, "And God said" is repeated eight times. Genesis 1:28 adds the blessing to that phrase, plus the preposition and pronominal suffix: "God blessed them and said to them." The additional preposition in Hebrew, *lhm* ("to them"), adds a new dimension to the spoken word of God. This is direct address, something entirely new, the first direct address of God to humans in the Bible. To be made in God's image is thus to be capable of understanding and responding to God. This first divine address to humans indicates dialogue and communion. Even though they are created beings, humans are God's counterpart, God's colleagues, not in the sense of equals but in the sense of legitimate sharers in relationship. Similar language is used in Gen 5:3. Genesis links God's blessing with the image of God in this second example. Adam has a son in his own image. Adam's son was a part of, or better yet, a counterpart to Adam. In the third example above, humans are to be protected from murder because there is something special about them; they are God's complement.[24] The first and last examples convey the divine commission to be fruitful and multiply a component of blessing language in the Old Testament.

The psalmist expresses this important relationship between humans and God in this way:

> When I look at your heavens, the work of your fingers,
> the moon and the stars, which you have set in place,
> what is man that you are mindful of him,
> and the son of man that you care for him?
> Yet you have made him a little lower than the heavenly beings
> and crowned him with glory and honor.
> You have given him dominion over the works of your hands;
> you have put all things under his feet. (Ps 8:3–6, ESV)

From an Old Testament perspective, being made in the image of God does not necessarily mean, however, that humans are innately eternal beings. This may sound strange in light of the teachings of the Christian church because of the New Testament—teachings that are heavily dependent on the church's witness of resurrection and Jesus's proclamation of eternal life. From the outset, however, the Old Testament makes it clear that humans are finite and that their time on this earth limited. The biblical word to denote humanity's finite nature is *bśr*, or "flesh." The first and only commandment to the human couple in the garden was that they refrain from eating of the tree of knowledge. God warned the couple that on the day that they ate of it, they would certainly die. From the perspective of the story of the fall, humankind is cursed with the curse of death. The results of sin in the garden yield cataclysmic consequences. The couple hides from God in humiliation and guilt. The man blames the woman, and the woman blames the serpent and ultimately God. Separation from God,

24. Stendeback, "*ṣlm*."

from one another, and from the soil are all examples of these negative consequences. The ultimate consequence, however, was promised before they partook of the fruit of the tree of knowledge: death. The theme of death reigns in the Old Testament, first through the primeval story and then in the Torah, Prophets, and Writings. Genesis 6:3 states, "My spirit shall not abide in man forever, for he is flesh: his days shall be 120 years" (ESV). In spite of being created a little lower than the angels, and in spite of being infused with the breath of God, human life is limited. Ecclesiastes 3:1–11 makes it clear that God has set eternity in the human heart, a desire and longing for eternal life. The Apostle Paul calls death the final enemy (1 Cor 15:26). Tragically, humans cannot understand or change the predetermined paths of life and are confined to a limited existence. Psalm 144:3–4 reflects both sides: the divine breath given to humans and the brevity of life: "Lord, what are human beings that you care for them, mere mortals that you think of them? They are like a breath; their days are like a fleeting shadow." The brief glimpses of resurrection in the Old Testament are only that. Yet they are mere whispers of that longing for eternal life.

From the outset, the Bible portrays humans as relational beings. They relate to the earth from which they originated, to the plants and animals that share this world with them; to their spouses, families, tribes, and kingdoms; and most important, they relate to God. The creation of a body and the possession of the very breath of God, which made the first human a living soul, are the elements that allow humans to relate to the world around them, to one another, and to God. The second creation story explicitly states that "it is not good for the man to be alone." The created order was a start to meeting that elemental human need for relationship, yet it fell short of what God intended and human need demanded. The Bible says that there was "no helper suitable for him." So God created the woman from the side of man to be his companion. Genesis emphasizes relationships: between spouses, brothers, families, tribes, kingdoms, and ultimately relationships between humans and the whole earth.

Ultimately, the need to relate is something innate in every human: to God, to other humans, to the world around them. The Old Testament is clear that a person's real purpose is external to themselves. Humans live a life of fullness to the extent that they fulfill the purpose that God intended for them. God established a purpose for each person, frankly, without consulting them. The prophet Jeremiah, for example, was informed that before he was even born, God had determined his purpose. The Old Testament is clear that some simply did what was right in their own eyes(Judg

16:7), but those who were truly fulfilled discovered God's purpose for them and were obedient to that purpose.

Finally, humans are accountable. Even though humans are finite and cannot always understand the eternity that God has set in their hearts, God still holds them accountable for their actions. Threat of curse in these texts, in part, highlights that accountability. Throughout the Old Testament humans are held responsible for their actions. The prophet Ezekiel, for example, argues that each individual is responsible for his or her own actions. The soul who sins will die (Ezek 18:4). The sin/punishment/grace theme prominent in the Old Testament highlights this important truth.

5

"I Will Bless Those Who Bless You and Curse Those Who Curse You"

Election and the Ancestral Narratives

ABRAHAM, THE PEOPLE OF GOD, AND THE PEOPLES OF THE EARTH

GERHARD VON RAD STATED that God's promise extends through the ancestral stories like a red line.[1] This promise could never be fulfilled in the lifetime of its recipient, so it had to be accepted by faith. Furthermore, this promise is preceded by the command to forsake all, a command that typifies Yahweh's actions with humans. Yahweh utters the divine promise to Abram in language of blessing and curse in Genesis 12:1–3. On five separate occasions the Hebrew root *brk* is used in regards to Abraham in the ancestral narratives (Gen 12:3; 18:18; 22:18; 26:4–5; 28:14), which run counter the five curses of the primeval history (Gen 3:14, 17; 4:11; 8:21; 9:25). God uses potent verbs to declare this promise: "I will show you the land," "I will make you a great nation," "I will bless you," "I will make of you a great name," "I will bless those who bless you," and "I will curse those who curse you." From the standpoint of election, blessing and curse are divine prerogatives first and foremost. Ultimately the promise of

1. Von Rad, *Genesis*, 166. See Gen 12:1–3; 13:14–17; 14:15–20; 15:4–7; 15:18–21; 22:17; 26:24; 28:3ff, 28:13–15; 32:12; 35:9–12; 46:3–4; 48:16.

blessing is not Abraham's alone, nor that of his family and descendants. It is something that extends to all the people of the earth. The promise of peoplehood and international blessing are linked together in unique ways that will be explored in this chapter.

After the Babel tragedy, God adopts a strategy with a narrower perspective. God will bless the peoples through one family. The promise of Abraham has the final word with blessing as its aim.[2] Set in opposition to Genesis 1–11, which shows that something has gone dreadfully wrong with this world, Gen 12:1–3 becomes the theological blueprint for the redemption of the world. This universal blessing is based on Abraham's obedient response to Yahweh's summons and is repeated later to Abraham after he demonstrates his obedient willingness to sacrifice his own son Isaac (Gen 22:18).[3] God also offers blessing to Abraham's son Isaac (Gen 26:4) and his grandson Jacob (Gen 28:14).

> And the angel of the LORD called to Abraham a second time from heaven and said, "By myself I have sworn, declares the LORD, because you have done this and have not withheld your son, your only son, I will surely bless you, and I will surely multiply your offspring as the stars of heaven and as the sand that is on the seashore. And your offspring shall possess the gate of his enemies, and in your offspring shall all the nations of the earth be blessed, because you have obeyed my voice." (Gen 22:15–18, ESV)

> And behold, the LORD stood above it and said, "I am the LORD, the God of Abraham your father and the God of Isaac. The land on which you lie I will give to you and to your offspring. Your offspring shall be like the dust of the earth, and you shall spread abroad to the west and to the east and to the north and to the south, and in you and your offspring shall all the families of the earth be blessed. Behold, I am with you and will keep you wherever you go, and will bring you back to this land. For I will not leave you until I have done what I have promised you." (Gen 28:13–15, ESV)

The promises to Abraham and the other ancestors of Israel employ images that exceed all bounds. Their descendants will be as numerous as the stars (Gen 15:5; 26:4), as common as dust (Gen 13:16; 22:17; 28:14; 32:13), a great people (Gen 12:2; 18:18; 46:3), and a multitude of peoples

2. Dumbrell, *Covenant and Creation*, 65.
3. Yarchin, "Imperative and Promise in Genesis 12:1–3."

(Gen 17:4–6; 35:11).[4] In response to God's sovereign call, Abraham's departure from Haran is the human trigger that releases the divine blessing.[5] Theologically, Gen 12:1–3 has nothing less in mind than the complete recovery of divine purpose for the cosmos. Therefore, the ancestral blessing is bound up with a theology of history. In the New Testament, this theology of history begins with Abram and culminates in Jesus the Messiah. Note the Apostle Paul's direct link between Abraham's call, the blessing to the peoples of the earth, and the call to believe.

> So also Abraham "believed God, and it was credited to him as righteousness." Understand, then, that those who believe are children of Abraham. Scripture foresaw that God would justify the Gentiles by faith, and announced the gospel in advance to Abraham: "All nations will be blessed through you." So those who have faith are blessed along with Abraham, the man of faith. (Gal 3:6–9)

The Hebrew blessing-promise to the peoples in Gen 12:3 has both a passive and reflexive dimension. The passive "All the peoples on earth will be blessed through Abraham," and the reflexive "all the peoples on earth will bless themselves through Abraham" reveal two dimensions of the blessing-promise.[6] This promise brings Abraham into relationship with all people outside his chosen family and is therefore a missional utterance. This blessing links all the ancestral narratives together and also connects them with the primeval history. Those peoples who operate in cooperation with Abraham's descendants are to be blessed.

But there is threat along with blessing: "The one who curses you I will curse" (Gen 12:3; cf. Deut 5:9–10; 7:9–10). Is this warning a free-standing promise of its own, or is it secondary to the previous promise? Frankly, it can be read either way. The passive voice in Gen 12:3 ("all the peoples of the earth will be blessed through you") implies that Abraham is the conduit through which the rest of the world is blessed. Reading the reflexive voice in Gen 12:3 may imply that others can be blessed in the same

---

4. Rendtorff, *The Canonical Hebrew Bible*, 25.

5. Wright, *The Mission of God*, 202.

6. The Niphal form of *brk* that occurs only in the blessing-promise to Abraham (Gen 12:3; 18:18; 28:14) must be juxtaposed with the Hithpael, which appears twice in the statement of the promise (22:18; 26:4). The Hithpael of *brk* occurs in four other verses (Deut 29:19; Ps 72:17; Isa 65:16; Jer 4:2), and in each case the stem appears to be reflexive, not a passive. For all the possible syntactical options, see Williamson, *Abraham, Israel, and the Nations*, 220–34.

way that Abraham is blessed.[7] This second reading of Gen 12:3 ("all the peoples of the earth will bless themselves through you") does not deny the missional sense of Abraham's commission but does broaden election beyond Abraham's family. Regardless, threat of curse is explicit. There is a connection between promise and blessing, between promise and curse. Neither is independent of the other. Neither can one be understood without the other. The tragedy of Israel's history was that instead of drawing the foreign peoples to the ways of Yahweh, Israel was drawn to the ways of those peoples.[8]

This blessing in Genesis 12–50 can be sharply contrasted with the attempt in the Babel story to establish an order based on human achievement and solidarity alone. Theologian Langdon Gilkey once observed four traits of a Babel worldview.[9] The first trait is lawlessness. In this worldview, each individual is a law unto him- or herself. The human tendency to shun accountability and refuse moral restrictions is rampant regardless of culture, education, or religion. The second trait is relativity; basically this is the idea that there is really only one moral virtue: openness. When openness becomes the only virtue, it becomes a vice, leading to a society ruled by public opinion, where one's self-absorbed freedom is the only absolute. The third trait is contingency. Everything is caused by some natural trigger, and the supernatural is denied. Contingency makes practical atheists out of those who hold such views. The fourth trait is temporality: the overriding concern for the present. Nietzsche once quipped that the newspaper had replaced prayer in the lives of believers so that temporality brackets out eternal concerns; only what one does today matters. The promise to Abram nullifies and defies this kind of Babel-based worldview. The blessing promise is tied to Abram's submission and obedience to God's sovereign call. He is summoned to iconoclasm, called to leave behind the trappings of his culture and his religious worldview. And he is to face a hard-nosed realism that acknowledges that his present decisions directly impact generations after him and peoples completely unrelated to him.

Outside the book of Genesis, the blessing for the world is a vision fitfully observed in the Old Testament, prominent in some books and completely absent in others. Yet perhaps even at its faintest this vision has always imparted some sense of mission to Israel.[10] Throughout the ances-

---

7. Moberly, *The Bible, Theology, and Faith*, 120–27.

8. Chester and Timms, *Total Church*, 48.

9. Gilkey, *Reaping the Whirlwind*, 210–16, 236–38.

10. Kidner, *Genesis*, 114.

tral narratives God affirms and reaffirms for each successive generation the fourfold promise of land, descendants, name, and blessing to the peoples. The role of Israel is to participate in the mission of God (*missio Dei*). Thus the people of God are at the very heart of the universal purpose of God. God does not choose to go it alone.

The ancestral narratives provide a new dimension to God's blessing, not seen in the primeval history. In the primeval history, God's blessing constituted general realities like fertility, prosperity, and success. At times in the ancestral narratives as well, sometimes God's blessing includes these elements (Gen 27:27–29). Yet there is also a narrowing of that blessing, representing God's constitutive promise to the particular family initially through Abraham (Gen 12:1–3; 15:4–5, 18–21) and broadened to his descendants (Gen 26:3–4, 24; 28:13–14; 35:10–12). Creation blessings alone are life exalting and life enhancing but not sufficient for the fullest life possible.[11]

The only reversal of this blessing in Genesis is with Melchizedek (Gen 14:18–20). Rather than Abraham's being a source of blessing to other peoples as was promised, the tables are turned, and he is himself blessed by this enigmatic king of Salem. Thus, the blesser can be blessed:

> Then Melchizedek king of Salem brought out bread and wine.
> He was priest of God Most High, and he blessed Abram, saying,
> "Blessed be Abram by God Most High,
>   Creator of heaven and earth.
> And blessed be God Most High,
>   who delivered your enemies into your hand." (Gen 14:18–20)

This account follows directly after Abraham's successful rescue of Lot from the Canaanite kings. Melchizedek is a truly enigmatic figure, mentioned only twice in the Old Testament; here and Ps 110:4, a messianic psalm. His name is similar to that of the Canaanite king Adoni-Zedek in Josh 10:1, which means "my king is righteousness." The Hebrew priestly name Zadok also derives from the root (2 Sam 8:17; 15:24–25). Because of these linguistic links of his name to royal and priestly ones, the mysterious figure Melchizedek may have been, at least metaphorically, a precursor of both royal and priestly lines. He is called the king of Salem. One reading of this geopolitical title not universally accepted is to interpret Melchizedek as king of Jerusalem. If Melchizedek was a priest, as the name Zadok implies, then the meal with Abraham was a sacred act, part of the blessing that followed. Regardless, this account relates directly back to Genesis 12. In

---

11. Fretheim, "Which Blessing," 282.

the context of the ancestral history, Abraham has just cleared the land of the opposition from Canaanite kings. The poetry in v. 19 demonstrates the reciprocal nature of the blessing from God, through Abraham, to Melchizedek; then a reversal of that blessing from Melchizedek, through Abraham, back to God.[12] This story, by the way, contrasts with many of the negative depictions of foreigners in the Genesis accounts. This outsider becomes a source of blessing to Abraham. Therefore, the non-elect are not exclusively dependent on the elect for many forms of blessing.[13] Just as the rain falls on the just and the unjust, so at times the non-elect may even mediate blessings to the elect.

Isaac typifies the results of the blessing. There is a similar pattern but a reversal of order from Abraham's story to Isaac's story: blessing-promise, command, journey, famine.

> Now there was a famine in the land, besides the former famine that was in the days of Abraham. And Isaac went to Gerar to Abimelech king of the Philistines. And the LORD appeared to him and said, "Do not go down to Egypt; dwell in the land of which I shall tell you. Sojourn in this land, and I will be with you and will bless you, for to you and to your offspring I will give all these lands, and I will establish the oath that I swore to Abraham your father. I will multiply your offspring as the stars of heaven and will give to your offspring all these lands. And in your offspring all the nations of the earth shall be blessed, because Abraham obeyed my voice and kept my charge, my commandments, my statutes, and my laws. So Isaac settled in Gerar. (Gen 26:1–6, ESV)

> From there he went up to Beersheba. That night the LORD appeared to him and said, "I am the God of your father Abraham. Do not be afraid, for I am with you; I will bless you and will increase the number of your descendants for the sake of my servant Abraham." (Gen 26:23–24)

In between these two verbal blessings to Isaac lies the charming story designed to demonstrate some of the tensions as well as the collegiality between Abraham's family and outsiders. Drought shoves Isaac to Gerar in the region of the Philistines. While there, Isaac, like his father before him, fears for his life in the presence of foreigners, so he tries to pass off his wife, Rebekah, as his sister. Abimelech, the anachronistic king of the Philistines,

12. Fretheim, *The Book of Genesis*, 1:442.
13. Fretheim, "Which Blessing," 281.

is possibly the same rather gullible person who had been victimized by Abraham. He realizes quite by accident that Rebekah is Isaac's wife and immediately gives orders that none of his people should molest her. His resentment against Isaac, however, is explicit. Abimelech berates Isaac for putting the existence of his very community in danger. Someone might have taken liberties with Rebekah, and brought God's judgment down on his people.[14]

The blessing of productivity (Gen 26:3) even in the midst of famine made Isaac's flocks numerous. In Gen 26:12–13, Isaac reaps a hundredfold harvest. Isaac's great wealth is mentioned three times in a single verse: "The man became rich and his wealth continued to grow and he became very wealthy" (Gen 26:13). Such wealth, however, does not always win friends.[15] Tensions over pastureland and water drive a wedge between Isaac's and Abimelech's herdsmen. Abimelech demands that Isaac move away, so Isaac moves up the valley, which resolves little. He opens old wells, renames them, and digs new ones. His herdsmen continue to quarrel with the herdsmen of Abimelech, so he returns to Beersheba. Now at a safer distance, Abimelech feels secure enough to make a covenant with Isaac: "So we said, let there be a sworn pact between us, between you and us, and let us make a covenant with you, that you will do us no harm, just as we have not touched you and have done to you nothing but good and have sent you away in peace. You are now the blessed of the LORD" (Gen 26:28b–29, ESV). Therefore the cordial relationship between Isaac and the Philistines is repaired. God's appearance at Beersheba establishes it as a cultic center.

Beside the call to Abraham in Genesis 12, perhaps the most monumental episode related to the blessing-and-curse theme in the ancestral history is found in the story of Isaac's blessing of Jacob. There are actually two stories that illustrate God's purpose of election for Jacob: the birthright and the blessing. There is a clear play on words between these two themes. The birthright (*bkrh*) conferred the rights of the eldest son (Gen 25:29–34), and the blessing (*brkh*) was the father's last will and testament and amounted to the inheritance (Gen 27:27–29). This pun is made explicit in Esau's complaint: "He took my birthright (*bkrh*) and now he's taken my blessing! (*brkh*)" (Gen 27:36). The first episode is somewhat short and

14. Biddle, "The 'Endangered Ancestress' and the Blessing for the Nations."

15. Sylva points to numerous other characteristics that make Isaac a man who is wrapped up in his own appetites; a little man governed by little goals with little closeness to bequeath to the next generation (Sylvia, "The Blessing of a Wounded Patriarch)," 270, 273.

rather cryptic. The possession of the birthright included a double share of the inheritance. The second episode is quite detailed. The blessing and curse really make up the central issue between Jacob and Esau. Many have cited this example to illustrate the unyielding magical power of the spoken word—that once uttered cannot be revoked. Indeed the text implies as much when Esau begs for a blessing of his own. But Isaac replies, "I have made him lord over you and have made all his relatives his servants, and I have sustained him with grain and new wine. So what can I possibly do for you, my son?" (Gen 27:37). Some suggest this is the only unqualified example of a magical blessing in the Old Testament. But a better solution is to understand Isaac's blessing from the perspective of a speech act, similar to deathbed blessings in Genesis 48–49 and Deuteronomy 33. A deathbed blessing or curse is a performative utterance. Note the highly ritualized nature of this last-will-and-testament blessing. Multiple signs of conventional ritual appear here: a summons from the father, an offering of an animal from the son, a shared meal of food and wine, a kiss from the father, and a pronouncement of blessing. The stylized ritual here is similar to Jacob's blessing of Ephraim and Manasseh in Genesis 48.[16] Isaac, suspicious but confused, utilizes the various stages of this ritual to ask probing questions regarding the identity of his deceitful son. This illocutionary speech act is irreversible, not because the magical notion of word power, but because of the performative word power uttered in accordance with specific social conventions. Note the echoes of Genesis 12 in the blessing:

> Ah, the smell of my son
> > is like the smell of a field
> > that the LORD has blessed.
> May God give you of heaven's dew
> > and of earth's richness—
> > an abundance of grain and new wine.
> May nations serve you
> > and peoples bow down to you.
> Be lord over your brothers,
> > and may the sons of your mother bow down to you.
> May those who curse you be cursed
> > and those who bless you be blessed." (Gen 27:27–29)

Almost as soon as Isaac voices the blessing, Esau enters from a successful hunt, prepares a meal, and brings it to his father. The rest of the story is painfully told, as the reader knows without even going further that Esau's

---

16. Bell, *Ritual Theory, Ritual Practice*, 16.

blessing has already been given to his fraudulent brother. There is no retrieving it. What, then, does Esau receive? A curse, with only a back-handed hint of blessing,

> Your dwelling will be
>> away from the earth's richness,
>> away from the dew of heaven above.
> You will live by the sword
>> And you will serve your brother
> But when you grow restless,
>> you will throw his yoke
>> from off your neck. (Gen 27:39–40)

This story makes modern readers incredulous. How is it that Esau could not also have had a blessing? Imagine the analogy of an Olympic athlete who won a gold medal, and it is revealed later that he cheated. His medal would be stripped and given to another competitor. But this is not the case with Jacob. The reason has less to do with the notion of word magic than it does the fact that there were different conventions operating in his ancient society. There was simply no social convention for the withdrawal of the blessing. Nevertheless, for Jacob the blessing turns out to be no picnic. Richard Briggs astutely observes that Jacob's blessing, like stolen cash, "makes it difficult to deploy as part of a life of praise and thanksgiving to God."[17]

In spite of a most unlikely beginning, the Joseph story also takes up the theme of universal blessing. But the blessing is covert and comes only after a slow, twisting, narrative plot. God never appears to Joseph personally. Never. His purpose for Joseph is revealed in Joseph's dreams, but nowhere is the blessing-promise given to Joseph directly and verbally from God. It is in this narrative context that God transforms Jacob's name to Israel. This change is highly transitional from the standpoint of the blessing and curse. Instead of God's uttering the blessing face-to-face with Joseph, it is Jacob/Israel who tells Joseph that God appeared to him. It is Jacob/Israel who blesses Pharaoh. It is Jacob/Israel who blesses Joseph and his sons. It is Jacob/Israel who blesses his own twelve sons—just as it was Jacob/Israel who blessed Esau (Gen 33:11). As promised, God's blessing will come to others through Israel.

The blessing on Joseph's sons begins with Jacob's testimonial of his own history: "God Almighty appeared to me at Luz in the land of Canaan, and there he blessed me and said to me, 'I am going to make you fruitful

17. Briggs, "Speech-Act Theory," 84.

and will increase your numbers. I will make you a community of peoples, and I will give this land as an everlasting possession to your descendants after you'" (Gen 48:3-4). The case of Ephraim and Manasseh presents an interesting and unique situation. It is interesting because this reads like an adoption of sorts. Their mother is an outsider, an Egyptian. The flaw of marrying an outsider was a source of humiliation for Isaac and Rebekah when Esau married outside the clan, but this flaw is completely overlooked in the Joseph tale. It is unique because these marginal outsiders, Joseph's sons, are brought under the blessing. Using many of the same ritualized actions, including the kiss, the placing of the right hand on the head, and the proclamation, the blessing of inheritance has clear cultural conditions,

> Then he blessed Joseph and said,
> May the God before whom my fathers
> Abraham and Isaac walked,
> the God who has been my shepherd
> all my life to this day,
> the Angel who has delivered me from all harm
> —may he bless these boys.
> May they be called by my name
> and the names of my fathers Abraham and Isaac,
> and may they increase greatly
> upon the earth." (Gen 48:15-16)

The blessing, however, goes well beyond the scope of the two sons. By metonymy, they themselves will become a blessing to the entire people, because they have been so blessed.

> He blessed them that day and said,
> In your name will Israel pronounce this blessing:
> May God make you like Ephraim and Manasseh. (Gen 48:20)

There is a second blessing that falls on the heels of the blessing in Genesis 48. Genesis 49, probably written soon after the events portrayed in the poetry, draws upon images of a lion, a donkey, a snake, a deer, a fruit tree, and a wolf to depict the victory of the tribes over their enemies. The enemies of these twelve tribes are never named. While Simeon and Levi are marginalized by a curse of sorts, the other tribes are given unqualified blessings.

Theologically, God is behind the blessings of the ancestral family. Because that family is blessed, outsiders around them are not just potentially blessed but actually blessed as well. Joseph declares to his brothers: "So then, it was not you who sent me here, but God. He made me father to

Pharaoh, lord of his entire household and ruler of all Egypt" (Gen 45:8–9). Joseph's dreams show that Yahweh is determined to bless the people of Israel no matter what. Despite Israel's attempts to destroy the one through whom the blessing will come, that individual still brings reconciliation and healing, not only for the peoples but also for Israel itself.

Outside the ancestral history, Gen 12:1–3 may have helped shape Isaiah's vision for the future. Isaiah 2:2–4 dreams of a day when the peoples of the earth will stream to the mountain of Yahweh,

> In the last days
> the mountain of the LORD's temple will be established
>   as chief among the mountains;
> it will be raised above the hills,
> and all nations will stream to it.
>
> Many peoples will come and say,
> "Come, let us go up to the mountain of the LORD,
>   to the house of the God of Jacob.
> He will teach us his ways,
>   so that we may walk in his paths."
> The law will go out from Zion,
>   the word of the Lord from Jerusalem.
> He will judge between the nations
>   and will settle disputes for many peoples.
> They will beat their swords into plowshares
>   and their spears into pruning hooks.
> Nation will not take up sword against nation,
>   nor will they train for war anymore. (Isa 2:2–4)

A similar use of this theme permeates the entire book of Isaiah (Isa 12:4–5; 19:24–25; 42:10–13; 45:22–25; 66:19–23). In Isa 49:6 the Servant will be a light for the foreign peoples (cf. Jer 4:2):

> It is too small a thing for you to be my servant
>   to restore the tribes of Jacob
>   and bring back those of Israel I have kept.
> I will also make you a light for the Gentiles,
>   that you may bring my salvation to the ends of the earth.

Psalm 67 also reshapes Abraham's (and Aaron's) blessing upon the people and gives it a universal focus. The intent of God's blessing is that God's people will experience the presence of God and all the ends of the earth will honor and fear him:

> May God be gracious to us and bless us
> > and make his face shine upon us,   *Selah*
> > so that your way may be known on earth,
> > your salvation among all nations.
>
> May the peoples praise you, God;
> > may all the peoples praise you!
> May the nations be glad and sing for joy,
> > for you rule the peoples with equity
> > and guide the nations of the earth. *Selah*
> May the peoples praise you, God;
> > may all the peoples praise you.
>
> The land yields its harvest;
> > God, our God, blesses us.
> God bless us still,
> > so that all the ends of the earth will fear him. (Ps 67:1–7)

ABRAHAM, FOREIGN PEOPLES, AND THE THEOLOGY OF MARGINALIZATION

Several markers in the book of Genesis delineate the cultural and religious boundaries between Israel and its neighbors. Genealogies, ethnic stereotypes, and the ritual practice of circumcision are three prominent ways of defining cultural identities in the Genesis accounts. The genealogies, for example, mark the boundaries of those inside and outside the community of Abraham's family. The *toledoth* formula (translated "this is the generation/account of") occurs ten times, and demarcates the genealogical self-definition of Israel. In modern Hebrew, the word *toledoth* simply means "history," but in the book of Genesis these genealogies have a social function. Furthermore, these genealogies form the literary backbone to the structure of the entire book, with the formula providing a break between most of the major narrative units. These genealogies place the Genesis narratives in the context establishing a cultural and religious identity for Israel.

Israel cherished a shared belief in a common story. In this story, Israel's neighbors are often portrayed with some kind of stereotypically negative trait. More than meets the eye, individuals in Genesis usually loom large as more than mere individuals. They often represent foreign groups, whereby the traditional shortcomings of these outsiders are woven into individual characterizations of the Genesis narratives. If a biblical story discredited the ancestor of one of these outsiders, it consequently discredited the entire people that descended from that ancestor. In the primeval history, for example, the narrator denigrates the Kenites, Canaanites, and Babylonians through the stories of Cain (Gen 4:1–24), Ham and Canaan (Gen 9:18–25), and Babel (Gen 11:1–9) respectively. Because Cain murdered his brother, he was estranged from his country and condemned to be a wanderer, east of Eden. Cain was the eponymous ancestor of the Kenites, a marginal group of metalworkers mentioned in several biblical texts. God promises Abraham that he will one day possess their land (Gen 15:19). Noah curses Canaan, the eponymous ancestor of the Canaanites, because of the actions, or inactions, of his father, Ham. Discrediting the Canaanites' ancestors had the sociological function of marginalizing Israel's most immediate nemesis, implying Canaanite subjugation to Israel. In these texts the theological swerves toward the political.[18] The play on words in the story of Babel is clearly intended to belittle the cultural religious traditions of Babylon, including their tendency to erect gigantic monumental shrines of worship.

In the ancestral narratives, Abraham, Isaac, and Jacob are often contrasted with wild and unsavory characters whose descendants would eventually become the next-door neighbors of Israel. In the case of Abraham, his nephew Lot is portrayed almost entirely in a negative light. Early in the narrative, his herdsmen quarrel with the servants of Abraham over territory and water. Abraham magnanimously gives Lot the choice of the any portion of the land. Lot selfishly, not to mention foolishly, chooses the fertile Jordan River valley, completely unaware that his own life will be threatened as a result. In what is often depicted as an example of Near Eastern hospitality, Lot callously offers his own virgin daughters to the men of Sodom, who come to his house seeking sex with his guests. In the narrative context, however, this act does not function as an act of hospitality at all, but it functions quite differently; it makes Lot look absolutely pathetic. He is plucked from death by Abraham prior to the destruction of Sodom and Gomorrah, kicking and screaming, wheedling out one last concession after another. His wife dies in the evacuation. Ultimately, after the destruction of Sodom, his own daughters have sex with him to carry on the family line. Two baby boys, Moab and Edom, are the result of this perverse incestuous relationship. This is clearly not the most edifying of

18. Clines, "Biblical Interpretation in an International Perspective," contends that ideology expresses the self-interest of one group at the expense of the other.

origin stories for these two close neighbors of Israel (Gen 19:30–38). Other stories later in the Pentateuch offer further evidence of the unworthiness of these neighbors, but the etiology of their origins condemns them from the outset.[19]

Next, Ishmael and Isaac are portrayed in ways that minimize the importance of Ishmael. The older ends up subservient to the younger. Ishmael is the firstborn but stands condemned from the start; he is the son of an Egyptian slave woman, and a wild donkey of a man (Gen 16:12). The curse-blessing concludes that he will always be at odds with all his relatives. His hand will be against everyone and everyone's hand will be against him. Yet, later in the narrative, he receives a rather insidious blessing of his own. He will become a great people (Gen 17:20). It is interesting to see how later literature in Judaism, Christianity, and Islam has interpreted the Ishmael and Isaac narratives. For Judaism, Isaac is the child of the promise, not Ishmael. For Christianity, Isaac is the son of the promise, who, deserving nothing by his own merit, still receives the blessing from God. Christians, consequently, are like Isaac, who do not trust in their own merits but rely on the gracious forgiveness of God through the sacrificial death of the Messiah, Jesus. In Islam, Ishmael is given the honor due to the firstborn. It is Ishmael, not Isaac, whom Abraham offers to God as a sacrifice. And it is Ishmael and Abraham together who build the *Kaaba* in Mecca. Many of the names in the genealogy of Ishmael are Arab names, giving credence to the Arab tradition that Ishmael is their ancestor (Gen 25:12–18).

Finally, Jacob and Esau are portrayed as being at odds with one another, even in the womb. Before either is born, the narrative makes clear that the older will serve the younger (Gen 25:23). Esau is born first, with Jacob grasping at his heel. Esau, or Edom, another neighbor of Israel, to the east, is so wild and impetuous that he trades his birthright for a bowl of red stew (Gen 25:27–35). There is much more happening in this story than merely a lapse in Esau's judgment. He marries outside his own people, one of the daughters of the Hittites, causing grief to his mother and father (Gen 26:34–35). Jacob filches the blessing out from under the nose of the unsuspecting Esau and must flee for his life as a consequence. Yet, later in the narrative these two estranged brothers are reconciled, albeit with Jacob's superiority to Esau clearly intact. Esau receives a blessing of his own, but that blessing is not from the mouth of God. It is a second-tier blessing from the lips of Jacob:

19. Heyler, "The Separation of Abraham and Lot."

Jacob said, "No, please, if I have found favor in your sight, then accept my present from my hand. For I have seen your face, which is like seeing the face of God, and you have accepted me. Please accept my blessing that is brought to you, because God has dealt graciously with me, and because I have enough." And he urged him, and he took it. (Gen 33:11, ESV)

Circumcision is a third marker of cultural identification in the narratives of Genesis. Many modern readers are surprised to learn that nearly all Israel's neighbors practiced circumcision. Egypt, Edom, Ammon, and Moab all circumcised males, perhaps for hundreds, if not thousands of years prior to Israelite practice. Among the neighbors in the immediate vicinity of Israel, the Philistines were the exception. The Philistines migrated from the Aegean around the same time that Israel entered Canaan and settled along the Mediterranean coast.[20] The derogative marker "uncircumcised" often precedes a mention of the Philistines in the Old Testament (Judg 15:18; 1 Sam 14:6; 31:4). Circumcision, the physical marker of the covenant in Genesis 17, was intended to signify the consecration of one's offspring and all he possessed in obedience and service to Yahweh. The Philistines are unequivocally condemned for not practicing circumcision. Consequently, circumcision was not only the sign of the covenant but a vehicle of marginalization.

Genesis presents some major exceptions to the disparagement of foreigners, yet even the foreigners mentioned there are marginalized in some respects. The most notable are in the Joseph narrative. The Egyptian Tamar entices her father-in-law, Judah, to sleep with her, and successfully preserves the ancestral line from which David the king would later emerge. Joseph marries an Egyptian woman without the slightest condemnation in the biblical narrative. This glaring example of exogamy in the ancestral narratives would disconcert postexilic Israelites. This exception to usual marriage customs led to later traditions in the Second Temple period that attempted to justify how a righteous Israelite like Joseph could have married outside his own people. The second-century-BCE story *Joseph and Asenath* goes to great lengths to depict Asenath's repentance and conversion to Judaism prior to their wedding. A third positive example of a foreigner in Genesis (mentioned above) is Melchizedek. An extremely popular figure in later Second Temple Jewish literature and in Christian literature, Melchizedek is not mentioned again in Genesis after chapter 14. A final example is Abimelech, who keeps Isaac and his herdsmen at

20. Dothan and Dothan, *People of the Sea*, 13–28, 257–59.

arm's length, yet goes out of his way to make sure that Isaac and his wife, Rebekah, are protected from any violations committed by his own people.

The examples above illustrate a rather uneasy truce between Israel and many of its neighbors. A fine line runs between cooperation and separation. Being a blessing to the foreign peoples and receiving blessing from foreign peoples does not mean outright identification and assimilation with the surrounding peoples. The relations of God's chosen with Lot, Abimelech, and Esau illustrate some of this tension. At the end of the Joseph story, Jacob and his extended family arrive in Egypt, yet tellingly they do not live among the Egyptians. Even though Joseph has charge over all Egypt, his family's occupation as herdsmen is "loathsome" to the Egyptians. So they live in Goshen, still under Pharaoh's protection but away from the Egyptian leader who had been blessed by Israel. This sense of autonomy in the midst of cooperation underscores the strained attempt at being a blessing to all the peoples of the earth.

ABRAHAM'S BLESSING IN REVERSE: BLESSING COMES TO ISRAEL THROUGH A GENTILE

The story of Ruth is one of the most tightly and beautifully crafted stories in the Bible. While the genealogical connection that concludes this short story highlight's Ruth's prominence and David's lineage, the book of Ruth is as much or more about Naomi than it is about Ruth. The tale is a wonderful composition in which blessing comes full circle despite a life of tragic hardship. In it are six blessings (Ruth 1:8–9; 2:12, 19–20; 3:10; 4:11–12, 14–15). Some of these blessings are freely composed (1:8–9; 2:12, 19–20; 4:11–12) and others adopt the popular *brk* formula (3:10; 4:14–15). Note the circular nature of God's blessing in this narrative: Naomi blesses Ruth (1:8–9), Ruth blesses Boaz (2:12), Naomi blesses Ruth (2:19–20), Boaz blesses Ruth (3:10), all the people and the elders bless Ruth (4:11–12), and the women of Bethlehem bless Naomi (4:14–15). Naomi is thus both blesser and blessed. But in the end, she is a qualitatively different sort of Naomi, barely recognized by her friends. Her experience with the hardships of life has even given her a new name, Mara. The tone at the end of the tale is not of triumphal blessing but of one who has been blessed but has also gone through the agonies of life.[21] Such blessings are similar to the blessing of other foreigners in the Old Testament like Melchizedek, Jethro, Balaam, and the queen of Sheba. Consequently the story of Ruth

21. Moore, "Ruth the Moabite and the Blessing of Foreigners," 212.

demonstrates Abraham's blessing in reverse: God blesses Israel through a Gentile.

COVENANT THEOLOGY AND COVENANT SIGNS

Ever since Walther Eichrodt's magisterial volumes on Old Testament theology, the concept of covenant has been at the forefront of theological discussions. The history of scholarly research on the topic of covenant is extensive.[22] Eichrodt understood the root *bryt* in a broad sense as the relationship between God and his people, God and the world, God and humans.[23] A covenant is essentially a fictive kinship. It depicts a relationship that would not otherwise normally exist. Adoption would be a good parallel today. The primeval and patriarchal stories of the Old Testament tell of three covenants, each having their own individual covenant sign. Note the threefold pattern to each of these covenants: first, the creation covenant, which includes a blessing, a charge to be fruitful and multiply, and an accompanying sign of Sabbath rest; second, the Noahide covenant, which also includes a blessing, a charge, and the accompanying sign of the rainbow; and finally, the Abrahamic covenant, with its own blessing, charge, and accompanying sign of circumcision. These covenants do not supersede each other but do maintain historical and theological trajectories through the rest of the Old Testament, and even into the New Testament as well. Each of these covenants is rooted in the sovereign choice and grace of God. Yet they also contain a charge entailing human responsibility. Last, in one sense, each of these covenants leads to a fourth covenant—the Mosaic covenant, which would eventually be established at Mount Sinai.

The grace of God is first made evident in the creation covenant. This covenant is firmly rooted in God's blessing. God twice declares to the human couple, "*I have given* all kinds of grain and fruit for you to eat . . . and *I have given* grass and leafy plants for food" (cf. Gen 1:29). The consequence of this gift to the crown of creation was that everything was "very good." Humans have the God-given responsibility over creation to have dominion and to subdue the earth. The charge to have dominion is no less a covenant of grace—but of the kind of divine grace that ultimately leads to human responsibility. Thus, the first creation account ends with God's completing all work in six days and resting on the Sabbath. This first covenant sign,

22. Hillers, *Covenant*; McCarthy, *Treaty and Covenant*; Mendenhall, *The Tenth Generation*; Nicholson, *God and His People*.

23. Eichrodt, *Theology of the Old Testament*.

Sabbath, is tantamount to all other covenants. Creation theology fore-shadows Mosaic covenantal theology. What was anticipated in creation and demonstrated by the deity himself is ultimately fulfilled in the Mosaic covenant. Note the rationale given by Moses for this lasting covenant at Sinai (cf. Lev 24:8): "The Israelites are to observe the Sabbath, celebrating it for the generations to come as a lasting covenant (*bĕrît 'ôlām*). It will be a sign between me and the Israelites forever, for in six days the LORD made the heavens and the earth, and on the seventh day he abstained from work and rested" (Exod 31:16–17). In spite of the uncreation motif in the flood, the blessing is reaffirmed to Noah. The two commissions below illustrate the parallel between creation blessing and Noah's blessing:

> As for you, be fruitful and increase in number; multiply on the earth and increase upon it. (Gen 9:7)

> God blessed them and said to them, "Be fruitful and increase in number; fill the earth and subdue it. Rule over the fish of the sea and the birds of the air and over every living creature that moves on the ground." (Gen 1:28)

The second covenantal sign, the Noahide covenant, is the rainbow, which God hangs in the sky as a sign of peaceful coexistence with the human community and as a promise that the world will never again be destroyed by water. The bow, which ordinarily served as a symbol of war-fare (Ps 7:12–13; Hab 3:9–11) is hung in the sky, a perpetual promise that it will not be used again. The Noahide covenant stresses the universality of God's grace. Additionally it emphasizes reverence for animal life (Gen 9:4–5) and the dignity of the human community (9:5–6). The blood—the symbol of life—is to be hallowed. Hallowing the blood honors the visible life-form from which the blood has come, as well as God, the giver of life. Like the covenant at creation, this Noahide covenant is with all people, not exclusively with descendants of Israel. This covenant is a (*bĕrît 'ôlām*), an everlasting covenant,

> And when the LORD smelled the pleasing aroma, the LORD said in his heart, "I will never again curse (*lĕqallēl*) the ground be-cause of man, for the intention of man's heart is evil from his youth. Neither will I ever again strike down every living creature as I have done. While the earth remains, seedtime and harvest, cold and heat, summer and winter, day and night, shall not cease." (Gen 8:21–22, ESV)

The third covenant, between God and Abraham and recounted (twice in quite different ways) in Genesis 15 and 17, builds on God's promise to Abraham in Genesis 12. Early source critics suggested that these two covenants came from different authors with entirely diverse theological perspectives from different periods in the history of Israel. Yet in the Bible they were both left intact, in spite of some of the difficulties in harmonizing these very dissimilar texts. Again, these two covenants are marked by grace. The command of God—"walk before me"—does not need to obeyed in order for the covenant to be in force but is an expression of the need to conform to God's character. Genesis 15 contains a most unusual ceremony of covenant ratification. Source critics have traditionally ascribed most of this chapter to the Yahwist. The narrative begins as Abraham rightfully expresses doubts about the viability of the promise: specifically that he would have many descendants. This is actually the first dialogue between Abram and God in the Bible. God reveals himself in standard covenantal form: "I am Yahweh, who brought you out of Ur of the Chaldeans" (see also Exod 20:2 and Deut 5:6). Abraham argues that he has no heir, so according to custom, the heir must come through his servant, Eliezer of Damascus. The Lord corrects Abram's logical but fallacious assumption. Eliezer will not be the heir. God says, "Look toward heaven and number the stars, if you are able to number them . . . so shall your offspring be" (Gen 15:5, ESV) Abram's response is in a sense rather surprising; it is one of simple faith: "And he believed the Lord, and he counted it to him as righteousness" (ESV). In the Bible, righteousness means both right relationship and right conduct. Abram's response is genuinely surprising because there is really nothing in his present situation that provides a reason to believe.

The rest of chapter 15 describes a covenant ceremony modeled after many in the ancient Near East.[24] Jeremiah 34:18–20 provides a biblical analogy to the rite. A sacrifice would be made and the two parties participating in the covenant would pass between two split portions of the sacrifice, enacting that horrible fate which would befall anyone who would violate the covenant. This ritual act of both word and deed was essentially a self-curse, invoking death on the participant who violated the covenant.

> And the men who transgressed my covenant and did not keep
> the terms of the covenant that they made before me, I will make
> them like the calf that they cut in two and passed between its

---

24. Several have observed parallels to royal land grants: Weinfeld, "The Covenant of Grant in the Old Testament"; Niehaus, *God at Sinai*, 175; Wenham, "The Symbolism of the Animal Rite."

> parts—the officials of Judah, the officials of Jerusalem, the eunuchs, the priests, and all the people of the land who passed between the parts of the calf. And I will give them into the hand of their enemies and into the hand of those who seek their lives. Their dead bodies shall be food for the birds of the air and the beasts of the earth. (Jer 34:18–20, ESV)

Yet in this case, Abraham does not participate, but Yahweh alone ratifies the covenant in the theophany of a smoking firepot and torch that passes between the pieces. Thus, the covenant is unilateral and unconditional. All Abraham has to do is believe. Yahweh promises, "to your descendants I give this land, from the river of Egypt to the great river, the river Euphrates, the land of the Kenites, the Kenizzites, the Kadmonites, the Hittites, the Perizzites, the Rephaim, the Amorites, the Canaanites, the Girgashites, and the Jebusites" (Gen 15:19–20, ESV). This unconditional promise of a land with very specific boundaries includes this list of ten peoples as God's gift to Abraham. The purpose of the dream sequence and the thick imagery of the dreadful darkness demonstrates that this promise of land will be a long time in coming. Abraham will not see it in his lifetime. But it will happen. What are we to make of this oath of self-imprecation that God utters? With the imagery of smoke and fire passing between the two parts of the animal, the oath resurrects images of Near Eastern covenant curses.[25] How far is God willing to go to bring this promise to completion? The oath of self-imprecation offers divine vulnerability. This oath foreshadows suffering and death on behalf of the promise.

Genesis 17, ascribed by source critics to the Priestly source, begins with the blessing language of the creation account and the blessing-promise of Genesis 12:

> Then Abram fell on his face. And God said to him, "Behold, my covenant is with you, and you shall be the father of a multitude of nations. No longer shall your name be called Abram, but your name shall be Abraham, for I have made you the father of a multitude of nations. I will make you exceedingly fruitful, and I will make you into nations, and kings shall come from you. And I will establish my covenant between me and you and your offspring after you throughout their generations for an everlasting covenant, to be God to you and to your offspring after you. And I will give to you and to your offspring after you the land of your sojournings, all the land of Canaan, for an everlasting possession, and I will be their God." (Gen 17:3–8, ESV)

25. Wenham, "The Symbolism of the Animal Rite."

God revises the elements of the earlier tradition in Genesis 15 and adds the third covenantal sign, the sign of circumcision, as the required expression of the covenant. The story of the birth of Ishmael in Genesis 16 separates these two covenants. Sixteen years pass between Ishmael's birth and this covenant. This covenant differs from the one in Genesis 15 in that it focuses less on land and more on Abram's becoming a father to a multitude of peoples. It also differs from the previous covenant in its focus on the sign of circumcision. Every male eight days old and older was to be circumcised. including Abram's family and all the servants of Abram's household. Those who refused the sign of circumcision were to be cut off from the people of God (Gen 17:14). This is significant, as the covenant sign of circumcision is extended beyond Abram's own family to slaves and foreigners living with him. Having symbolically broadened the understanding of family, and as a reflection of the significance and breadth of this new covenant, God changes Abram's name to Abraham, meaning "father of peoples." In this way the narrator makes explicit the link between circumcision and the broadening of the promise to other peoples.[26] Circumcision opens the door to outsiders. Since Abraham is already a father, the promise narrows to his wife Sarai. Sarai is blessed twice and destined to be a mother of peoples, so her name is changed to Sarah. It is through her, not Hagar, that the promise will prevail. All this happens prior to the birth of Isaac. This covenant is referred to as an "everlasting" covenant (*běrît 'ôlām*) three times in this account (Gen 17:7, 13, 19).[27] It is common for Westerners to think of eternity as longitudinal time. But *'ôlām* is best translated "perpetual" rather than "eternal," and denotes a qualitative as well as a quantitative sense. Texts like Isa 24:5 make it clear that an eternal covenant can indeed be broken, resulting in a curse:

> The earth is defiled by its people;
>> they have disobeyed the laws,
>> violated the statutes
>> and broken the everlasting covenant.
> Therefore a curse consumes the earth;
>> its people must bear their guilt.
> Therefore earth's inhabitants are burned up,
>> and very few are left. (Isa 24:5–6)

26. Alexander, "Royal Expectations in Genesis to Kings."

27. See also Gen 9:16; 17:7, 13, 19; 2 Sam 23:5; 1 Chr 16:17; Ps 105:10; Isa 24:5; 55:3; 61:8; Jer 32:40; 50:5; Ezek 16:60; 37:26.

In one last attempt at equivocation, Abraham cites the procreative impossibility of his old age and suggests that perhaps his firstborn son, Ishmael, the son of Hagar, would be the one to carry on this great promise. God's response is that indeed there is a blessing and promise for Ishmael as well, but the narrative is clear that Sarah will have a son of her own. The blessing to Ishmael also adopts creation-blessing language, "As for Ishmael, I have heard you; behold, I will bless him and make him fruitful and multiply him exceedingly; he shall be the father of twelve princes, and I will make him a great people. But I will establish my covenant with Isaac, whom Sarah shall bear to you at this season next year" (Gen 17:20–21, RSV). Abraham is less than convinced but immediately circumcises Ishmael and his entire household in obedience to the command of the covenant.

There are clear limitations to the covenant sign of circumcision. While circumcision opens the door to the outsider, it closes the door to women; women are included in the covenant only by virtue of living in a household where males are circumcised. This physical sign has other limitations. Physical circumcision alone can never substitute for a changed heart of faith and faithfulness. Talk of an uncircumcised heart is present in both Law and Prophets (Lev 26:41–42; Deut 10:16; 30:6; Jer 4:4; 9:25; Ezek 44:7–9).[28] Physical circumcision alone is an empty sign without this spiritual dimension of a changed life. The New Testament also adopts spiritual circumcision as a living sign of the people of God (Phil 3:3; Col 2:11–13).

In some ways the covenants of Noah and Abraham foreshadow the Mosaic covenant, particularly in the story of the people's reception of the Book of the Covenant (within our book of Exodus). For example, the Noahide covenant warns against the shedding of blood because the blood signifies the source of life, both for animals (Gen 9:4) and for humans (Gen 4:10). Even prior to that, blood is requisite in Abel's sacrifice, and Cain's crime of shedding innocent blood elicits a cry to Yahweh from the ground. In Genesis 15 and 17 the separation of the animal carcasses between which Yahweh passed and the sign of circumcision both required blood: in the first case from the victims of the sacrifice, and in the second from the males who were circumcised. In the book of Exodus, after what is commonly called the Book of the Covenant (Exod 20:22—23:19), Moses reads that code to the people, which he calls the Book of the Covenant. The people affirm that they will be obedient by proclaiming that they will

28. W. Lemke argues that circumcision of the heart is a biblical metaphor for spiritual renewal: "Circumcision of the Heart."

do everything that is required in the covenant. Moses then takes a portion of the blood from the sacrifice and scatters it over the people as a sign of that covenant relationship. Note Exodus 24:

> When Moses went and told the people all the LORD's words and laws, they responded with one voice, "Everything the Lord has said we will do." Moses then wrote down everything the LORD had said.
>
> He got up early the next morning and built an altar at the foot of the mountain and set up twelve stone pillars representing the twelve tribes of Israel. Then he sent young Israelite men, and they offered burnt offerings and sacrificed young bulls as fellowship offerings to the LORD. Moses took half of the blood and put it in the bowls, and the other half he sprinkled on the altar. Then he took the Book of the Covenant and read it to the people. They responded, "We will do everything the LORD has said; we will obey.
>
> Moses then took the blood, sprinkled it on the people and said, "This is the blood of the covenant that the LORD has made with you in accordance with all these words." (Exod 24:3–8)

The special symbolism of blood continues in the Torah legal codes. No one was to eat meat that still had the blood in it (Lev 17:10–12; Deut 12:23–24). The altars were prepared and made ritually ready by the sprinkling of blood (Lev 1:5–9; 4:3–7; 6:24–30; 8:15), and the priests anointed themselves with blood so they would be fit to serve in the presence of Yahweh (Exod 29:19–21; Lev 8:22–30). Even in the account of the exodus from Egypt, the people of Israel were to spread blood on their doorposts to protect themselves as the angel of death passed by.

These four covenants have many parallels to the Davidic covenant, to be discussed later. The theology of election is also classically stated in exodus story. God's covenant with his people in the desert and God's promise of an eternal covenant with David raise the question about the relationship between peoplehood and international blessing. In Paul's Letter to the Ephesians, in the New Testament, he takes on this theme of covenant and election in the early chapters of the book. Ephesians 1:3–14, a single sentence in the Greek, is an exquisitely elaborate blessing describing all the benefits that come to the believer through faith in the Messiah: "Blessed be the God and Father of our Lord Jesus Christ, who has blessed us in Christ with every spiritual blessing in the heavenly places . . ." (Eph 1:3–4, ESV). The blessings of predestination, adoption, redemption, forgiveness, grace, inheritance, and salvation, are part of Paul's long list of covenantal benefits. Ephesians 2:1–10 follows by describing how a person individually moves from death to life by the grace of God. Finally, Eph 2:12ff essentially encompasses a redefinition of election around the Messiah. The Gentiles, or the "uncircumcision," who were alienated from the commonwealth of Israel and strangers to the covenant of promise, have been brought near to God by the blood of the Messiah, Jesus. The Messiah has effectively completed that for which Israel was chosen in the first place. The Messiah's death provides the atonement through which all peoples, not just Israel, are redeemed. Consequently, the dividing wall of hostility between Jew and Gentile has been broken down, and all have been reconciled to God through the cross, thereby erasing hostility. Using mixed metaphors, Paul broadens the idea of the elect, and Christ becomes a cornerstone of a completely new household, a new people of God, a living holy temple to the Lord.

Blessing, Curse, and Election

The notion of election is central to the Old Testament's message. The blessings and curses of the ancestral narratives raise the stakes for the importance of the doctrine of election. Readers encounter the doctrine of election in the ancestral narratives before the Bible ever unambiguously defines it. The primeval history and ancestral narratives never use the root "to choose" (*bḥr*), nor do they present an explicitly theological rationale for election as the books of Deuteronomy and Isaiah do (Deut 7:6–11; Isa 41:8–9; 42:1; 44:1–2; 45:4). A handful of character pairings illustrate the theology of election in Genesis. Cain and Abel, Ishmael and Isaac, Hagar and Sarah, Jacob and Esau, Joseph and his brothers: within these pairs, one member is always pitted against the other. But these competitions are not between equals. Joel Kaminsky states, "favoritism, though highly unpalatable to most people living in a modern democratic world, is at the very center of the Bible's theology and points toward a profound intuition about God's relationship to the human community."[29] Often these stories raise the ire of modern readers, who shy away from anything that smacks of particularism. Postmodernism has even less of a taste for such notions of God's choosing one over another. But the modern world's acquired blindness toward particularism does serious injustice to material in Old Testament. Take a few examples from the book of Genesis. God's mysterious favoritism of Abel is never really explained in the biblical narrative.

29. Kaminsky, *Yet I Loved Jacob*, 17

Mountains of commentaries and articles try to explain why God would be inclined to accept Abel's offering while decisively rejecting Cain's. The observations that Abel's offering is accepted because it is a blood sacrifice or because he offers his firstfruits are only educated guesses attempting to come to grips with a text that is maddeningly inexplicit. God simply accepts one brother's offering over the other's. Even murdering the elect fails to gain Cain the elect's favored status. This theme of divine preference is repeated among the other pairings in the ancestral narratives. Another good example is Ishmael. Ishmael's status of election is strikingly ambiguous. He is blessed, but only in a *second-tier,* derivative sense. Isaac, on the other hand, is clearly the child of the promise, even though he is Abraham's younger son. In Abraham's case, his own bold departure from Haran releases the blessing. One could argue that the pioneering accomplishments of a man like Abraham were due to his daring obedience. But Isaac seemingly does nothing remarkable to bring his own election to fulfillment; he is simply the child of promise, a fact that the Apostle Paul gives much theological weight in the New Testament. This begs the question, does election once initiated by God require human action to bring it to fulfillment? Jacob is an even more startling example. Jacob's status as the blessed son over Esau is morally complicated, to say the least, as his own treachery actually brings God's purposes in election to pass. The storyteller magnificently weaves together the two doctrines of providence and election in the Joseph story. As Joseph looks back on the ups and downs of his life, he knows that God's providence has brought him to his place of standing as Pharaoh's prime minister. He also knows that everything that his brothers had intended for his harm eventually worked out for his benefit. But the *why* of that providence has no definitive logical explanation. God has chosen a particular family to be a blessing to the peoples of the earth. While many of the characters in Genesis take on an ethnic quality, and the blessings and curses carry over to later generations, election is not merely an issue of ethnic superiority. While the non-elect are typically non-Israelites, a nonchosen sibling is not necessarily excluded from divine favor. Ishmael and Esau are prime examples. Their lives are often also part of God's story for humankind, but not as the elect. Also, possessing the blessing of election does not mean a life without strife and turmoil. Common in these ancestral stories is a recurring theme of the elect child being put in grave peril.[30] On one hand, human fate and destiny are divinely determined by a sovereign, omnipotent God. Yet, God's foreknowledge

---

30. Hauge, "The Struggles of the Blessed in Estrangement I," 1–30.

does not preclude human freedom. The dichotomy of blessings and curses illuminate the power of self-determination and the ability to choose between conflicting courses of action.

What is the purpose of election in these narratives? Is election instrumental or intrinsic? Horst Dietrich Preuss's two-volume *Old Testament Theology* takes up the theme of election as the "center" for his theology: "Yahweh's historical activity of electing Israel for communion with this world."[31] Preuss candidly admits that the Old Testament is remarkably reserved as to the motives for election.[32] The Bible never says why God calls Abraham. The book of Deuteronomy is more explicit regarding the ground for the election of Israel, as it is God's love for this "fewest of all peoples" (Deut 7:7). But that is no reason. Even though election is introduced in the primeval and ancestral narratives, it is the exodus event that is the leading vehicle of election. In the exodus, Yahweh fights for his people and snatches them right out from under the noses of the Egyptians. A host of Old Testament texts portray the exodus as the foundational election event of the Bible (Num 23:21–22; 1 Kgs 12:28; Isa 10:26; Jer 2:6; Ezek 20:5; Hos 2:17; 11:1, 12:10, 13:4; Amos 9:7). The hopeful themes of a new exodus in Isaiah resurrect the dormant notion that God's choice of Israel, which began with the exodus, still had implications after the exile (Isa 40:3–5; 41:17–20; 43:16–21; 48:20–22; 49:7–13; 51:9–11; 52:10). It is this election blessing in the book of Exodus to which we now turn.

31. Preuss, *Old Testament Theology*, 1:25, 38.
32. Ibid., 38.

6

"Bless Me Also"

Divine Presence and Divine Glory in Exodus

The Exodus Story and Divine Blessing

THE BOOK OF EXODUS opens with the poignant memory of the blessing uttered by God in the Genesis 1 creation account: "But the people of Israel were fruitful and increased greatly; they multiplied and grew exceedingly strong, so that the land was filled with them" (Exod 1:7, ESV).[1] The opening verses of Exodus recollect two common refrains of the primeval blessing: "be fruitful and increase" (Gen 1:22, 28; 9:1; 17:6, 20; 26:22; 28:3; 35:11; 41:52; 47:27) and "multiply your offspring" (Gen 1:22, 6:1, 8:17, 9:1,7; 16:10, 17:20, 26:4, 24; 28:3; 35:11; 48:4). The Genesis blessing is uttered to all humanity at creation and is more narrowly articulated in the ancestral narratives to Abraham's family. Rather than moving from particularism toward universalism, these texts move toward universalism through an ever-deepening particularism. For example, the multiplication of Abraham's descendants harkens back to Genesis 22.

> I will surely bless you, and I will surely multiply your offspring
> as the stars of heaven and as the sand that is on the seashore.
> And your offspring shall possess the gate of his enemies, and

---

1. On the exodus theme throughout the Bible see Clifford, "The Exodus in the Christian Bible."

in your offspring shall all the nations of the earth be blessed,
because you have obeyed my voice." (Gen 22:17–18, ESV)

Genesis 15:13 mentions the oppression and exodus revealed to Abram in
advance.

> Then the LORD said to Abram, "Know for certain that your off-
> spring will be sojourners in a land that is not theirs and will
> be servants there, and they will be afflicted for four hundred
> years. But I will bring judgment on the nation that they serve,
> and afterward they shall come out with great possessions. (Gen
> 15:13–15, ESV)

In the exodus story, Pharaoh recognizes the threat of the multiplication of the people of Israel: "Come let us deal shrewdly with them, lest they
multiply, and, if war breaks out, they join our enemies and fight against
us and escape from the land" (Exod 1:10, ESV). Pharaoh takes drastic
measures to eliminate this danger of multiplication. He decides to murder
all newborn male Hebrew children. Yet in spite of this oppression, the Israelites increase even more, and the book of Exodus reminds readers that
what Pharaoh fears most ultimately comes to pass. Some four hundred
years after Joseph, a key tenet of God's promise to Abraham, Isaac, and
Jacob has already been fulfilled: exponentially. Israel is now a numerous
people—so numerous, in fact, that they constitute a looming threat to the
Egyptians' security.

The theme of blessing and curse is not prominent in the book of Exodus as it is in Genesis; yet where it does appear in several key texts, it appears at crucial seams in the narrative that are important to the theological
interpretation of the book. This blessing theme appears at the following
major transitions in the narrative: at the beginning of the exodus story
(Exod 1:10), at the end of the plagues (Exod 12:31–32), at the beginning
and end of the Book of the Covenant (Exod 20:22–25; 23:23–27), and
at the completion of the tabernacle at the end of the book (Exod 39:43).
Additionally, the threat of curse from within the community of God is
made explicit in the story of the golden calf. The book of Exodus also
demonstrates how peoples who curse Abraham's descendants are in fact
themselves cursed.

In spite of the predicament in which Israel finds itself, the blessing alluded to in the opening chapter of Exodus remerges in the narrative of the
plagues at a key juncture. Pharaoh has repeatedly denied Moses's requests
to allow Israel to go to the wilderness to sacrifice to Yahweh, and has lived
to regret it. Plague after plague brings devastation and desolation to Egypt

but still does not alter Pharaoh's defiant opposition to Moses. Yet there are signs that Pharaoh begins to soften—or break—as the plagues continue. At several junctures he asks Moses to pray for him (Exod 8:28; 9:28; 10:17). Finally, after the last plague—the death of the firstborn—Pharaoh urgently summons Moses and Aaron and gives them permission to leave, yet with an extraordinary request, "Up, go out from among my people, both you and the people of Israel; and go, serve the LORD, as you have said. Take your flocks and your herds, as you have said, and be gone, and bless (*wbrktm*) me also!" (Exod 12:31–32, ESV). Pharaoh begs Moses to bless him? This odd and compelling request reveals what readers already suspect: those who curse the people of God will be cursed, and those who bless this emergent people will be blessed. This last-ditch attempt at blessing reveals that Pharaoh has now seen the light. He now knows by personal experience that Yahweh is the Lord—not as a statement of faith by any means, but by experiencing God's opposition to a life of fullness. The antithesis of Pharaoh's (a Gentile's) request for blessing is represented in Jethro's blessing of Yahweh:

> Jethro said, "Blessed (*bārûk*) be the LORD, who has delivered you out of the hand of the Egyptians and out of the hand of Pharaoh and has delivered the people from under the hand of the Egyptians. Now I know that the LORD is greater than all gods, because in this affair they dealt arrogantly with the people." And Jethro, Moses' father-in-law, brought a burnt offering and sacrifices to God; and Aaron came with all the elders of Israel to eat bread with Moses' father-in-law before God. (Exod 18:10–12, ESV)

Jethro is one of several outsiders who utter a blessing to God in the presence of a famous Israelite. Melchizedek (Gen 14:19–20), Balaam (Num 22–24), the queen of Sheba (1 Kgs 10:9), and Hiram (2 Chr 2:11–12) are other examples.[2] The closest parallel to Jethro's blessing is found in the Melchizedek story. Both stories have an officiating priest and a blessing to Yahweh, followed by a shared meal. Mitchell has warned that the *brk* formula is not necessarily a statement of faith.[3] Nebuchadnezzar's blessing upon Yahweh affirms the providence and protection of the young men (Dan 3:28) but is certainly no real monotheistic confession. Yet there appears to be more in the case of Jethro than a greeting. Jethro's "Now I know that the LORD is greater than all other gods" (Exod 18:11) and Rahab's

2. Moore, "Ruth the Moabite and the Blessing of Foreigners."
3. Mitchell, *The Meaning of BRK 'to Bless' in the Old Testament*, 156–57.

"I know that the LORD has given you this land" (Josh 2:9) are both pronouncements of faith.

The book of Exodus explicitly links the exodus story with the blessing at creation and the ancestral blessings to Abraham, Isaac, and Jacob. The plagues provide moving evidence as to exactly how peoples who curse Abraham will themselves be cursed. These plagues differ considerably from the covenant curses in Leviticus 26 and Deuteronomy 27–28, even though there is some overlap in the plagues of boils, locusts, and pestilence.[4] Yet the Exodus plagues also present an opportunity for the mixed multitude of Egypt to join this covenant community in the experience of that blessing (Exod 12:38). The key transitional promise of Exod 19:2–6 demonstrates specifically how Israel's life is to mediate the presence of Yahweh around them:

> They set out from Rephidim and came into the wilderness of Sinai, and they encamped in the wilderness. There Israel encamped before the mountain, while Moses went up to God. The LORD called to him out of the mountain, saying, "Thus you shall say to the house of Jacob, and tell the people of Israel: You yourselves have seen what I did to the Egyptians, and how I bore you on eagles' wings and brought you to myself. Now therefore, if you will indeed obey my voice and keep my covenant, you shall be my treasured possession among all peoples, for all the earth is mine; and you shall be to me a kingdom of priests and a holy nation. These are the words that you shall speak to the people of Israel. (Exod 19:2–6, ESV)

This passage adds a new element to election from what was related less explicitly in the ancestral narratives. Election leads to divine service. The Old Testament doctrine of election is not merely intrinsic; it is instrumental. Israel represents Yahweh to all peoples. As God's unique treasure, they enjoy a privileged relationship to God. Israel maintains a unique standing before God. Yet they are to be a kingdom of priests. As God's people, this new people is to provide a twofold ministry of mediation and service. This passage also clarifies exactly how a narrowing of God's promise to the descendants of Abraham in the ancestral narratives leads to a broadening missional purpose. As Abraham was to become a great people and be a blessing to all peoples, so Israel is a treasured possession among all peoples. The *entire people* serves as a priesthood and the entire people is holy to Yahweh.

4. Zevit, "Three Ways the Look at the Ten Plagues."

This blessing of God's people reemerges in Exodus at another crucial point in the narrative. Exodus 20:24, a key transitional text, introduces God's blessing at the beginning of the earliest law code in the Bible, called the Book of the Covenant. God's blessing to Israel is directly linked to guidelines for faithful worship. While scholars have hotly debated the sources behind Exodus 20–24, chapters 20:22 to 23:33 clearly contain an ancient collection of laws embedded within the narrative framework that the Bible itself calls "the Book of the Covenant"(*sēpher habĕrît*).[5] Note that an explicit blessing marks the beginning of this law code:

> And the LORD said to Moses, "Thus you shall say to the people of Israel: You have seen for yourselves that I have talked with you from heaven. You shall not make gods of silver to be with me, nor shall you make for yourselves gods of gold. An altar of earth you shall make for me and sacrifice on it your burnt offerings and your peace offerings, your sheep and your oxen. In every place where I cause my name to be remembered I will come to you and bless (*ûbēraktîkā*) you." (Exod 20:22–24, ESV)

Just after the close of the Book of the Covenant, Yahweh makes the blessing explicit:

> But if you carefully obey his voice and do all that I say, then I will be an enemy to your enemies and an adversary to your adversaries. When my angel goes before you and brings you to the Amorites and the Hittites and the Perizzites and the Canaanites, the Hivites and the Jebusites, and I blot them out, you shall not bow down to their gods nor serve them, nor do as they do, but you shall utterly overthrow them and break their pillars in pieces. You shall serve the Lord your God, and he will bless (*ûbērak*) your bread and your water, and I will take sickness away from among you. None shall miscarry or be barren in your land; I will fulfill the number of your days. I will send my terror before you and will throw into confusion all the people against whom you shall come, and I will make all your enemies turn their backs to you. (Exod 23:22–27, ESV)

---

5. Julius Wellhausen argued that Exodus 20–23 originated with the Yahwist in the tenth century BCE. Martin Noth was convinced that Exod 20:22—23:33 was a self-contained literary unit that was inserted into the narrative, and George Fohrer later labeled this the "Covenant Code." Recent scholars have had much less confidence in source criticism and argue for a sophisticated structure and a literary unity. See the discussion in Hoffmeier, *Ancient Israel in Sinai*, 181–83.

These two texts demonstrate that God's blessings serve as bookends, defining the beginning and end of the Book of the Covenant. Theologically, these two bookends mark the Book of the Covenant as one means by which God's blessing can be appropriated to Israel.

A final blessing in the book of Exodus is strategically placed at the end of the book. When the tabernacle is finally completed, Moses blesses the people: "And Moses saw all the work, and behold, they had done it; as the LORD had commanded, so had they done it. Then Moses blessed (*waybārek*) them" (Exod 39:43, ESV). This blessing, based on the finished construction of the tabernacle, prompts the final phase of the tabernacle's completion in the last chapter of the book of Exodus; God's glory fills the empty vessel of the tabernacle with a palpable presence.

THE THREAT OF CURSE FROM WITHIN: THE GOLDEN CALF

The story of the golden calf demonstrates a dangerous tendency among the people of God, repeated later in the Balaam story and replayed over and over again in the Deuteronomistic History. That tendency is Israel's penchant for turning God's blessing into curse. Simultaneously, as Moses is on the mountain receiving instructions from God regarding the means by which God will mediate divine presence among the people, Israel lapses into idolatry and misdirected worship. This sudden turn is made explicit through the ironic contrast between the last words uttered by Israel when the covenant was confirmed—"All that the LORD has spoken to us we will do and we will be obedient" (Exod 24:7, ESV)—and the very next words uttered by Israel—"Up, make us gods who shall go before us" (Exod 32:1, ESV). It is important not to miss the connection between covenant making, covenant breaking, and covenant renewal. Israel breaks the covenant before it is even finalized. Surely this is a negative omen of things to come. But in a strange turn, it is also a profound statement of God's grace toward the ever failing human race. God forgives the people before Moses ever confronts them with their sin.

Israel feels threatened by the absence of their leader. "We do not know what has become of him," they cry. Israel's naivete is remarkable, because at this exact moment their missing leader is receiving God's plan for a perpetual meeting place. Israel utterly fails to live up to the conditions of covenant. They fashion an idol, build an altar, proclaim a feast, and get down to business. The interplay between Yahweh and Moses on the mountain strikes at the very nature of God's covenant promise of blessing to Abraham and his descendants. God intends to completely wipe out this disobedient people, tragically returning to the futility of the primeval human community before the covenant existed. It is as though neither God nor Moses wants to take ownership of this disobedient bunch. Yahweh commands Moses to go down from the mountain because *"your people* have become corrupt"* (Exod 32:7). Not to be outdone, Moses implores Yahweh, "why should your wrath burn hot against *your people*, whom you brought out of Egypt with great power and a mighty hand?" (Exod 32:11). In an unsurpassed moment of human mediation with the divine, Moses appeals to God's oath given to the ancestors that Israel would multiply and ultimately inherit the land of promise. The shoe is now on the other foot. Now Yahweh backs down and relents from the promised disaster, yet even then the Levites slay three thousand men and a plague breaks out among the people (Exod 32:28). A remnant remains and God issues the command to leave Sinai. Détente is finally reached between Moses and Yahweh, yet even Moses is leery of taking ownership of this wayward horde. Moses says to Yahweh, "See, you say to me, 'Bring up *this people*,' but you have not let me know whom you will send with me" (Exod 33:12, ESV). God promises that his presence will go with Moses and that he will have rest. Moses is not so sure. He ends the discussion by protesting that God should not bother to lead them out from Sinai if God is simultaneously unwilling to be present among the people.

After Moses initially hears of Israel's sin and returns to confront them, Exodus records the following unusual punishment enacted by Moses:

> When Joshua heard the noise of the people as they shouted, he said to Moses, "There is a noise of war in the camp." But he said, "It is not the sound of shouting for victory, or the sound of the cry of defeat, but the sound of singing that I hear." And as soon as he came near the camp and saw the calf and the dancing, Moses' anger burned hot, and he threw the tablets out of his hands and broke them at the foot of the mountain. He took the calf that they had made and burned it with fire and ground it to powder and scattered it on the water and made the people of Israel drink it. (Exod 32:17–20, ESV)

On a day that should have been a time of blessing, three thousand men fall. The Bible does not explain why Moses requires that the people drink the water, but the episode stands as a conspicuous parallel to the water ordeal of Numbers 5. This water ordeal is used in Numbers to determine the guilt of a woman accused by her husband of adultery. There has been no human witness, but the divine observer sees all. The priest is to take holy water in an earthenware vessel, scoop some of the dust from the floor of the tabernacle and mix it with this water. The accused woman drinks this "water of bitterness that brings the curse" (Num 5:19, ESV) If she is innocent of the accusation; she is free from the water of bitterness that brings the curse. Nothing malevolent happens. If guilty, the woman becomes a metonym, a curse and an oath among the people, and her "thigh will fall away and body swell" (Num 5:21, ESV). It is not certain exactly what this expression means. One possibility is a reference to miscarriage and barrenness: Num 5:28 states that the woman who is innocent retains the ability to have children. Back in Exodus in the account of the golden calf, the narrator uses three descriptive verbs to show what Moses does to the calf. He burns it, grinds it into powder, and scatters it on the water.[6] In an intriguing Ugaritic parallel to the three verbs above, Anath kills Mot with a sword, burns the body, grinds, it and scatters it.[7] But it is really impossible to tell if there is any explicit literary connection between Numbers and the Ugaritic. Finally, Moses forces the people of Israel to drink their own idolatrous brew. What is the intent of Moses's strange command? Is his intention to eradicate the guilt in Israel, or as in the example above from Numbers 5, to determine it? Israel chokes on her own perversion. The symbolism is palatable—literally. The Book of the Covenant, which began and ended with a blessing, lies broken in pieces on the ground. The thick tension between blessing and curse is revealed in what happens next.

> Then Moses stood in the gate of the camp and said, "Who is on the LORD's side? Come to me." And all the sons of Levi gathered around him. And he said to them, "Thus says the LORD God of Israel, 'Put your sword on your side each of you, and go to and fro from gate to gate throughout the camp, and each of you kill his brother and his companion and his neighbor.'" And the sons of Levi did according to the word of Moses. And that day about three thousand men of the people fell. And Moses said, "Today you have been ordained for the service of the LORD, each one at the cost of his son and of his brother, so that he might bestow a blessing upon you this day." (Exod 32:26–29, ESV)

6. On the difficulties as to how one might burn and grind gold, see Hamilton, *Exodus*, 542–45.

7. Childs, *The Book of Exodus*, 569.

What is clear is that the Levites go throughout the camp killing their brothers and companions. What is unclear is whether these killings are random or intentionally selective. It is hard to imagine that these murders are completely random, but the text does not say. Perhaps those who were most guilty of the offense were killed. Exodus 32:2 implies that all the people were complicit in the rebellion, but perhaps some less than others. Yet, the final words of Moses are revealing: "Today you have been ordained for the service of the LORD, each one at the cost of his son and his brother, so that he might bestow a blessing upon you this day" (Exod 32:29, ESV). Why the use of the language of ordination? This is a strange ordination to be sure, and an even stranger blessing! Is this as simple as saying that God used these leaders to purge the infidelity from the midst of God's people, or is there something more? Moses states, "You have been set apart for the LORD today" (Exod 32:29). It is ironic that in this case, the Levites are blessed for their violence while their ancestor, Levi, was cursed for his own similarly violent acts (cf. Gen 49:7).

The threat of curse from within looms large in the Sinai and wilderness stories. Yet in spite of the repeated disobedience of the people of God, the blessing-promise to the ancestors ultimately prevails. The positive side of the golden-calf episode reveals the pervasive stubbornness of this promise that refuses to be extinguished. Not only is the covenant broken before it is completed, but by God's grace and mercy God's people are saved before they even know they are damned.

The next divine command after this pathetic episode is for the people to leave Sinai and go to the promised land. God swears that he will not, however, go up with the people. Moses once again intercedes; God reconsiders, and promises his divine presence for the journey.

> And the LORD said to Moses, "This very thing that you have spoken I will do, for you have found favor in my sight, and I know you by name." Moses said, "Please show me your glory." And he said, "I will make all my goodness pass before you and will proclaim before you my name 'The LORD.' And I will be gracious to whom I will be gracious, and will show mercy on whom I will show mercy. But," he said, "you cannot see my face, for man shall not see me and live." And the Lord said, "Behold, there is a place by me where you shall stand on the rock, and while my glory passes by I will put you in a cleft of the rock, and I will cover you with my hand until I have passed by. Then I will take away my hand, and you shall see my back, but my face shall not be seen. (Exod 33:17–23, ESV)

DIVINE NAME/DIVINE PRESENCE/DIVINE GLORY

Strange as it may sound, theologically, the book of Exodus is not primarily about the exodus from Egypt.[8] It is mostly about the divine presence of Yahweh, a presence mediated primarily by five manifestations of divine glory: the burning bush, the plagues, the cloud and fire, and the ark/tabernacle, and the angel of the Lord.[9] Another way of saying this is that the book of Exodus is about knowing God through personal experience. The divine presence of Yahweh does redeem Israel out of the hands of the Egyptians to be sure. But that redemption is an important indication of divine presence. Another name for this visible manifestation of God's presence is *glory*.

Divine Name

Theologically, the book of Exodus posits two questions of identification: Who is Yahweh? And, who is Moses?[10] The main antagonist in the story, Pharaoh, asks the first question with stinging sarcasm, "Who is the LORD that I should heed his voice and let Israel go? I do not know the LORD, and moreover I will not let Israel go" (Exod 5:2, ESV). His initial question demonstrates ignorance about divine character. But the following statement, "I do not know the LORD," flatly rejects divine authority. The final challenge, "I will not let Israel go," reflects Pharaoh's harsh restriction on the activities of Yahweh's representatives. Moses himself asks this same question when God calls him to deliver Israel from the hands of the Egyptians: "If I come to the people of Israel and say to them, 'The God of your fathers has sent me to you,' and they ask me, "What is his name?' what shall I say to them?" (Exod 3:13, ESV). Consequently, the book of Exodus is ultimately about the revelatory presence of Yahweh. The answer to Pharaoh's question, who is Yahweh?, is rendered sixteen times in the book: "I am the LORD."

The second question, who is Moses?, is equally important for the theological message of the book of Exodus. The exchange in Exodus 3 between Yahweh and Moses over the divine call is almost as much about who Moses is as it is about who Yahweh is. Moses asks Yahweh, "Who am

---

8. Gowan's insightful theological commentary is structured by a helpful inclusio: Exodus 1–2 is reviewed under the title, "The Absence of God," and the chapter over Exodus 32–34 is titled, "The Distancing of God" (Gowan, *Theology in Exodus*).

9. Bosman, "The Absence and Presence of God."

10. Mann, *The Book of the Torah*, 106.

I that I should go to Pharaoh and bring the Israelites out of Egypt?" (Exod 3:11). At the height of the exodus story when Israel is finally delivered out the hand of the Egyptians, the Israelites look at the slain Egyptian bodies washed ashore from the Red Sea. The writer of Exodus comments: "And Israel saw the great work that the Lord did against the Egyptians, and the people feared the Lord; and they believed in the Lord *and in his servant Moses* (Exod 14:31 ESV; italics added). These two questions of identity are worthy of a more detailed exploration.

Divine Identity

Much in the book of Exodus, then, boldly welcomes the challenge of identifying Yahweh head on. And God said to Moses,

> I am the LORD. I appeared to Abraham, to Isaac, and to Jacob, as God Almighty, but by my name the Lord I did not make myself known to them. I also established my covenant with them, to give them the land of Canaan, the land in which they dwelt as sojourners. Moreover, I have heard the groaning of the people of Israel whom the Egyptians hold in bondage and I have remembered my covenant. (Exod 6:2–5, ESV)

The expression "they/you will know that I am Yahweh" occurs regularly in the exodus narrative (Exod 6:7; 7:5, 17; 8:10; 10:2; 14:4, 18; 16:12; 29:46; 31:13), as does the expression "I am Yahweh" (Exod 6:2, 6, 8, 29; 12:12; 15:26; 20:2; 29:46). "Who among the gods is like you, LORD?" (Exod 15:11) is also pivotal a rhetorical question that reveals Yahweh's sovereign, uncontested authority.

The revelation of the divine name to Moses through the burning bush resides at the heart of the theology of the exodus. As Walter Brueggemann observes, this theophany is an abrupt intrusion into the life of Moses and the life of Israel.[11] Just as the Genesis creation accounts show, so the theophany at the bush also shows that God is "underived" and capable of direct imposition into the workings of human history. Yet the difference between the creation accounts and the exodus story is significant. God's entry into history here is in direct response to a human cry.

---

11. Brueggemann, *Old Testament Theology: An Introduction*, 23. Here Brueggemann posits three "primal revelations" of YHWH in Exodus (3:1–4:17; 19:1–24:18; 33–34).

> During those many days the king of Egypt died, and the people
> of Israel groaned because of their slavery and cried out for help.
> Their cry for rescue from slavery came up to God. And God
> heard their groaning, and God remembered his covenant with
> Abraham, with Isaac, and with Jacob. God saw the people of
> Israel—and God knew. (Exod 2:23–25, ESV)

The two texts in Exodus 2 and Exodus 6 quoted above flatly connect the exodus story with the ancestral narratives. All of Israel's history
falls under the promise of God. Humans have an innate desire to name all
kinds of things, yet there is a reticence about disclosing the divine name.
The first man was entrusted with naming the animals, and the early ancestral stories show how God changed human names at will. But for God to
reveal his own name—that is another matter. As Paul Tillich states, "there
is sublime embarrassment when we mention the name of God."[12] Since
names were used in blessings and curses as sources of power, some have
suggested that accessing the name of the deity was related to accessing the
power of that deity. To the ancestors of Israel, God revealed himself by designations such as Eternal God (*El Olam*) or God Almighty (*El Shaddai*).
Later in Exodus, Moses prays to God, "Show me your glory," to which God
responds: "I will make all my goodness pass before you, and will proclaim
before you my name 'The LORD': and I will be gracious to whom I will
be gracious, and I will show mercy on whom I will show mercy" (Exod
33:19, ESV). The acts that deliver Israel from Egypt were ways of guar-
anteeing that Pharaoh, the Egyptians, and even Moses would "know that
I am Yahweh" (Exod 7:5, 18; 8:10; 14:4, 18). The explicit purpose of the
plagues harkens back to theme of knowing Yahweh (Exod 7:17; 8:10, 22;
14:4, 18). God's presence in the plagues also echoes throughout the Psalms
(Ps 78:42–52; 105:26–38; 135:8–9; 136:10). In answer to Moses's question
about who it is sending him to deliver God's people, God responds, "Say
this to the people of Israel, 'The LORD, the God of your fathers, the God
of Abraham, the God of Isaac, and the God of Jacob, has sent me to you.'
This is my name forever, and thus I am to be remembered throughout all
generations" (Exod 3:15–16, ESV). When Moses first returns to Egypt, he
gathers the elders of Israel and gives an account of how Yahweh appeared
to him on the holy mountain. Their response was ultimately to believe
(Exod 4:31).

---

12. Church, *The Essential Tillich*, 62.

Mosaic Identity

Who is Moses? This question of Moses's identity is also essential to the theology of the exodus story. His central role in receiving the law is unquestioned in the canonical text. In the opening chapters of Exodus his life is in peril and his identity ambivalent. A Hebrew baby rescued from almost certain death, Moses is raised in Pharaoh's household but weaned by his Hebrew mother. Moses grows up in a multicultural setting. He is raised as an Egyptian and visibly recognized as such (Exod 2:14, 19). Even before Yahweh calls to him through the burning bush, his identity is challenged in the narrative. "Who made you a prince and judge over us?" is a direct challenge that Moses has no business interfering with matters pertaining to the Israelites. Jethro's daughters from Midian also recognize Moses as an Egyptian (Exod 2:19). In light of these ambiguities, the two questions that Moses presents to Yahweh—who am I? and, who are you?—are both pivotal. Moses speaks as the very voice of Yahweh prior to the miracles that ultimately destroy the Egyptians, and these miracles are enacted by the hand of Moses. "See, I have made you like God to Pharaoh (Exod 7:1, ESV). Plus, it is Moses, not Yahweh, who risks having an audience with the powerful Pharaoh.

The narrator casts the story of Moses's birth in light of the roles of five women archetypes: the Hebrew midwives, the daughter of Pharaoh and her slave, Moses's mother, and Moses's sister. These two midwives represent the path of defiant resistance against an evil oppressor. They are the only two of these women whose names are recorded: Shiprah and Puah. The fear of God fueled their resistance, and because they daringly spared the lives of the Hebrew boys, a prophet was born who would ultimately lead the entire people to freedom. Pharaoh's daughter represents the merciful Gentile, who takes pity on the Israelite baby and raises him as her own. Her slave represents one who in her retrieval of the baby obeys her mistress but at the risk of retaliation from Pharaoh. Moses's sister is the ultimate opportunist, who watches from afar, seizes the moment, and acts in behalf of her brother. Moses's mother sacrificially gives up her son, not once, but twice, in order to preserve his life.

Moses is a paradigmatic figure in the Old Testament in many respects. First, Moses represents the ultimate mediator. He arbitrates between Yahweh and Israel, Yahweh and Pharaoh, and Israel and Pharaoh. Moses's central role is as the mediator of the covenant (Exod 19:19; 20:18; 33:11; 34:29). The law of Moses equates to nothing less than the law of God. He alone approaches God when others either fear to do so or are strictly commanded against doing so. In Exod 24:4 Moses is the one who writes down all the words of the covenant (cf. Deut 31:24). The Old Testament ends with the command, "Remember the law of my servant Moses, the statutes and rules that I commanded him at Horeb for all Israel" (Mal 4:4). The story of Moses's mediation against the Amalekites recounts another famous example of this important role (Exod 17:8–16), but perhaps Moses's finest hour is his mediation on behalf of the Israelites in the incident of the golden calf (Exodus 32).

Second, Moses represents the archetypal prophet. The book of Exodus first records this preeminent role repeated throughout the Old Testament, "Thus the Lord used to speak to Moses face to face, as a man speaks to his friend" (Exod 33:11, ESV). Note the two later articulations about Moses's prophetic role, in Numbers and Deuteronomy:

> And he said, "Hear my words: If there is a prophet among you, I the Lord make myself known to him in a vision; I speak with him in a dream. Not so with my servant Moses. He is faithful in all my house. With him I speak mouth to mouth, clearly, and not in riddles, and he beholds the form of the Lord. Why then were you not afraid to speak against my servant Moses?" (Num 12:6–9, ESV)

> The Lord your God will raise up for you a prophet like me from among you, from your brothers—it is to him you shall listen— just as you desired of the Lord your God at Horeb on the day of the assembly, when you said, "Let me not hear again the voice of the Lord my God or see this great fire any more, lest I die." And the Lord said to me, "They are right in what they have spoken. I will raise up for them a prophet like you from among their brothers. And I will put my words in his mouth, and he shall speak to them all that I command him. And whoever will not listen to my words that he shall speak in my name, I myself will require it of him. But the prophet who presumes to speak a word in my name that I have not commanded him to speak, or who speaks in the name of other gods, that same prophet shall die." And if you say in your heart, "How may we know the word that the Lord has not spoken?"—when a prophet speaks in the name of the Lord, if the word does not come to pass or come true, that is a word that the Lord has not spoken; the prophet has spoken it presumptuously. You need not be afraid of him. (Deut 18:15–22, ESV)

The background of Moses as paradigmatic prophet and mediator makes a look at the story of divine opposition to Moses in Exod 4:24–26 that much more surprising.

> At a lodging place on the way, the LORD met [Moses] and was about to kill him. But Zipporah took a flint knife, cut off her son's foreskin and touched [Moses's] feet with it. "Surely you are a bridegroom of blood to me," she said. So the Lord let him alone. (At that time she said "bridegroom of blood," referring to circumcision.)

Like many perplexing texts of the Old Testament, this little enigmatic episode is devoid of background. The statement that God intended to kill Moses is as categorical as it is vague. There is no blessing or promise, only opposition to a life of fullness. God is a dangerous God, untamed and a threat even to the one instrumental in the deliverance of God's own people. Most important, however, this episode adds to our present question, who is Moses? Zipporah bequeaths Moses yet another moniker, "a *bridegroom of blood* to me." The connection to the circumcision of Moses's son is the key to God's release. The parenthetic note of explanation proves that the narrator is also well aware that this story is undeniably obscure.

Third, Moses is paradigmatic of the prophetic call found throughout the prophetic literature of the Old Testament.[13] The typical pattern of prophetic call went as follows: The prophet-to-be has an encounter with Yahweh, either through a vision, a dream, or a message received. God calls the prophet to deliver God's message to Israel or Judah. Typically, the prophet expresses reluctance to the call. Moses, for example, feels that he does not possess the skills to speak before Pharaoh and Israel (Exod 3:11). Jeremiah argues that he is merely a youth (Jer 1:6), Isaiah states that he is a man of unclean lips (Isa 6:9–13), and Amos finds the message too dreadful to announce (Amos 7:2). After these expressions of reluctance, typically Yahweh affirms that he will be with the prophet at every turn when the prophet delivers the divine warning. Ultimately, the prophet capitulates and bears the message of God to the people.

Finally, Moses is paradigmatic of the human who experiences and enacts with the presence of God. This is revealed numerous times in the life of Moses—from his encounter with Yahweh at the burning bush to his interactions with God on the holy mountain. Perhaps the most telling example of Moses's encounter with divine presence results in a radiant transformation to his face when Moses comes down from the mountain

---

13. Habel, "The Form and Significance of the Call Narratives."

with the two tablets of the testimony in his hands. Moses's personal presence is so changed by his encounter with God that Aaron and the leaders of the community are afraid of him.

In the New Testament, the Apostle Paul recalls this episode and uses it to highlight the contrast between the covenant written on stone and the new covenant of the Spirit.

> Now if the ministry of death, carved in letters on stone, came with such glory that the Israelites could not gaze at Moses' face because of its glory, which was being brought to an end, will not the ministry of the Spirit have even more glory? For if there was glory in the ministry of condemnation, the ministry of righteousness must far exceed it in glory. Indeed, in this case, what once had glory has come to have no glory at all, because of the glory that surpasses it. For if what was being brought to an end came with glory, much more will what is permanent have glory. Since we have such a hope, we are very bold, not like Moses, who would put a veil over his face so that the Israelites might not gaze at the outcome of what was being brought to an end. But their minds were hardened. For to this day, when they read the old covenant, that same veil remains unlifted, because only through Christ is it taken away. Yes, to this day whenever Moses is read a veil lies over their hearts. But when one turns to the Lord, the veil is removed. Now the Lord is the Spirit, and where the Spirit of the Lord is, there is freedom. And we all, with unveiled face, beholding the glory of the Lord, are being transformed into the same image from one degree of glory to another. For this comes from the Lord who is the Spirit. (2 Cor 3:7–18, ESV)

The Glory of Yahweh

Glory is the manifestation of divine presence. The book of Exodus is filled with examples of visible manifestations of God's presence. The pillars of fire and cloud, the angel of the Lord, and the tabernacle—not to mention the burning bush and the plagues—are all manifestations of God's glory in the exodus story. Even Moses manifests God's glory as he enters the cloud, receives the law, and returns physically transformed. The crux of the exodus story is that even the pharaoh of Egypt is the foil of God's glory (Exod 14:17–18). All these symbols—fire, cloud, angel, tent, bush, and Moses—come together in the exodus story, the wilderness narratives, and the events at Sinai. They merge in a way that can only be described as theologically crowded. These multiple vehicles overlap regularly to display the palpable presence and glory of God.

First, a note on the theme of glory in Exodus. The height of the exodus proper is the Passover and deliverance through the sea (Exodus 12–14). Here Yahweh explicitly reveals the terse theological high-water mark of the book of Exodus: "The Egyptians will know that I am Yahweh, when I have gotten glory over Pharaoh" (Exod 14:4, 17, my translation). The Songs of Moses and Miriam both celebrate this glory (Exod 15:6, 11, 21). While Moses is on the mountain, he prays that Yahweh will show him his glory (Exod 34:17). And last, when the tabernacle is complete, Yahweh's glory fills the tabernacle, so much so that even Moses himself cannot enter it because of the "heavy" visible presence of God (Exod 40:34–38). In the discussion of the language of cursing, we observed that the root of the Hebrew word for "glory" (*kbd*) is an antonym of the word often translated "curse," or "to be light" (*qll*). Glory conveys the sense of gravity. The glory of God is the honor and dignity due divine majesty. The weightiness of God's character is conveyed by the idea of God's glory.

Notice how these visible symbols of God's presence are cluttered together in the wilderness stories in Exodus. A few short excerpts, which will be sorted out below, illustrate the interwoven and at times overlapping relationship between these visible manifestations of divine presence and divine glory: The Lord resides in, looks down from, and goes ahead of the pillars of fire and cloud (Exod 13:21; 14:24). The angel of God who had been traveling in front of Israel's army with the cloud withdraws and moves behind the people to protect them from Pharaoh's approaching armies (Exod 14:19). Simultaneously, the pillar of cloud also moves from in front of the people and stands behind them. The glory of the Lord appears in the cloud (Exod 16:10). At Mount Sinai, God promises his presence: "I am going to come to you in a dense cloud" (Exod 19:9). Moses himself enters the cloud (Exod 24:18), and upon his return his countenance is changed. The tent of meeting is to be consecrated by God's glory (Exod 29:44–46). After the tent of meeting is complete, the cloud settles on it (Exod 40:34–38). The glory of the Lord fills the tabernacle. These disparate phrases show that God's presence, God's direction, and God's protection are all conveyed by the multiple manifestations of cloud, fire, angel, Moses, and tent.

In Deuteronomy, the divine name—an important theme in the exodus story—is directly associated with divine presence at the central shrine (Deut 12:5, 11). While the traditional Priestly source of the Pentateuch uses the root "glory" (*kbd*) to convey divine presence in the tabernacle, the Deuteronomic source uses the word "name" (*šm*) to convey that presence in the chosen place. Consequently God's name and God's glory are interchangeable concepts to express the majesty of divine power. The proclamation of God's name throughout the world in Exod 9:16 is identical with the proclamation of God's glory among the foreign kingdoms at the close of the book of Isaiah:[14]

> I will set a sign among them, and I will send some of those who survive to the nations—to Tarshish, to the Libyans and Lydians (famous as archers), to Tubal and Greece, and to the distant islands that have not heard of my fame or seen my glory. They will proclaim my glory among the nations. And they will bring all your brothers, from all the nations, to my holy mountain in Jerusalem as an offering to the LORD—on horses, in chariots and wagons, and on mules and camels, says the LORD. They will bring them, as the Israelites bring their grain offerings, to the temple of the Lord in ceremonially clean vessels. And I will select some of them also to be priests and Levites, says the LORD. As the new heavens and the new earth that I make will endure before me, declares the LORD, so will your name and descendants endure. From one New Moon to another and from one Sabbath to another, all mankind will come and bow down before me, says the LORD. And they will go out and look upon the dead bodies of those who rebelled against me; their worm will not die, nor will their fire be quenched, and they will be loathsome to all mankind. (Isa 66:19–24)

Let us take a few of these symbols individually. In the Old Testament, fire and smoke are often signals of the presence of God (Gen 15:17–18; Exod 3:2, 19:16–19; Judg 13:20–21; Isa 6:4). The symbolism of the smoke is logical. Smoke conceals as much as it reveals. Therefore, smoke is a metaphor for God's identity as well as God's mystery. This theophany of Yahweh's presence first appears in Gen 15:7 in association with the covenant, as the smoking oven and burning torch move between the two pieces of the sacrifice. The storyteller associates these two manifestations of fire and cloud with all the major themes of the book of Exodus: the deliverance from Egypt, guidance in the wilderness, and the giving of the law at Sinai. Thick clouds, thunder, lightning, smoke, and fire shrouded the mount from which Moses receives Yahweh's instructions (Exod 19:9, 16, 18). Fire

14. Weinfeld, *The Book of Exodus*, 1:37.

and smoke billow up as in a furnace in Exod 19:18, which harkens back to the parallel of Sodom and Gomorrah (Gen 19:28).

God's presence (theophany) is also connected with the story about the giving of the law. The book of Exodus outlines the connection between theophany and law by three revealing mountain appearances. First, in Exodus 3 there is the appearance of the angel of the Lord in the burning bush. The storyteller recounts a theophany of God, the ground becomes holy because of the divine presence, and Moses receives a commission to deliver Israel from the Egyptians. Second, in Exodus 19, Moses makes three round trips up and down Mount Sinai. (Traditional source-critics had a heyday with this chapter!)[15] The storyteller includes a theophany with thunder, lightning, cloud, smoke, and trumpet. There is a warning for the people of Israel not to ascend the mount, and a commission to Israel to be a kingdom of priests and a holy people. The third story of ascent is in Exodus 24, as Moses also records multiple ascents and descents of the holy mountain. Moses tells the people all the words of the law, builds an altar and offers a blood sacrifice. Moses and the leaders of Israel observe the following divine theophany: "Moses and Aaron, Nadab and Abihu, and the seventy elders of Israel went up and saw the God of Israel. Under his feet was something like a pavement made of sapphire, clear as the sky itself. But God did not raise his hand against these leaders of the Israelites; they saw God, and they ate and drank" (Exod 24:9–11).

The tabernacle and ark are further manifestations of the glory of God. Moses receives explicit instructions about the tent, the ark, the tables, the lampstands, the two altars, and the basins; about garments for Aaron, garments for the Levites, the oil, and the incense. The tent of meeting and the tabernacle perhaps reflect a blending of two distinct ancient traditions, yet they are separated in the narrative. Regardless, these two symbols are mediums of revealing God's glory. God identifies the tabernacle with divine presence: "There I will meet with you, and from above the mercy seat, from between the two cherubim that are upon the ark of the testimony, I will speak with you of all that I will give you in commandment for the people of Israel" (Exod 25:22, ESV). The fellowship meal also indicates God's presence: "And you shall set the bread of the Presence on the table before me always" (Exod 25:30 ESV). Also, note the common expressions: "I will meet with you" (Exod 25:22; 29:42, 43; 30:6, 36), and "I will dwell in their midst" (Exod 25:8; 29:45–46). In Exodus, the tabernacle was designed to be a place consecrated by God's glory. Like the story of Moses

---

15. Childs, *The Book of Exodus*, 340–51.

and the burning bush, God imparts holiness where he appears (Exodus 3; Joshua 5:15). God's presence makes a place holy (1 Kgs 9:3). That holiness is not something that lingers after God leaves. Holiness, then, is another way to convey the abiding presence of God.[16] After the tent of meeting was completed, the glory of the Lord filled it so majestically that even Moses could not enter it.

> It shall be a regular burnt offering throughout your generations at the entrance of the tent of meeting before the LORD, where I will meet with you, to speak to you there. There I will meet with the people of Israel, and it shall be sanctified by my glory. I will consecrate the tent of meeting and the altar. Aaron also and his sons I will consecrate to serve me as priests. I will dwell among the people of Israel and will be their God. And they shall know that I am the LORD their God, who brought them out of the land of Egypt that I might dwell among them. I am the LORD their God. (Exod 29:42–46, ESV)

> Then the cloud covered the tent of meeting, and the glory of the Lord filled the tabernacle. Moses could not enter the tent of meeting because the cloud had settled upon it, and the glory of the LORD filled the tabernacle. In all the travels of the Israelites, whenever the cloud lifted from above the tabernacle, they would set out; but if the cloud did not lift, they did not set out—until the day it lifted. So the cloud of the LORD was over the tabernacle by day, and fire was in the cloud by night, in the sight of all the house of Israel during all their travels. (Exod 40:34–38)

THE ANGEL OF YAHWEH

The expression "the medium *is* the message" was never more true than with the topic of the angel of the Lord. The "angel of the Lord," "the angel of God," and the "angel of his presence" (Isa 63:9) all refer to appearances of a divine messenger who shares the nature and power of God, and is a medium for divine revelation. This angel serves as Yahweh's personal agent, and is often virtually identified with God. This angel speaks in the name of God, and does so in the first-person singular, as though God were speaking. Those who encounter the angel of the Lord in the biblical tradition often marvel that they have seen God (Judg 13:21–22). Unconfined

---

16. Niehaus, *God at Sinai*, 25–26.

to a particular place or a prescribed ritual enactment, the angel of Yahweh often announces and executes deliverance for the people of God.

There are a handful of primary episodes in which the angel of God appears. The first is to Hagar as she flees to the wilderness from her mistress, Sarah (Gen 16:7–15). Here the angel of Yahweh encourages Hagar to return to her mistress, proclaiming this indirect blessing,

> I will so greatly multiply your descendants that then cannot be numbered for multitude . . . Behold, you are with child, and shall bear a son; you shall call his name Ishmael, because the LORD has given heed to your affliction. He shall be a wild ass of a man, his hand against every man and every man's hand against him; and he shall dwell over against all his kinsmen. (Gen 16:10–12, ESV)

After this, Hagar wonders in amazement how it is that she has seen God. In the *akedah*, the account of Abraham's offering of his son Isaac as a sacrifice to God (Gen 22), the angel of Yahweh appears not in a visible, earthly encounter but as a voice from heaven. This messenger rescues Isaac from the hand of his own father. After Isaac's life is spared and the appropriate sacrifice made, the angel returns to Abraham a second time and reaffirms the blessing once given to the ancestor. To Jacob the angel of Yahweh speaks in a dream and tells him to leave Laban, his uncle, and return to Canaan (Gen 31:13). The famous account of the revelation to Moses at the burning bush (Exodus 3) also depicts God's revelation through the appearance of the angel of Yahweh. This text contains some of the most unequivocal and direct revelation of God to humans, and it is mediated through the agency of the angel of Yahweh. One other example comes from the exodus story in Exod 14:19–20:

> Then the angel of God, who had been traveling in front of Israel's army, withdrew and went behind them. The pillar of cloud also moved from in front and stood behind them, coming between the armies of Egypt and Israel. Throughout the night the cloud brought darkness to the one side and light to the other side; so neither went near the other all night long.

Last the angel appears to Gideon to announce that God will deliver Israel from the Midianites through him and assures Gideon of God's continued divine presence (Judg 6:11–16). In each of these examples the angel of the Lord is God's personal agent who incarnates the speech and actions of the deity.

Yet there are as many examples where the angel of Yahweh is clearly distinct from God. The angel of destruction in 2 Sam 24:16 and 2 Kgs 19:35, the angel who supports Elijah in 1 Kings 19:6–7, and the angel who accompanied Daniel into the furnace and the lions' den in Dan 3:25, 28; 6:23, are not as closely associated with the literal presence of God as the texts cited above. The role of the angel of Yahweh in the Balaam story is also rather ambiguous (Num 22:22). In this case, the angel stands in direct opposition to a prophet. In two additional accounts, a human figure serves as God's representative. The ancestor Jacob wrestles with a man until daybreak and demands to know his name, and a man speaks to Joshua promising deliverance to him (Josh 5:34). In both of these instances the specific term, angel, however, is not used.

One key theme in nearly all of these accounts is deliverance from danger. In these critical texts, the angel of the Lord promises and executes deliverance to individuals: Hagar, Isaac, Jacob, Moses, Daniel, Gideon, and even the people of Israel. Another common characteristic emerging from the angel's presence is a delivery of a commission (1 Kgs 13:18; 1 Chr 21:18; 2 Kgs 1:3). One of the most important texts dealing with the angel of the Lord is found in the night visions of Zechariah 1–6. In these chapters, it is the angel of the Lord, as well as other interpreting angels, who reveal the future restoration of Israel, primarily through the completion of the temple. The angel of the Lord (Zech 1:12; 3:1, 3, 5, 6; 5:1) and the "angel who talked with me" (Zech 1:19, ESV; 2:3; 4:1; 5:5; 5:10; 6:4) reveal that the completion of the temple will be a turning point in the restoration of Israel. God will use Zerubbabel and Joshua to bring about this magnificent reversal of fortune. The presence of interpreting angels is also felt in Ezekiel 40–48 and in the book of Daniel. In all of these cases, the identification of the angel of Yahweh with Yahweh himself is not pressed, as it is in the ancestral history and the book of Judges.

At the height of these eight visions is the flying curse of Zechariah 5, a picture of divine cleansing and renewal. Here a flying scroll with curses on both sides comes from the air, suggesting it is from God. The scroll moves through the earth to punish thieves and those who swear falsely—two important objects of many ancient Near Eastern curse texts. The book of Zechariah ends with the promise that Jerusalem will one day dwell in security and peace, and that there will no longer be any curse.

Jewish and Christian commentators alike have struggled to make sense of the theology implied by the appearances of the angel of Yahweh. The patristrics, of early Christianity, identified the angel of Yahweh with the preexistent Christ, a practice still common in many circles today. The root *ml'k* essentially means "messenger" and only secondarily means "angel." Claus Westermann begins with this assertion, arguing that at its essence the angel of Yahweh is first and foremost a messenger.

> It is important that in the early narrative the *ml'k yhwh* is the one who meets. He is there only in the meeting. He is not a figure, nor a representative, nor some manifestation of God; he is only the one who meets. This is comprehensible only in the context of the religion of the patriarchs where the figure of a mediator between God and man does not yet appear. One can receive a divine oracle neither through a man of God, nor a seer or prophet, nor through a cultic institution; on each occasion the oracle can proceed *only from God* by means of a messenger who is a person like anyone else. There is only one way in which he differs from others—he is unknown; he comes from and returns into the unknown. This is a trait common to all narratives about the *ml'k yhwh*. His coming and going are part of the message of the *ml'k yhwh*. His coming is often accompanied by a greeting; this is to state that he meets a person as a person. Only at his departure is he recognized as a messenger of God.[17]

For Westermann, God is primarily present in the message that comes only from God, not in the messenger. While this view does not account for the responses of those who clearly were convinced they had been in the very presence of God, it does take seriously the reality of the message itself. As to the identity of the angel with the deity, it is important to remember that messengers can often be identified with those they represent, particularly if they serve the wishes of royalty. An ambassador, for example, does not merely speak for a people; by metonymy the ambassador not only represents but embodies the policies, speech, and actions of that government. The common Christian position of equating the angel of Yahweh with the preexistent Christ fails in not understanding the important concept that representation does not necessarily imply ontological identification. More important the equation of the angel and the preexistent Christ runs the danger of emasculating the Christian doctrine of the incarnation by making all too common the appearances of Jesus in the Old Testament.

---

17. Westermann, *Genesis 12–36*, 243 (italics added).

7

"I Set Before You Today
The Blessing and the Curse"

Deuteronomic Theology and Worldview

Blessings and Curses in Deuteronomy

THE WORD *DEUTERONOMY* MEANS "second law." The expression actually comes from a Greek mistranslation of Deut 17:18, where the king is to write for himself on a scroll a "copy" of the law. Theologically, Deuteronomy as *retelling* is an important concept in the book, in spite of this error. From a noncritical perspective, this law is secondary only because the exodus generation perished in the desert. A new generation, no longer at Sinai, now camps in a new setting on the plains of Moab. The retelling of the law gives allows them their own place in the Torah story. Modern criticism has tended to view this book as a hinge of sorts, looking back at God's past deliverance and care, and forward to life in the new frontier. Gerhard von Rad reads the Pentateuch as an incomplete story without the book of Joshua, which describes the conquest of the promised land. He preferred to speak of a Hexateuch (Genesis—Joshua), which takes the blessing-promise of descendants, land, name, and blessing in Genesis 12 to its completion. Joshua 24 is a fitting end to this story, as Israel renews the covenant with God at Shechem. Martin Noth generally agreed with von Rad, arguing that the book Deuteronomy by itself added little to the narrative that ends in Numbers. Noth preferred, however, to use the language of a Tetrateuch (Genesis through Numbers). For Noth, Deuteronomy was better suited as a prologue for the narrative from Joshua through Kings rather than as the conclusion of the narrative from Genesis through Numbers. Noth envisioned a single author who penned Joshua through Kings. Most scholars today argue that both perspectives (as prologue or conclusion) reflect the message of Deuteronomy, which is both retrospective and prospective. This view embraces the theological affirmation that there is a providential relationship between the present moment, events leading up to that moment, and the ripe anticipation of the future.[1]

The academic study of the book of Deuteronomy reveals a rich history of scholarly research. In the middle of the twentieth century, scholars compared the general structure and content of the book with Near Eastern suzerainty treaties. Evidence indicates that these treaty patterns undoubtedly had some influence on the book. Yet, despite its attractiveness, the claim that the treaty form can cover the diversity of structure in Deuteronomy is difficult to sustain.[2] One of the most notable characteristics of these treaties is the blessings and curses that occur at the end of the legal stipulations. These blessings and curses were intended to reinforce the laws contained in the document, and ensure that those exposed to these laws would be motivated to keep them. Blessing and curse served as carrot and stick respectively, but the stick was much bigger than the carrot. Therefore these blessings and curses established social control and also specified exactly what moral and ethical standards were to be followed by the people: Blessing would lead to success, security, and status. Curse would lead to a miserable life, devoid of the fullness of blessing.

While the book of Deuteronomy undoubtedly shares elements of the treaty pattern, there are other ways at looking at the structure of the book. The rhetorical force of the book derives from four sermons given by Moses.[3] This is the simplest way of understanding the structure of the book. The genre of Deuteronomy could be called preached Torah. Moses makes four addresses (1:1—4:40; 5:1—26:19; 27:1—28:68; 29:1—30:20) to the people of Israel while they are in Moab, poised just across the Jordan, anticipating entry into the land of promise. These four sermons are followed by a few appendixes: Moses's song (Deuteronomy 32), Moses's

---

1. Craigie, *The Book of Deuteronomy*, 327.

2. Vogt, *Deuteronomic Theology and the Significance of Torah*, 26. Also see Christensen, "Form and Structure in Deuteronomy 1–11," 135.

3. Weinfeld, *Deuteronomy and the Deuteronomic School*, 157.

blessing (Deuteronomy 33), and Moses's death (Deuteronomy 34). In keeping with the idea that the book of Deuteronomy is a metaphorical hinge, the speeches are also both retrospective and prospective. In addition to structural indicators based on the addresses of Moses, there are other ways of defining the structure of the book. The title of the book in Hebrew comes from its opening phrase: "these are the words" (ĕlleh haddbārîm).[4] Similar expressions are found in Deut 4:44–45, 6:1, 12:1, 29:1, and 33:1. Some have taken these as indicators of major divisions in the book. Moshe Weinfeld interprets Deuteronomy as nothing less than a theological revolution.[5]

How might the theme of blessing and curse merge with the four sermons and delineate a fresh way of looking at the structure of the book of Deuteronomy? First, in the historical review of God's deliverance in Deuteronomy's opening chapters, the following expression summarizes God's providential care of Israel in the wilderness: "The LORD your God has blessed you in all the work of your hands. He has watched over your journey through this vast wilderness. These forty years the LORD your God has been with you, and you have not lacked anything" (Deut 2:7). This retrospective summary nicely distills the first four chapters of the book. Similarly, Deuteronomy 7 reflects back on God's oath to the ancestors, yet also looks forward with the command to observe the laws of the covenant:

> If you pay attention to these laws and are careful to follow them, then the Lord your God will keep his covenant of love with you, as he swore to your forefathers. He will love you and bless you and increase your numbers. He will bless the fruit of your womb, the crops of your land—your grain, new wine and oil— the calves of your herds and the lambs of your flocks in the land that he swore to your forefathers to give you. You will be blessed more than any other people; none of your men or women will be childless, nor any of your livestock without young. The LORD will keep you free from every disease. He will not inflict on you the horrible diseases you knew in Egypt, but he will inflict them on all who hate you. You must destroy all the peoples the LORD your God gives over to you. Do not look on them with pity and do not serve their gods, for that will be a snare to you. (Deut 7:12–16)

4. On speaking and writing law, see Knight, *Law, Power, and Justice in Ancient Israel*, 87–114.

5. Vogt, *Deuteronomic Theology and the Significance of Torah,* 1; Weinfeld, "Deuteronomy's Theological Revolution."

The core of the book of Deuteronomy comes from the covenant stip-ulations in chapters 12–26. Jeffrey Tigay has observed that Deut 11:26–30 and Deuteronomy 27, while not part of this legal code, nicely frame these laws that make up the legal code.[6] The warning of blessing and curse in Deuteronomy 11 and the covenant ceremony of blessings and curses in Deuteronomy 27 encompass the Deuteronomic law code of chapters 12–26. At several summarizing stages in the book, Moses invokes bless-ings and curses as reminders for the people to keep the law and as threats of what might happen to them if they disregard the commands given in the book of the law:

> Behold I set before you a blessing and a curse: the blessing, if you obey the commandments of the LORD your God, which I command you this day, and the curse, if you do not obey the commandments of the LORD your God, but turn aside from the way which command you this day, to go after other gods which you have not known. And when the LORD your God brings you into the land which you are entering to take possession of it, you shall set the blessing on Mt. Gerazim and the curse on Mount Ebal. (Deut 11:26–29, RSV)

Craigie pursues further this sandwiching structure—the laws sur-rounded by blessing and curse.[7]

- The blessing and the curse in the *present* renewal of the covenant (11:26–28)

- The blessing and the curse in the *future* renewal of the covenant (11:29–32)

- The specific legislation (12:1—26:19)

- The blessing and the curse in the *future* renewal of the covenant (27:1–26)

- The blessing and the curse in the *present* renewal of the covenant (28:1—29:1)

Deuteronomy 10–11 appear after a lengthy retrospective historical review of God's acts done on behalf of his people, in Deuteronomy 8–9. At the close of that review, the choice of blessing or curse is now prospective. What are the commands that God requires the people to observe?

---

6. Tigay, *Deuteronomy*, 116.

7. Craigie, *The Book of Deuteronomy*, 212.

Rhetorically, the blessings and curses of Deuteronomy 27 and 28 place a capstone on the legal materials presented in the book. Yahweh promises blessings if the commands of the covenant are kept, and threatens curses if these commands are broken. The blessing and curse blocks in Deuteronomy 27 and 28 should first be considered individually, since they most likely derived from two independent traditions. Deuteronomy 27 is particularly intrusive as it actually interrupts the flow of the narrative in chapters 26 and 28. Deuteronomy 27 also differs from chapter 28 in time and place. In time, Deuteronomy 27 speaks of the future, "the day when you cross . . . ," while chapters 26 and 28 use the temporal expression "today" (Deut 26:16, 18; 28:1). In place, the setting for Deuteronomy 27 is Shechem as opposed to Moab. Yet in spite of its intrusive character, the chapter itself makes sense as a unified whole.[8] One lurking irony is that in Deuteronomy 27 is an explicit call for blessings in vv. 12–13, but in actuality no blessings are uttered, only curses. What can be made of this omission? The short answer is, no one has any idea. Unless one wants to revert back to the sleepy-editor theory, the omission is the editor's patently negative tipping of the cards, a revelation of Israel's future demise.

Notice the highly ritualized nature of the covenant ceremony in keeping with the performative thrust of blessing and curse speech acts. This ceremony roughly parallels the one in Exod 24:11–13. First, the participants were to set up stones and coat them with plaster. Then they were to build a separate altar of unhewn stones at Mount Ebal and there inscribe all the words of "this teaching." No iron tools were to be used in the preparation of this altar. There is no reason mentioned for this prohibition other than perhaps the existence of a biblical parallel where Israel had to rely on the Philistines to sharpen their iron implements (1 Sam 13:19–23). Perhaps this restriction agaunst using iron tools was to prevent association with these outsiders. Note that everyone has a role in the ceremony, including Moses, priests, Levites, and people.

The place of this ritual is highly significant.[9] Moses charges the people that when they arrive in the land of promise, they should enact a covenant renewal ceremony at Shechem.[10] Why Shechem and not another location? For a variety of good reasons. Shechem lies at the foot of Mount

---

8. Hill, "The Ebal Ceremony as Hebrew Land Grant."

9. Ralph Hawkins argues that the site of this ceremony is on Mt. Ebal, not Shechem, *The Iron Age I Structure on Mt. Ebal.*

10. Richard Nelson discusses the competition between the Shechem tradition and the Gilgal tradition visible in the text of Deuteronomy 27 (*Deuteronomy*, 316).

Ebal. At 3,083 feet / 940 meters, it is the highest mountain in the vicinity. That places Shechem in the only east-west pass in the central mountain range. Shechem has a rich tradition in the Old Testament and is therefore a lively theological metaphor: it is a place for a new beginning; it is a place to return to; and it is place to show that one has the right to rule. A few quick examples illustrate these three facets of Shechem theology. Shechem was the first place where Abram stopped after arriving in Canaan, and it was the first city where he built an altar. Shechem was also the first place in Canaan where God spoke the Abram. And it was the first place where Abram identified the land as his own.

Next, Shechem was the ultimate place to come back to. When Jacob returned after his sojourn in Haran, he purchased the first plot of land for the ancestral family. Where? At Shechem. Joseph made his family swear that they would not leave his bones in Egypt, so four hundred years later, the Israelites took his remains with them to the new land and buried Joseph's bones at Shechem. There is nothing in Joshua about the conquest of this town, so we can assume that there was no conflict over Shechem. After Israel possessed the land, they returned to Shechem to renew the covenant (Joshua 24).

Third, Shechem was the place to go to show that one had the right to rule. In Judges 9, Abimelech is inaugurated as king near the oak at Shechem. In 1 Kgs 12, Rehoboam goes to Shechem for his own inauguration as king over all Israel. After the split between the northern and southern kingdoms, Shechem becomes the first capital of Jeroboam's northern kingdom. Again, Shechem is the location for the ceremony of Deuteronomy 27, whereas Moab is the location for the blessings and curses of Deuteronomy 28.

The priests and Levites were to station themselves on two prominent mountains that overlooked Shechem: Mount Gerizim and Mount Ebal. Six tribes stood on the greener slopes of Gerizim, which was the locus of blessing. Six other tribes uttered the curse from the more barren, but slightly taller, Ebal. The ark was probably stationed in the middle. The priests presumably proclaimed a blessing, and the Levites proclaimed a curse upon anyone who might violate the commands mentioned in the statutes of the covenant. There might have been a bit of insidious favoritism among the participating tribes. The tribes that stand for the blessing are the sons of Rachel and Leah, Jacob's wives. The tribes that stand for the curse are the sons of Bilhah and Zilpah, Jacob's wives' slaves.[11] So the illocutionary force

11. Seebass, "Garizim und Ebal," 22–31, argues that the "curse" tribes were eventually lost.

of exclusion is potent even in the utterance of these blessings and curses. All twelve tribes were to be assembled for this ceremony. No blessing is recorded, but as the curses are pronounced, the people's amen turns the twelve imprecations into effective self-curses, presumably one for each of the twelve tribes.[12] Most of these curses cover clandestine sins not typically detected in the normal course of events. As individuals participate in these sins, the curse clings to each and God's judgment would be unleashed, but not in some magical sense. The highly ritualized nature of this ceremony gives the spoken word performative power in society. Theologically, this particular list of curses conveys that God's authority extends well into the hidden places of one's life. Note the private nature of the sins these curses enforce:

- Setting up an idol in secret
- Treating father or mother with contempt
- Moving a neighbor's boundary marker
- Leading astray a blind person
- Perverting justice for the alien, orphan, or widow
- Having sex with one's father's wife
- Having sex with an animal
- Having sex with a sister or half-sister
- Secret, physical assault
- Taking a bribe to shed innocent blood
- Failing to uphold all the words of the law

Rhetorically, Deuteronomy 28 follows on the end of chapter 26 (Deuteronomy 27 is clearly an insertion). In Deuteronomy 28, blessings and curses are uttered in two stages, but note the lack of a highly ritualized structure. First, Moses utters a series of six blessings for those who obey the covenant and do all the things recorded there. God promises that if they obey the covenant, he will place them "high above all the nations of the earth." Among these six blessings, Moses recalls all manner of prosperity that will influence nearly every area of society. Note the broad gamut of blessing theology:

12. Barker argues that this omission is theologically intentional (Barker, "The Theology of Deuteronomy 27").

- Progeny   v. 4
- Produce   v. 5
- Protection   vv. 6–7
- Prosperity   v. 8
- Prominence   vv. 9–10
- Preeminence vv. 12–13

Six curses are similarly pronounced on those who might disobey the covenant.[13] These curses are arranged in the opposite order as the blessings. Moses reveals with a long list of examples how the curses might be unleashed. The list of the specific consequences due to curses is about three times longer than the list of blessings, something not unusual in ancient Near Eastern blessing-and-curse texts. These disproportionate curses contrast with what one finds in Genesis which uses the root for bless (*brk*) seventy-three times and the word for curse (*'rr*) a mere nine times. There are two groups of threats: vv. 20–44 describe natural calamities, disease, and military reversals; vv. 45–57 describe calamities resulting from conquest by other peoples and the consequences of those conquests. Richard Nelson has argued that there are two distinct genres in Deuteronomy 28. Verses 3–6 and 16–19 are "blessings and curses" in the proper sense. They have a declaratory shape, use a participial verbal form, and do not mention Yahweh. Nelson distinguishes these blessings and curses from "promises and threats," which use finite verbs and make up much of the rest of the chapter.[14] Nelson pushes the distinction too far, however. Yahweh is the subject of these threats as well. But it is possible to read these curses as part of the sermon, not the ceremony.

The people that would ignore God's commands will experience drought, warfare, sickness of all kinds, exile, and death. Inherent in this ideal is a theology of double agency. Human agents can and do actually execute God's judgment. God will punish violators of the covenant by using other peoples. The conditional clause of Deut 28:15 shows the open-endedness of the covenant: "However, if you do not obey the LORD your God and do not carefully follow all his commands and decrees I am giving you today, all these curses will come upon you and overtake you." Deut

---

13. On curses being a motivating factor in ancient law codes and treaties, see the Vassal Treaties of Esarhaddon (*ANET*, 534–41); Parpola and Watanabe, eds., *Neo-Assyrian Treaties and Loyalty Oaths*, 28–58.

14. Nelson, *Deuteronomy*, 328.

28:45–46 echoes 28:15–16: "All these curses will come upon you. They will pursue you and overtake you until you are destroyed, because you did not obey the LORD your God and observe the commands and decrees he gave you. They will be a sign and a wonder to you and your descendants forever." So not only at the close of the Deuteronomic law code but at other crucial junctures in the narrative, the blessings and curses are appealed to as motivation to keep the law.[15] These curses convey collective responsibility and promise communal consequences of rebellion.

The final speech of Moses (Deut 29:1—30:20) profoundly sums up the blessing-and-curse theology of the entire book. There is some question whether Deut 29:1 begins a new section, which looks forward, or whether Deut 29:1 is better placed as retrospective, closing comments from chapter 28, before Moses summons Israel in 29:2.[16] The superscriptions in Deut 1:1, 4:44, 29:1, and 33:1 all point forward, and it makes better sense to read chapters 29 and 30 in this prospective way. The "words of the covenant" in 29:1 refer primarily to curses. The covenant at Moab is beautifully ordered by the repeated use of the second-person personal pronoun:

- "You Have Seen"   Personal Experience   Deut 29:2–9
- "You Stand Today"   Corporate Identity   Deut 29:10–15
- "You Know Well"   Covenant Curse   Deut 29:16–29

First, there is a difference between the ability to see and the will to do so. Before their very eyes the exodus generation had seen the things Yahweh did in Egypt, to Pharaoh and the land. Yet, those Israelites did not really have a mind to understand or eyes to see. God provided them with clothing, food, water, and protection from enemies while they were in the wilderness. Finally, God gave the next generation the land that had been promised to their ancestors. But this text hints that the exodus generation never really *saw* all that God had done.

Second, Moses addresses the nature of communal identity. This new community is as vibrant as it is diverse—made up of chiefs, elders, officers, children, women, and aliens. This second generation after the exodus enters into the covenant curse to establish themselves to be God's people, the very people God promised the ancestors would be. Yet the curse extends even further, to those "who are not standing here today." Future generations are also bound by this covenant. Third, the phrase "You know well,"

15. Olson, "How Does Deuteronomy Do Theology?," argues that the Moab Covenant of chapters 29–31 is an integral part of the literary strategy of Deuteronomy.

16. Van Rooy, "Deuteronomy 28:69—Superscript or Subscript?"

alludes to the practices of the peoples around this new community. This new generation is to beware of turning away from God toward the gods of these peoples. Note the warning against those who might see themselves as exempt:

> When such a person hears the words of this oath, he invokes a blessing on himself and therefore thinks, "I will be safe, even though I persist in going my own way." This will bring disaster on the watered land as well as the dry. The LORD will never be willing to forgive him; his wrath and zeal will burn against that man. *All the curses* written in this book will fall upon him, and the LORD will blot out his name from under heaven. The LORD will single him out from *all the tribes* of Israel for disaster, according to *all the curses* of the covenant written in this Book of the Law. (Deut 29:19–21)

Future generations will look at the misery and calamity brought about by the consequences of the curse, and will wonder how God could have allowed such a thing to happen. The answer? Israel turned their backs on God's covenant. The pervasiveness of the curse is demonstrated by the threefold use of the word "all" (*kl*): "all the curses," "all the tribes," and "all the curses." Deut 29:29 is a perplexing text: "The secret things belong to the LORD our God, but the things revealed belong to us and to our children forever, that we may follow all the words of this law." Here is the bottom line: Some things about God will never be known. God's direction of the future is one of these things. An ominous tint clouds the future. But the present is known. It has been revealed, so for the present, Israel is commanded to keep the law now.

Moses is not very confident about this future. There is an awful inevitability to the theology of blessing and curse. In Deuteronomy the curses are assumed to have already taken place. A new tone begins chapter 30 with similarities to Deut 4:29–31. After this awful inevitability of curse, a complete renewal and return to God is not only a potentiality, but likely. Obedience becomes second nature. Circumcision of the heart is a reality (cf. 10:16). Curses are now transferred to Israel's enemies. The matter is still one of individual choice. The phrase "I set before you" is found three times (Deut 30:1, 15, 19). That choice is now. The word, "today" is used seven times (vv. 2, 8, 11, 15, 16, 18, 19). Similarly, at the end of Moses's final sermon (in Deut 29:1—30:20) comes a reminder of the consequences of either blessing or curse for those who have a definitive choice to make. The appeal is not just for consent but obedience,

> See, I have set before you this day life and good, death and evil. If you obey the commandments of the LORD your God which command you this day, by loving the LORD your God, by walking in his ways, and by keeping his commandments and his statutes and his ordinances, then you shall live and multiply, and the LORD your God will bless you in the land which you are entering to take possession of it. But if your heart turns away, and you will not hear, but are drawn away to worship other gods and serve them, I declare to you this day that you shall perish; you shall not live long in the land which you are going over the Jordan to possess. I call heaven and earth to witness against you this day, that I have set before you life and death, blessing and curse; therefore choose life, that you and your descendants may live. (Deut 30:15-19, ESV)

This new tone of restoration and renewal is also discernible the closing chapters of the book. It is tempting to read chapters 32, 33, and 34 as simple appendixes that some slovenly editor slapped on the end of the book. But if Moses is the prophet par excellence, then his last recorded words in the Bible ought to be read as important. Moses's last words are a blessing—one for each of the twelve tribes.[17] This literary collage is similar to Jacob's blessing at the end of Genesis. The similarity between Deut 32-34 and Genesis 49 is structural and rhetorical. Literally, it says, "This is the blessing with which Moses the man of God blessed the people of Israel before his death" (Deut 33:1).

Blessings and curses in the book of Deuteronomy are theologically significant. They create a somber tone for the book. In spite of God's choice of Israel among the peoples, Israel itself has a choice to make. Deuteronomy brings together creation and covenant in chapters 27-30. If Israel obeys, the created order and promised land will be abundantly fruitful. If Israel does not obey, the land itself will turn against them. They can adhere to God's covenant and experience the blessing of God, or they can depart from the covenant and God's blessing will also depart. For the Deuteronomist, Yahweh is behind both blessing and curse. Note the language of potent curse: "The LORD will send you curses, confusion, frustration in all that you undertake to do, until you are destroyed and perish quickly, on account of the evil of your doings because you have

---

17. Fleming posits that Deuteronomy 33 is dominated much more by the notion of blessing, and the divine involvement that accompanied that blessing, than Genesis 49; *The Legacy of Israel in Judah's Bible*, 88.

forsaken me" (Deut 28:20, RSV). Walter Brueggemann delineates this act/consequence scheme:

> The sanctions of covenant curse, punishment for those who violate oaths of obedience, may be enacted in a variety of ways, though Deuteronomy 28 and Leviticus 26 suggest a rather stock inventory of penalties and punishments. Israel envisioned a precise symmetry of acts and outcome, so that those who obeyed received all the blessings of life—well being, prosperity, fruitfulness, security and land—and those who disobeyed received a negation of life, whether by extermination, exile, barrenness, or natural disaster (cf. Deut 30:15–20). The commands, together with the sanctions, constituted the life-world in which Israel proposed to live. That life-world offered its adherents enormous blessing and was known to be morally reliable. The violator of that life-world as willed by Yahweh was commensurately to receive all the deathliness that came with a denial of the governance of Yahweh.[18]

God is the Lord over the world of nature and Lord over history.[19] There is no sphere of life wherein one can escape God. There is no halfway house. Every people and the course of nature itself are under God's authority.

The final chapter of this work will deal in detail with Paul's explicit reinterpretation of Deuteronomy 27–30 in the books of Galatians and Romans. For the time being, suffice it to say that Galatians 3 is an explicit interpretation of Deuteronomy 27 and Romans 10 provides an equally explicit interpretation of Deuteronomy 30. Galatians 3 also refers to God's promise to Abraham in Genesis 12 and 15. Galatians revisits the lives of Abraham, Isaac, Sarah, and Hagar. But the key interpretive context for Paul's argument in Galatians 3 comes from Deut 27:26: "Cursed is the man who does not uphold all the words of this law by carrying them out." Paul's conviction is that God preached the gospel beforehand to Abraham by stating that all the peoples on earth would be blessed through him. Through the Messiah Jesus, the blessing of Abraham comes to the Gentiles, to anyone who has the same faith Abraham did. The Messiah, through the cross, took on the curse of the law reflected in Deuteronomy 27. Jesus redeemed all who were born under the law as well (as all Gentiles who demonstrate faith) from this curse of the law (Gal 3:13). In Romans 10, Paul explicitly quotes and interprets Deuteronomy 30's promise of restoration and return

---

18. Brueggemann, *Theology of the Old Testament*, 196.

19. Craigie, *The Book of Deuteronomy*, 43–44.

from exile. The promises of return are fulfilled by the death and resurrection of Jesus the Messiah. God fulfills his promise by bringing back
his people from exile after a long curse. But Paul's iconoclastic midrash
contends that exile did not begin in Babylon; it began at Sinai.[20]

FIVE IMPERATIVES OF DEUTERONOMIC THEOLOGY

While blessings and curses provide an overall theological context for the
book of Deuteronomy, deuteronomic theology is reflected in five common
imperatives used rather liberally in the book: *choose, hear, remember, love,*
and *watch.*[21] In a very real sense, these imperative verbs constitute five different ways of saying exactly the same thing. Each of these five imperatives
illustrates the divine mandate to God's people to obey divine law reflected
throughout the book. The new community at Moab faces the hopeful
promise of blessings and imminent threat of curses depending on how
it responds to covenantal law. All five of these verbs are used reciprocally
denoting both divine initiation and human response.

Choose

The Hebrew root, "to choose" (*bhr*) is employed many times in the book of
Deuteronomy, most often as a reflection of Yahweh's choice of two things:
a people who will serve him and a place where he will be worshiped. God
reveals the election of Israel as an act of unconditional love and a choice
of divine sovereignty. This explicit revelation of election happens well after
God demonstrates that election love during the exodus. Moses instructs
the tribes that it is not because of their greatness or special merit that God
chose them to be the reflection of his nature and purpose among the peoples. It is simply because of God's choice. Election is a divine prerogative:

> It was not because you were more in number than any other
> people that the LORD set his love upon you and chose you, for
> you were the fewest of all peoples, but it is because the LORD
> loves you and is keeping the oath which he swore to your fa-
> thers, that the LORD has brought you out with a mighty hand
> and redeemed you from the house of bondage, from the hand of
> Pharaoh, king of Egypt.

20. Wright, *Paul in Fresh Perspective,* 138–39.

21. On repetition and its rhetorical and theological impact in Deuteronomy, see
Strawn, "Keep/Observe/Do—Carefully—Today!"

> And because you hearken to these ordinances, and keep and
> do them, the LORD your God will keep with you the covenant
> and the steadfast love which he swore to your fathers to keep;
> he will love you, bless you, and multiply you; he will also bless
> the fruit of your body and the fruit of your ground your grain
> and your wine and your oil, the increase of your cattle and the
> young of your flock in the land which he swore to your fathers to
> give you. You shall be blessed above all peoples . . . (Deut 7:7–8,
> 12–13a, ESV)

Another important term is the Hebrew root *nḥlh*, which refers to
Israel as Yahweh's inheritance (Deut 4:20; 9:26; 32:9) or *sglh* (Deut 7:6;
14:2; 26:18), which describes Israel as a special people. Robert Miller mentions several other verbs that speak of God's covenant election.[22] Election
is based on God's sovereignty alone. While election is recounted in the
narratives of Genesis and Exodus, it is made theologically explicit in Deuteronomy. God has selected Israel in his sovereign choice. Yet what has
surprised commentators is that divine election is mentioned so casually
and unemphatically (Deut 4:37; 7:6ff; 10:15; 14:2).[23] Regardless, God has
chosen a people Israel from among a group of peoples, so that they will be
blessed above all peoples. Deuteronomy 26:5–11, Gerhard von Rad's ancient credo, summarizes Israel's own understanding of their chosenness.

Another example of divine sovereignty relates to the centralization
of worship, a doctrine at the heart of the book of Deuteronomy.[24] This
doctrine is distinctive to Deuteronomy. God has chosen a single place for
worship, a place not yet mentioned by name. The opening section of the
Deuteronomic law code (Deut 12–26) emphasizes this point at length.
Unlike the peoples around them, who worship at the high places and in
multiple locations, Israel is to worship (in particular, sacrifice) only at a
place that will be revealed to them after they enter the land: "the place
[God] will choose as a dwelling for his Name." (See also Deut 14:21, 23;
15:20; and 16:6).

> You shall not do according to all that we are doing here today,
> everyone doing whatever is right in his own eyes, for you have
> not as yet come to the rest and to the inheritance that the LORD
> your God is giving you. But when you go over the Jordan and

---

22. Miller, *Covenant and Grace in the Old Testament*, 196–97.

23. Seebass, "*bḥr*," 83

24. Wenham, "Deuteronomy and the Central Sanctuary," 109–16, argues that Deuteronomy envisions a central but not a sole sanctuary.

live in the land that the LORD your God is giving you to inherit, and when he gives you rest from all your enemies around, so that you live in safety, then to the place that the LORD your God will choose, to make his name dwell there, there you shall bring all that I command you: your burnt offerings and your sacrifices, your tithes and the contribution that you present, and all your finest vow offerings that you vow to the LORD. And you shall rejoice before the LORD your God, you and your sons and your daughters, your male servants and your female servants, and the Levite that is within your towns, since he has no portion or inheritance with you. Take care that you do not offer your burnt offerings at any place that you see, but at the place that the LORD will choose in one of your tribes, there you shall offer your burnt offerings, and there you shall do all that I am commanding you. (Deut 12:8–14, ESV)

Worship at the local shrines and on the high places is strictly prohibited in Deuteronomic theology. Oddly enough, theologically, this prohibition led in the opposite direction to a kind of practical secularization. If a person actually obeyed this command, it tended to remove a sacral dimension from the life of most Israelites.[25] What common person could afford to journey to a central shrine every time he wanted to offer a sacrifice? Wouldn't such a command drive ordinary people toward the use of household shrines, localized cultic practices, and sacred high places?[26]

God's choice of grace is reciprocal and always involves a human response. At the climax of the book of Deuteronomy, Moses charges the people with these words: "I call heaven and earth to witness against you this day, that I have set before you life and death, blessing and curse; therefore choose (ûbāhartā) life, that you and your descendants may live" (Deut 30:19). Mosaic legislation involving human choice is the constitutional blueprint for how Israel should live in their new divinely granted home in Canaan. Von Rad says it well: "The meeting with Yahweh meant a decision about life and death. When Isreal heard this utterance, she was put in a position from which there was no more going back. Both Deuteronomy and the Holiness Code make blessings and curses follow on proclamation of commandments."[27]

25. Tigay, *Deuteronomy*, xvii.

26. On the evidence for family and household religion, see Albertz and Schmitt, *Family and Household Religion in Ancient Israel and the Levant*, 172–75, 474–95.

27. Von Rad. *Old Testament Theology*, 1:196.

Hear

At many crucial junctures in the book of Deuteronomy, the Hebrew root "to hear" *šmʿ* is employed to denote the human capacity to hear and respond to the voice of God. Every parent knows that there is a difference between a child's capacity to hear and the choice to do so. In this case as well, the command to hear has less to do with the capacity to hear than it does with the intentional and personal choice to obey the commands of God. The command "to hear" is noteworthy at several crucial junctures in the book (Deut 4:1; 5:1; 6:4; 9:1; 27:9). Deuteronomy 5 contains a record of the Ten Commandments, repeated with some important changes from Exodus 20. It begins with this exhortation: "Hear O Israel, the statutes and the ordinances that I speak in your hearing today" (Deut 5:1, ESV). When a parent raises her voice toward her unresponsive child and asks, "Do you hear me?," she is not asking about the capacity to hear but demanding a response of obedience. In another important text, perhaps one of the most influential texts of the Hebrew Bible, the command "Hear!" is used by Moses to declare the essential elements of Israelite faith, namely, that God is one and that his people are to love him with their entire being:

> Hear, O Israel: The LORD our God, the LORD is one. Love the LORD your God with all your heart and with all your soul and with all your strength. These commandments that I give you today are to be upon your hearts. Impress them on your children. Talk about them when you sit at home and when you walk along the road, when you lie down and when you get up. Tie them as symbols on your hands and bind them on your foreheads. Write them on the doorframes of your houses and on your gates. (Deut 6:4–9, ESV)

The theological theme here is that Yahweh alone is God; if you will, a monotheistic consciousness.[28] Note the language of exclusivity: "For the LORD your God is God of gods and Lord of lords, the great God, mighty and awesome, who shows no partiality and accepts no bribes" (Deut 10:17). This verse is in keeping with the vehement campaign in Deuteronomy to keep Israel away from pagan worship. Commands requiring execution of Israelites who worship other gods, and the requirement to destroy all the Canaanites so they don't influence Israel away from the one God, are in keeping with this monotheistic consciousness.

---

28. Rofé, *Deuteronomy*, 9.

The blessings and curses of Deuteronomy 27–28 also employ this verb *šmʿ*. Prior to the ceremony at Mount Gerizim, God's people are instructed to "keep silence and hear O Israel: this day you have become the people of the LORD your God" (Deut 27:9, ESV). And in Deuteronomy 28, "Whereas you were as the stars of heaven for multitude, you shall be left few in number; because you did not obey (*šmʿ*) the voice of the LORD your God" (Deut 28:62, ESV). Finally, the summative exhortation in Deut 11:27–28 directly links blessings and curses with the verb "to hear." The theology is profoundly simple: Hearing God's voice means keeping the Torah.

> See, I am setting before you today a blessing and a curse—the blessing if you obey (*tišmĕû*) the commands of the LORD your God that I am giving you today; the curse if you disobey (*lōʾ tišmĕûʿ*) the commands of the LORD your God and turn from the way that I command you today by following other gods, which you have not known. (Deut 11:26–28)

Remember

The command to remember (*zkr*) and its negative parallel "Do not forget," (*lōʾ šākahʿ*) unequivocally dominate the book of Deuteronomy (Deut 5:15; 7:18; 8:18: 9:7, 27; 15:15; 16:3, 12; 24:9, 18, 22; 25:17, 32:7). As this new covenant community would eventually enter the land and settle it, they would be tempted to settle into their lives and businesses and to forget the blessings that God had given them along the way. "But remember the LORD your God, for it is he who gives you the ability to produce wealth, and so confirms his covenant, which he swore to your ancestors, as it is today" (Deut 8:18). This command to remember is particularly linked with the capacity and will to remember how God had delivered Israel from slavery in Egypt (Deut 5:15; 15:15; 16:12; 24:19). The command to remember is never an injunction to remember a historical event for its own sake, but a means to an obedient response to covenant.[29]

One major difference between the Ten Commandments in Deuteronomy and the earlier version in Exodus is that here in Deuteronomy the motivation for the Sabbath command was rooted in Israel's own history. Israel is to remember that they were once slaves themselves in Egypt. Thus, their own servants are to be given rest. The magnificent deeds of God are

29. Yerushalmi, *Zakhor*; and Myers, "Remembering Zakhor," 129–46.

also to be remembered, particularly all the ways that God had led them as a people up to this point in their history as a people (Deut 8:2, 18). Most of all, Yahweh himself is to be remembered (Deut 4:9–14). To remember is both a retrospective and prospective act.

One final oddity in the book of Deuteronomy is the command to remember Amalek, or to put it another way, to blot out the memory of Amalek:

> Remember what the Amalekites did to you along the way when you came out of Egypt. When you were weary and worn out, they met you on your journey and cut off all who were lagging behind; they had no fear of God. When the LORD your God gives you rest from all the enemies around you in the land he is giving you to possess as an inheritance, you shall blot out the memory of Amalek from under heaven. Do not forget! (Deut 25:17–19)

Readers will recall the story of Moses and the battle against the Amalekites in the book of Exodus. Kaminsky's excellent study on election distinguishes between what he calls the "anti-elect" and the "non-elect."[30] The anti-elect, one might say, were the ancient "axis of evil": the Amalekites, Canaanites, and to a somewhat lesser extent, the Midianites. The non-elect were those kingdoms such as Edom and Moab, who had not received the promise but still had a closer family kinship and a more benevolent connection to Israel than the anti-elect. In Deuteronomy, Israel is commanded to never forget to blot the memory of Amalek from under heaven. This command would influence later stories and events in the Old Testament: Saul disobediently spares the life the Amalekite king, Agag, which allows for the line of Amalek to not be wiped out. Centuries later Esther's obedience leads to the death of Haman, the Agagite, who determined to exterminate every Judean living under Persian hegemony.

Love

The Hebrew root "to love" (*'hb*) is also prominent in the book of Deuteronomy in a reciprocal relationship of election and faithfulness: God's unconditional love for Israel and also Israel's faithful love towards God and others.[31] The theme is found explicitly in five places in Deuteronomy

---

30. Kaminsky, *Yet I Loved Jacob*, 12.

31. McCarthy, "Notes on the Love of God in Deuteronomy," 144–47.

(Deut 4:37–38; 7:7–10, 13; 10:14–19; 23:6), but is largely absent in the rest of the Old Testament, save in the striking exception of the prophet Hosea, where the theme appears on nearly every page (Hos 1:6–7; 2:4, 19, 23; 4:1; 6:4; 9:1, 15; 10:2; 12:6; 14:4). With God as the subject, *'hb* is used ten of eighteen times in Deuteronomy and Hosea.[32] God's action in behalf of God's people is the prototype for covenant relationship. In the Ten Commandments (Deut 5:10), Yahweh is one who shows love to the thousandth generation to those who love him. This same covenant of love to the thousandth generation is also mentioned in Deut 7:9–16 and is linked with the promise of blessing. In the *shema*, Israel is to love the Lord their God with all their heart, soul, and strength. This love is not some amorphous friendship, however. To love Yahweh is to behave in specific ways.[33] This has typically meant that to love Yahweh refers more to conduct and obedience and less to an affective relationship. But even given the ambiguity of the word, Bill Arnold contends that while the word denotes more than affection, it certainly indicates not less than affection.[34] And in the climactic passage of Deut 30:19–20, several of these key words come together in a reminder of the responsibility of God's people back to Yahweh: "Choose life, that you and your offspring may live, loving (*'hb*) the LORD your God, obeying (*šmʿ*) his voice, and holding fast to him for he is your life and length of days" (ESV). Israel is to "hold fast" to God. (See also Deut 4:4, 10:20, 11:22, and 19:9.)

Watch

The Hebrew root *šmr* can be translated in several ways: "watch," "observe," "guard," or "obey." The word is used more in the book of Deuteronomy than in any book of the Bible.[35] In Deuteronomy, the root *šmr* entails the idea of vigilant watchfulness to exercise great care in following the commands given in the covenant. The use of this word is particularly prominent in the covenant blessings and curses of Deuteronomy 28 (28:1, 13, 15, 58), but is perhaps best expressed in the following examples:

32. Vang, "God's Love according to Hosea and Deuteronomy," 173–94.

33. Biddle, *Deuteronomy*, 406.

34. Arnold, "The Love-Fear Antinomy in Deuteronomy 5–11," 560.

35. Some other examples include Deut 5:28; 6:2; 8:1, 6; 10:12–13; 11:1, 13, 22; 12:28; 15:5; 16:12; 17:19; 19:9; 28:1, 15; 30:10, 16; 31:2.

You shall therefore keep (*ûšmartem*) all the commandment which I command you this day, that you may be strong, and go in and take possession of the land which you are going over to possess, and that you may live long in the land which the LORD swore to your fathers to give to them and to their descendants, a land flowing with milk and honey.

For if you will be careful to do (*šāmōr tišmĕrûn*) all this commandment which I command you to do, loving the LORD your God, walking in all his ways, and cleaving to him, then the LORD will drive out all these nations before you. (Deut 11:8–9, 22–23, RSV)

Essentially, all these active imperatives signify the same thing: Israel must pay close attention so that they do not neglect their covenant with God. They neglect this covenant to their peril, not only as a people, but also as individuals, families, and tribes. Israel should be careful when they arrive in this new land to keep God's covenant. At the close of the Deuteronomic law code, note how the Deuteronomic reciprocal theme of God's election and human response are interwoven:

The LORD your God commands you this day to follow these decrees and laws; carefully observe (*wĕšāmartâ*) them with all your heart and with all your soul. You have declared this day that the LORD is your God and that you will walk in his ways, that you will keep (*wĕlišmōr*) his decrees, commands and laws, and that you will obey (*wĕlišmōaʿ*) him. And the LORD has declared this day that you are his people, his treasured possession as he promised, and that you are to keep (*wĕlišmōr*) all his commands. He has declared that he will set you in praise, fame and honor high above all the nations he has made and that you will be a people holy to the LORD your God, as he promised. (Deut 26:16–19)

Sadly, Deuteronomy 31 says bluntly what the reader suspects might happen, given all these warnings against disobedience:

The LORD said to Moses, "Now the day of your death is near. Call Joshua and present yourselves at the Tent of Meeting, where I will commission him." So Moses and Joshua came and presented themselves at the tent of meeting.

Then the LORD appeared at the tent in a pillar of cloud, and the cloud stood over the entrance to the Tent. And the Lord said to Moses: "You are going to rest with your fathers, and these people will soon prostitute themselves to the foreign gods of the land they are entering. They will forsake me and break the covenant I made with them. On that day I will become angry with them and forsake them; I will hide my face from them, and they will be destroyed. Many disasters and difficulties will come upon them, and on that day they will ask, 'Have not these disasters come upon us because our God is not with us?' And I will certainly hide my face on that day because of all their wickedness in turning to other gods.

"Now write down this song and teach it to the Israelites and have them sing it, so that it may be a witness for me against them. When I have brought them into the land flowing with milk and honey, the land I promised on oath to their forefathers, and when they eat their fill and thrive, they will turn to other gods and worship them, rejecting me and breaking my covenant. And when many disasters and difficulties come upon them, this song will testify against them, because it will not be forgotten by their descendants. I know what they are disposed to do, even before I bring them into the land I promised them on oath." So Moses wrote down this song that day and taught it to the Israelites. (Deut 31:14–22)

Deuteronomic Theology in the Deuteronomistic History

The book of Deuteronomy's influence on the Former Prophets (Joshua through Kings) is pervasive. Ever since Martin Noth argued that Deuteronomy through Kings is the work of a single historian, many have observed numerous similarities in language and theology in these books.[36] The books of Deuteronomy through Kings represents about one-fourth of the Old Testament and are quoted regularly in the New Testament. The prophets Jeremiah and Hosea also share a similar worldview to the one presented in these books. It is almost universally acknowledged that when Hilkiah found the Book of the Law in the temple during the reign of Josiah, what he found was most likely a portion of Deuteronomy that propelled a reformation initiated by the Judean king, Josiah. The Huldah prophecy makes it explicit that the curses in Deuteronomy jarred

---

36. Noth, *The Deuteronomistic History*. For a recent survey of the state of scholarship on the Deuteronomistic History see Römer, *The So-Called Deuteronomistic History*. For a catalog of Deuteronomic phraseology, see Weinfeld, *Deuteronomy and the Deuteronomic School*, 320–65.

Josiah to initiate this well-intended but unsuccessful series of reforms (2 Kgs 22:14–20). We know this because many of his reforms have direct parallels to the prohibitions mentioned in the legal code of Deuteronomy as well as the blessings and curses at the end of the book. The story recounted in the so-called Deuteronomistic History is nothing less than a working out of the blessings and curses of Deuteronomy. Another way of saying this is through Walter Brueggemann's contention that the Deuteronomistic History recounts the Israelite monarchy's a steady abandonment of the radical nature of the Mosiac vision.[37]

The ominous shadow of Sinai looms over this history of covenant breaking in Joshua through Kings. Jon Levenson observes that the curses and blessings of the covenant formulary enable the prophets of Israel to provide their own theology of history. This theology is also replete in the Deuteronomistic History. All these calamities—adversity, drought, famine, epidemic, or defeat—could be accounted for by reference to a violation of covenant obligations. Conversely, the prosperity and tranquility of either the past or the coming age could be seen as a positive consequence of faithful partnership with God. This made for a nice, tidy theology of retribution. What covenant theology could not tolerate was the inability to correlate the two: the observation that the just suffer and the wicked thrive, and that Israel may indeed have a just claim against God.[38]

Significantly, explicit references to the Book of the Law begin (Josh 1:8) and end (2 Kgs 22:11) the Former Prophets. In Josh 1:8, the new leader of the Israelite people is charged, "Do not let this Book of the Law depart from your lips; meditate on it day and night, so that you may be careful to do everything written in it. Then you will be prosperous and successful" (Josh 1:8). The Josianic reforms come at the close of the book of Second Kings and also include several explicit references to the Book of the Law. Second Kings recounts that after he heard the words of the Book of the Law, Josiah tore his clothes, fearful that God kindled divine wrath against the kingdom because they had not obeyed covenant law. After summoning the people, Josiah begins a series of drastic reforms to Israel's customary religious practices. At least this is the account given in the book of Kings. The problem with this account is that there is no mention of any of Josiah's reforms in the prophets, and archaeology bears little evidence of such late reforms as destruction of high places, desecration of pagan temples, or the like. Yet, the vigorous monotheism presented here

---

37. Brueggemann, *The Prophetic Imagination*, 22.

38. Levenson, *Sinai and Zion*, 55.

fits an eighth- and seventh-century-BCE context well, although many of the laws presented in the book are far less advanced than the political and social situation characterized by seventh-century Judah. The laws in Deuteronomy, for example, are primarily about farmers and herders, not merchants, soldiers, or royal professionals. Regardless of whether Josiah's reforms were superficial or systemic, the destruction by Babylon comes immediately after these reforms were enacted by King Josiah. The question of the extent of Josiah's reforms is moot, and Josiah's reforms were obviously too little and too late.

How then might the book of Deuteronomy have influenced the theological worldview of Joshua through Kings? Moshe Weinfeld suggests nine theological tenets that grew out of Deuteronomic style and reflected the innovative religious upheaval of seventh and sixth centuries BCE: struggle against idolatry; centralization of the cult; exodus, covenant and election; the monotheistic creed; observance of the law and loyalty to covenant; inheritance of the land; retribution and material motivation; fulfillment of prophecy; and election of the Davidic dynasty.[39] Examples of these theological tenets can be seen on nearly every page of the Deuteronomistic History. How can one explore connections between historiography and theology? Bernhard Anderson, building on Noth, has suggested several fruitful avenues that contain marked theological perspectives in Joshua through Kings.[40] He suggests that divine addresses, climactic speeches/prayers by Israel's leaders, and interpretive summaries by the storyteller provide the clearest expressions of the theology of the Deuteronomistic History. We will briefly summarize these three, plus add a fourth fruitful theological avenue worth taking: covenant renewal ceremonies.

Divine Addresses

Yahweh speaks directly to Joshua, Gideon, Samuel, David, and Solomon in the Deuteronomistic History. With a brief comparison of these instances of of divine address, a vital theology emerges. In two appearances of Yahweh to Joshua, Yahweh addresses the nature of the covenant gift of land to Israel. First, God clarifies the dimensions of the land that he promised to God's people (Josh 1:1–9). God encourages Joshua to be strong, and promises that if he demonstrates such courage, Israel will have victory over all enemies and will take possession of the land of promise. Adherence to the

39. Weinfeld, *Deuteronomy and the Deuteronomic School*, 1
40. B. W. Anderson, *Contours of Old Testament Theology*, 166.

Book of the Law is prerequisite to actualizing and retaining these divine promises. God provides the promise of his abiding presence to Joshua with these words: "I will be with you." Later, however, after initial victories at Jericho, Israel stumbles, and suffers a horrible setback at Ai. They are routed before their enemies, because Achan, one of the Israelite soldiers, had stolen some of the booty from Jericho that was supposed to be dedicated to Yahweh. God appears to Joshua a second time to confirm Israel's sin. It is this sin that is the source of their defeat at Ai. God uses robust language: Israel has become a thing for destruction. The words of Yahweh stand in sharp contrast to his initial promise: "I will be with you no more unless you destroy the devoted things" (Josh 7:12, RSV). These two appearances clarify Deuteronomic thinking about the covenant promise of land. The land is a gift that must be taken and retained. Like the possession of the land, its retention is dependent on Israel's covenant faithfulness. The story of Gideon illustrates this powerfully as Yahweh speaks to Gideon with repeated instructions about how his army should prepare to face the Midianites (Judg 7:1-9).

Yahweh's addresses to Samuel begin when he is a child (1 Sam 3; 8:7-9, 10-18). Yahweh reveals to Samuel as a young boy that the end was near for the family of Eli the priest. Because Eli's sons violate the law by committing blasphemy and because Eli does not restrain them, Yahweh promises to punish the house of Eli for its depravity. Later, God's message to Samuel not only proves that the people had categorically rejected God by longing after a king, but God's lengthy tirade against the abuses of the monarchy is modeled almost entirely after Deuteronomy 17 (1 Sam 8:7-9). The king would take sons and daughters for his own service, a portion of the harvest, and the choicest fields. In other words, having a king would come at Israel's expense.

With David (2 Sam 7:5-17) and Solomon (1 Kgs 9:1-9), Yahweh's addresses focus on the promise of a dynasty that will last forever. Yahweh promises David that he will make a great name for him—language similar to the promise made to Abraham. God vows to appoint a place for the people and to give them rest from all their enemies. In spite of sin and shortcomings, God announces that while he would chasten David's descendants for acts of sinfulness, he would never remove his love. The covenant that God makes with David is remarkable. In spite of God's misgivings regarding the monarchy, God's promise to David is unconditional and eternal, similar to covenants to Noah and Abraham. For Solomon Yahweh reaffirms the promise that there would never fail to be a man on the throne from the house of David. Yet with Solomon, the dark side of God's potential punishment for sin is more pronounced. Yahweh promises that if God's people turn aside from the covenant, he will cut them off entirely from the land. Israel will become a heap of ruins, a proverb and byword among foreign peoples (cf. Deut 28:37). Everyone who looks at this people will hiss because God's people forsook the one who had been faithful to them. As unusual as it might sound, Yahweh's addresses to Joshua, Gideon, Samuel, David, and Solomon clarify the conditionality of the unconditional promise. God's gift does not preclude human freedom. These leaders of Israel are held accountable to a standard of obedience and faithfulness.

Climactic Speeches and Prayers by Leaders of Israel

With the exception of Gideon, these same individuals—Joshua, Samuel, David, and Solomon—make lengthy addresses to their people and also utter prayers to God. These speeches and prayers are dense theologically and are similar to programmatic speeches in Judith 8:11–27; 9:2–14, and in 1 Maccabees 2:48–67 and to those scattered throughout the book of Acts. Joshua's speech comes as his farewell address, prior to the renewal of the covenant at Shechem. Once again, he charges Israel with the responsibility to keep the covenantal commands (Josh 23:6). This means undiluted devotion to Yahweh and absolute separation from other gods. Separation from other gods also means separation from intermarrying with people from foreign peoples that worship such gods. Joshua strictly forbids such relationships. Joshua ties the successes of the people in the conquest of the land directly to the promises made to the ancestors by Yahweh. "Not one thing has failed of all the good things which the LORD your God promised concerning you" (Josh 23:14, NRSV). As has been seen so many times in a Deuteronomic worldview, Joshua also is realistic about the consequences of disobedience. Just as God brought about so much good, he also is just as capable of bringing evil, should Israel choose to transgress the covenant.

Samuel's address to the young people (1 Sam 12:1–25) begins on a negative note. He reviews the sad cycle recounted in the book of Judges so many times: sin, oppression, deliverance, peace, and sin once again. The promise of God's blessing and curse are clearly denoted. Israel is encouraged to fear the Lord and serve him faithfully. If Israel fears the Lord, it will go well with them. If they do not listen to God's voice, they will be punished. Yahweh promises that if Israel persists in wickedness, it will be swept away—both the people and their king. David's (2 Sam 7:18–29) and Solomon's (1 Kgs 8:12–53) speeches center primarily on the Davidic monarchy and its extravagant success. David thanks God for bringing him as far as he has. David emphasizes the uniqueness of God and the uniqueness of God's people in all the earth. David requests God's blessing on his house:

> O Sovereign LORD, you are God! Your words are trustworthy, and you have promised these good things to your servant. Now be pleased to bless the house of your servant, that it may continue forever in your sight; for you, O Sovereign LORD, have spoken, and with your blessing the house of your servant will be blessed forever. (2 Sam 7:28–29)

The theology expressed by Solomon himself is remarkably similar to the theology expressed in divine addresses to Solomon. Before the people he blesses the Lord and points to God's choice of David as the forerunner of an eternal dynasty. Solomon announces that he has built a house for the name of Yahweh. In his prayer, however, he is explicit about the impending consequences for sin, including defeat by enemies, drought, famine, pestilence, blight, mildew, sickness and captivity—all of which are mentioned in Deuteronomy 28.

Interpretive Summaries

The Former Prophets contain two interpretive summaries that reveal some of the richest theological material in the Former Prophets: the summary of the Judges Cycle (Judg 2:11—3:6) and the summary depicting the reasons for the fall of Samaria (2 Kgs 17:7–23). The summary in the book of Judges introduces a cycle that recurs some thirteen times in the narrative of the book. Israel forsakes Yahweh by following after other gods, thus provoking the deity. Yahweh then delivers Israel over to an oppressive foreign power. The expression "Yahweh was against them for evil" expresses the power of the covenant curses. Yahweh then raises up judges who save Israel from the hands of their enemies. In spite of the fact that Israel still does not listen to God, God provides peace as long as the judge is alive. After the death of the judge, Israel once again follows after other gods, turns back , and actually becomes worse than before—once again provoking the deity and starting the cycle anew. In many ways the book of Judges entails a theology of a failed conquest. Many of the peoples that are said to be done away with in Joshua rise once again in Judges, with a vengeance. In the book of Judges the expression "so the LORD left those nations, not driving them out at once" is noteworthy.

While the actual siege and destruction of Samaria, the capital of the northern kingdom, is given little attention in the biblical narrative, the explanation for exactly why this kingdom is destroyed is pointedly emphasized. Israel sins by walking in the customs of foreign peoples. Many of these sins are secret sins, known only to God. They set up and serve idols at will. Even though prophets warn them repeatedly, they ignore them and still continue in their sinful ways. They despise the covenant by making molten images and other gods; they even burn their sons and daughters in the fire to worship Baal. Consequently, God's punishment is complete: "So the LORD was very angry with Israel and removed them from his presence" (2 Kgs 17:18). The introductory and concluding royal summary for each reign of a northern king are also schematically structured and serve as theologically latent interpretive material. These mechanical royal summaries (1 Kgs 14:21–24, 29–31; 15:1–8, 25–32) illustrate that apostasy is a dominant theme in the narrative from Joshua through Kings. That structure, however, is less ridged and more subtle; some evil kings do have prayers answered.[41]

Covenant-Renewal Ceremonies

There are four explicit covenant-renewal ceremonies in the so-called Deuteronomistic History, plus intriguing parallels in covenant-renewal ceremonies at Qumran. The first two are prompted by Joshua: one after the conquest of Ai (Josh 8:30–35) and the other after the division of the land among the twelve tribes after the possession of Canaan (Joshua 24). The third ceremony is Samuel's renewal of the covenant at Gilgal (1 Sam 11:14—12:25), and the fourth is when Josiah is abruptly confronted by Israel's persistent inability to keep the covenant after the book of the law is discovered in the temple and was read to him (2 Kgs 23:1–3).[42] In these cases the leaders typically summon the people to hear the words written in the book of the law. The account of the covenant ceremony in Joshua is given much more detail, but the response of King Josiah after he completed the ceremony is awarded more detail in the Kings account.

Both covenant-renewal ceremonies in Joshua take place at Shechem, and both specifically mention covenant blessings and curses. In the

---

41. Birch et al., *A Theological Introduction to the Old Testament*, 265.

42. Paul, "King Josiah's Renewal of the Covenant (2 Kgs 22–23)."

episode after the victory at Ai, Joshua builds an altar of uncut stones as prescribed in the law. He writes a copy of the law on stones in the presence of all Israel, including native-born Israelites, sojourners, women, children, elders, officers, and judges. With the ark in between two groups, the people divide themselves and stand on opposite sides: half in front of Mount Gerizim and half in front of Mount Ebal. Josh 8:34–35 say, "Afterward, Joshua read all the words of the law—the blessings and the curses—just as it is written in the Book of the Law. There was not a word of all that Moses had commanded that Joshua did not read to the whole assembly of Israel." Joshua 24 describes a similar gathering, but here Joshua utters a lengthy restatement of Israel's own history, from Abraham to their present day. He summons Israel to put away foreign gods and serve Yahweh only. The people promise to do exactly that, but Joshua, like Moses, has his own premonitions that such was not to be the case. In this context, Joshua writes the words of the law in books, not on stones, and sets up a stone under a sacred tree (Josh 24:26).[43] This stone constitutes a witness against Israel. Deuteronomic theology has now raised three sensory witnesses against Israel: the written law at Sinai, the song of Moses at Moab, and the sacred stone at Shechem.

It is unclear whether the ceremony in Joshua 4 at Gigal describes a simple memorial or a covenant-renewal ceremony. But Samuel's ritual in 1 Samuel 11–12, located at Gilgal, is clearly a covenant-renewal ceremony where the first memorial on Israelite soil originally was erected. Samuel's defensive self-interest is apparent from the beginning. He gathers all the people together and forces them to swear an oath to Yahweh that he has done nothing to abuse his office. The people obviously comply. Samuel begins his historical recital, not with Abraham but with Jacob, and continues well into the period of the judges, the context of his own time. It is now apparent that Israel has their king. Samuel applies the Deuteronomistic law of succession equally to both people and king. If Israel disobeys the voice of Yahweh, the hand of Yahweh will be against them. With a show of arrogant and defiant hostility, Samuel calls upon the thunder and rain and terrifies the people. Now they know for sure that they have rejected Yahweh by seeking a king, yet Samuel also promises that God will not forsake his people. He assures Israel that he will do two things: pray for them and instruct them in the way.

Joshua's covenant-renewal ceremonies took place at Shechem, Samuel's at Gilgal, and Josiah's at Jerusalem. The discovery of the Book of the

43. Dafni, "The Supernatural Characters and Powers of Sacred Trees."

Law in the temple spurs this last covenant-renewal ceremony. Huldah the prophetess confirms that the covenant curse looms in Israel's future, but luckily not in Josiah's time. "Because your heart was responsive and you humbled yourself before the LORD when you heard what I have spoken against this place and its people, that they would become accursed and laid waste, and because you tore your robes and wept in my presence, I have heard you, declares the LORD" (2 Kgs 22:19). Josiah's response includes activities well outside of Jerusalem as well as within the city. He burns all the vessels that were used for the worship of Baal and Asherah and deposes the priests who cared for these shrines. He blackens the Asherah poles, breaks down the houses of the cult prostitutes as well as the high places where they served. He destroys the pagan altars on the roof of the palace. He tears down the altar at Bethel and burns the bones in the tombs nearby. Finally, he slaughters the high priests serving at that shrine at Bethel. He also puts away the mediums and wizards in the land. Closer to home, he reinstitutes the Passover. The writer of Kings makes this glowing assessment of Josiah in words that directly parallel the *Shema* in Deut 6:4: "Before him there was no king like him, who turned to the LORD with all his heart and with all his soul and with all his might, according to all the Law of Moses, nor did any like him arise after him" (2 Kgs 23:25, RSV).

These covenant renewal ceremonies bear close parallels to Qumran. At Qumran, the blessings and curses in the covenant renewal ceremony of 1QS 2, 4Q280, and 4Q286–90 reflect rich intertextuality with various traditions of the Hebrew Bible, including the priestly blessing in Numbers, the blessings and curses of Leviticus and Deuteronomy, and the covenant-renewal ceremony in Joshua 24. These blessings and curses are uttered within a theatrical ritual with clearly defined elements of a processional, stylized recitation of the blessing and curse by proper leaders of the ritual, and an affirmation of acceptance by the participants by means of a self-curse or oath. This intramural event was repeated every year, probably the day of or before Shavu'ot (Weeks): "all the days of Belial's dominion," for veterans and new initiates alike (1QS 2:19–20). While the ceremony is patterned after the one at Gerazim and Ebal, the community adapted both content and form of blessings and curses to its own needs.

Several important events and individuals are conspicuously absent from these divine addresses—addresses and prayers of Israel's leaders, interpretive summaries, and covenant-renewal ceremonies. Most notable is King Saul. God does not speak to him as to David and Solomon, nor do we have any record of a lengthy address or enactment of covenant renewal.

There is also no divine address to Josiah, no lengthy speech or prayer by Josiah on behalf of the people. But perhaps the most conspicuous omission is the lack of any sustained theological reflection on the destruction of Jerusalem by King Nebuchadnezzar. Unlike the destruction of the northern kingdom, in which the narrator quite explicitly details the many shortcomings of the kingdom, things are noticeably different when the southern kingdom is destroyed. Yet, one could easily argue that the entire Deuteronomistic History is a sustained reflection on the destruction of Jerusalem.

Based on the analysis of these four sources for theological reflection (divine addresses, climactic speeches by leaders, interpretive summaries, and covenant-renewal ceremonies), a number of important themes emerge that illustrate the influence of Deuteronomic theology on the material of Joshua through Kings: evidence of Yahweh's past faithfulness, the tension between the promise of the land and the tentative nature of its possession, ambivalence to the monarchy, the promise of blessing and the threat of curse, the overriding principle that apostasy leads to devastation, and the importance of human choice. Succinctly, Joshua provides a theology of conquest, Judges a theology of *failed* conquest, Samuel and Kings the culmination of conquest. The book of Kings ends with the tiniest note of hope that the Davidic dynasty is not entirely dead. This odd ending finishes a story that comes begging for a sequel. From the perspective of the canon of the Old Testament, the end of Joshua–Kings harkens back to the end Genesis 1–11. Both units culminate in Babylon and end tragically.[44] The rhetorical power of the theme of blessing and curse drives the story of the Deuteronomist. Bernhard Anderson comments:

> Here is a history that speaks powerfully to people who have the freedom to shape their destiny, at least in some degree. Why wait until it is too late, when catastrophe falls, pitifully and ominously? The alternatives of life and death, of blessing and curse, are set before a people. Why follow national policies that are suicidal, policies that will not bring the blessing of peace but the curse of violence and warfare? The question is still relevant in out time of economic imbalances and alarm about the future of the earth. Crisis is a time of opportunity; the future is open, not fatalistically predetermined. Therefore choose life, not death.[45]

44. On the ambiguity of the ending of 2 Kings, see Janzen, "An Ambiguous Ending."
45. B. W. Anderson, *Contours of Old Testament Theology*, 167.

8

"The Sword Will Never Depart"

Saul, David, and Solomon

SAUL UNDER BLESSING ... SAUL UNDER CURSE

Is Saul among the Prophets?: The Blessing

TODAY, ON A SPUR of the Gilboa range lies Mount Shaul, the traditional location where Israel's first king, Saul, and his sons were killed in a memorable battle by the Philistines. In Arabic, the name of the mountain is *Tel Kholila*, or "Mountain of the Curse," a play on the Arabic cognate of the Hebrew word *qll*. What can we make of this strange association of Israel's first king with a curse?[1] Saul is an enormously important, yet tragic figure in the Old Testament. There are more chapters in the Bible dealing with Saul than any of the four gospel accounts of Jesus. Yet Saul is portrayed as an enigma.[2] On one hand, he is a modest, handsome, and courageous young warrior. In a reign characterized by war, he maintains a very simple court, responds quickly and fights valiantly against the Philistine threat. Yet, he has also been characterized as possessing the dangerous

---

1. Robert Polzin observes that Israelite kings are special objects of God's curse, "Curses and Kings."

2. Steven L. McKenzie said that Saul could best be described as ambivalent ("Saul in the Deuteronomistic History," 61). See also Van Seters, *In Search of History*, 250–63..

combination of driving ambition and an inferiority complex.[3] From his presumptuous sacrifice and imprudent curse on his own son to his suspicion of David, his gradual and pitiful decline is pointedly documented in 1 Samuel. His precipitous downfall and imminent doom is predicted during his covert encounter with a medium, a direct violation of his own statutes prohibiting consultation with such intermediaries. The Philistines mortally wound Saul, and he ends up taking his own life so the Philistines cannot humiliate him. Saul's death marks the sudden end of Israel's first , brief dynasty. His tragic reign is part of a larger drama, and he personally exemplifies the Bible's ambiguity about the establishment of the monarchy in Israel. In that sense, Saul functions as a paradigm for the shortcomings of the monarchy and as a portent of horrible things to come.

In spite of the biblical narrator's misgivings about the monarchy, the initial accounts of Saul's activities are essentially positive. Note that the language describing Saul's election as king is reminiscent of the language describing Israel's greatest prophet, Moses, who received the divine commission to lead Israel out of slavery in Egypt:

> Now the day before Saul came, the LORD had revealed this to Samuel: "About this time tomorrow I will send you a man from the land of Benjamin. Anoint him leader over my people Israel; he will deliver my people from the hand of the Philistines. I have looked upon my people, for their cry has reached me." (1 Sam 9:15–16)

When Samuel anoints Saul as king, his rhetorical question is loaded with promise: "Has not Yahweh anointed you a ruler over his inheritance?"(1 Sam 10:1). The narrative specifically notes Saul's imposing physical presence, yet his noble birth and heroic stature uniquely qualify him to fill the tragic role.[4] A divine assignment leads initially to divine provision. The storyteller uses two remarkably similar accounts of Saul's involvement in prophetic ecstasy to mark the divide between Saul's promising beginnings and his pitiful descent into madness. Note Samuel's instructions to Saul, below:

> After that you will go to Gibeah of God, where there is a Philistine outpost. As you approach the town, you will meet a procession of prophets coming down from the high place with lyres, tambourines, flutes and harps being played before them, and they will be prophesying. The Spirit of the LORD will come upon

3. Bright, *A History of Israel,* 191–95.
4. Humphreys, *The Tragic Vision and the Hebrew Tradition,* 38.

you in power, and you will prophesy with them; and you will be changed into a different person. Once these signs are fulfilled, do whatever your hand finds to do, for God is with you. Go down ahead of me to Gilgal. I will surely come down to you to sacrifice burnt offerings and fellowship offerings, but you must wait seven days until I come to you and tell you what you are to do. (1 Sam 10:5–8)

Like the great prophet Moses, who received power to perform prophetic signs before the Israelites and Egyptians, so Saul, Israel's first king, received power to prophesy mightily among the people:

As Saul turned to leave Samuel, God changed Saul's heart, and all these signs were fulfilled that day. When they arrived at Gibeah, a procession of prophets met him; the Spirit of God came upon him in power, and he joined in their prophesying. When all those who had formerly known him saw him prophesying with the prophets, they asked each other, "What is this that has happened to the son of Kish? Is Saul also among the prophets?" (1 Sam 10:9–11)

So drastic was this change in Saul's character that his contemporaries quipped, "Is Saul also among the prophets?" This could be merely a matter of extreme incongruity. Another way of saying it is, "What on earth is Saul doing among the prophets?"[5] Yet, there is more to this question, as it is repeated verbatim later in the narrative as an integral part of the literary design of the story. This same Spirit came upon Saul mightily early in his reign, allowing him to deliver Israel from the Ammonites and to secure initial successes against the Philistines.[6] Saul also boldly rescued the city of Jabesh-Gilead and magnanimously spared those who had earlier questioned his status as king (1 Sam 11:12). His dual status as king and prophet set him apart doubly as God's anointed: first by Samuel as a king and then by the Spirit of God as a prophet. In this case, Saul's reckoning among the prophets is an optimistic and positive sign of God's blessing. But prophesying can be an ambiguous gift, as we shall see.

---

5. Alter, *The David Story*, 56.

6. Edelman argues that Saul pretended to be a member of the prophetic guild in order to assassinate the Philistine prefect (*King Saul in the Historiography of Judah*, 993).

Is Saul among the Prophets?: The Curse

Yet this early blessing heartbreakingly transforms to a curse. Tragically, Saul is a model of human failure. Saul was a victim of both himself and Samuel. Unsupported by Samuel, fearful of the people, and eventually threatened by the popularity of David, Saul loses his influence, which slowly disintegrates into depravity. The narrative provides some early hints of Saul's disastrous end. For those familiar with the Deuteronomistic History, the story of Saul's selection as king reads remarkably like another story, but one with a completely different ending. In Joshua 7, Israel is soundly defeated at Ai after a decisive victory against Jericho. Why? An unknown perpetrator had violated the ban and stolen forbidden valuables. The story of how Achan is singled out from among the tribes as the source of all the evil that had come upon the people (Josh 7:10–26) reads remarkably like the account of the process by which Saul is selected as king,

> In the morning therefore you shall be brought near by your tribes. And the tribe that the LORD takes by lot shall come near by clans. And the clan that the LORD takes shall come near by households. And the household that the LORD takes shall come near man by man. And he who is taken with the devoted things shall be burned with fire, he and all that he has, because he has transgressed the covenant of the LORD, and because he has done an outrageous thing in Israel." So Joshua rose early in the morning and brought Israel near tribe by tribe, and the tribe of Judah was taken. And he brought near the clans of Judah, and the clan of the Zerahites was taken. And he brought near the clan of the Zerahites man by man, and Zabdi was taken. And he brought near his household man by man, and Achan the son of Carmi, son of Zabdi, son of Zerah, of the tribe of Judah, was taken. (Josh 7:14–18, ESV)

Then Samuel brought all the tribes of Israel near, and the tribe of Benjamin was taken by lot. He brought the tribe of Benjamin near by its clans, and the clan of the Matrites was taken by lot; and Saul the son of Kish was taken by lot. But when they sought him, he could not be found. So they inquired again of the LORD, "Is there a man still to come?" and the LORD said, "Behold, he has hidden himself among the baggage." Then they ran and took him from there. And when he stood among the people, he was taller than any of the people from his shoulders upward. And Samuel said to all the people, "Do you see him whom the LORD has chosen? There is none like him among all the people." And

> all the people shouted, "Long live the king!" (1 Sam 10:20–24, ESV)

No wonder Saul is found hiding in the baggage! Before David even appears on the scene, Saul makes several unfortunate decisions. His first royal acts begin in 1 Samuel 13. The Philistines assemble against Israel with three thousand chariots and six thousand charioteers and soldiers: "as numerous as the sand on the seashore." Saul had been instructed by Samuel to wait for seven days to engage the Philistines so that Samuel could offer the appropriate sacrifice prior to battle. When the appointed time had elapsed and there was no sign of Samuel, Saul saw that many of his troops were beginning to flee in fear. Taking matters into his own hands rather than waiting, he offered the sacrifice, completing it at precisely the moment when Samuel arrived. Timing is everything. Saul's presumptuous sacrifice leads to the first indication from Samuel that Saul's kingdom would not endure. Because of this infraction, Samuel charges that Saul will be replaced by a man who has God's own heart (1 Sam 13:14). But how serious was such an infraction? David Gunn has contended that Saul's culpability is more technical than anything of any real moral substance, and that his condemnation is clearly out of balance with the nature of his crimes. Rather, God is predisposed to reject him as king and chooses to find him guilty.[7] Yet, even if the reader is willing to let Saul off the hook for his initial unfortunate statesmanship in 1 Samuel 13, Saul's character gets more dubious as the story unfolds.

On the heels of Saul's fateful act, Saul's son Jonathan takes his armor bearer, enters a Philistine camp at Micmash, and single-handedly slays twenty Philistine soldiers. Panic strikes the Philistine camp, and Saul's enemies flee from Jonathan. Saul's lookouts observe all this and report to Saul that the enemy is scattering. Ignorant of what is really happening, Saul rashly proclaims a curse on any Israelite soldier who would eat before evening. Saul does this so that he can have vengeance on his enemies. Jonathan, who knows nothing of his father's curse, has stopped along the way to eat some honey and revive his strength. When Saul discovers that his own son has violated the oath, Saul surprisingly appears to be quite willing to take Jonathan's life just to honor his own foolish curse. Jonathan's comment reveals Saul's dubious character: "my father has troubled the land" by his curse (1 Sam 14:29, RSV). The Hebrew word here for

---

7. Gunn, *The Fate of King Saul*, 124. For another interpretation that the biblical portrayal of Saul is a negative distortion, see Simcha, *Saul and the Monarchy*.

"troubled" literally means to "muddy up" (Judg 11:35). Saul has mucked it up for the entire land.

> Now the Israelites were in distress that day, because Saul had bound the people under an oath, saying, "Cursed be (*'ārûwr*) any man who eats food before evening comes, before I have avenged myself on my enemies!" So none of the troops tasted food. The entire army entered the woods, and there was honey on the ground. When they went into the woods, they saw the honey oozing out, yet no one put his hand to his mouth, because they feared the oath (*haššĕbū'â*). But Jonathan had not heard that his father had bound the people with the oath (*bĕhašbîa'*) so he reached out the end of the staff that was in his hand and dipped it into the honeycomb. He raised his hand to his mouth, and his eyes brightened. Then one of the soldiers told him, "Your father bound the army under a strict oath (*hašbēa' hišbia'*), saying, 'Cursed be (*'ārûwr*) any man who eats food today!' That is why the men are faint." Jonathan said, "My father has made trouble for the country. See how my eyes brightened when I tasted a little of this honey. How much better it would have been if the men had eaten today some of the plunder they took from their enemies. Would not the slaughter of the Philistines have been even greater?" (1 Sam 14:24–30)

Yet because of the persuasive veto of the people, Saul relents from his curse. The power of the spoken word literally has no power. In the end, the people rule, not the king.[8]

The pivotal scene that ultimately leads to Yahweh's rejection of Saul is his encounter with the Amalekites and their king, Agag. According to various biblical accounts, the Amalekites were a nomadic people descended from Esau who attacked Israel when they were on their way to Sinai from Egypt. Moses ordered Joshua to go up against the Amalekites at Rephidim while he watched from the high vantage point. Exodus records that from a hilltop Moses raised his hands in intercession, gaining victory in battle (Exod 17:8–16). When Moses's hands were raised, Joshua and the Israelites would prevail. When Moses grew weary and his hands lowered, the Amalekites would prevail. Aaron and Hur held up Moses's hands until Joshua had brought about a complete victory. After the victory, Yahweh promises "to be at war against the Amalekites from generation to generation." So pronounced was this animosity between Israel and Amalek that Deuteronomy records the following:

8. Gunn, *The Fate of King Saul*, 69.

> Remember what the Amalekites did to you along the way when
> you came out of Egypt. When you were weary and worn out,
> they met you on your journey and cut off all who were lagging
> behind; they had no fear of God. When the LORD your God
> gives you rest from all the enemies around you in the land he
> is giving you to possess as an inheritance, you shall blot out the
> memory of Amalek from under heaven. Do not forget! (Deut
> 25:17–19)

This "third straw" of Saul's demise begins as he is ordered by Yahweh
to punish the Amalekites and to completely destroy everything that belongs to them. Saul is to dedicate everything to the ban and spare nothing.
While he is indeed victorious, he also spares the life of the Amalekite king.
Saul is unwilling to destroy everything but keeps the best of the calves,
lambs, sheep, and cattle for himself. Tellingly, as ancient Near Eastern
kings were prone to do after a successful battle, he also sets up a monu-
ment in his own honor. As Samuel arrives, Saul blesses him with these
words, "The LORD bless you! I have carried out the LORD's instructions"
(1 Sam 15:13). Samuel confronts Saul with his disobedience and promises
once again that Yahweh will take the kingdom from him. This time the
matter is settled. As Samuel turns to leave, Saul reaches out for the hem
of his robe and catches hold of it so that it tears. Samuel poignantly announces that as of that very day, Yahweh has torn the kingdom from Saul.

This crucial act of Saul's willful disobedience introduces a new
phase of the story, delineated by the second account of his involvement in
prophetic activity. In place of the Spirit that empowered Saul to perform
mighty accomplishments early in his reign, an evil spirit from Yahweh
now terrorizes him (1 Sam 16:14, 23; 18:10). Saul becomes a foil for the
man who is now under God's blessing: David.[9] The storyteller uses the
Goliath episode to highlight this new dichotomy between Saul and David.
Paralyzed with fear, Saul and his troops are humiliated daily by the taunt-
ing of the champion of Gath. David will have no such indecisiveness. He
takes matters into his own hands, slays Goliath, and leads Israel in triumph
over the Philistines (1 Samuel 17). What is worse, Saul seems to already
perceive that Yahweh has left him and now resides with David instead (1
Sam 18:10). This realization only aggravates Saul's hatred for David. Saul
becomes increasing irrational and insanely jealous. Tensions mount and
David must flee for his life.

---

9. Humphreys, *The Tragic Vision*, 63.

It is here that the narrator inserts the second account of Saul's prophetic activity. Like the first example, the account ends with the incredulous question, "Is Saul also among the prophets?" This doublet is no editorial slip up; it provides a strong frame for Saul's pitiful transfer from blessing to curse,

> Now David fled and escaped, and he came to Samuel at Ramah and told him all that Saul had done to him. And he and Samuel went and lived at Naioth. And it was told Saul, "Behold, David is at Naioth in Ramah." Then Saul sent messengers to take David, and when they saw the company of the prophets prophesying, and Samuel standing as head over them, the Spirit of God came upon the messengers of Saul, and they also prophesied. When it was told Saul, he sent other messengers, and they also prophesied. And Saul sent messengers again the third time, and they also prophesied. Then he himself went to Ramah and came to the great well that is in Secu. And he asked, "Where are Samuel and David?" And one said, "Behold, they are at Naioth in Ramah." And he went there to Naioth in Ramah. And the Spirit of God came upon him also, and as he went he prophesied until he came to Naioth in Ramah. And he too stripped off his clothes, and he too prophesied before Samuel and lay naked all that day and all that night. Thus it is said, "Is Saul also among the prophets?" (1 Sam 19:18–24, ESV)

The tables have turned. The concluding question, "Is Saul among the prophets?" implies a completely negative depiction of Saul. The episode's setting is clear. Saul is out to kill David. He hears the whereabouts of this renegade and sends his men to capture him. Ironically, the prophet Samuel, who had originally anointed Saul, has now been engaged in helping Saul's enemy. Samuel has already anointed David as the new king. In his last encounter between Saul and his mentor, the storyteller reveals that Samuel will never see Saul's face again (1 Sam 15:35). Yet, here Samuel is standing among these prophets as Saul's men approach. The 3+1 model is similar to the Balaam pronouncement of blessing in Numbers 22–24, where three attempts at cursing are foiled by God's blessing. Balaam adds a fourth unsolicited curse-utterance against Moab. Similarly, three times Saul's men approach the prophets, and in all three cases, they are swept up in the prophetic frenzy. Finally, Saul himself goes to see things with his own eyes. The spirit of prophecy that marked out his election as king now serves a completely different purpose. There is no question that Saul's prophecy is evaluated negatively by the storyteller.[10] In Samuel's very presence Saul prophesies, rips off his clothes, and lies naked. The symbolism of his nakedness has implications for the monarchy: Saul divests himself of the kingship as he divests himself of his clothing.[11] The question of the people, "Is Saul also among the prophets?" is a sarcastic, derogatory taunt. Now Saul, no longer empowered with the divine Spirit, becomes a "self-lacerating, babbling, whirling exhibitionist."[12]

The end for Saul is now only a matter of time. It is not enough that Samuel is engaged in helping Saul's enemy; his own son Jonathan also participates in aiding David to escape (1 Sam 20:13). Paranoia increases, Saul accuses the priests of Nob of treason (1 Sam 22:6–23) and orders the execution of their whole lot. David now retreats into the Judean wilderness, but the tables have already turned. In 1 Samuel 24–25, Saul is now the one who is vulnerable and at David's mercy. The roles of pursued and pursuer are reversed. David has two opportunities to kill Saul but chooses not to. Saul momentarily expresses his regret and acknowledges that he has wronged David, but in the end there has been no genuine change. Saul even implies that he is completely aware that David will be the king (1 Sam 24:20, 26:25). Nabal's curses (*brk*!) are a mere bump along the road to David's greatness, and serve only to enhance David's stature and lead to Saul's own demise (1 Sam 25:14).

The final dialogues between Saul and David, in 1 Sam 26:17–25 represent Saul as cursed, while David is blessed,[13]

> Saul recognized David's voice and said, "Is that your voice, David my son?"
>
> David replied, "Yes it is, my lord the king." And he added, "Why is my lord pursuing his servant? What have I done, and what wrong am I guilty of? Now let my lord the king listen to his servant's words. If the Lord has incited you against me, then may he accept an offering. If, however, men have done it, may they be cursed (*'arûrîm*) before the LORD! They have now driven me from my share in the Lord's inheritance and have said, 'Go, serve other gods.' Now do not let my blood fall to the ground far from the presence of the LORD. The king of Israel has come out

10. Wilson, "Prophecy and Ecstasy."

11. Perry includes a chapter, "On Proverb Formation: Is Saul Too among the Prophets?," that grapples with the change in Saul's character (*God's Twilight Zone*, 77–91).

12. Mobley, "Glimpses of the Heroic Saul," 86.

13. Carlson, *David, the Chosen King*, 47.

to look for a flea—as one hunts a partridge in the mountains." Then Saul said, "I have sinned. Come back, David my son. Because you considered my life precious today, I will not try to harm you again. Surely I have acted like a fool and have erred greatly." "Here is the king's spear," David answered. "Let one of your young men come over and get it. The LORD rewards every man for his righteousness and faithfulness. The LORD delivered you into my hands today, but I would not lay a hand on the LORD's anointed. As surely as I valued your life today, so may the LORD value my life and deliver me from all trouble." Then Saul said to David, "May you be blessed (*brk*), my son David; you will do great things and surely triumph." So David went on his way, and Saul returned home. (1 Sam 26:17–25)

After this encounter, the narrator escalates Saul's demise. Every deed is a mockery of his intentions, as he struggles with the foreknowledge that he is a dead man, and consults a medium at Endor. In this interaction Yahweh is completely silent, so Saul must bring up Samuel from the dead for help. The story of the encounter with the medium is a lesson about someone driven to something he once despised as evil. Saul had already banished all mediums from Israel, yet he himself resorts to one in his own time of peril. While desperation can at times be a powerful positive force, desperation can also drive people to do things that they themselves find appalling and would never have dreamed of even considering under other circumstances. Later, Saul's mortal wound in battle and subsequent suicide bring his tragic story to a tragic end. In his death is the stench of curse (Deut 21:23). The story takes a final, ironic twist: While alive, Saul had exposed himself under prophetic impulse; in death, his headless body and those of his sons are exposed—fastened to the wall—at Beth Shean (1 Sam 31:10).

DAVID UNDER BLESSING, DAVID UNDER CURSE

Nathan's Blessing

During Saul's last direct exchange with David, Israel's first king says, "May you be blessed (*bārûk*), my son David; you will do great things and surely triumph" (1 Sam 26:25). This is an understatement. It is difficult to underestimate the significance of this man who would eventually be Israel's second king. He came to be known as the greatest of Israel's kings, as he took a small people and made it a world power. Under David's leadership

Israel for the first time secures rest from all enemies. A great leader with a tremendous ability to inspire loyalty, a talented musician and gifted poet, David ushers in the golden age of Israel's history. His ascension to power has an earthiness reminiscent of an Abraham Lincoln. Born in obscurity as the youngest of seven sons, he was among the least likely to ascend to greatness. This pattern of the older serving the younger has already been repeated many times in the Old Testament: Isaac and Ishmael, Jacob and Esau, Joseph and his brothers. Samuel anoints David secretly as king before anyone in Israel really knows anything about him. He first makes a name for himself through his heroic defeat of the Philistine's great warrior, Goliath. With only a sling and a few stones David brings victory to the entire house of Israel. This act is witnessed by the armies of friend and foe alike, right under the nose of Saul. Saul almost immediately becomes jealous of David's instant popularity and begins to seek ways to remove him. Saul even provided his daughters Merab and Michal in marriage to David, thinking they would be a snare and draw the ire of the Philistines (1 Sam 18:17–29). The bride price—foreskins of one hundred Philistine warriors—clearly reveals Saul's motives. David's intimate friendship with Saul's son Jonathan, the heir, only adds fuel to the fire. Twice, Jonathan alone rescues David from certain death. Jonathan's gift of his robe and armor to David symbolize that Jonathan understands the inevitable; David will be the next king.

David ultimately has to flee for his own life from Saul. Joined by other outcasts, he becomes a roving fugitive, living in the desert of Judea and even among the Philistines, as Saul tries to eliminate him. On two occasions David spares Saul's life. These two acts are not only signs of respect for the current king but also an unmistakable message to his own supporters about the importance of unflinching loyalty to the monarchy. Saul, on the other hand, relentlessly pursues David, dissuaded only briefly by David's acts of mercy. The Deuteronomistic author goes out of the way to defend David from the accusation that he has wrested control of the throne from Saul by surreptitious means.

After the death of Saul and Jonathan, David reigns for two years in Hebron over Judah alone as he waits for those loyal to him to eliminate Ish-Bosheth, Saul's son and the rightful heir of the throne. After the death of Ish-Bosheth, David continues to reign in Hebron for five more years over all Israel. It was only after seven years that he captures the Jebusite fortress in Jerusalem and makes it his capital. Centrally located, heavily fortified, and possessing plenty of water, Jerusalem was an excellent choice for the new king's capital. (Interesting is that the first mention of Jerusalem outside the Bible is from an Egyptian execration text from Sakkara Egypt, dated to the eighteenth century BCE. It is intriguing that the first mention of Jerusalem—Rusalimum—comes in a curse.) Nevertheless, it is in this city that Yahweh makes a covenant with David; his descendants will always be on the throne. This covenant is one of the most prominent in the Old Testament, and has attracted attention of students of the Old and New Testaments alike. The claim of royal theology that God has chosen David as his permanent agent for the exercise of divine rule on earth directly leads to later developments of the messianic hope.[14] The promise to David is quite a contrast to the view of the monarchy described in 1 Samuel 8, where Samuel unveils the dangers of having a king as all the peoples do. Samuel warns that all kinds of personal and civil liberties will be forever lost if Israel goes the route of establishing an empire. In spite of the warnings about the abuses of the monarchy, David appears unaware and uninvolved in all kinds of extraordinary deaths that happen to those around him.[15]

The story of David's blessing and curse is told by means of two messages that the prophet Nathan receives from God and announces to David. In 2 Samuel 7, David informs Nathan of his plan to build a house for Yahweh. At first, Nathan appears to be happy with this plan. But he receives a word from Yahweh to the contrary. It is Yahweh who will build a house for David, not the other way around. The language of Nathan's message here is remarkably similar to God's promise to Abram in Genesis 12, "Now I will make your name great, like the names of the greatest men on earth" (2 Sam 7:9).[16] The promise that follows is one of the most central texts in all of Judaism and Christianity.

> Moreover, the LORD declares to you that the LORD will make you a house. When your days are fulfilled and you lie down with your fathers, I will raise up your offspring after you, who shall come from your body, and I will establish his kingdom. He shall build a house for my name, and I will establish the throne of his kingdom forever. I will be to him a father, and he shall be to me a son. When he commits iniquity, I will discipline him with the rod of men, with the stripes of the sons of men, but my steadfast love will not depart from him, as I took it from Saul, whom I put

14. Roberts, *The Bible and the Ancient Near East*, 361.

15. Halpern, *David's Secret Demons*; McKenzie, *King David: A Biography*.

16. Kaiser drew together a list of eight connections between the blessing of Abraham and the blessing of David; *Toward an Old Testament Theology*, 153.

> away from before you. And your house and your kingdom shall be made sure forever before me. Your throne shall be established forever." In accordance with all these words, and in accordance with all this vision, Nathan spoke to David. (2 Sam 7:11b–17, ESV)

Note the double theme of Yahweh's house and David's house raised by the narrative. The Lord promises that one of David's own offspring will succeed him and build a house for Yahweh's name.[17] This is no pre-Solomonic antitemple ideology but indicates a bit of presumption on David's part that he will be the one to build a temple for the Lord. Yahweh's promise to David is a promise about both houses. When the temple will be built, it will be more than a token of God's indwelling among his people, but will signal a divine underwriting of David's house, the Davidic dynasty.[18] There will be periods of fidelity and infidelity on the part of Israel's leaders, but this covenant promises that God's love will never depart as it had in the case of Saul. David's house will be established forever (*ʿabdĕkā lĕʿôlām*). Second Samuel 7:25–29 (cf. 1 Chr 17:27) is an equally important text.

> And now, LORD God, keep forever the promise you have made concerning your servant and his house. Do as you promised, so that your name will be great forever. Then men will say, "The LORD Almighty is God over Israel!" And the house of your servant David will be established before you. "O LORD Almighty, God of Israel, you have revealed this to your servant, saying, 'I will build a house for you.' So your servant has found courage to offer you this prayer. O Sovereign LORD, you are God! Your words are trustworthy, and you have promised these good things to your servant. Now be pleased to bless(*ûbārēk*) the house of your servant, that it may continue forever in your sight; for you, O Sovereign LORD, have spoken, and with your blessing (*ûmibbirkātkā yĕbōrak*) the house of your servant will be blessed (*mwbr ŝtk ybrk*) forever." (2 Sam 7:25–29)

Yahweh's promise to David is phrased in the language of blessing. The word *to bless* is found three times in the final sentence. The house that God promises to build for David refers to a lasting dynasty, where a descendant would be on the throne forever.[19] This term occurs seven times in 1 Samuel chapter 7. The kingdom will continue in perpetuity. This

17. Schniedewind, *Society and the Promise to David*, 35.

18. Alter, *The David Story*, 232.

19. Levenson, "The Davidic Covenant and Its Modern Interpreters."

sentiment represents quite a change from the strong reluctance of Samuel to the very idea of the monarchy. The chapters that follow portray David as a man who can do no wrong. Second Samuel 8 recounts list after list of David's victories over the peoples around him. David reigns over all Israel and "administers justice and equity to all his people" (2 Sam 8:15). David restores broken relationships with Saul's family and subjugates the Ammonites and Syrians to his popular rule (2 Samuel 9). There is seemingly no stopping him . . . or is there?[20]

Nathan's Curse

R. A. Carlson's classic traditio-historical study on the life of David divides the reign of this great king in to two periods: David under the blessing and David under the curse.[21] In spite of David's widespread popularity and wide-scale successes, the inescapable fact is that the so-called Deuteronomistic Historian interprets the fundamental character of the monarchy as apostasy from Yahweh. This narrator lays the blame for the destruction of the kingdom at the feet of the kings (2 Kgs 17:7ff.). David is no exception.[22] The watershed event in David's reign is his adulterous affair with Bathsheba and the murder of her husband Uriah (2 Samuel 11). These two flagrant sins were intentional, calculated, cold-blooded acts of a despot with unlimited power . . . almost. David is confronted with his sin by the prophet Nathan, who delivers confrontation and condemnation in equal measure. But he also delivers more . . . a curse. Nathan's role is absolutely instrumental in both the promise of the eternal covenant and the curse that the sword will never depart from David's house. In the first instance of Nathan's message to David, mentioned above, the word of the Lord comes to Nathan at night with the instructions to relay to David the promise of the eternal covenant. Nathan is the immediate messenger of the blessing-promise. Likewise, the Lord now sends Nathan to David after Uriah's death with the following message of divine displeasure:

> Nathan said to David, "You are the man! Thus says the Lord, the God of Israel, 'I anointed you king over Israel, and I delivered you out of the hand of Saul. And I gave you your master's house and your master's wives into your arms and gave you the

20. See Linafelt et al., *The Fate of King David*.

21. Carlson, *David, the Chosen King*.

22. Van Seters observes that the biblical portrayal of David as a model king is hardly uniform; "David: Messianic King of Mercenary Ruler?"

house of Israel and of Judah. And if this were too little, I would add to you as much more. Why have you despised the word of the LORD, to do what is evil in his sight? You have struck down Uriah the Hittite with the sword and have taken his wife to be your wife and have killed him with the sword of the Ammonites. Now therefore the sword shall never depart from your house, because you have despised me and have taken the wife of Uriah the Hittite to be your wife.' Thus says the Lord, 'Behold, I will raise up evil against you out of your own house. And I will take your wives before your eyes and give them to your neighbor, and he shall lie with your wives in the sight of this sun. For you did it secretly, but I will do this thing before all Israel and before the sun.'" (2 Sam 12:7–12 ESV)

Note the paralleled contrast between Nathan's first message and his second: "my mercy will not depart (*lō' āsûr*) from him" (2 Sam 7:15), and "the sword will not depart (*lō' āsûr*) from your house" (2 Sam 12:10). The sword curse corresponds as the antithesis to the mercy blessing. David's callous reply to Joab after his general confirms that Uriah was indeed dead is, "the sword devours one as well as another" (2 Sam 11:25). This cold remark is thrown back in David's face: "the sword will never depart . . ."

The later part of David's reign basically amounts to a series of personal catastrophes—the consequences of stereotyped curses.[23] The episode with Bathsheba inaugurates a pattern of cause and effect that is thoroughly Deuteronomstic and continues not only through David's life but throughout the reigns of the subsequent kings of Judah.[24] Volumes have been written on Nathan's Davidic blessing covenant of 2 Samuel 7, but interpreters have been less captivated with Nathan's curse in 2 Samuel 12. To be blunt, the Deuteronomist appears to be as interested in cursing David's dynasty as in blessing it.[25] The charge "indeed you did it secretly, but I will do this thing before all Israel, and under the sun" is reminiscent of Deut 27:24: "Cursed is the man who kills his neighbor secretly." The sword curse leads to an extended chain of misfortunes: the unnatural death of four sons; the revolts of Absalom, Sheba, and Adonijah; the rape of David's own concubines in broad daylight; famine and pestilence; and the curse of Shimei. Whatever the meaning of God's eternal covenant with David, these misfortunes are all remarkably synonymous to the maladictory triad of sword, famine, and pestilence in Deuteronomy 28:15ff.

23. Lamb cites seven Deuteronomic prophecies of judgment against the house of David in "The Eternal Curse," 325.

24. Carlson, *David, the Chosen King*, 25.

25. Lamb, "The Eternal Curse," 317.

At the height of David's troubles within his own family, he is forced to flee Jerusalem to escape from his very own son, Absalom.[26] This episode reads like an account of a group of exiles marching away from their homeland. The narrative slows to a snail's pace. Second Samuel 16 is an account of David's exchanges with the last remnants of Saul's household. Earlier in his reign, David had looked for survivors from the house of Saul so he could show them kindness for Jonathan's sake (2 Sam 9:1–2). Mephibosheth, son of Jonathan, was lame in both feet. In an act of kindness to honor Jonathan, David brought Mephibosheth to his own table, where he would eat like one of the kings own sons. The story concludes: "Mephibosheth lived in Jerusalem, for he ate always at the king's table." In the follow up account in 2 Samuel 16, David has just fled the city and crossed the Kidron. He is met along the way by Ziba, servant of Mephibosheth. Ziba has two donkeys saddled with supplies for David and his entourage. Ziba, however, has lied to David and said that Mephibosheth remained in Jerusalem in hopes of receiving back the kingdom that had belonged to his grandfather Saul. David consequently gives title of everything he had given Mephibosheth to his servant Ziba. As David continues, another family member from Saul's household approaches David with a string of vehement curses:

> As King David approached Bahurim, a man from the same clan as Saul's family came out from there. His name was Shimei son of Gera, and he cursed (*wmqll*) as he came out. He pelted David and all the king's officials with stones, though all the troops and the special guard were on David's right and left. As he cursed (*bqllw*), Shimei said, "Get out, get out, you man of blood, you scoundrel! The LORD has repaid you for all the blood you shed in the household of Saul, in whose place you have reigned. The LORD has handed the kingdom over to your son Absalom. You have come to ruin because you are a murderer!" Then Abishai son of Zeruiah said to the king, "Why should this dead dog curse (*yĕqallēl*) my lord the king? Let me go over and cut off his head." But the king said, "What does this have to do with you, you sons of Zeruiah? If he is cursing (*yĕqallēl*) because the LORD said to him, 'Curse (*qallēl*) David,' who can ask, 'Why do you do this?'" David then said to Abishai and all his officials, "My son, who is of my own flesh, is trying to kill me. How much more,

26. See Polzin's discussion of David's flight from Jerusalem and the observation that David was one of the favorite targets of curses by several individuals: Goliath (1 Sam 17:43), Michal (2 Sam 6:22), and Shimei (2 Sam 16:5–13); Polzin, "Curses and Kings," 213–26.

> then, this Benjamite! Leave him alone; let him curse (*wîqallēl*), for the LORD has told him to. It may be that the Lord will look upon my misery and restore to me his covenant blessing instead of his curse (*qillātô*) today." (2 Sam 16:5–12)

There are two accounts of David's relationship with the house of Saul in 2 Samuel. (The literary barrier between these two accounts is the Bathsheba episode.) The context of this particular, second episode reads like an account of exile. Exile and curse join in Old Testament theology. In spite of this vehement rhetoric, there is a certain passivity to David's response.[27] He doesn't even deny the validity of the curse. Now is not the time for David to take vengeance on Shimei's hostility, but the time will come. A ruler's last recorded words are important, and David's last words are his instructions to Solomon to take vengeance against Shimei for his insolent curses. One of Solomon's first acts is to abide by David's last words and have Shimei killed, but with Solomon's own twist on blessing theology: "The king also said to Shimei, 'You know in your heart all the wrong you did to my father David. Now the LORD will repay you for your wrongdoing. But King Solomon will be blessed, and David's throne will remain secure before the Lord forever'" (1 Kings 2:44–45).

Solomon Under Blessing, Solomon Under Curse

Solomon under Blessing (1 Kings 1–8)

Unlike David, Solomon does not rise from anonymity to become the king of Israel. And also unlike David, he has rest from his enemies throughout his entire reign. The writer of the book of Kings summarizes the early years of Solomon's reign with pleasure: "Judah and Israel were as numerous as the sand on the sea; they ate and drank and were happy (1 Kgs 4:20, RSV). Yet Solomon's name is conspicuously absent from the list of Israel's good kings in the apocryphal book written by Jesus ben-Sirach around 200 BCE (Sir 49:4). Some of the possible reasons for that omission will be explored below by reviewing the Deuteronomistic account of Solomonic sovereignty. His reign can be surveyed under four themes: his consolidation of power, his foreign policy, his domestic agenda, and the burden of the monarchy.

---

27. Fokkelman, *King David*, 201.

When David died, for a brief period of time Israel wavered between two potential successors to Israel's most popular king: Adonijah and Solomon. Adonijah, the elder brother of Solomon, had the support of David's selfless general, Joab, as well as his high priest Abiathar. Solomon, on the other hand, had the support of his mother, Bathsheba, and Nathan, the southern prophet who had confronted David after the king's illicit sexual liaison with Bathsheba. Bathsheba and Nathan persuaded David to produce some visible demonstration that Solomon was his chosen successor. David had his own mule prepared for Solomon to ride in a showy inaugural procession down to Gihon to be anointed king by Nathan the prophet and another priest, Zadok. The opening chapters of Kings describe how Solomon consolidates his throne by murdering his rival Adonijah (1 Kgs 2:25), as well as David's faithful general Joab (1 Kgs 2:34). Not wanting to murder a high priest, he banishes Abiathar to the village of Anathoth in Judah. He restricts Shimei, the sole remaining descendant of Saul, to Jerusalem and later kills him.

Free from the burden of warfare, Solomon could turn his attentions to pursuing his international and domestic agendas. Solomon's foreign policy was characterized by prolific reinforcement of domestic defenses, and establishing and strengthening foreign alliances by marrying the daughters of foreign leaders. He fortified many cities (1 Kgs 9:15), expanded the cavalry and chariot base (1 Kgs 10:26), and even established a navy for the first time in Israel's history at Ezion-Geber (1 Kgs 9:26). Through intermarriage, he established foreign alliances with Egypt (1 Kgs 3:1), Tyre (1 Kgs 5:11), as well as several other countries (1 Kgs 11:1).[28]

At home, Solomon astutely created a way of emasculating old tribal loyalties and consolidating state power. He carved Israel into twelve administrative districts (1 Kgs 4:1–19) along lines quite different from the borders of the traditional twelve tribes. Each of these administrative districts provided revenue and labor for Solomon's enterprises for one month out of each year. This new political structure supplied needed capital and centralizes the political structure by removing the geopolitical barriers based on tribal loyalties. Interestingly, his tribe, Judah, was not included as one of the twelve administrative districts that provided revenue for the empire. This undoubtedly led to tensions between north and south. The book of Kings records the extravagances of Solomon's palace needs.

28. Such is the view of the biblical historian. For the current state of Solomonic research, see Handy, ed., *The Age of Solomon.*

> Judah and Israel were as many as the sand by the sea. They ate and drank and were happy. Solomon ruled over all the kingdoms from the Euphrates to the land of the Philistines and to the border of Egypt. They brought tribute and served Solomon all the days of his life. Solomon's provision for one day was thirty cors of fine flour and sixty cors of meal, ten fat oxen, and twenty pasture-fed cattle, a hundred sheep, besides deer, gazelles, roebucks, and fattened fowl. For he had dominion over all the region west of the Euphrates from Tiphsah to Gaza, over all the kings west of the Euphrates. And he had peace on all sides around him. (1 Kgs 4:20–24, ESV)

Such extravagance carried with it the burdensome consequences of supporting such a lavish lifestyle.

Solomon entered into many business enterprises to develop and diversify his kingdom's economy. He established horse-and-chariot trades and solidified control of the trade routes that passed through Israel. He commissioned a fleet of ships and developed copper mines. Because Solomon was not distracted by warfare, he is able to devote most of his energies to major building projects such as fortifying the major cities of Israel, stables for his chariot army, and most important a permanent temple in Jerusalem. The writer of Chronicles mentions that David had wished to build this temple, but was not allowed to because he was a man of warfare (1 Chr 22:6–10). David did, however, establish the original site for the temple at the threshing floor at Araunah, where today the Dome of the Rock—the second-most sacred shrine to Muslims—stands upon the platform of Harem es-Sharif. But David went no further than that, other than to procure finely hewn ashlar masonry to be used in the construction. To date, there are no archaeological remains of the Solomonic temple, but examples of this masonry can be found at Megiddo, Hazor, Gezer, and elsewhere in Israel. Such construction is typical of royal building projects. The construction of the temple began in the fourth year of Solomon's reign (1 Kgs 6:1) and took seven years to complete.

Solomon called on one of his important political allies, Phoenicia, to provide workers and timber for the seven-year temple project. Hiram of Tyre, a Phoenician artisan, furnished the bronzework for the temple (1 Kgs 7:13–47). The Phoenicians also provided much of the gold used to overlay the magnificent vessels and furnishings of the temple. Israel provided their own stoneworkers for the project (1 Kgs 5:15–18). The book of Kings describes the phases of construction in great detail. Finally, the project was complete. Solomon assembled all the elders of Israel and heads of all the tribes, brought the ark into the temple, sacrificing many sheep and oxen along the way. Solomon blessed Yahweh (1 Kgs 8:14–15), acknowledging that God has been faithful to fulfill his promise to David that a son would complete a house for the name of the Lord. The three prayers of Solomon (1 Kgs 8:15–21, 23–53, 56–61) constitute a pastiche of blessing promises from the Torah,

> As for the foreigner who does not belong to your people Israel but has come from a distant land because of your name—for they will hear of your great name and your mighty hand and your outstretched arm—when he comes and prays toward this temple, then hear from heaven, your dwelling place, and do whatever the foreigner asks of you, so that all the peoples of the earth may know your name and fear you, as do your own people Israel, and may know that this house I have built bears your Name. (1 Kgs 8:41–43)

> He stood and blessed (*wybrk*) the whole assembly of Israel in a loud voice, saying,

> "Praise be (*brwk*) to the LORD, who has given rest to his people Israel just as he promised. Not one word has failed of all the good promises he gave through his servant Moses. (1 Kgs 8:55–56)

> . . . so that all the peoples of the earth may know that the LORD is God and that there is no other. But your hearts must be fully committed to the LORD our God, to live by his decrees and obey his commands, as at this time." (1 Kgs 8:60–61)

The blessing in 1 Kings 8 affirms that God had fulfilled all the promises made to Moses, and these blessings extend not only to Israel but to all the peoples on earth. The rest that Yahweh had given alludes to the language of Deut 12:9 and Josh 21:45, where the themes of rest and God's chosen place are brought together.[29] First Kings 8 is truly the high point of Solomon's role as Israel's second king.

Solomon under Curse (1 Kings 9–11)

Doublets in the stories of Saul, David, and Solomon delineate the positive and negative characteristics of the reigns of the kings of the united monarchy. Saul's two encounters with a prophetic band in 1 Samuel 10 and 19 conclude with the question, "Is Saul also among the prophets?" The first

---

29. McCarter, *II Samuel*, 204.

time this question is asked, it is a wholly positive reflection on Saul. The second time the question comes up, it is patently negative. In David's case, Yahweh visits Nathan twice and sends him on missions with messages to David in 2 Samuel 7 and 12. In 2 Samuel 7, Nathan informs David that his son will be the one to build a temple for Yahweh, and that David's dynasty will be marked by the grace and favor of God eternally. After David's sin with Bathsheba and the subsequent murder of her husband, Uriah, Nathan confronts David with his sin and announces the curse that the sword will never depart from his house. In the case of Solomon, the Lord appears to Solomon on only two specific occasions. In 1 Kings 3:13, Yahweh promises to award Solomon with a wise and discerning heart, riches and honor, and (with qualification) a long life. In 1 Kings 9 Yahweh appears to Solomon a second time (1 Kgs 9:2) with a rather different take: a deconstruction, if you will, of the unconditional covenant to David,

> And as for you, if you will walk before me, as David your father walked, with integrity of heart and uprightness, doing according to all that I have commanded you, and keeping my statutes and my rules, then I will establish your royal throne over Israel forever, as I promised David your father, saying, "You shall not lack a man on the throne of Israel." But if you turn aside from following me, you or your children, and do not keep my commandments and my statutes that I have set before you, but go and serve other gods and worship them, then I will cut off Israel from the land that I have given them, and the house that I have consecrated for my name I will cast out of my sight, and Israel will become a proverb and a byword among all peoples. And this house will become a heap of ruins. Everyone passing by it will be astonished and will hiss, and they will say, "Why has the Lord done thus to this land and to this house?" Then they will say, "Because they abandoned the Lord their God who brought their fathers out of the land of Egypt and laid hold on other gods and worshiped them and served them. Therefore the Lord has brought all this disaster on them." (1 Kgs 9:4–9, ESV)

The promise begins similarly to the covenant given to David. But the second appearance of Yahweh to Solomon is patently conditional. If he or his sons turn away from Yahweh, Israel will be cut off from the land and the temple rejected. In the language of the Deuteronomic curses, Israel will become "a byword, an object of ridicule among all peoples" (Deut 28:37). In a negative twist on the Abrahamic blessing, all the peoples on earth will observe with their own eyes the horrors that happen to Israel.

By metonymy, Israel is not only cursed, but becomes a curse and object of ridicule among all peoples.

Immediately after Yahweh's second appearance to Solomon, 1 Kings 9 hints that things are beginning to unravel. Solomon's longtime ally, Hiram is finally paid for the cedar and cypress timber and gold that he supplied Solomon for the construction projects of temple and palace. Solomon gave him twenty cities in the Galilee. Hiram is not impressed. Unhappy with the land Solomon had given him, he derogatorily calls his payment the land of Cabul.[30] First Kings 9 also gives an account of the forced labor Solomon required for all his building projects. Not surprisingly, along with all these advances came the burden of the monarchy. This monumental construction activity led to heavy taxation of the people (1 Kgs 4:7). Over thirty thousand laborers assisted with these projects (1 Kgs 5:13). Those from the northern tribes bore the brunt of economic and labor support for these projects. Given Israel's painful history as slaves, this practice could only be seen as oppressive, especially to those from the north. Deuteronomy's warning about the monarchy has clear parallels to Solomon's excesses:

> You may indeed set a king over you whom the LORD your God will choose. One from among your brothers you shall set as king over you. You may not put a foreigner over you, who is not your brother. 16 Only he must not acquire many horses for himself or cause the people to return to Egypt in order to acquire many horses, since the Lord has said to you, 'You shall never return that way again.' 17 And he shall not acquire many wives for himself, lest his heart turn away, nor shall he acquire for himself excessive silver and gold. (Deut 17:15–17, ESV)

The sheer numbers of these excesses are staggering. The book of Kings records that Solomon had forty thousand stalls of horses for his chariots and twelve thousand horsemen. He also had a harem of seven hundred princesses and three hundred concubines.

The visit of the queen of Sheba provides another opportunity for an accounting of Solomon's wisdom and wealth. Her words are a blessing of the Lord:

> How happy your people must be! How happy your officials, who continually stand before you and hear your wisdom! Praise (*brk*) be to the LORD your God, who has delighted in you and placed you on the throne of Israel. Because of the LORD's eternal

30. Josephus (*Ant.* 8.142) interpreted this as "The land of good for nothing."

> love for Israel, he has made you king, to maintain justice and
> righteousness."
>
> And she gave the king 120 talents of gold, large quantities
> of spices, and precious stones. Never again were so many spices
> brought in as those the queen of Sheba gave to King Solomon.
> (1 Kgs 10:8–10)

The queen of Sheba gives Solomon the same amount given to him by
Hiram (1 Kgs 9:14). Yet a rather cryptic and guarded gift from Solomon
rebounds back to the queen: "King Solomon gave the queen of Sheba all
she desired and asked for, besides what he had given her out of his royal
bounty. Then she left and returned with her retinue to her own country"
(1 Kgs 10:13).

Religious apostasy (1 Kgs 11:1ff.) was also a part of the burden of the
monarchy. While Solomon's regression is hinted at after 1 Kings 9, 1 Kgs
11:1–4 marks the real transition to Solomon's apostasy. George Mendenhall comments that the reversion to ancient paganism reaches its climax
in the reign of Solomon.[31] As Solomon entered into alliances with other
kingdoms, he married wives of other leaders and took many concubines
into his palace. This recalls the prohibition in Deut 7:3 not to intermarry
with the indigenous inhabitants of Canaan, as well as parallels to Joshua's
farewell speech in Josh 23:2–16.[32]

> But if you turn away and ally yourselves with the survivors of
> these nations that remain among you and if you intermarry with
> them and associate with them, then you may be sure that the
> LORD your God will no longer drive out these nations before
> you. Instead, they will become snares and traps for you, whips
> on your backs and thorns in your eyes, until you perish from
> this good land, which the Lord your God has given you. (Josh
> 23:12–13)

In addition to the temple, Solomon erected many other pagan temples
and shrines for his wives. Neh 13:26–27 condemn Solomon's intermarriage with foreign women:

> Was it not because of marriages like these that Solomon king of
> Israel sinned? Among the many nations there was no king like
> him. He was loved by his God, and God made him king over all
> Israel, but even he was led into sin by foreign women. Must we

31. Mendenhall, *The Tenth Generation*, xiv.
32. Knoppers, "Solomon's Fall and Deuteronomy."

hear now that you too are doing all this terrible wickedness and are being unfaithful to our God by marrying foreign women?

Walter Brueggemann noted three dimensions of Solomonic achievement: well being and affluence not democratically shared, an oppressive social policy that produced social stratification, and static religion where the sovereignty of God was subordinated to the purpose of the king.[33] Solomon's fiscal policies deprived the people, and in many ways he became a despot just like the leaders of all the other kingdoms. Instead of modeling practices unique among the kingdoms of the world, Israel's king established practices that mirrored the other kingdoms of the ancient Near East. While Solomon was alive, his absolute power was able to keep resistance at bay, but immediately after his death, the oppression of his reign birthed open revolt. First Kings 11:9 specifically mentions the two earlier divine appearances to Solomon. In this final account, God speaks but does not appear to Solomon,

> So the Lord said to Solomon, "Since this is your attitude and you have not kept my covenant and my decrees, which I commanded you, I will most certainly tear the kingdom away from you and give it to one of your subordinates. Nevertheless, for the sake of David your father, I will not do it during your lifetime. I will tear it out of the hand of your son. Yet I will not tear the whole kingdom from him, but will give him one tribe for the sake of David my servant and for the sake of Jerusalem, which I have chosen." (1 Kgs 11:11–13)

Furthermore, there is an explicit biblical connection between Solomon's sins in the tenth century BCE and Josiah's reforms in the seventh century.[34]

> [Josiah] pulled down the altars the kings of Judah had erected on the roof near the upper room of Ahaz, and the altars Manasseh had built in the two courts of the temple of the Lord. He removed them from there, smashed them to pieces and threw the rubble into the Kidron Valley. The king also desecrated the high places that were east of Jerusalem on the south of the Hill of Corruption—the ones Solomon king of Israel had built for Ashtoreth the vile goddess of the Sidonians, for Chemosh the vile god of Moab, and for Molech the detestable god of the people of Ammon. Josiah smashed the sacred stones and cut down the

---

33. Brueggemann, *The Prophetic Imagination*, 24.
34. Knoppers, "Solomon's Fall and Deuteronomy," 408.

Asherah poles and covered the sites with human bones. (2 Kgs
23:12–14)

Cuius regio, eius religio. This medieval slogan "whose rule, his religion" speaks to the power of a king in setting the religious direction for the
entire kingdom. Such was true in the case of Solomon.[35] Solomon's sins ultimately brought desolation and curse to his kingdom. A close reading of
the biblical narrative about the lives of Saul, David, and Solomon reveals
a profound ambiguity toward the monarchy. On one hand, this period
of a little over a century represents the only time in the entire historical
metanarrative of Israel when there was a single king reigning independ-
ently and freely over the entire people. Even though the promises to the
ancestors never mention a king, the territories governed by David and
Solomon, as well as by several later kings, approach those geographical
boundaries promised to Israel in the wilderness. Yet in the lives of these
three early leaders of Israel is a conspicuous and troubling pattern. All
three leaders begin relatively well but finish horribly. Their reigns are paradigmatic for the entire unfolding of the kingdom that overpromised but
underperformed. David's story begins with an unparalleled and hopeful
promise. There will always be someone on the throne of David. But if the
lives of these three are any indication, the actual future is not bright. The
deconstruction of the Davidic covenant in God's second appearance to
Solomon provides a corrective to the exaggerated language of the unconditional promise to David. Here it is clear that the actions of the king can
lead to loss of the kingdom, or at least parts of it.

Even though the thrust of the narrative moves from blessing to curse
in all three kings of the united monarchy, this does not mean that the only
reading of these kings is a diachronic one. The message is not entirely negative. Whereas Jeroboam (the first ruler of the separate, northern kingdom
of Israel) is condemned throughout the Old Testament as the stereotypical
bad king, there is no mention of Saul, and almost nothing about Solomon
in the Prophets. The Writings associate Solomon with wisdom, but the
condemnation for his idolatry is completely ignored. Of the three kings
of the united monarchy, David fares the best in the rest of the Old Testament. Jeremiah 33:17 echoes the Davidic covenant: the line of David will
never fail to have a man sit on the throne of that house And the prophet
Zechariah imagines high times for the house of David:

35. Steven Weitzman suggests that there was something illicit and dangerous hidden in Solomon's quest for unattainable wisdom, a curiosity gone wildly astray, that led
to his apostasy; *Solomon: The Lure of Wisdom*, 162, 166.

The LORD will save the dwellings of Judah first, so that the honor of the house of David and of Jerusalem's inhabitants may not be greater than that of Judah. On that day the LORD will shield those who live in Jerusalem, so that the feeblest among them will be like David, and the house of David will be like God, like the angel of the LORD going before them. On that day I will set out to destroy all the nations that attack Jerusalem.

And I will pour out on the house of David and the inhabitants of Jerusalem a spirit of grace and supplication. They will look on me, the one they have pierced, and they will mourn for him as one mourns for an only child, and grieve bitterly for him as one grieves for a firstborn son. On that day the weeping in Jerusalem will be great, like the weeping of Hadad Rimmon in the plain of Megiddo. The land will mourn, each clan by itself, with their wives by themselves: the clan of the house of David and their wives, the clan of the house of Nathan and their wives, the clan of the house of Levi and their wives, the clan of Shimei and their wives and all the rest of the clans and their wives. (Zech 12:7–14)

9

Damned If You Don't

Blessings and Curses and the Prophetic Tradition

From Blessing to Threat of Desolation

The Israelite Monarchy and the Rise of Hebrew Prophetism

IT IS NO COINCIDENCE that Abraham, the one who received God's promise of blessing through whom all the peoples of the earth would be blessed or cursed is the first individual to be called a prophet in the Old Testament (Gen 20:7). While he is typically not considered when studying the phenomenon of prophecy in ancient Israel, the figure of Abraham is essential. One of the hallmarks of Abraham's life is his calling. He, like other prophets portrayed in the Old Testament, obeyed in response to a divine summons. God directs Abraham to leave his family and his country and to go to a place unknown to him that would only be revealed in the future. Abraham is called to be the forerunner who would one day father a people as numerous as the stars in the sky and the sand on the seashore. That people was to represent Yahweh—to become God's representatives among the peoples of the world. God promises them a land, a name, and a universal blessing. Therefore they often need individuals from among their own ranks to reawaken their sense of identity as God's people. Such is the calling of prophets.

The prophet par excellence in the Old Testament is Moses. Moses's calling was in many ways similar to Abraham's. Walter Brueggemann's classic, *The Prophetic Imagination*, captures the essence of the Mosaic call.[1] Moses was to bring the people out of Egypt, but this coming out was more than any mere exodus from slavery. Like Abraham, he also is a pivotal figure in Israel's blessing and curse. The prominent ritual blessings and curses of Leviticus 26 and Deuteronomy 27–28 emerge as Yahweh commands Moses to speak to the children of Israel (Lev 25:1; Deut 27:11). The blessings and curses of Leviticus 26 end with this concluding statement: "These are the decrees, the laws and the regulations that the LORD established on Mount Sinai between himself and the Israelites *through Moses*" (Lev 26:46; italics added). Following the groundbreaking studies of George Mendenhall and Norman Gottwald, Brueggemann argued that Moses was summoned to create not only a countercommunity but also a counterconsciousness.[2] This could never be done through any type of social action alone, but by creating a new imaginative social consciousness characterized by three traits:

1. A radical break from the imperial reality that promotes a religion of state triumphalism and the politics of oppression.

2. An alternative consciousness that criticizes an idolatrous status quo and energizes the community to be built up in a way that makes a genuine break from imperial reality.

3. A lively prophetic imagination that uses memory to evoke hope of a new community that is defined by and at the disposal of God who is unco-opted by the empire.[3] This prophetic imagination is devoted to the pathos and passion of a divine covenant relationship with his people. The laws of Sinai were to be the bedrock upon which this community was based, and covenantal demands expressed these laws.

Samuel is another key prophetic figure in the premonarchic period. Samuel served at the enigmatic cult center of Shiloh, which would eventually become a sign of Yahweh's curse on a disobedient people (Jeremiah 7). Samuel's call as a child entailed a message that the covenant had been abandoned, even by the religious establishment who served in the land

1. Brueggemann, *The Prophetic Imagination*.

2. Mendenhall, *The Tenth Generation*; Gottwald, "Domain Assumptions and Societal Models."

3. Brueggemann, *The Prophetic Imagination*, 5–19.

that God had given Israel (1 Samuel 3). Yahweh told Samuel that Eli's house would come to an end because of the sinfulness of Eli's sons, and because Eli himself did nothing to stop such abominations. As an adult, Samuel called the people back to covenant, to once again become the countercommunity God had originally intended them to be: "If you are returning to the LORD with all your hearts, then rid yourselves of the foreign gods and the Ashtoreths and commit yourselves to the LORD and serve him only, and he will deliver you out of the hand of the Philistines" (1 Sam 7:3). A transitional figure in his own right, Samuel anointed the first two kings of Israel, in spite of his own ambivalence to the monarchy.

The testimony of the Deuteronomistic History is a testimony to the failure of Israel to return to the covenant of God. For Walter Brueggemann, King Solomon is the paradigm of the imperial reality that led to this slow abandonment of the Mosaic vision. If Moses was the prophet par excellence, Solomon represents all that led to the "paganization of Israel."[4] Just as he described the Mosaic reality in three traits, so Brueggemann describes this imperial reality in three dimensions: the economics of affluence, the politics of oppression, and a religion of immanence and accessibility. Israel had become just like all of its neighbors, and its king was an imperial despot with incredible wealth, a huge harem, and an uncritical confidence in his religion. It is within the context of the monarchy that the prophetic movement emerges in earnest.

Prophets appear prior to the rise of the monarchy, but a groundswell of prophetic activity bursts on the scene during the divided monarchy, particularly from the ninth to the seventh centuries BCE. Numerous prophets, named and unnamed, suddenly appear in the texts of the Deuteronomistic History and in written prophecies of the writing prophets. What was it about the monarchy that awakened such a vibrant prophetic response? In part, the royal consciousness of the monarchy led to a spiritual malaise or numbness that had to be burned away by prophetic criticism. Recent archaeological work suggests that the monarchy produced a gradual socioeconomic stratification of society marked by a growing divide between lower and upper classes.[5]

Using performative language that was expressive and often overstated, the prophets spoke as if the sky were to collapse. They were shadowy

4. Brueggemann's use of Mendenhall's language in his *Prophetic Imagination*, 24–25.

5. Faust, "Socioeconomic Stratification in an Israelite City"; Joffee, "The Rise of Secondary States in the Iron Age Levant"; Dever, "Social Structure in Palestine."

figures who often had no name and appeared briefly, only to disappear just as quickly. The Bible refers to these individuals by a variety of terms: *prophet, seer, visionary, man of God*, or *sons of the prophets*. The most common root is the term *nby'*, which is used over two hundred times, mostly in the Deuteronomistic History and Jeremiah.[6] This link with Deuteronomic theology is telling, as the prophets are ubiquitous in the Deuteronomistic History. There is no single definition of what it meant to be a prophet but rather a complex unfolding of the use of the term over centuries. These prophets are typically peripheral, challenging the established power structure of the time.[7] The prophetic perspective mediated between Yahweh and the people of Israel and Judah. They spoke the very words of God to humans. Their speech was performative speech. After the exile, when the monarchy was no longer in existence, prophetic activity as a movement waned.

The prophetic message summoned Israel back to covenant, but it also negated the very covenant that the prophets appealed to through their prophecies, calling the vitality of the covenant into question. The salvation election history so touted in the Bible is questioned, critiqued, and often denied by the prophets: "So that is the new, hard message of the classical prophets. God's great history of salvation with Israel, which began with the Exodus from Egypt and received a final seal in the election of Jerusalem, will be pushed inexorably to its end."[8] This prophetic negation of the covenant could be summed up in the curse-laden message of Jeremiah: "I am watching over you for evil" (Jer 44:27).

The theological message of the prophets has its roots in the prophetic call, which itself was anchored in the divine presence of Yahweh (Amos 7, Isaiah 6, Jeremiah 1, Ezekiel 1–3, Isaiah 40, Hosea 1, and Micah 3). The broader prophetic call in the Old Testament is based on the Mosaic model provided in the book of Exodus. Moses, Isaiah, and Jeremiah most clearly represent the five-fold call sequence discussed earlier, but traces of that sequence are present with Ezekiel, Amos, Hosea, and Micah. Even the book of Jonah presents a parody on the prophetic call. In this book the prophet receives a command from God to proclaim a message of repentance to the people he despises. Because of his seething hatred for them, he immediately bolts in the opposite direction. The recalcitrant prophet

---

6. Wilson, *Prophecy and Society in Ancient Israel*, 136.

7. Birch et al., *A Theological Introduction to the Old Testament*, 270.

8. Wolff, "Prophets from the Eighth through the Fifth Centuries," 87.

shows no expression of reluctance, no sense of reassurance—only defiant disobedience.

Covenant Blessings and Curses and the Prophetic Message

The authority of the prophetic message derived from an urgent call summoning Israel back to covenant, which had its origins in the covenant love of Yahweh. Covenant love implied covenant demands. Scholars have long noted parallels between prophetic rhetoric and covenantal language—whether in Deuteronomy, in the Deuteronomistic History, or in the covenantal blessings and curses in Leviticus 26. One question has been whether the writing prophets drew on the covenantal legal traditions, or whether these legal traditions were written later, with the prophecies of the prophets in mind.[9] Regardless, no one contests the obvious links between the language of the writing prophets and covenantal blessings and curses in Leviticus 26 and Deuteronomy 28. Deuteronomy 28:1–13 describes a blessed life characterized by fertility (vv. 4–5, 8, 12), prosperity (vv. 3, 11), security (vv. 6–7), and authority (vv. 10, 12, 13).[10]

> If you fully obey the LORD your God and carefully follow all his commands I give you today, the LORD your God will set you high above all the nations on earth. All these blessings (*habbĕrākôt*) will come upon you and accompany you if you obey the LORD your God: You will be blessed (*bārûk*) in the city and blessed (*ûbārûk*) in the country. The fruit of your womb will be blessed (*bârûk*), and the crops of your land and the young of your livestock—the calves of your herds and the lambs of your flocks. Your basket and your kneading trough will be blessed (*bārûk*). You will be blessed (*bārûk*) when you come in and blessed (*ûbārûk*) when you go out. The LORD will grant that the enemies who rise up against you will be defeated before you. They will come at you from one direction but flee from you in seven. The LORD will send a blessing (*habbĕrākâ*) on your barns and on everything you put your hand to. The LORD your God will bless (*ûbērakkâ*) you in the land he is giving you. The LORD will establish you as his holy people, as he promised you on oath, if you

---

9. The conflicting views are presented in detail by Carroll, *Jeremiah*, 38–50, 65–82; Bright, *Jeremiah*, lv–lxxiii; J. A. Thompson, *The Book of Jeremiah*, 27–49; Clements, *Jeremiah*, 10–12; and Holladay, *Jeremiah 2*, 10–24, 53–64.

10. See McKeown's excellent theological discussion of blessing and curse in *Genesis*, 219–40.

keep the commands of the Lord your God and walk in his ways. Then all the peoples on earth will see that you are called by the name of the Lord, and they will fear you. The Lord will grant you abundant prosperity—in the fruit of your womb, the young of your livestock and the crops of your ground—in the land he swore to your forefathers to give you. The Lord will open the heavens, the storehouse of his bounty, to send rain on your land in season and to bless (*ûlbārēk*) all the work of your hands. You will lend to many nations but will borrow from none. The Lord will make you the head, not the tail. If you pay attention to the commands of the Lord your God that I give you this day and carefully follow them, you will always be at the top, never at the bottom. (Deut 28:1–13)

The Deuteronomist lavishly describes this extravagant blessing primarily in terms of fertility: fruitful families, fruitful land, and fruitful livestock. Israel's enemies will be defeated, fleeing even when only few are pursuing. Israel will be esteemed as the head of peoples, never the tail. Leviticus 26 also mentions a similar set of blessings, but adds the fifth blessing of the continued presence of God. God is the agent through which blessing occurs. Theologically, the priestly writer links the language of divine blessing with the notion of divine providence in Leviticus 26.

I will turn to you and make you fruitful and multiply you and will confirm my covenant with you. You shall eat old store long kept, and you shall clear out the old to make way for the new. I will make my dwelling among you, and my soul shall not abhor you. And I will walk among you and will be your God, and you shall be my people. I am the Lord your God, who brought you out of the land of Egypt, that you should not be their slaves. And I have broken the bars of your yoke and made you walk erect. (Lev 26:9–13, ESV)

However, if the agent of the blessing chooses to remove that blessing, then a horrible curse ensues. To portray this horrible threat, the prophets used many stock phrases shared with Deuteronomic and Levitical blessings and curses.[11] Some stereotyped phrases of blessing include "to dwell in the land," "to be God's people," "to be fruitful and multiply," "to possess trees that yield abundant fruit," "to bless the work of one's hands," and "to remember the covenant." Some stock phrases of curses are "to set God's

11 Hillers, *Treaty-Curses and the Old Testament Prophets*; Weinfeld, *Deuteronomy and the Deuteronomic School*; Weinfeld, "Ancient Near Eastern Patterns in Prophetic Literature," 187.

face against you"; "to be beset by sword, famine, and pestilence"; "to be scattered among the nations"; "to be uprooted from the land"; "to have an iron yoke"; "to harvest no new wine"; "to be devoured by swarms of locusts"; "to send one's daughters into captivity"; "to face blight and mildew"; and "to suffer from sores from the soles of one's feet to the top of one's head."

But perhaps the three most notable curse texts that influenced prophetic rhetoric are from Deut 28:25, Deut 28:37, and Lev 26:30–34:

> The LORD will cause you to be defeated before your enemies. You will come at them from one direction but flee from them in seven, and you will become a thing of horror to all the kingdoms on earth. (Deut 28:25–26)

> You will become a thing of horror (*lĕšamâ*) and an object of scorn and ridicule to all the nations where the LORD will drive you. (Deut 28:37)

> I will destroy your high places, cut down your incense altars and pile your dead bodies on the lifeless forms of your idols, and I will abhor you. I will turn your cities into ruins and lay waste (*wahăšimmōtî*) your sanctuaries and I will take no delight in the pleasing aroma of your offerings. I will lay waste (*wahăšimmōtî*) the land, so that your enemies who live there will be appalled (*wĕšāmmû*). I will scatter you among the nations and will draw out my sword and pursue you. Your land will be laid waste (*šĕmāmâ*), and your cities will lie in ruins. Then the land will enjoy its Sabbath year all the time that it lies desolate (*hŏššammâ*) and you are in the country of your enemies, then the land will rest and enjoy its sabbath. (Lev 26:30–34)

These texts in particular serve the prophets well in their castigation of the people. Yet the prophets are not slavishly dependent on the covenantal threat of curses and withdrawn blessings for their harsh messages. Note a few Deuteronomic and Levitical blessing and curse phrases not present in prophetic parallels: "the fruit of your womb and the crops of your ground" (Deut 28:11); "five of you shall chase a hundred and a hundred ten thousand" (Lev 26:8); "blessed/cursed when you come in and blessed/cursed when you go out" (Deut 28:6); "the sky over your head will be bronze and the ground beneath you iron" (Deut 28:23); "your sons and daughters will be given to another nation and you will wear out your eyes watching for them" (Deut 28:32); "they will be a sign and wonder to you" (Deut 28:46); "God will bring on you all the diseases of Egypt" (Deut 28:60); "there will be no resting place for the sole of your foot" (Deut 28:65)—to name more than a few.

Vineyard Imagery and Blessings and Curses.

Notions of building and planting are prominent and persistent themes in the prophets. The threat of curse is poignant in Deut 28:30b: "You will plant a vineyard, but you will not even begin to enjoy its fruit." The same threat is also reflected in Lev 26:16: "You will plant seed in vain, because your enemies will eat it." One of the major targets of prophetic attack is the fertility of the ground. Just as in the early chapters of Genesis the ground was the object of both blessing and curse, so in the prophets imagery of vines, vineyards, grapes, and wine communicate Yahweh's blessing and judgment (Amos 5:11; Zeph 1:13; Jer 6:1–13; 29:5, 28; 31:4; Deut 20:5–6; 28:30; Isa 62:6–9; 65:21; Ezek 28:26; 36:36).[12] The curse came to symbolize the horrible repercussions of a successful siege, notably deportation from the land and the destruction of agriculture. Isaiah's beautifully poetic critique of Israel's precarious place as God's people resonates in the Song of the Vineyard:

> I will sing for the one I love
>   a song about his vineyard;
> My loved one had a vineyard
>   on a fertile hillside.
> He dug it up and cleared it of stones
>   and planted it with the choicest vines.
> He built a watchtower in it
>   and cut out a winepress as well.
> Then he looked for a crop of good grapes,
>   but it yielded only bad fruit.
>
> Now you dwellers in Jerusalem and men of Judah,
>   judge between me and my vineyard.
> What more could have been done for my vineyard
>   than I have done for it?
> When I looked for good grapes,
>   why did it yield only bad?
> Now I will tell you
>   what I am going to do to my vineyard:
> I will take away its hedge,

12. Walsh, *The Fruit of the Vine.*

> and it will be destroyed;
> I will break down its wall,
>   and it will be trampled.
> I will make it a wasteland,
>   neither pruned nor cultivated,
>   and briers and thorns will grow there.
> I will command the clouds
>   not to rain on it."
>
> The vineyard of the Lord Almighty
>   is the house of Israel,
> and the men of Judah
>   are the garden of his delight.
> And he looked for justice, but saw bloodshed;
>   for righteousness, but heard cries of distress. (Isa 5:1–7)

There is a ringed structure to this exquisite song. The opening (vv. 1–3) and closing (v. 7) reflect the words of the prophet, but the message's center contains an illocutionary utterance of Yahweh. The prophet presses the covenantal theme that God has done just about everything one can do for Israel and Judah. God picked a fertile environment, protected it carefully, and prepared expectantly for a fruitful harvest—to no avail. This wayward vineyard yielded only *bad* grapes. (The Hebrew word *bĕ'ušîm* denotes something rotten and smelly. The same word is used in Exodus to describe the smell of the Nile after the plague of blood [Exod 7:18, 21], and the word describes the stinking manna hoarded by the greedy Israelites [Exod 16:20].) God pleads through the prophet: "What more could I have done?" Consequently both safety and fertility are now at dire risk. God promises to remove the vineyard's hedge and walls and to make it a wasteland (*bātâ*—a word that is used only here in the Old Testament). Jeremy Smoak has revealed that the Song of the Vineyard and numerous other parallels adopt the imagery of building houses and planting vineyards as an ancient Israelite wartime curse.[13] (Comparing biblical texts with relevant Assyrian sources underscores that the imagery of this curse came to symbolize all kinds of horrors associated with being under siege.) In case there is any doubt for hearers or readers of Isaiah's song about who is to blame for the curse, Isaiah makes the parable explicit. Israel and Judah are to blame (vv. 6–7). Isaiah's play on words in Hebrew is powerful: "he looked for justice (*lĕmišpāṭ*), but saw bloodshed (*mišpâ*); for righteousness (*lĕṣdāqâ*) but heard cries of distress (*ṣĕ'āqâ*)." The fertile vineyard in which

13. Smoak, "Building Houses and Planting Vineyards."

so much had been invested would come to devastation and ruin. Just as in Genesis the curse begins with the ground (Gen 3:17), so here Isaiah targets the land in this prophetic metaphor: loss of the land's fertility of, the land's destruction, expulsion from the land, dispersion from the land, and removal of God's presence from the land.

Isaiah's vineyard song is followed by six woes that vividly describe the specific moral conditions that have led to God's abandonment of his vineyard. Greed (v. 8), carousing (v. 11), defiance (v. 18), perversion (v. 20), arrogance (v. 21), and corruption (v. 23) all lead to desolation.[14] Isaiah intentionally takes up the desolation language of Deut 28:30: "Surely the great houses will become desolate (*lĕšammâ*), the fine mansions left without occupants" (Isa 5:9). In addition to this vivid language of desolation, four therefores point to impending exile (v. 13), death (v. 14), devastation (v. 24), and wrath (v. 25). The scathing language of Isaiah 5 is similar to Amos 5:11 (ESV), which also bears clear allusions to the curse of Deut 28:30.[15]

> Therefore because you trample on the poor
>   and you exact taxes of grain from him,
> you have built houses of hewn stone,
>   but you shall not dwell in them;
> you have planted pleasant vineyards,
>   but you shall not drink their wine.

Vineyard imagery depicting threatening curses is also used in a negative way in Amos 4 as famine (v. 6), drought (v. 7), mildew (v. 9), and plagues (v. 10)—all of which lead to the overthrow of Israel, which is like the demise of Sodom and Gomorrah (v. 11). The prophet Joel also describes the locust invasion as recounted in Deut 28:38–42 (ESV):

> You shall carry much seed into the field and shall gather in little, for the locust shall consume it. You shall plant vineyards and dress them, but you shall neither drink of the wine nor gather the grapes, for the worm shall eat them. You shall have olive trees throughout all your territory, but you shall not anoint yourself with the oil, for your olives shall drop off. You shall father sons and daughters, but they shall not be yours, for they shall go into captivity. The cricket shall possess all your trees and the fruit of your ground.

14. Chaney, "Bitter Bounty"; Silver, *Prophets and Markets,* 49–52.

15. Also, parallels in Mic 6:15 and Zeph 1:13 echo this curse in Deut 28:30 and Lev 26:16.

The Blessing and the Curse

Joel's wartime curse links the locust invasion with the marauding Assyrian army (Joel 1:6–7, 11–12, 16–17). The people will sow their seed in vain. They will sow wheat but reap thorns. Jeremiah uses strikingly similar vineyard imagery in Jer 2:20–21.

> Long ago you broke off your yoke
>   and tore off your bonds;
>   you said, "I will not serve you!"
> Indeed, on every high hill
>   and under every spreading tree
>   you lay down as a prostitute.
> I had planted you like a choice vine
>   of sound and reliable stock.
> How then did you turn against me
>   into a corrupt, wild vine? (Jer 2:20–21)

Here Jeremiah describes the vine as wild—literally "foreign" or "strange." As in Isaiah's Song of the Vineyard, here in Jeremiah Yahweh asks the crucial question: how did you turn against me into a corrupt, wild vine? Hosea also engages the imagery of the vineyard.

> Israel was a spreading vine;
>   he brought forth fruit for himself.
> As his fruit increased,
>   he built more altars;
> as his land prospered,
>   he adorned his sacred stones.
> Their heart is deceitful,
>   and now they must bear their guilt.
> The LORD will demolish their altars. (Hos 10:1–2)

Ezekiel, in his rather pessimistic evaluation of Jerusalem, makes explicit usage of the vineyard imagery and desolation language in chapters 15 and 17. Twice Yahweh promises that he will "set his face against them"—the people in Jerusalem (Ezek 15:7), and that the land will be a desolation (šĕmāmâ, Ezek 15:8). In addition to desolation language, the theme of God's setting his face against his own people derives directly from Lev 26:33:

> The word of the LORD came to me: "Son of man, how is the wood of a vine better than that of a branch on any of the trees in the forest? Is wood ever taken from it to make anything useful? Do they make pegs from it to hang things on? And after it is thrown on the fire as fuel and the fire burns both ends and chars

the middle, is it then useful for anything? If it was not useful for anything when it was whole, how much less can it be made into something useful when the fire has burned it and it is charred? Therefore this is what the Sovereign LORD says: As I have given the wood of the vine among the trees of the forest as fuel for the fire, so will I treat the people living in Jerusalem. I will set my face against them. Although they have come out of the fire, the fire will yet consume them. And when I set my face against them, you will know that I am the LORD. I will make the land desolate (*šěmāmâ*) because they have been unfaithful, declares the Sovereign LORD." (Ezek 15:1–8)

The oddity of this parable is interesting. Five staccato-like questions keep Ezekiel on his heels. No one has ever really seriously argued that the wood of a vine is comparable to that of a tree. Whether or not a vine can, like a tree, be turned into useful objects is not the point. The real point is that the vine's value depends not on what one can make from the vine itself but on the fruit that the vine produces.[16] As Isaiah had earlier, so Ezekiel characterizes the inhabitants of Jerusalem as useless because of their lack of fruit. And as it is within the Song of the Vineyard, so in Ezekiel a consuming fire is the medium of judgment (cf. Isa 5:24). The verdict is condemnation, and God has already decided what must be done with this people.

In Ezekiel 17 the house of Israel is the object of great expectations for blessings. The soil is good, water abounds, and God expects bountiful production. Yet this tragic vine will be uprooted, will be stripped bare, and will and wither. This allegory has a number of similarities to Jotham's fable and curse in Judg 9:8–15. Note again the use of the staccato rhetorical questions.

> The word of the LORD came to me: "Son of man, propound a riddle, and speak a parable to the house of Israel; say, Thus says the Lord God: A great eagle with great wings and long pinions, rich in plumage of many colors, came to Lebanon and took the top of the cedar. He broke off the topmost of its young twigs and carried it to a land of trade and set it in a city of merchants. Then he took of the seed of the land and planted it in fertile soil. He placed it beside abundant waters. He set it like a willow twig, and it sprouted and became a low spreading vine, and its branches turned toward him, and its roots remained where it stood. So it became a vine and produced branches and put out boughs.

16. Eichrodt, *Ezekiel*, 193–95.

And there was another great eagle with great wings and much plumage, and behold, this vine bent its roots toward him and shot forth its branches toward him from the bed where it was planted, that he might water it. It had been planted on good soil by abundant waters, that it might produce branches and bear fruit and become a noble vine. Say, Thus says the LORD God: Will it thrive? Will he not pull up its roots and cut off its fruit, so that it withers, so that all its fresh sprouting leaves wither? It will not take a strong arm or many people to pull it from its roots. Behold, it is planted; will it thrive? Will it not utterly wither when the east wind strikes it—wither away on the bed where it sprouted?" (Ezek 17:1–10, ESV)

A theme recurs in all these passages presented so far: Israel is a vineyard that bears no fruit. Consequently it will become a desolate wasteland. Yet the allegory below is quite different. Here the vineyard metaphor is pressed into speaking about a single individual, Zedekiah the king. The reference in Ezek 19:11 to a single vine among many branches and the references to a ruler's scepter are informative. The rapid succession of verbs in v. 12 leads to the common theme of fire being the instrument of God's justice.

Your mother was like a vine in your vineyard
    planted by the water;
it was fruitful and full of branches
    because of abundant water.
Its branches were strong,
    fit for a ruler's scepter.
It towered high
    above the thick foliage,
conspicuous for its height
    and for its many branches.
But it was uprooted in fury
    and thrown to the ground.
The east wind made it shrivel,
    it was stripped of its fruit;
its strong branches withered
    and fire consumed them.
Now it is planted in the desert,
    in a dry and thirsty land.
Fire spread from one of its main branches
    and consumed its fruit.
No strong branch is left on it
    fit for a ruler's scepter. (Ezek 19:10–14)

Yet no passage better portrays this threat of desolation than Jeremiah 12.

> Many shepherds will ruin my vineyard
>> and trample down my field;
> they will turn my pleasant field
>> into a desolate wasteland (*lĕmidbar šĕmāmâ*).
> It will be made a wasteland (*lĕšmāmâ*),
>> parched and desolate (*šĕmēmâ*)before me;
> the whole land will be laid waste (*nāšammâ*)
>> because there is no one who cares.
> Over all the barren heights in the desert
>> destroyers will swarm,
> for the sword of the LORD will devour
>> from one end of the land to the other;
>> no one will be safe.
> They will sow wheat but reap thorns;
>> they will wear themselves out but gain nothing.
> So bear the shame of your harvest
>> because of the LORD's fierce anger. (Jer 12:10–13)

No fewer than four occasions this prophecy refers to the waste or wasteland resulting from the covenant curse. The cumulative result of all these prophetic texts is to discover that the word *šmmh* is one of the favorite terms in the prophets to denote the desolation caused by disaster. This word is used 195 times in the Hebrew Bible—most liberally in the prophetic books of Isaiah, Jeremiah, Ezekiel, Hosea, Joel, Micah, Nahum, and Zephaniah. The language of desolation and waste is derived from covenantal blessing and curse texts such as Lev 26:33 and Deut 28:37, and such language also appears in 2 Kgs 22:19 and 2 Chr 30:7. It is reflective of Exod 23:25–32, which notes that Israel will drive the Canaanites out of the land little by little so that the land does not become desolate and so that wild animals don't overtake the land.

> Worship the LORD your God, and his blessing (*ûbērak*) will be on your food and water. I will take away sickness from among you, and none will miscarry or be barren in your land. I will give you a full life span. I will send my terror ahead of you and throw into confusion every nation you encounter. I will make all your enemies turn their backs and run. I will send the hornet ahead of you to drive the Hivites, Canaanites and Hittites out of your way. But I will not drive them out in a single year, because the land would become desolate (*šĕmāmâ*) and the wild animals too numerous for you.

The lively word *šĕmāmâ* overlaps semantically with the root *ḥrb*, which is also used liberally in the prophets (Isa 64:10; Lam 1:4; Ezek 6:4; Joel 1:7, 2:3). It is also often paired up with *qll* and *'lh*, which are often translated "curse" (2 Kgs 22:19; Jer 25:18, 44:22). False prophets question such hardened pessimism: "Why should this city become a desolation?" (Jer 27:17). But the prophets know where the kingdom is headed. Even Daniel uses the root four times in the Polel stem to refer to the abomination that causes desolation (Dan 8:13; 9:27; 11:31; 12:11). As tragic as it sounds, it is one thing to experience desolation. It is quite another to become the very spectacle of desolation.

The Metonymical Curse and the Spectacle of Desolation

In some cases, a blessing or curse is not a verbal imprecation. In some cases a blessing or cuse operates by metonymy and refers to a person or group who experiences wonderful prosperity (blessing) or horrible misfortunes (curse). A metonym is a trope or figure of speech in which the name of one thing substitutes for the name of another thing, where both names are associated. This can take place in several ways. For example, an adjunct can stand for a whole. In the case of "The White House said yesterday," the adjunct "White House" (the adjunct) substitutes for the administration of the presidency (the whole). Metonymy can also be employed when a cause is substituted for effect or an effect for a cause. It is this substitution that has important implication in the prophets, particularly in Jeremiah and Ezekiel. Josef Scharbert has argued that blessing and curse terminology in the Old Testament can sometimes be employed metonymically as "a noun for persons on whom the curses come as devastating calamities."[17] These unfortunate individuals and peoples actually become a curse because they are in such a horrific situation that their whole existence could be considered cursed. They so embody the results of curse that they have become a spectacle of desolation. In short, because they have been cursed, they become a curse.

In some prophetic texts in Jeremiah and Ezekiel, the people of Jerusalem and Judah are not just recipients of the covenant curse; they actually are a curse. These Judeans inhabit the land of the curse and have themselves become a curse for all the peoples of the earth. Theologically, this is highly ironic. Those originally intended to be a metonymical blessing to all the peoples of the earth (Gen 12:3) are now described as a curse among

17. Scharbert, "'*lh*," 264–65.

all the peoples of the earth.[18] The use of metonymy in such a curse recalls the enigmatic text in Numbers 5, where a woman suspected of adultery drinks the water that brings a curse, and the priest says, "The LORD make you a curse and an oath." Similarly, Isa 65:15 states, "you shall leave my name for my chosen ones to use in their curses."

Jeremiah and Ezekiel in particular string together a clichéd chain of synonyms to colorfully convey the horror and shock of Judah's looming desolation in well over a dozen texts.[19] English translators grope for enough synonyms to graphically portray the horror: "reproach," "condemnation," "byword," "taunt," "curse," "hissing," "oath," "desolation," "waste," "execration," and "horror" are all terms piled up in derisive portents of doom. In several of these passages, the prophets combine the Deuteronomic object of horror with the Levitical malevolent triad of "sword, famine, and plague" to make the language that much more polemical. Note these thirteen scathing examples below.

- I will make them abhorrent and an offense to all the kingdoms of the earth, a reproach and a byword, an object of ridicule and cursing (*lĕḥerpâ ûlmāšal lišnînâ wĕliqlālâ*) wherever I banish them. I will send the sword, famine and plague against them until they are destroyed from the land I gave to them and their fathers. (Jer 24:9–10)

- "I will summon all the peoples of the north and my servant Nebuchadnezzar king of Babylon," declares the LORD, "and I will bring them against this land and its inhabitants and against all the surrounding nations. I will completely destroy them and make them an object of horror and scorn and everlasting ruin (*lĕšammâ wĕlišrĕqâ ûlḥārĕbôt 'ôlām*). I will banish from them the sounds of joy and gladness, the voices of bride and bridegroom, the sound of millstones and the light of the lamp. This whole country will become a desolate wasteland (*lĕḥārĕbâ lĕšammâ*), and these nations will serve the king of Babylon seventy years." (Jer 25:9–11)

- So I took the cup from the LORD's hand and made all the nations to whom he sent me drink it: Jerusalem and the towns of Judah, its kings and officials, to make them a ruin and an object of horror and scorn and cursing (*wĕliqlālâ*), as they are today. (Jer 25:17–19)

18. Pedersen, *Der Eid bei den Semiten*, 73–74.

19. J. S. Anderson, "The Metonymical Curse as Propaganda in the Book of Jeremiah."

- Then I will make this house like Shiloh and this city an object of cursing (*liqlâlâ*) among all the nations of the earth. (Jer 26:6)

- I will pursue them with the sword, famine and plague and will make them abhorrent to all the kingdoms of the earth and an object of cursing and horror, of scorn and reproach (*lĕʾālâ ûlšammâ wĕliqlālâ ûlḥerpâ*), among all the nations where I drive them. (Jer 29:18–19)

- This is what the LORD Almighty, the God of Israel, says: "As my anger and wrath have been poured out on those who lived in Jerusalem, so will my wrath be poured out on you when you go to Egypt. You will be an object of cursing and horror, of condemnation and reproach (*lĕʾālâ ûlšammâ weliqlālâ ûlḥerpâ*); you will never see this place again. (Jer 42:18)

- Therefore, my fierce anger was poured out; it raged against the towns of Judah and the streets of Jerusalem and made them the desolate ruins (*liḥārbâ lišmāmâ*) they are today.

  Why provoke me to anger with what your hands have made, burning incense to other gods in Egypt, where you have come to live? You will destroy yourselves and make yourselves an object of cursing and reproach (*liqlālâ ûlḥerpâ*) among all the nations on earth. (Jer 44:6, 8)

- I will take away the remnant of Judah who were determined to go to Egypt to settle there. They will all perish in Egypt; they will fall by the sword or die from famine. From the least to the greatest, they will die by sword or famine. They will become an object of cursing and horror, of condemnation and reproach (*lĕʾālâ lĕšammâ wĕliqlālâ ûlḥerpâ*). I will punish those who live in Egypt with sword, famine, and plague, just as I punished Jerusalem. (Jer 44:12–13)

- When the LORD could no longer endure your wicked actions and the detestable things you did, your land became an object of cursing and a desolate waste (*lĕḥārbâ ûlšammâ wĕliqlālâ*) without inhabitants, as it is today. Because you have burned incense and have sinned against the LORD and have not obeyed him or followed his law or his decrees or his stipulations, this disaster has come upon you, as you now see. (Jer 44:22–23)

- I swear by myself, declares the LORD, that Bozrah will become a ruin and an object of horror, of reproach and of cursing (*lĕšammâ lĕherpâ lĕhōreb wĕliqlālâ*); and all its towns will be in ruins forever. (Jer 49:13)

- I will make you a ruin and a reproach among the nations around you, in the sight of all who pass by. You will be a reproach and a taunt, a warning and an object of horror (*ûmšammâ*) the nations around you when I inflict punishment on you in anger and in wrath and with stinging rebuke. I the LORD have spoken. (Ezek 5:14–15)

- Let the priests, who minister before the LORD,
    weep between the temple porch and the altar.
  Let them say, 'Spare your people, O LORD.
  Do not make your inheritance an object of scorn (*lĕherpâ*),
    a byword among the nations.
  Why should they say among the peoples,
  'Where is their God?'" (Joel 2:17)

- As you have been an object of cursing (*qĕlālâ*) among the nations, O Judah and Israel, so will I save you, and you will be a blessing (*bĕrākâ*). Do not be afraid, but let your hands be strong. (Zech 8:13)

In Jeremiah, this clichéd string of derogatory words appears in three definable units of prose: chapters 24–29 (Jer 24:9; 25:17–18; 26:6; 29:19), a unit that begins and ends with the metaphor of the rotten figs; chapters 42–44 (Jer 42:18; 44:8, 12, 22), part of the biographical prose narrative of Jeremiah; and once in the prophecies against the kingdoms in 49:7–22 (49:13). The prophecy in Ezekiel is directed against Jerusalem, as is Joel's call for a solemn assembly in Zion. Many would argue that in the case of Jeremiah, all of these examples are fraught with Deuteronomic language.[20]

What is most striking is who these curses are directed against. In the exilic and postexilic periods, three broad Jewish communities emerged after the devastating destruction by Babylon: the remnant in Judah, those who fled to Egypt, and the community in Babylon. In all of these instances, the language describing this spectacle of desolation—the rotten figs—applies to the non-Babylonian Jewish communities in Judah and Egypt. The fusion of sword, famine, and plague with the language of the curse leaves the Judeans who remained in Judah, the Judeans who fled to Egypt, and

---

20. Stulman, *The Prose Sermons of the Book of Jeremiah*; and Thiel, *Die deuteronomistische Redaktion von Jeremia 26–45*.

even Judah's enemies as cursed. But more than cursed, they *are* a curse. It is obvious that the postexilic tensions between the returning exiles from Babylon and those who remained in Judah are present in these prose sections of Jeremiah. Let us consider a few examples.

The Vision of the Rotten Figs: Jeremiah 24:1–10

In this symbolic vision, the exiles of Judah who were deported to Babylon are the "good figs" and those who remained in Judah and those who fled to Egypt are the "bad figs."

> Then the LORD asked me, "What do you see, Jeremiah?" "Figs," I answered. "The good ones are very good, but the poor ones are so bad they cannot be eaten."
>
> Then the word of the LORD came to me: "This is what the LORD, the God of Israel, says: 'Like these good figs, I regard as good the exiles from Judah, whom I sent away from this place to the land of the Babylonians. My eyes will watch over them for their good, and I will bring them back to this land. I will build them up and not tear them down; I will plant them and not uproot them. I will give them a heart to know me, that I am the LORD. They will be my people, and I will be their God, for they will return to me with all their heart.
>
> 'But like the poor figs, which are so bad they cannot be eaten,' says the LORD, 'so will I deal with Zedekiah king of Judah, his officials and the survivors from Jerusalem, whether they remain in this land or live in Egypt. I will make them abhorrent and an offense to all the kingdoms of the earth, a reproach and a byword, an object of ridicule and cursing wherever I banish them. I will send the sword, famine and plague against them until they are destroyed from the land I gave to them and their fathers.'" (Jer 24:3–10)

These bad figs are described in scathing language: "I will make them abhorrent and an offense to all the kingdoms of the earth, a reproach and a byword, an object of ridicule and cursing, wherever I banish them. I will send the sword, famine and plague against them until they are destroyed from the land I gave to them and their fathers." The hope of the prophets was that the people of God would experience only temporary exile. There would be a time when they would return and rebuild. In Ezekiel 11, for example, it says, "This is what the Sovereign LORD says: I will gather you from the nations and bring you back from the countries where you have been scattered, and I will give you back the land of Israel again" (Ezek 11:17).[21] Yet there are clear polemical implications in the vision of the rotten figs. It is only the returnees who participate in the rebuilding of the kingdom who will be blessed. The Judeans who remain in the land and those who fled to Egypt are an object of ridicule and cursing.

The Temple Sermon: Jeremiah 26:1–24

Jeremiah 26 is a narrative reporting the disturbance provoked by Jeremiah's temple sermon, leading to the demand from the priests and false prophets that Jeremiah be killed for blasphemy. Chapter 26 bears numerous parallels to the famous temple sermon in chapter 7 and is integrally related to the larger section of material in Jeremiah 26–29. The primary theme of this larger unit is to distinguish between true and false prophecy, and to point out Judean rejection of Jeremiah's words. Chapter 26 depicts the confrontation between Jeremiah and the prophets and priests at the temple. This unit begins (Jer 26:6) and ends (Jer 29:18, 22) with a curse. Jeremiah proclaims the metonymical curse in 26:6: "Then I will make this house like Shiloh and this city an object of cursing among all the nations of the earth." Just as Shiloh had once been the place where Yahweh caused his name to dwell before the place destroyed, so Jerusalem will likewise suffer the same fate of destruction[22] The once thriving cult center would become desolate. To curse the temple and city was equivalent to blasphemy. Jeremiah's highly provocative words spark a riot and the leaders demand Jeremiah's death.

The Letter to the Exiles: Jeremiah 29:16–19

A similar viewpoint is confirmed in the letter to the exiles. Jeremiah draws a sharp contrast between the exiles, whose future is peaceable, and the remnant of Judah, who will utterly be driven from their land. The image of the rotten figs in chapter 24 reappears but is used in a different way. Here

21. Other texts promising restoration to Israel are Isa 2:2–4; 49:6; Jer 16:15; 23:8; 31:27–34; Ezekiel 34–37; Amos 9:11–15; Sir 48:10; *Ps. Sol.* 17–18; *1 Enoch* 24–25; Tob 13–14.

22. Schley, *Shiloh*, 178–82. Schley argues that the references to Shiloh in Jer 26:6 and Jer 7:12–15 pertain to the destruction concurrent with the fall of Samaria, not during a hypothetical Philistine invasion around 1050 BCE. In either case Shiloh became a paradigm for a desolate cult center.

Jeremiah describes the Judean community as vile figs that cannot be eaten: "I will pursue them with the sword, famine, and plague and will make them abhorrent to all the kingdoms of the earth and an object of cursing and horror, of scorn and reproach, among all the nations where I drive them" (Jer 29:17–18).

The Judeans in Egypt: Jeremiah 42–44

More than ten years later, after the fall of Jerusalem and the subsequent murder of Gedaliah, Johanan and his forces, worried about the reprisals of the Babylonians, ask Jeremiah whether they should flee to Egypt. Jeremiah warns against this, stating that those who flee to Egypt will become an object of cursing and horror, of condemnation and reproach (Jer 42:18). The order of events described in chapters 42 and 43 is in some doubt, but a rough reconstruction of the depicted events is as follows: Jeremiah promises that only those who remain in Judah will be spared. Johanan accuses Jeremiah of lying and flees to Egypt anyway, along with the entire remnant of Judah (Jer 43:5). Jeremiah confirms that the cities of Judah are a desolation and no one dwells in them (Jer 44:2). There is literally no one left in the land.[23] Such a recollection is reminiscent of the deserted land in Leviticus 26:43a, "for the land will be deserted by them and will enjoy its Sabbaths while it lies desolate without them."

Later, after Johanan forces Jeremiah to accompany them to Egypt, he summons all the Judean communities in Egypt (Jeremiah 44) and chides them for continuing to burn incense to other gods, again citing the formula that they will be cut off and become a curse and a taunt among all the kingdoms of the earth (Jer 44:12). Finally the land of Judah, which they left, is depicted as "an object of cursing and a desolate waste without inhabitants, as it is today. Because you have burned incense and have sinned against the LORD and have not obeyed him or followed his law or his decrees or his stipulations, this disaster has come upon you, as you now see" (Jer 44:22–23). Relegating to the curse both the land in which they live (Egypt) and the land from which they fled (Judah), this rhetoric effectively cuts off any alternative for both Judean communities: the Judeans in Egypt and the inhabitants of Judah. Nicholson comments that those who fled to Egypt are condemned in "language that is amongst the most bitter and vehement in the whole book."[24] Elsewhere Jeremiah has announced that

23. Smith-Christopher, *The Religion of the Landless*, 133–36.
24. Nicholson, *Preaching to the Exiles*, 110.

people will travel from all around the world to come see the horror that God has unleashed on the kingdom (Jer 16:16; 18:16, 19; 22:8).

Prophecies against the Kingdoms: Jeremiah 49:7–22; 51:37–41; and 25:15–38

Three additional pertinent texts relate to this clichéd string of invectives that describe the spectacle of desolation for Edom and Babylon. In Jeremiah 49:7–22, a prose insertion to the poetic prophecy states, "Bozrah will become a ruin and an object of horror, of reproach and of cursing; and all its towns will be in ruins forever" (Jer 49:13). The disdain for Edom is well attested elsewhere in the Old Testament.[25] Babylon also bears the brunt of such invective:

> Babylon will be a heap of ruins,
>   a haunt of jackals,
> an object of horror and scorn,
>   a place where no one lives.
> Her people all roar like young lions,
>   they growl like lion cubs.
> But while they are aroused,
>   I will set out a feast for them
>   and make them drunk,
> so that they shout with laughter—
>   then sleep forever and not awake,"
>   declares the LORD"
> I will bring them down
>   like lambs to the slaughter,
>   like rams and goats.
> "How Sheshach
>   will be captured,
>   the boast of the whole earth seized!
> What a horror Babylon will be
>   among the nations! (Jer 51:37–41)

---

25. Bozrah is associated with the Edomite kings in Gen 36:33 and 1 Chr 1:44. The only references in the Old Testament to Bozrah are in the prophecies against foreign kingdoms (Isa 34:6; 63:1; Jer 49:13, 22; Amos 1:12; and possibly Mic 2:12).

ISRAEL'S RETURN FROM DESOLATION BACK TO BLESSING

Jeremy Smoak's work has also revealed that the relatively imprecise and vague nature of vineyard curse imagery allows the same imagery to be retooled and transformed into a promise of return, which allows for a social setting characterized by security and stability.[26] Nearly all the prophets long for a return to blessing, when Israel and Judah will once again be united, when the land will be full of produce and fruitfulness. This will be a time when Jerusalem will no longer be called desolate. Just as before, the peoples saw Judah's public humiliation of desolation, so now the foreigners will see Zion's splendor.

> For Zion's sake I will not keep silent,
> for Jerusalem's sake I will not remain quiet,
> till her righteousness shines out like the dawn,
> her salvation like a blazing torch.
> The nations will see your righteousness,
> and all kings your glory;
> you will be called by a new name
> that the mouth of the LORD will bestow.
> You will be a crown of splendor in the LORD's hand,
> a royal diadem in the hand of your God.
> No longer will they call you Deserted,
> or name your land Desolate (*šāmāmâ*).
> But you will be called Hephzibah,
> and your land Beulah;
> for the LORD will take delight in you,
> and your land will be married.
> As a young man marries a maiden,
> so will your sons marry you;
> as a bridegroom rejoices over his bride,
> so will your God rejoice over you. (Isa 62:1–5)

Amos 9:11–15 reformulates the curse of Amos 5 into a blessing. The northern kingdom of Israel will be restored. Cities will be rebuilt and vineyards replanted. Such is the image of Eden free of curse. Yahweh promises that he will replant Israel on their ground (*'admātām*, echoing the threat in Amos 5:2 that Yahweh will abandon Israel on her land [*'admātām*]). Even if these verses are a later addition, as some think, this reversal of the curse leads to a restoration of the lost territories of Israel,[27]

26. Smoak, "Building Houses and Planting Vineyards," 35. Also see Head, "The Curse of Covenant Reversal."

27. Schniedewind, *Society and the Promise to David*, 63–65.

In that day I will restore David's fallen shelter. I will repair its broken walls, restore its ruins—and build it as it used to be, so that they may possess the remnant of Edom and all the nations that bear my name," declares the Lord, who will do these things. "The days are coming," declares the Lord, "when the reaper will be overtaken by the plowman and the planter by the one treading grapes. New wine will drip from the mountains and flow from all the hills. I will bring back my people Israel back from exile; they will rebuild the ruined (*nĕšammôt*) cities and live in them. They will plant vineyards and drink their wine; they will make gardens and eat their fruit. I will plant Israel in their own land, never again to be uprooted from the land I have given them," says the Lord your God. (Amos 9:11–15)

The dual imagery of replanting and rebuilding is in direct contrast to Amos 4 with its descriptions of famine, drought, blight, mildew, and plague. The poignant imagery is of a harvest so incredible that as soon as the produce is harvested, the farmer is already sowing seed for the next one. This imagery is reminiscent of Lev 26:4–5, "I will send you rain in its season, and the ground will yield its crops and the trees of the field their fruit. Your threshing will continue until grape harvest and the grape harvest will continue until planting, and you will eat all the food you want and live in safety in your land." Amos makes the point specific by playing on the two themes of planting vineyards and *planting* Israel, never to be uprooted.

Zechariah 8 also promises that the time of humiliation is over and the days will return when life for Israel and Judah will be blessing, a time of fertility, prosperity, safety, authority, and divine presence. This theme of reversal which contrasts the gloomy picture presented in Zech 7:13–14 is a most fitting conclusion to Zechariah 1–8.[28] The era when Judah and Israel are objects of the curse has now concluded. Using the vine and vineyard imagery already noted, Zechariah's promise of blessing is clear.

"Thus says the Lord: I have returned to Zion and will dwell in the midst of Jerusalem, and Jerusalem shall be called the faithful city, and the mountain of the Lord of hosts, the holy mountain. Thus says the Lord of hosts: Old men and old women shall again sit in the streets of Jerusalem, each with staff in hand because of great age. And the streets of the city shall be full of boys and girls playing in its streets. Thus says the Lord of hosts: If it is marvelous in the sight of the remnant of this people in those days, should it also be marvelous in my sight, declares the Lord

28. Ollenburger, *The Book of Zechariah*, 796.

of hosts? Thus says the Lord of hosts: Behold, I will save my people from the east country and from the west country, and I will bring them to dwell in the midst of Jerusalem. And they shall be my people, and I will be their God, in faithfulness and in righteousness."

Thus says the Lord of hosts: "Let your hands be strong, you who in these days have been hearing these words from the mouth of the prophets who were present on the day that the foundation of the house of the Lord of hosts was laid, that the temple might be built. For before those days there was no wage for man or any wage for beast, neither was there any safety from the foe for him who went out or came in, for I set every man against his neighbor. But now I will not deal with the remnant of this people as in the former days, declares the Lord of hosts. For there shall be a sowing of peace. The vine shall give its fruit, and the ground shall give its produce, and the heavens shall give their dew. And I will cause the remnant of this people to possess all these things. And as you have been a byword of cursing among the nations, O house of Judah and house of Israel, so will I save you, and you shall be a blessing. Fear not, but let your hands be strong." (Zech 8:3–13, ESV)

The announcement "this is what the Lord Almighty says" recurs ten times in this chapter. Many interpreters read chapter 8 as a sermon. Reflecting a similar promise in Zech 1:16, this sermon notes the return of the divine presence of Yahweh to the holy mountain of Zion, consistent with Joel 4:17 and Ezek 48:35. Jerusalem is given a new character and new nicknames. Instead of an object of cursing among the peoples, it is now a City of Truth and God's holy mountain. Jerusalem, once a portrait of abject horror, has become a place of safety. The blissful picture of old men and women sitting surrounded by children playing in the "open places" is a great reversal of the former exile and destruction.[29] The writer of 1 Maccabees employs similar language to depict the period of peace and safety won by Simon when he secured political independence from the Seleucids: "Old men sat in the streets; they all talked together of good things, and the youths put on splendid military attire" (1 Macc 14:9, NRSV). Yahweh's rhetorical question of v. 6 recalls Jer 32:15: "Houses, fields, and vineyards will again be bought in the land." Instead of the language of Zechariah 7, with Israel being scattered, strangers, and desolate, new imagery ushers in a time of bounty and prosperity.

29. Meyers and Meyers, *Haggai–Zechariah 1–8*, 416.

The entire sermon of Zechariah 8 is replete with language from the blessings of Leviticus 26. Twice in this passage Yahweh proudly announces a return to Zion. Yahweh will dwell in the middle of the city (Lev 26:11). Citing the covenant formula, Yahweh declares that Jerusalem will once again house the people of God (Lev 26:12). There will be a universal gathering of God's people to live in Jerusalem (cf. Isa 11:11–12; 43:5–7; Jer 30:8–11; 31:7–8). The immediate setting of the Zechariah 8 sermon relates to the laying of the foundation for the temple. This risky undertaking has led to a new promise of blessing and peace. This promise should encourage the completion of this important task. Zech 8:10 reflects Deuteronomy 28:6, contrasting the former desperate times when people could not "go out or come in" because there was no peace. The word *šlwm* is used four times in Zechariah 8—in verses 10, 12, 16, and 19.

Verses 11–13 ascribe the language of blessing to both Israel and Judah. The people who were once an object of Yahweh's curse are now blessed. Note the parallel in Zechariah 2.

> Sing and rejoice, O daughter of Zion, for behold, I come and I will dwell in your midst, declares the LORD. And many nations shall join themselves to the LORD in that day, and shall be my people. And I will dwell in your midst, and you shall know that the LORD of hosts has sent me to you. And the LORD will inherit Judah as his portion in the holy land, and will again choose Jerusalem." Be silent, all flesh, before the LORD, for he has roused himself from his holy dwelling. (Zech 2:10–13, ESV)

Ezekiel 34–36 describes the hill of blessing and takes up the covenant blessings of fertility, prosperity, safety, and divine presence.

> I will make a covenant of peace (*běrît šālôm*) with them and rid the land of wild beasts so that they may live in the desert and sleep in the forests in safety. I will bless (*běrākâ*) them and the places surrounding my hill. I will send down showers in season; there will be showers of blessing (*běrākâ*). The trees of the field will yield their fruit and the ground will yield its crops; the people will be secure in their land. They will know that I am the LORD, when I break the bars of their yoke and rescue them from the hands of those who enslaved them. They will no longer be plundered by the nations, nor will wild animals devour them. They will live in safety, and no one will make them afraid. I will provide for them a land renowned for its crops (*maṭṭâ lěšēm*), and they will no longer be victims of famine in the land or bear the scorn of the nations. Then they will know that I, the LORD their God, am with them and that they, the house of Israel, are

> my people, declares the Sovereign LORD. You my sheep, the
> sheep of my pasture, are people, and I am your God, declares
> the Sovereign LORD. (Ezek 34:25–31)

Note Eichrodt's comment: "It can hardly be said that this passage is remarkable for definitiveness in division or for clarity of construction. Familiar features expressive of prophetic eschatological expectation come one on top of another, without any effort at completeness or systematic arrangement."[30] Yet that is exactly the point. The language is over the top . . . loaded down with varied imagery of the blessing. The covenant of peace of Ezek 34:25 is associated with the one forged at Sinai.[31] Yet the renewal language of Ezekiel 34 is no mere reinstitution of the Sinai covenant. It is something new altogether (cf. Ezek 36:22–32).[32] The renewal described by Ezekiel is nothing less than a complete transformation of nature.[33] Verse 26, "my hill of blessing" (*gib'ātî běrākâ*) is vague, perhaps intentionally so. One obvious possibility is that the hill denotes Jerusalem and the Temple Mount. As seen previously, the entire unit is replete with language and language reversals of Leviticus 26. Ezek 34:28 in particular converts the curses of Lev 26:5–6 into their opposite blessings (cf. Jer 30:10; Mic 4:4; Zeph 3:13). The expression in Ezek 34:27, "when I break the bars of their yoke," is an expression found only here and in Lev 26:13. Moshe Greenburg notes that along the lines of the blessings and curses of Deut 28 and Lev 26, the welfare of the restored community will be a direct providence of God.[34] The covenant curse of Lev 26:22 regarding ravenous beasts is coupled with the promise of blessing in Lev 26:6. Yahweh also eradicates the dangerous animals from this restoration land: "A land renowned" depicts a reversal of the curse. Instead of being a metonymical curse among all the peoples of the earth, Israel will never again be the butt of insults from foreign peoples.

Ezekiel 36 also highlights this reversal of the curse. Here the imagery of a time before the curse in the Garden of Eden. Those cities which were once laid waste are now a fruitful garden. This is nothing less than

---

30. Eichrodt, *Ezekiel*, 475.

31. Darr, *The Book of Ezekiel*, 6:1472, argues that the linking of these text with Ezekiel 16:60 is strained. Rather, the covenant of peace is associated with the covenant forged at Sinai (Leviticus 26; Deuteronomy 28).

32. Such imagery is also present in Isa 29:17ff.; 32:15ff; and Jer 31:4ff.

33. See Kelle, "Dealing with the Trauma of Defeat."

34. Greenburg, *Ezekiel 21–37*, 703, 707.

a complete reversal of desolation language. Note the parallels to Amos 9 described above.

> This is what the Sovereign LORD says: On the day I cleanse you from all your sins, I will resettle your towns, and the ruins (*hehŏrābôt*) will be rebuilt. The desolate land will be cultivated instead of lying desolate (*šĕmāmâ*) in the sight of all who pass through it. They will say, "This land that was laid waste (*hannĕšammâ*) has become like the Garden of Eden; the cities that were lying in ruins, desolate (*hehŏrābôt*) and destroyed, are now fortified and inhabited." Then the nations around you that remain will know that I the Lord have rebuilt what was destroyed and have replanted what was desolate (*wĕhanšamôt*). I the Lord have spoken, and I will do it. (Ezek 36:33–36)

The reversal of desolation imagery expands in Isaiah beyond a simple reunification of Israel and Judah. The wildly extravagant note of hopefulness now includes Isaiah's amazing promise that Egypt, Assyria, and Israel will all experience God's blessing. This international promise, among the loftiest of the entire Bible, is a "conscious fulfillment" of the original promise to Abraham.[35]

> In that day there will be a highway from Egypt to Assyria. The Assyrians will go to Egypt and the Egyptians to Assyria. The Egyptians and Assyrians will worship together. In that day Israel will be the third, along with Egypt and Assyria, a blessing (*bĕrākâ*) on the earth. The LORD Almighty will bless them, saying, "Blessed be Egypt my people, Assyria my handiwork, and Israel my inheritance." (Isa 19:23–25)

---

35. Muilenburg, "Abraham and the Nations," 396.

10

"May the Lord Bless You"

Blessings and Curses in Israel's Cult

Psalms and Theology

It is not insignificant that the oldest texts in both Old and New Testaments are songs.[1] Something about the combination of music and words makes for easy recall, touches the emotions as well as the mind, and can be passed along easily to others. William Hendricks often quipped that most people learn more theology from their worship songs than from the Bible.[2] Songs are not merely a product *of* theology but a source *for* theology. They don't just methodically enumerate life's experiences that God gives; they theologize about those experiences, good and bad. In the Bible, these songs celebrate God's superiority over every other power, known and unknown. They define the reason for God's kingship over the earth; they revel in the notion that God's kindness lasts forever. This kind of experiential knowledge is fundamental to the human consciousness. Giving praise is one of the most elementary characteristics of being alive.

Theologically, the Psalms are the densest material in the Old Testament.[3] Theology and doxology are two sides of a coin. Theology articulates the nature and character of God, and doxology is a way that

1. Jeremias, "Worship and Theology in the Psalms," 89.
2. Hendricks, *A Theology for Children.*
3. Goldingay, *Psalms,* 1:69.

242

humans celebrate God's nature and character. As a collection of literature espousing the interplay of theology and doxology, the psalter portrays a dichotomy: a life lived before God and a life lived in response to God.[4] The psalter reflects the gamut of human experiences and emotions—from the highest highs to the lowest lows. Like the music of any generation, songs are created primarily by individuals, but they are not typically merely about individual experiences and emotions; they function best in community. In other words, songs by nature are meant to be shared. Whether the cognitive content of the musical text is positive or negative, the songs in the Bible are rooted in emotive relationship—relationship with God and fellow human beings. Yet the psalms aren't merely secular songs. They assume all the complexities of a relationship with God; the psalmists are covenant writers. The content of these songs espouses the popular theology of the day, and like the theology of the rest of the Old Testament, the psalms are not abstract, intellectual speculations. They are intended to be imminently relevant to life lived in covenant with other people and in covenant with God. The psalms convey layers of theological meaning in a way that poetry combined with music only can. As one reads the collection of Israel's songs of worship, a point of view about God emerges, even given the diversity of that collection.

By the way, just because an emotion or attitude is found in the Bible, it doesn't mean that what a biblical character does or says is necessarily prescriptive to all generations. One of the problems of canon is that a canon tends to level everything to the same rank of authority. Just like there are people in the Bible who are not the best role models for us today so that their personal morality should not be emulated, so there are emotions expressed toward God and others in the Psalter that are not only not very Christian or Jewish; indeed they are not even very *human*. We will not flinch at some of these less than sublime expressions of hatred towards others, neither will we try to rationalize or explain away such emotionally loaded language. Nevertheless, we refuse to manipulate these wishes for the misfortune of others to be anything less than desperate, vengeful, and petty attempts by humans to force God to take their own side.

Patrick Miller categorizes some of these life experiences celebrated or denigrated in the psalms an awareness of the transiency of life, a declaration of the majestic glory of God, a feeling of godforsakenness, the lifelong confidence in the trustworthiness of God, the simple joy and blessing of children, the jarring moral outrage of sin, the human yearning to reach

---

4. Miller, *Interpreting the Psalms*, 19.

out for that which transcends ourselves, the anxiety and despair over a sense of feeling trapped in some present circumstance, the experience of God's repetitive help, and the common experience of low self-esteem and worthlessness.[5] Some of these experiences and emotions are not time bound, while others are given explicit concrete, historical situations. For Christians, these psalms enjoy a history of rich interaction with New Testament texts, not to mention their own reapplication and reinterpretation elsewhere in the Old Testament.

Form criticism has dominated the study of the book of Psalms for over a century. This has led to a great deal of attention to the literary type and character of each psalm. Erhard Gerstenberger expressed a sense of alarm about recent approaches that have shown no interest in the life and cultic setting of the psalms. He rightfully warns that approaches that neglect these backgrounds are irresponsible.[6] Instead he tries to develop a case for not isolating texts from their ground of origin. Context is essential because the closeness of these musical texts to life situations and ritual directly bears on theology. It is obvious, or should be, that religious songs sprang up from different social and cultic contexts. Neither should we try to pigeonhole every psalm into some kind of boilerplate genre. For example, some psalms appear to give instruction to the covenant community of faith about their own sacred history (Psalms 78; 105; 106; 136). Other psalms portray a pilgrimage of believers who have journeyed to the temple for festivals and worship (Psalms 23; 42–43; 113–118; 122).[7] Still others utter highest praises for a God who rules the world and who intervenes in human life in positive ways (Psalms 19; 146–150). Some mutter about God's abandonment and inattention to the plight of his own people (Psalms 3–7). And, notoriously, some invoke God's curse on their human enemies, hoping that God will snuff out their lives (Psalms 35; 58; 109). Like it or not, one can really find it all in the Psalms.

The book of Deuteronomy reveals an interesting exchange richly illustrating the interplay between written text and music relevant to the use of songs in cultic settings. This is important for the present study because of our interest in performative ritual and language associated with speech acts. In this exchange between Moses, Joshua, and the people, Moses writes down the law and gives it to the priests with the instructions that

5. Ibid., 20–25.

6. Gerstenberger, "Life Situations and Theological Concepts of Old Testament Psalms," 83.

7. Anderson, *Out of the Depths*; Smith, "The Psalms as a Book for Pilgrims."

every seven years the entire law should be read aloud before all Israel in a ritual context. People of all ages and both genders, as well as outsiders who live in their towns, are required to participate in the ritualized sabbatical reading of the written text. Then, somewhat surprisingly, Moses also instructs Joshua to write down the words of a song (yes, a song!) and to teach it to the people as well. This song is also intended to be a lasting witness for Moses against the people of Israel. When Israel disobeys God, which Moses seems to have a premonition they most certainly will, both the written law and the audible song will confront them as witnesses. The chapter concludes as Moses writes down the words of the Book of the Law, and then commands the priests to put it alongside the ark of the covenant as a witness against Israel. Then at the end of Deuteronomy 31 Moses subsequently introduces the words of the song that make up Deuteronomy 32.[8] What is informative for the use of songs in cultic settings is that the song in Deuteronomy 32 is treated with equal reverence to the written law. Frankly, the lyrics of this song are not very uplifting. One can only imagine whether a somber tune or chanted cadence matched the sober message. The song's main theme is that God is an unmovable, steady Rock (Deut 32:4, 15, 18, 30, 31, 37). The song draws from creation themes, when God divided all humanity into peoples and fixed the borders of kingdoms. His own portion from among the created peoples which he chose only for himself, was Israel. Sadly, the text of the song accuses the people of God of forsaking that Rock, unmindful of God's salvation. Because of their proven rejection, God promises to heap disaster on them (Deut 32:23). This is not a musical text that exudes a lot of confidence for the future of this burgeoning people. At the end of the narrative, Moses recites the words of this song, which one can read today in Deuteronomy 32. In this example, one can easily observe the interplay between ritual, music or chant, and written text in a cultic setting. David Carr has keenly observed that in the ancient Near East, writing possessed a numinous quality. Textuality and orality were two sides of a coin. The literacy that counted most in ancient societies was not the basic ability to read and write but an oral-written mastery of a body of texts, much like those in the Old Testament.[9] From the perspective of speech acts, the combination of the oral mastery of songs like the Song of Moses and the oral recapitulation of the Book of the Law held a performative function that served as a witness against Israel.

8. Thiessen contends that a number of various features of the Song of Moses are not explicable unless understood to have originated in the context of worship; "The Form and Function of the Song of Moses."

9. Carr, *Writing on the Tablet of the Heart*, 14.

PSALMS AND BLESSING

Frankly, there is only a loose connection between blessings and the structure of the book of Psalms, and there is no blindingly obvious connection between curses and the literary structure of the book at all, even though blessings and curses can be found in abundance throughout the Psalter. But the loose connections between blessings and the structure of Psalms are nevertheless worth exploring, because they carry with them some meaningful theological insights. It is well known that the book of Psalms is a composite work of five books made up of the following chapters: 1–41, 42–72, 73–89, 90–106, and 107–150. Theologically, this arrangement presents the reader with a Torah of David (the paradigmatic model king) alongside a Torah of Moses (the paradigmatic model prophet). Each of these five books ends with a doxology, and, as will be argued below, each ends with a specific blessing. Royal or messianic psalms are scattered throughout the book, particularly along the seams at the ends of the first three books.[10] These royal psalms begin book 1 and conclude books 2 and 3, and in some respects may even call for a response in books 4 and 5. The conclusion of book 2 makes it clear that the Davidic covenant has come to an end. How will Israel respond? Likewise, a number of psalms of cursing are scattered throughout the book but appear to have no relationship to the structure.

Eric Zenger has argued that these doxologies, even if they come from different hands, provide a way of interpreting the Psalms.[11] Many would agree with Zenger that these closing doxologies were not part of the original version of each psalm but were added later. Regardless, the ultimate canonical shape of the Psalms forces the reader to interact with the blessing theme in the book. With Psalm 1, the book of Psalms begins with a blessing and a curse: the blissfully blessed life of the righteous is sharply contrasted with the gloomy fate of the wicked. The opening expression, "Blessed is the one who does not walk in the counsel of the wicked," introduces this torah-wisdom psalm. The Hebrew here, translated as "happy is," or "blessed is" (*šry*) is relatively common in the Psalms, used some twenty-six time. Some have suggested that *šry* is a secular form of the more religious sounding *brk*, but that difference is overstated when one looks at the Psalms contextually.[12] The two words are synonyms, and both

10. Wilson, *The Editing of the Hebrew Psalter*, 207.

11. Zenger, *Der Psalter in Judentum und Christentum*, 1–57.

12. Cazelles, "*šry.*"

have theological significance. K. C. Hanson argues that these two words are largely misconstrued. They are thematically related but linguistically and contextually distinct. The word *'šry* entails a value judgment rooted in the value system of honor and shame rather than a pronouncement.[13] The English phrase "happy is," or "blessed is," using *'šry,* is found in a number of psalms related to spiritual matters like the one whose sins are forgiven (Ps 32:1–2), the one who fears God (Pss 112:1; 128:1), the one whose way is blameless (Ps 119:1), and as in the case of Psalm 1, the one who does not follow the ways of the wicked (Ps 1:1). In some sense, all the psalms vividly portray what it means to be happy or blessed.[14]

This specific expression of blessing also closes out Psalm 2: "Blessed are all who take refuge in him." Early Jewish and Christian interpreters, as well as most modern interpreters, regularly read Psalms 1 and 2 as one psalm. If Psalm 1 and 2 are read together, this blessing at the beginning of Psalm 1 and at the end of Psalm 2 forms a ring that opens up the larger book of Psalms. The keyword *hgh,* which is translated "meditate" in Psalm 1, repeats and is translated quite differently as "plot" in Psalm 2. Blessings also close out books 1 (Ps 41:13) 2 (Ps 72:18–19), 3 (Ps 89:52), 4 (Ps 106:48) and 5 (Ps 145:21).

Psalm 145 begins and ends with a blessing as do Psalms 1 and 2, but after this, the blessing-structure breaks down—that is, unless one reads the last five psalms as a separate unit. Psalm 146–150, five psalms of praise, form an elaborate conclusion to the book of Psalms. All these begin with the same opening: "Praise the LORD" (*halĕlû yāh*). They are clearly songs of praise that close out the Psalter on a high note (pardon the pun). If the last five psalms are read as a unit, then Psalm 145 has a heightened importance structurally.[15] Many have struggled to make some sense (with mixed success) of whether the individual psalms included in the five books are categorized in intentional ways.[16] It has been noted that most of the laments are in the first half of the book of Psalms, and that the collection seems to display momentum in a positive direction with more hymns of praise toward the end. This may or may not be the case. But in the case of blessings one is on solid ground to say that the blessing provides a loose

13. K. C. Hanson, "'How Honorable!' 'How Shameful!'"

14. McCann, *The Book of Psalms* 4:684.

15. Wilson argues that Psalm 145 is the theological climax of the fifth book; *The Editing of the Hebrew Psalter,* 225.

16. DeClaissé-Walford, *Reading from the Beginning.* Also see the series of essays in McCann, *The Shape and Shaping of the Psalter.*

structure to the five books within the larger whole, particularly if one reads Psalms 146–150 as a final musical movement to the book, leaving Psalm 145 as the psalm with the final blessing.

Most of the blessings in Psalms are directed in one of two ways: humans blessing Yahweh or humans being blessed by Yahweh. The expression "Blessed be Yahweh," or "Blessed be God" is found a dozen or more times in the Psalms.[17] Some translations render the phrase simply as, "Praise the LORD!" Blessed people are those who are righteous (Psalm 5), who have clean hands and a pure heart (Psalm 24), whose transgressions are forgiven (Ps 32), who take refuge in Yahweh (Psalm 34), who make Yahweh their trust (Psalm 40), who consider the poor (Psalm 41), who are disciplined by Yahweh (Psalm 94), who observe justice (Psalm 106), who fear Yahweh (Psalm 112) and whose help is the LORD (Psalm 146). Blessings are sung on behalf of the king, the temple, the family, the land, the covenant, God's people, and the kingdom. A sung or chanted blessing or curse is just as much an utterance as a spoken blessing if it meets with Austin's conventions of performative speech. Therefore the power of this kind of illocutionary language is formidable.

My argument so far is that blessings begin and end book 1. Blessings also conclude books 2, 3, and 4. We will argue that book 5 ends with Psalm 145 which also ends in blessing. Curses are scattered throughout the Psalter with little or no structural significance. Messianic psalms or royal psalms are also scattered about but appear to have more significance to the general structure of the book. The opening of the Psalter (Psalm 2) and the close of books 1 (Psalm 41), 2 (Psalm 72), and 3 (Psalm 89) can all be read as psalms blessing the king. Finally, the psalms that close out each book of the collection all use the Hebrew *ôlām*, the language of the perpetuity of Yahweh and his rule: "You . . . set me in your presence forever" (Ps 41:12), "may his name endure forever" (Ps 72:17), "blessed be his glorious name forever" (Ps 72:19, ESV), "steadfast love will be built up forever" (Ps 89:2, ESV), "Blessed be the LORD forever" (Ps 89:52, ESV), "his steadfast love endures forever" (Ps 106:1, ESV), "Blessed be the LORD, the God of Israel, from everlasting to everlasting" (Ps 106:48), "and let all flesh bless his holy name forever" (Ps 145:21, ESV). The significance of these examples will be examined below. The point of our examination is not to do a careful exegesis of each psalm but only to demonstrate how the theme of blessing engages with each psalm.

17. Pss 28:6; 31:21; 41:13; 66:20; 68:19, 35; 72:18; 89:52; 106:48; 124:6; 135:21; 144:1.

Psalms 1–2

Editors placed Psalm 1–2 at the beginning of the collection. This canonical assignment has given these two psalms a new function.[18] Neither of these two psalms has a title. They are framed by blessing formulas at 1:1, "Blessed is the man who does not walk in the council of the wicked," and 2:12 "Blessed are all who take refuge in him." The ancient Greek Codex D introduces Paul's citation of Psalm 2:7 as Psalm 1, indicating these two psalms were taken together rather early. The keyword *hgh*, translated "to meditate" in Ps 1:2 and "plot" in Ps 2:1, serves as a lynch pin joining the two psalms. In some ways, the two psalms couldn't be more different. Psalm 1 focuses completely on the individual while Psalm 2 is entirely international. Here the foreign kingdoms are furiously conspiring together to plot against Yahweh and his anointed. But read together, these two psalms suggest a reading for the whole book. Individual experience and edification with the Lord is juxtaposed alongside a volatile international context. That sentence describes the history of Israel and the church alike.

Psalm 1 is a torah-wisdom psalm. Like the book of Proverbs, with its two-way theology, Psalm 1 also sets a dichotomy between vv. 1–3 and 4–5: the way of the righteous and the way of the wicked. Christian scholars as early as Jerome observed parallels between Psalm 1 to Deut 30:15–20. Both passages set the challenge to choose the way of blessing or the way of curse.[19] The word *drk* ("way") is a dominant metaphor in Psalm 1. The blessed man keeps his distance from the wicked and draws closely to the law by meditating (*hgh*) on it day and night. God's torah, God's instruction, is where true righteousness can be found. The psalm exploits the contrast between the grounded, permanent productivity of the righteous versus the ephemeral uselessness of a life lived outside Yahweh's orientation of righteousness. Fertility language of blessing-and-curse permeates the psalm. The language relates to both conduct and destiny. The command to meditate on the law is reminiscent of Josh 1:7–8. While the Lord knows the way of the righteous, there is a certain amount of ambiguity in the psalm's claim that the way of the wicked "perishes." The wicked person's chaff-like fate drifts off into oblivion. This two-way theology that espouses a Deuteronomic approach to human decision making affirms the importance of life's perilous choices.[20] How life is lived is patently decisive.

---

18. Childs, *Introduction to the Old Testament as Scripture*, 513.
19. Waltke and Houston, *The Psalms as Christian Worship*, 118–19.
20. Mays, "The Place of the Torah-Psalms in the Psalter," 4–5.

Echoes of this psalm in the New Testament emerge in Jesus's Sermon on the Mount (Matt 5:17–20).

Psalm 2 links back to Psalm 1 by the lack of a superscription, the blessing clause at the end, and the reuse of the *leitwort hgh*. Now instead of a call to individual righteousness, we hear of the tumult of kingdoms, kings and empires; their clashes and conflict with Yahweh and his Messiah. The use of the word *hgh* in Ps 1:2 as quiet contemplative devotion versus its use again in Ps 2:1 as vain scheming against God's rule depicts a telling parallelism. The righteous individual ruminates on ways she can better apply God's law while the kings of the foreign kingdoms muse over how to develop coalitions against Yahweh and his anointed. Yahweh scoffs at such nonsense:

> The One enthroned in heaven laughs;
>> the LORD scoffs at them.
> Then he rebukes them in his anger
>> and terrifies them in his wrath, saying,
> "I have installed my King
>> on Zion, my holy hill."
>
> I will proclaim the decree of the LORD:
>
> He said to me, "You are my Son;
>> today I have become your Father.
> Ask of me,
>> and I will make the nations your inheritance,
>> the ends of the earth your possession.
> You will rule them with an iron scepter;
>> you will dash them to pieces like pottery." (Ps 2:4–9)

Why does Yahweh scoff? Because Yahweh has adopted the king as his son! This psalm displays a theology of an office where a king's installation is a divine act.[21] Like the wise individual in Psalm 1 who follows God's law, these foreign kings would be wise to not provoke God's adopted son. Psalm 2 depicts the sovereignty of God amid the conflicts and power struggles of human history. The promise in v. 8 to "make the nations your inheritance and the ends of the earth your possession" rings of God's promise to Abraham in Genesis 12.

Not surprisingly, the writers of the New Testament are enthralled with the theological implications of this messianic psalm. Mark 1:11 and Mark 9:7 and their parallels depict Jesus's baptism and transfiguration

21. Mays, *Psalms*, 47.

as moments when God's divine rule is visibly made known through his Son. Acts 13:33 states that just as promised, the resurrection of Jesus demonstrates God's power through his Son, and the quotation of this psalm in Heb 1:5 follows immediately after a passage with some of the highest Christology in the entire New Testament:

> Long ago, at many times and in many ways, God spoke to our
> fathers by the prophets, but in these last days he has spoken to
> us by his Son, whom he appointed the heir of all things, through
> whom also he created the world. He is the radiance of the glory
> of God and the exact imprint of his nature, and he upholds the
> universe by the word of his power. After making purification
> for sins, he sat down at the right hand of the Majesty on high,
> having become as much superior to angels as the name he has
> inherited is more excellent than theirs. (Heb 1:1–4, ESV)

Similarly, in the last book of the New Testament, "the kingdom of this world has become the kingdom of our Lord and Christ" (Rev 11:15). Finally, the conclusion of Psalm 2, "blessed are all who take refuge in him" is a warning as well as a promise.

Psalm 41

Psalm 41 opens "blessed (*šry*) is the one who has regard for the weak" and closes, "Blessed (*brk*) be the Lᴏʀᴅ, the God of Israel." Form critics have struggled with what to do with this psalm. It cannot be forced into any clean form-critical category. Perhaps it is best to follow Mowinckel's safer generalized designation as a "psalm of sickness." In one sense, this psalm mirrors the opening of the psalter in Psalm 1. Both songs begin with the good fortune of certain kinds of people. In Psalm 1 the person who follows God's instruction is blessed; the life lived in harmony with torah is a life of blessing. Yet in the psalms that follow immediately afterwards, the writers launch protest after protest that God does not always act that way. In this particular psalm, the opening blessing is on the one who sustains the poor/weak. In Hebrew this word is *dl*, and is most often rendered "poor," but can also be translated as "low" or "weak." Contextually, a translation of "poor" doesn't seem to fit the rest of the psalm. The basic thrust of the psalm is that one who has shown concern for the weak may expect God's blessing in their own time of weakness. In this case, that weakness refers to physical infirmity. There are three verbs of blessing in v. 2: "protect," "preserve," and "bless."

> Blessed (*ʾšry*) is the one who considers the poor!
> In the day of trouble the LORD delivers him;
> the LORD protects him and keeps him alive;
> he is called blessed (*ʾšry*) in the land
> and do not give him up to the will of his enemies..
> The LORD sustains him on his sickbed;
> in his illness you restore him to full health. (Ps 41:1–3, ESV)

This train of thought is similar to Jesus's words in the New Testament, "Blessed are the merciful for they shall be shown mercy" (Matt 5:7). Some have also read this psalm as a messianic or royal psalm. Such an interpretation is not decisive but is certainly possible.[22] The New Testament interprets it as such. Multiple references in the psalm to enemies who visit the speaker conjure up images of royal audiences, even from those who are secretly hoping that the king will never recover. There are references to the Lord's sustaining the psalmist on his sickbed. People come to visit him and utter empty words, then go out behind his back and talk about his bad prognosis for recovery. These "friends" are hovering around him like vultures waiting for him to die. Verse 5 contains a not-so-playful pun *mty ymwt*, "when will he die?" Just as it was for Job, so for the speaker of this psalm, even his close friends have turned on him:

> All my enemies whisper together against me;
> they imagine the worst for me, saying,
> "A vile disease has beset him;
> he will never get up from the place where he lies."
> Even my close friend, whom I trusted,
> he who shared my bread,
> has lifted up his heel against me. (Ps 41:7–9)

Verse 8 contains an interesting curse placed on the lips of his enemies: *dĕbar bĕliaʿal yāṣûq bô* ("may a Belial thing be poured out on him"). Belial was that mythological power associated with death and chaos. Later expressions in the Old Testament of "a son of Belial" or a "belial-like man" connote all kinds of derogatory conduct. His enemies are clearly longing for his destruction. Verse 9 is quoted in the New Testament book of John regarding Jesus's betrayal (John 13:18). Eating bread, part of a covenant rite is part of both the Old and New Testament contexts of this psalm. The prayer of vengeance that follows is inexcusable but makes perfect sense in light of the adversarial relationships described above. The psalmist wants vengeance, but more important, he does not leave that vengeance in the

---

22. Eaton, *Kingship and the Psalms*, 44–46.

hands of Yahweh. He wants to be raised up so he can extract revenge . . . personally.

Psalm 72

In principle, the king is to embody the rule of Yahweh. Psalm 72, in many respects, is a commentary on how that rule should be administered by the king. Israel's king is to judge all people, including the poor, righteously (v. 2), to defend the cause of the poor (v. 4), and to deliver the needy saving them from violence and oppression (v. 12). This blessing Psalm for the king was perhaps first written for an inauguration. One cannot say for sure. It begins as a prayer asking God to bestow certain blessings upon the king's rule. Twelve jussives delineate the content of these blessings: that the people fear him and his rule be one of peace, that he receive tribute from kingdoms far away, that he live a long life, that he receive blessings all day long, that there be plenty of grain, that there may be prosperity for his people, and that he will retain a name that endures for generations. The language of the psalm is expansive both geographically and temporally. Geographically, the blessing invokes that the king's domain extend from sea to sea, from the River (Euphrates) to the very ends of the earth (v. 8). Temporally, the king is to rule throughout all generations (*dôr dôrîm*), his name is to endure forever (*lĕʿôlām*), his fame is to endure as long as the sun continues to shine. Therefore the king represents the geographical and temporal expansiveness of Yahweh's reign on earth. Yahweh's glorious name is to be blessed forever (*lĕʿôlām*), and the whole earth will be filled with his glory. The psalm, which is a blessing throughout, concludes with the dual blessing of the king and the Lord.

> Long may he live!
> May gold from Sheba be given him.
> May people ever pray for him
>   and bless (*yĕbārakenhû*) him all day long.
> Let grain abound throughout the land;
>   on the tops of the hills may it sway.
> Let its fruit flourish like Lebanon;
>   let it thrive like the grass of the field.
> May his name endure forever;
>   may it continue as long as the sun.
> All nations will be blessed (*wĕyitbārkû*) through him,
>   and they will call him blessed (*yĕʾaššĕrûhû*).

> Praise (*barûk*) be to the L**ORD** God, the God of Israel,
>   who alone does marvelous deeds.
> Praise (*ûbārûk*) be to his glorious name forever;
>   may the whole earth be filled with his glory.
>
> Amen and Amen. (Ps 72:15–19)

One can hear echoes from Genesis 12, 2 Samuel 7, and 1 Kings 8 throughout the entire psalm. God's blessing is on his king and people, and that blessing carries over to all the kingdoms. Because the psalm closes with the sentence, "the prayers of David are ended" and because of the superscription of the song, Brevard Childs implies that it was sung by David for Solomon, perhaps at an inauguration.

The concluding two verses are a reminder that Yahweh is ultimately sovereign over all things. The double blessing formula depicts the stark contrast between the frailties of human kingship and the exclusive authority and comprehensive expansiveness of Yahweh's reign. Perhaps as worshipers recited the words of this psalm, they noted the contrast between how royal leaders were supposed to live as opposed to their actual behavior.

Psalm 89

Unlike the psalm above, Psalm 89 deconstructs Yahweh's covenant with David in 2 Samuel 7. It is a psalm of both praise and protest. A "Maskil of Ethan the Ezrahite" (1 Kgs 4:31), this psalm is one of the three or four longest psalms in the Bible. To say that the figure of Ethan the Ezrahite mentioned in Kings is also the author of Psalm 89 does not make sense in the context of the psalm, which is clearly much later and written in an entirely different historical context. There may be a possible play on the root *'zrh*, which means *native* "Israelite" (Lev 23:42; Num 15:13) and *'ytn*, which means "perennial." If so, a perennial Israelite would be contrasted with what the psalmist is presently experiencing: the collapse of the monarchy and the fall of Jerusalem. But almost nothing is certain. What is certain is that the psalm echoes the Davidic covenant of 2 Samuel 7: "You said, I have made a covenant with my chosen one, I have sworn to David my servant, I will establish your line forever and make your throne firm through all generations" (Ps 89:3–4). Notice the blunt accusation, "You said . . . ," which contrasts eternal God's promise with the current demise of the monarchy. This covenant also applies to the house of David. If his children violate the law, then they will be punished, but God will never remove his steadfast love from the house of David (Ps 89:20–37).

Like Psalm 19, this psalm displays dual themes of creation and covenant. Creation language is employed to denote Yahweh's incomparable power. He rules the raging sea, crushes Rahab like a carcass, and scatters his enemies. All heaven belongs to the Lord and every direction of the compass is under his sovereignty. Yahweh is praised among the heavenly beings and in the council of the holy ones, "Blessed (*ʾšry*) are those who learn to acclaim you, who walk in the light of your presence O LORD" (v. 15). The kingship is created by God's choice (vv. 19–20). God promises to be with the king against his enemies (vv. 21–27). God's blessing on David will be conferred on his descendants (vv. 28–37).

But . . . then the writer does a summersault. Yahweh has abandoned the king! The present situation is an incredible contradiction to what was supposed to characterize the monarchy. The covenant promise is in peril. In Ps 89:38–45 the psalmist angrily wonders how all these things can be happening in light of the covenant with David. The psalmist uses vivid language to portray the catastrophe. What has God done with his anointed? He is cast off, rejected, and God's wrath opposes him. His crown has been thrown in the dust, the city walls have been breached, he has been plundered by all who pass by, he is the scorn of all his neighbors, his enemies are thrilled with his dismal prospects, he has been forced to retreat in battle, his splendor has ceased, and his days cut short. The final line is perhaps the most damaging accusation against Yahweh: "you have covered him with shame" (Ps 89:45). To this, the psalmist asks, where is your faithfulness to the promise? How long must this go on? He takes the language of the geographical and temporal expansion of God's kingdom and turns it on its head. The word *ʿôlām* is used repeatedly: seven times in the psalm. God was supposed to establish the king's offspring forever (*ʿôlām*) and build his throne unto all generations. But now? The king's days have been "cut short." God has not honored the eternal covenant. Instead, the psalmist demands, "How long, O LORD? Will you hide yourself forever?" The use of creation language in the psalm implies that God has the power to do something about things but has chosen to remain inactive. Likewise, the root *ḥsd* is also used seven times (vv. 1–2, 14, 24, 28, 33, 49). In the first six instances God's loving faithfulness is affirmed and extolled. Yet after the transition in v. 38 the psalmist demands to know where this great love and faithfulness went. The psalm ends with a twofold plea for God to remember.

How long, O LORD? Will you hide yourself forever?
How long will your wrath burn like fire?
Remember how fleeting is my life.
For what futility you have created all men!
What man can live and not see death,
or save himself from the power of the grave?   *Selah*

O Lord, where is your former great love,
which in your faithfulness you swore to David?
Remember, Lord, how your servant has been mocked,
how I bear in my heart the taunts of all the nations,
the taunts with which your enemies have mocked, O Lord,
with which they have mocked every step of your anointed one.

Praise be to the LORD forever! (*bārûk yhwh lĕʿôlām*)
Amen and Amen. (Ps 89:46–52)

No wonder this psalm is typically read in Christian communities on Maundy Thursday! Originally the psalm was written in a clearly exilic context as a reflection on the humiliation of King Jehoiachin.

Psalm 106

Praise the LORD!
Give thanks to the LORD, for he is good;
his love endures forever.
Who can proclaim the mighty acts of the LORD
or fully declare his praise?
Blessed (*ʾšry*) are they who act justly,
who always do what is right. (Ps 106:1–3)

Even though Psalm 106 begins and ends with this blessing, it hits all the low points in Israel's pathetic history. It systematically recounts Israel's record of unfaithfulness, from their origins in Egypt until the exile; from their "desiring a desire" in the wilderness to the idolatrous golden calf to their refusal to enter the land and their infidelity at Baal Peor—this psalm reveals Israel's shortcomings. As a result, God has sent them into exile. The reasons for this exile are in clarified in vv. 34–39. Israel mixed with the foreign peoples and served their idols. They sacrificed sons and daughters to demons and shed innocent blood. God gave them into the hands of the nations who suppressed them under their power. The final blessing in verse 48 is paralleled in 1 Chron 16:36. The conclusion is a heartfelt plea for salvation. God forgave in the past, so why not now?

Many times he delivered them,
    but they were bent on rebellion
    and they wasted away in their sin.

Yet he took note of their distress
    when he heard their cry;
for their sake he remembered his covenant
    and out of his great love he relented.
He caused all who held them captive
    to show them mercy.

Save us, Lord our God,
    and gather us from the nations,
that we may give thanks to your holy name
    and glory in your praise.

Praise (*bārûk*) be to the Lord, the God of Israel,
    from everlasting to everlasting (*hā'ôlām wĕ'd hā'ôlām*).
Let all the people say, "Amen!"

Praise the Lord. (Ps 106:43–48, ESV)

Psalm 145

We have discussed the interplay between music and written text. As music, Psalm 145 is an overture to the final movement of the book of Psalms, Psalms 146–150. Like Psalm 1–2, 41, and 106, this psalm begins and ends with a blessing. But unlike any of the examples so far, the psalm is written as an acrostic. The inclusio "bless your name forever and ever (*lĕ'ôlām wā'ed*) in v. 1, and "let all flesh bless his holy name forever and ever (*lĕ'ôlām wā'ed*) in v. 21 recites the attributes that comprise the nature and character of God, from A to Z. The language is over the top. The root every/all (*kl*) is repeated 16 times in the psalm. The use of the entire Hebrew alphabet combined with the generous use of *kl* underscores the unlimited comprehensiveness of praise to Yahweh.[23] The final line, "all flesh will bless his holy name," reflects the universal scope of God's praise. The psalm describes the relation of God's acts of power and God's abundant goodness between earlier and midpoint of the psalm. The last line anticipates the book's final movement leading up to Psalm 150. Psalm 145:21 foreshadows 150:6; these two verses form an inclusio around this final musical movement.

---

23. The letter *n* is missing in the acrostic.

> My mouth will speak the praise of the LORD,
> and let all flesh bless his holy name forever. (Ps 145:21, ESV)

> Let everything that has breath praise the LORD. Praise the LORD!
> (Ps 150:6)

What conclusions can be made about the theme of blessing and its relationship to the structure of the book of Psalms? The blessing structure represents theologically prominent stages in Israel's history. The two blessings at the end of book 1 and book 2 (Psalms 41; 72) reflect the period of the united monarchy of David and Solomon; the close of book 3 (Psalm 89) is set in the context of the collapse of the monarchy, and the prayer of repentance and request for deliverance that ends book 4 (Psalm 106) describe the scattering of God's people in exile among the foreign peoples. Assuming that Psalms 146–150 are added as a single final exultation of praise to complete the Psalter, one can point to the last verse of book 5, which is a blessing: "My mouth will speak the praise of the LORD, and let all flesh bless his holy name forever and ever" (Ps 145:21, ESV). This universal injunction of blessing is to all humanity. Book 4 is the theological climax of the book of Psalms.[24] Israel is under judgment but not full abandonment. Messianic psalms figure prominently in this blessing structure.

CENSORED PSALMS

William Holladay has taken up the topic of censored Christian texts, particularly the exclusion of certain psalms from Christian worship.[25] Certain components of Roman Catholic liturgy are designed to cover the entire book of Psalms over a year. Yet the Roman Catholic liturgy of the hours completely omits Psalms 58, 83, and 109 altogether. There are also large-scale omissions: Psalm 35, 59, and 69, as well as verses here and there in other psalms (Pss 35:4–6; 139:19–20) that frankly do not read too well in Christian contexts. Patrick Miller shares this sense of discomfort. He has written a wonderful chapter on blessings and curses in his book on the form and theology of biblical prayer. Miller concedes that blessing is a vital part of Christian tradition. Cursing, on the other hand, is not only generally unfamiliar to the contemporary religious community as a prayer; it also seems to have no legitimate place in its life of prayer. No religious community engages in any kind of frequent or regular prayer for

24. Miller, *Interpreting the Psalms*, 92.
25. Holladay, *The Psalms through Three Thousand Years*, 304–15.

God to bring harm or trouble to others. And most persons would reject such prayer on any occasion. A curse prayer is theologically unacceptable and psychologically nearly impossible to utter—except under certain circumstances, which may be a clue to what is going on in such prayers.[26] For Miller, blessing and curse are not just two sides of the same coin.

Clearly, the New Testament has a different take on the issue of malevolent speech. Jesus tells his disciples to love their enemies and pray for those who persecute them (Matt 5:44). On the cross, Jesus prays for the forgiveness of his enemies (Luke 23:34). Paul encourages Roman believers to bless those who persecute: "bless and do not curse" (Rom 12:14). Last, Paul encourages Roman Christians to leave room for the vengeance of God.

> Repay no one evil for evil, but give thought to do what is honorable in the sight of all. If possible, so far as it depends on you, live peaceably with all. Beloved, never avenge yourselves, but leave it to the wrath of God, for it is written, "Vengeance is mine, I will repay, says the Lord." To the contrary, "if your enemy is hungry, feed him; if he is thirsty, give him something to drink; for by so doing you will heap burning coals on his head." Do not be overcome by evil, but overcome evil with good. (Rom 12:17–21, ESV)

Alex Luc has also tried to grapple with this sensitive topic. [27] He first suggests that imprecations in Psalms are not simply confined to the narrow form-critical category called "Imprecatory psalms" (e.g., Psalms 35; 58; 69; 83; 109; and 137). He convincingly argues that the category imprecatory psalms does not cleanly constitute a genre. Sometimes these curses are expressed as jussives (Ps 55:15), imperatives (Ps 59:11), or a mix of the two (Ps 109:6–9). Luc has shown that twenty-eight Psalms have at least one verse of imprecation. He agrees with what any fair-minded reader of the Psalms observes about these psalms: no one is comfortable with them. Some try to tone them down as prayers of lament or private expressions of anguish . . . not direct verbal attacks. But Luc contends that not all imprecations are prayers—that imprecation is not an indispensable part of a lament, and therefore many laments have no imprecations. Some scholars interpret these as prophetic predictions rather than personal sentiments. While Luc is completely comfortable with the idea of psalmists as prophets, he rightly contends that interpreting these psalms

---

26. Miller, *And They Cried to the Lord*, 281.

27. Luc, "Interpreting the Curses."

as predictions minimizes the jussives used regularly in the curses. Finally, he reviews and quickly dismisses interpretations by some who read Psalm 109 as the words of a psalmist's enemies and not of the psalmist. Others place these psalms in the context of covenant theology, particularly of the covenant curse from biblical law. Yet covenant provides a general biblical framework only, not an explicit literary point of contact with these psalms of cursing. Finally, Luc reviews a glaring problem for Christians: the New Testament alludes to Psalms 35, 69, and 109—some of the more notorious psalms of cursing. Jesus predicts that Jerusalem will fall and that its children will be the victims of its fall (Luke 19:44). Paul speaks of "delivering a man over to Satan" in 1 Corinthians (cf. Ps 109:6).

Luc's solution is to take up these curses in the context of their biblical basis in prophetic writings.[28] He argues that it is best to understand psalms of cursing as prophetic judgment proclamations. Just because the authors were writers of psalms does not mean they cannot also be prophets. Elements of punishment proclaimed in these judgments include shame, physical infliction, death, misfortune of family members, and unspecified retribution. Luc supports his case by finding parallels to these psalms of cursing in prophetic speech (Isa 26:11; Jer 17:18; 18:21). The locutionary content of these prophetic curses comes from prior biblical teaching. Luc agrees with most Christian commentators that imprecations as personal sentiments are inapplicable for Christians. But if these maledictions are read as prophetic judgment, then it is an entirely different story. To some extent, these psalms are limited by who they address as specific persons. From the New Testament perspective, enemies in the imprecatory psalms are enemies of Christ.

Luc's proposition that these curse texts are prophetic proclamations, though well presented, appears to me to be entirely out of character with the emotive nature of the Psalter. Good or bad, these troublesome psalms reflect genuine emotions and experiences. These curse texts are clearly invocations for God to bring horrible catastrophes upon one's enemies, not merely prophecies of things to come. To read these psalms as prophetic utterances changes the entire illocutionary force of these emotive texts. Thus, as much as we would like, we cannot let the psalmists off the hook by relegating these curse psalms to prophetic activity.

As I mentioned in an earlier chapter, Sigmund Mowinckel directly dealt with blessings and curses in the context of the cult, where people of prominence as cultic leaders, such as priests or Levites, have greater

28. Ibid., 395.

blessing or cursing power than those in ordinary life roles. His chapter titled "Psalms of Blessing and Cursing" reviews the pertinent imprecatory psalms.[29] Mowinckel's examples of psalms of blessing are Psalms 115, 118, 122, and 128. Examples of psalms of cursing are Psalms 35, 40, 55, 109, 129, and 137. These blessings pour out in all sorts of shapes and manifestations. One intriguing insight provided by Mowinckel has to do with the role of blessing and the temple of Yahweh. The place where Yahweh lives is the home of all blessing (Ps 133:3). Because of this connection, Yahweh's name as word of blessing is the strongest blessing that can be uttered: "Blessed be the name of Yahweh." For Mowinckel, the transfer of blessing was a holy, ritual act through the Israelite cult. Therefore, the Psalter provides a fitting context for blessings and curses. Mowinckel cites as the best ritual example of blessing Numbers 6 and as the best ritual example of cursing Deuteronomy 27. But Mowinckel takes a page from Pedersen: an evil curse will not affect person full of blessing. Mowinckel's contribution is that the curse also has its place in cult and among rites.[30] Before making some final comments on the theological nature of these psalms of cursing, an application of speech-act theory to the book of Psalms is in order.

Psalms as Speech Acts

The primary method employed in this study is to apply models of performative speech to the biblical theme of blessing and cursing as it appears along major seams in the Old Testament. The book of Psalms makes for an interesting exploration of this topic. Walter Brueggemann has broached this topic by talking about the "world making capacity of the psalms."[31] Liturgy, says Brueggemann, is performative enactment. "Liturgy is not an appeal to any enduring ontology, but is an enactment of a fresh drama in this moment."[32] Brueggemann is certainly onto something here. As performative speech, praise actually enthrones God for the community and creates a world that excludes other gods and allows worshipers to envision themselves more ably in a world where God is king. There is constitutive power in praise. Herbert Levine has made similar arguments examining

---

29. Mowinckel, *The Psalms in Israel's Worship*, vol. 2.

30. Ibid., 49.

31. Brueggemann, *Israel's Praise*, 12–28.

32. Ibid., 34.

psalms as speech acts.[33] Language has a way of making things happen in the world. Take two examples from the early chapters of Psalms:

> The LORD is King for ever and ever;
>   the nations will perish from his land.
> You hear, O LORD, the desire of the afflicted;
>   you encourage them, and you listen to their cry,
> defending the fatherless and the oppressed,
> so that mere earthly mortals
> will never again strike terror. (Ps 10:16–18)

> Therefore my heart is glad and my tongue rejoices;
>   my body also will rest secure,
> because you will not abandon me to the realm of the dead,
>   nor will you let your Holy One see decay.
> You have made known to me the path of life;
>   you will fill me with joy in your presence,
> with eternal pleasures at your right hand. (Ps 16:9–11)

Note how these two examples employ performative speech: in the first case to enact a world where God reigns, and in the second case to enact a world where God is aware of the plight of the psalmist. In an act of communal worship, a ritualized setting allows worshipers to speak a new world into being. Speech acts like this are often subversive illocutions. In an earlier work on Psalms, Brueggemann argues for three categories of psalm: psalms of orientation, disorientation, and new orientation.[34] Orientation is that foundational biblical worldview like the one described in Psalm 26: "My feet stand on level ground, in the great assembly I will praise the LORD" (Ps 26:12). It is a world where God is on the throne and all is well. Disorientation is the dissonance associated with the fact that humans experience things contrary to that general biblical orientation where God is king. Many times it looks as if God is not in control at all. How does one find a way through this experience of disorientation? A new orientation is attained via performative enactment through worship. This line of reasoning is similar to von Rad's take on the Psalter as "Israel before Yahweh: Israel's Answer."[35] These performative enactments are decisive moves of faith. They are not a once-for-all experience by any means but can be reenacted as situations and rituals demand. The new orientation

33. Levine, *Sing unto God a New Song.*
34. Brueggemann, *The Message of the Psalms.*
35. Von Rad, *Old Testament Theology,* 1:355–459.

is also a countercultural posture. For example, Psalm 19 describes God's orientation to this world through creation and Torah. Verses 1–6 speak the language of creation. God is over the entire created order. Verses 7–11 speak of covenant; Torah rewards those who endeavor to keep it. Verses 12–14 talk about how both together reveal sin and keep the believer from being dominated by sin. The dominion of Yahweh's creation and covenant trumps that competing dominion characterized by hidden and presumptuous faults. The context of ritualized public worship is a context in which the generativity of creation can be recognized and enhanced.[36] The premise of applying the notion of speech acts to the Psalms is that the language of worship affects the worshiper. Gordon Wenham has taken up speech-act theory and the use of the Psalms as prayers. [37] Praying the Psalms in public worship is akin to taking an oath in court: the words are addressed to God in the presence of human witnesses. In this way worshipers commit themselves to the words and attitudes of the Psalms in a strong way. Wenham cites an example:

> Not a word from their mouth can be trusted;
>> their heart is filled with destruction.
> Their throat is an open grave;
>> with their tongue they speak deceit.
> Declare them guilty, O God!
>> Let their intrigues be their downfall.
> Banish them for their many sins,
>> for they have rebelled against you. (Ps 5:9–10)

Wenham draws an analogy from this psalm to Deuteronomy 27. In the covenant ceremony at Shechem, saying the amen after the curse was in essence a commissive performative. One commits to the curse by means of the proclamation, "Amen!" Whereas merely listening to laws, proverbs, or stories involves passive engagement with religious teaching, praying or singing a psalm involves direct address to God. God, who knows whether or not the worshiper is sincere, evaluates that commitment. What may at first glance appear to be mere statements of fact are more than that.[38] Thus the singing of psalms enacts a new orientation in the life of the believer.

So, how can we apply this methodology of speech-act theory to psalms of cursing? While the Bible is always authoritative for Christian faith, it is not always prescriptive. Just because a Samson or a Solomon is

36. Brueggemann, *Theology of the Old Testament*, 532.
37. Wenham, "Reflections on Singing the Ethos of God."
38. See Evans, *The Logic of Self-Involvement*.

part of the Bible's story doesn't mean that one necessarily must emulate their moral character in every respect. The same thing is true with psalms of cursing. One of the first things to admit is that the imprecatory Psalms do not measure up to the ethics emulated in the vast majority of the Old and New Testaments. But what they do so well, sometimes all too well, is account for the experiences and emotions that everyone faces at certain points in their lives. Let us take one of the most challenging examples of imprecatory language in the psalms from two different perspectives: first, to see how the psalm describes the experiences and emotions of the author; second, to observe how performative curse speech *in a ritualized context* might present a different reading:

> Appoint a wicked man against him;
>> let an accuser stand at his right hand.
> When he is tried, let him come forth guilty;
>> let his prayer be counted as sin!
> May his days be few;
>> may another take his office!
> May his children be fatherless
>> and his wife a widow!
> May his children wander about and beg,
>> seeking food far from the ruins they inhabit!
> May the creditor seize all that he has;
>> may strangers plunder the fruits of his toil!
> Let there be none to extend kindness to him,
>> nor any to take pity on his fatherless children!
> May his posterity be cut off;
>> may his name be blotted out in the second generation!
> May the iniquity of his fathers be remembered before the LORD,
>> and let not the sin of his mother be blotted out!
> Let them be before the LORD continually,
>> that he may cut off the memory of them from the earth!
> (Ps 109:6–15, ESV)

To make a bad interpretive situation worse, this song is strongly Yahwistic. There is simply no denying it. The appeal here is for Yahweh's direct intervention for evil in the life of one's enemies. It is impossible to miss the emotional elocution here. One can easily see that this is an unblessing. The author expresses in the form of a jussive the following consequences for his enemy: May that person face evil enemies, live a short life, have no grandchildren, leave poverty as an inheritance to his family, face humiliation, and have no posterity. The emotive tone of the psalm as originally composed is vengeful animosity. The context of communal worship, however, as both Miller and Wenham contend, is one giant step removed from the malevolence of the original historicized setting of the psalm's composer. The psalm was originally composed in the context of one person's absolute desire for vengeance against his personal enemy. But chanted or sung in the context of corporate worship changes things; if not dramatically, significantly. This new collective context makes it nearly impossible to utter such a cry for vengeance corporately.

Miller is absolutely right that a curse prayer is theologically unacceptable and *psychologically nearly impossible* to utter. Miller is also correct that no Christian religious community engages regularly in this kind of malevolent speech. Then how does one read this psalm? What are worshipers enacting with such strong language? First, they are appealing to Yahweh for justice and restitution.[39] They want the guilt of their offender to be brought into the open, even though in a corporate setting that offender is completely different from the enemy the original composers had in mind. They also want restitution. Therefore, if it only ended there, the psalm of cursing is an act of liberation, a new orientation, a powerful way of speaking a new world into being. Sadly, however, the invocation does not end there. It goes well beyond equitable restitution. The psalmist's demand for payment, death, no posterity, poverty, and the like clearly outweighs the offense.[40] Yet in an odd way, the new corporate, ritualized context makes the utterance of the prayer border on the absurd.

Frankly, there is no easy solution or justification for the psalmist's prayer. Here is where such corporate unrestraint is tempered by the nature and character of God. God is a worthy match for such unrestrained demand for retaliation. God does not implement the violent yearning. The worshiper, by necessity, leaves Yahweh to govern as he will. At best, such performative speech releases the worshiper to live unencumbered by the demand for revenge. Vengeance, by necessity, is left in the hands of God; and frankly, God appears not to be doing much about it.

The sad fact is that the practice of "praying your enemies to death" has a long and controversial history in the Christian church. Athanasius and Augustine read Psalm 109 as referring to Judas. This led, by metonymy, to a substitution of the Jews for the persona of Judas, leading to the use of this particular psalm in pogroms against Jews. Psalm 109 became its own performative speech act, as it was often uttered regularly in liturgical contexts against hated enemies of the faith. These historical abuses have led some interpreters to throw up their hands in frustration and claim that

39. Barker, "Divine Illocutions in Psalm 137."
40. Britt, "Curses Left and Right."

the psalmist is actually quoting others and has no such hateful feelings in his own heart. Again, such interpretation is wishful thinking that passes over the emotive nature of these potent speech acts.

Another example of a psalm of cursing is Psalm 137. This is one of the few psalms with a specific historical content. This specific historical content raises significant hermeneutical implications. It requires Christians to face the essential Jewishness of these psalms.[41] This particular psalm was written by a Judean who had lived in Babylonian exile for a long time. This is no immediate or impulsive reaction to a sudden loss. The curse in this psalm is an embarrassment, but only to detached elitists who have never had their homes burned or their wives raped—who have never faced the humiliation of having been forced to flee from their homeland. Only a post-Holocaust reading can help the twenty-first-century interpreter understand this psalm in its original historical context. Few people in the Western world have the experiential background to engage with this psalm. Eric Zenger comments:

> Psalm 137 is not the song of people who have power to effect a violent change in their situation of suffering, nor is it the battle cry of terrorists. Instead, it is an attempt to cling to one's historical identity even when everything is against it. Still more, it is an attempt in the face of the most profound humiliation and helplessness, to suppress the primitive human lust for violence in one's own heart by surrendering everything to God—a God whose word of judgment is presumed to be so universally just that even those who pray the psalm submit themselves to it.[42]

What is striking is the nontheological nature of this psalm. Only v. 7 is addressed directly to God. The rest is mostly contemplative language. Yet, in spite of Zenger's comments above, there is no dancing around the blessing upon child murderers present in vv. 8–9: "happy they shall be who take your children and smash them against the stones."[43] Yet, the psalmist takes no direct action against the little ones, and as the example above, leaves things in God's hands.

> Remember, O LORD, against the Edomites
>   the day of Jerusalem,
>   how they said, "Lay it bear, lay it bear
>   down to its foundations!"

41. Brueggemann, *The Message of the Psalms*, 74.

42. Zenger, *A God of Vengeance?*, 48.

43. Ibid.

O daughter of Babylon, doomed to be
    destroyed
    blessed shall he be who repays you
    with what you have done to us!
Blessed shall he be who takes your little ones
    and dashes them against the rock! (Ps 137:7–9, ESV)

THE PRIESTLY CURSE, THE PRIESTLY BLESSING (NUMBERS 5–6)

The Priestly Curse

The priestly curse and blessing in Numbers 5–6 belong an entirely differ-ent ritual-cultic context.[44] Numbers 5 is an odd blend of magic, cult, and ethics.[45] The setting of this highly specialized ritual is as follows: a woman is pregnant and the husband is not sure he is the father. Consequently, his wife is subjected against her will to the conditional curse of an oath (*'lh*) of innocence. That oath is substantiated by a water ordeal, which acts very much like a trial where the accused utters a solemn statement of in-nocence. Water ordeals such as the one here were not at all unknown in the ancient Near East. Typically, the accused is subject to some kind of physical test, and usually given some sacred food or drink. If the accused is innocent, there is no ill effect from the food or drink. If guilty, these hallowed substances cause irredeemable disorders that lead to sickness or death.[46] River ordeals and fire ordeals were even more dramatic.[47]

---

44. Catherine Bell has argued that ritual is a type of critical juncture wherein some pair of opposing social or cultural forces comes together. Ritualization involves the differentiation and privileging of particular activities. These activities may use a delin-eated and structured space, may occur at special periodic times, may involve restricted codes of communication or distinct and specialized personnel, may use objects, texts, and dresses designated for use in these activities, and may involve a particular con-stituency not necessarily assembled for any other reason. Ritualization is basically a "way of acting," which, according to Bell, lies below the level of discourse; *Ritual Theory, Ritual Practice*, 16.

45. Brichto plays down magic here unfortunately: *The Problem of Curse in the He-brew Bible*, 82.

46. Van der Toorn, "Theology, Priests, and Worship in Canaan and Ancient Israel," 2051.

47. Levine, *Numbers 1–20*, 204–5.

The specific process is described in Numbers 5. The suspicious husband drags his accused wife to the sanctuary along with a cultic remembrance offering of grain. The priest officiates over the ordeal. He prepares the "water that brings the curse" (*hammayim haměˇārrîm hāˇēlleh*) by mixing the holy water with dust from the floor of the tabernacle. The priest positions the woman before the Lord and makes her take a verbal curse-oath while she holds the grain offering in her hand. The priest also utters an oath and the suspected woman acknowledges the oath with an amen,

> Here the priest is to put the woman under this curse (*bišĕbuˇat hāˇālâ*)—"may the LORD cause you to become a curse (*lĕˇlh wlšbˇh*) among your people when he makes your womb miscarry and your abdomen swell. May this water that brings a curse (*hamārrîm hāˇēlleh*) enter your body so that your abdomen swells or your womb miscarries." "'Then the woman is to say, "Amen. So be it." (Num 5:21–22)

After the amen, the accused woman is then given the potion of holy water mixed with dust from tabernacle floor.[48] The priest writes various curses in ink, which dissolve in the water-dust concoction.[49] He takes the grain offering and burns it on the altar and makes the woman drink the water of the ordeal. If she is innocent, the woman suffers no ill effects. If she is guilty, then Num 5:24 reads as a possible euphemism for miscarriage: "He shall make the woman drink the bitter water that brings a curse, and this water that brings a curse and causes bitter suffering will enter her." Verdict and penalty come together:

> If she has made herself impure and been unfaithful to her husband, this will be the result: When she is made to drink the water that brings a curse and causes bitter suffering, it will enter her, her abdomen will swell and her womb will miscarry, and she will become a curse. If, however, the woman has not made herself impure, but is clean, she will be cleared of guilt and will be able to have children. (Num 5:27–28)

Like covenant curses, the ordeal is based on the theological assumption that Yahweh is omniscient. God sees crimes that may have been committed in secret: "The eyes of the LORD are everywhere, keeping watch on the wicked and the good" (Prov 15:3). This was a way for humans to

---

48. Feinstein, "The 'Bitter Waters' of Numbers 5:11–31."

49. In the Rabbinic Period, the rabbis required that the ink had to completely dissolve in the water. No trace could remain on the parchment (Mishnah, *Sotah* 2.4).

involve God in determining innocence and guilt in a supernatural process outside the regular modes of juridical process. The event is highly ritualized and decidedly stylistic, but theologically this ritual transfers jurisdiction to Yahweh alone. There is no reason to think the priest has added anything to the water. There is no human jury. Only God can decide the fate of the woman. God's "ruling," however, is subject to delay. That delay is also up to God and may take days, weeks, or months. Imagine the psychological anguish of a woman waiting day after day, even month after month, to see if the curse will cause her to miscarry, become infertile, or even worse. Note the similar language in a psalm of cursing: "He wore cursing as his garment; it entered into his body like water, into his bones like oil" (Ps 109:18).

The emphasis is entirely on the woman's guilt, but there is no provision that a wife has a reciprocal right to put her husband through a similar ordeal. The husband apparently faces no penalty if the ordeal proves her to be innocent. She must render herself completely vulnerable. The uncovering and unbinding of her hair by someone other than her husband is an act of shaming. Nevertheless, one wonders about the likelihood of drinking a little muddy water really impacting a pregnancy. In an oblique way, some have suggested that this ritual protects the woman from a lynch-mob mentality and places her case in the hands of the divine judge. I would love to think that that is the case. Yet, the woman has no voice. She must give consent to the ritual with the words, "Amen, Amen." The context of the book of Numbers is also interesting here. The people of God are just about to set out on an epic journey. This journey will either lead to victory and entry into the land, or bitter defeat. Yet the preparations for that journey are almost entirely cultic. McKane has noted parallels between this water ordeal and the imagery in the prophetic literature about drinking the cup of God's wrath (cf. Jer 9:15, 23:15),

> Why are we sitting here?
>   Gather together!
> Let us flee to the fortified cities
>   and perish there!
> For the LORD our God has doomed us to perish
>   and given us poisoned water to drink,
> because we have sinned against him. (Jer 8:14)

There are also some clear similarities to the golden-calf story, where Moses forces Israel to drink the dust of their own gods. This act was intended to bring Israel's judgment on itself by the drinking the poisonous water. The imagery of the water ordeal is opposite to the communal meal, the celebration of fellowship through eating together. McKane calls it the "anti-banquet."[50] Further parallels with various "cup of wrath" passages (Isa 51:17–23; Jer 25:15–29; Ezek 23:31–34; Hab 2:15–16) depict the judgment of God entering the innermost parts of the human body. Paul conveys a similar interpretation in 1 Cor 11:28–30 of why some believers are getting sick or even dying: "A man ought to examine himself before he eats of the bread and drinks of the cup. For anyone who eats and drinks without recognizing the body of the Lord eats and drinks judgment on himself. That is why many among you are weak and sick, and a number of you have fallen asleep."[51]

The Priestly Blessing

Aaron's priestly blessing is one of the best-known and regularly recited texts in the entire Old Testament. The ritual context is clear, as the priests were to utter this blessing upon God's people.[52] Regularly recited at the end of the synagogue service and in churches around the world, this blessing exhibits a balance of literary artistry and poetic design. In Hebrew there are three lines, with three, five, and seven words respectively. The number of consonants for each line is fifteen, twenty, and twenty-five. The first and last clauses contain seven syllables each, the perfect number.

> The LORD said to Moses, "Tell Aaron and his sons,
> 'This is how you are to bless the Israelites. Say to them:
>
> The LORD bless you
>   and keep you;
> the LORD make his face shine upon you
>   and be gracious to you;
> the LORD turn his face toward you
>   and give you peace.
> So they will put my name on the Israelites, and I will bless them.
> (Num 6:22–27)

---

50. McKane, "Poison, Trial by Ordeal, and the Cup of Wrath."

51. Another intriguing parallel are the so-called purgatorial prayers uttered in the context of sacral jurisdiction. In these prayers, there is a hint of some kind of nightly ordeal with resolution the next morning (Pss 3:5–6; 4:8; 5:3; 7:6; 17:13; 57:1, 8; 139; 142); Schmidt, *Das Gebet der Angleklagten im Alten Testament*, 1–46.

52. Milgrom, *Numbers*, 360.

The phrase "May Yahweh keep you" speaks to the protection and posterity that God will provide the community, and the expression "make his face shine" connotes God's active presence among his people. The light of God's face connotes clarity, warmth, and brightness. The ultimate goal of the blessing is peace. The Hebrew *šlwm* entails more than mere lack of conflict; it conveys assurance of all the elements of blessing: prosperity, progeny, prominence, and productivity.

In 1979, archaeologists excavated two silver inscriptions from Ketef Hinnom, an ancient burial complex near Jerusalem's city walls.[53] The Ketef Hinnom inscriptions are the earliest known artifacts that document a passage from the Bible. Each of the two inscriptions quote from the famous priestly blessing in Num 6:24–26. While the inscriptions are highly unusual, the nature of these inscriptions is even more unusual. The two inscriptions are etched on tiny silver amulets that were rolled up tightly like mini scrolls. They were delicately unwound and cleaned by a team at the Israel Museum. Based on script and archaeological context, these two inscriptions date from the seventh or sixth century BCE. One of the difficulties in unrolling and translating was that they are so incredibly small, and in some cases individual letters are not much wider than the width of a hair. The largest inscription is 97 millimeters long, smaller than a cigarette. These inscriptions demonstrate that the Aaron's priestly blessing may have been used to ward off evil, thus affirming the power of the priestly blessing.

In the cult of ancient Israel, blessing is offered upon entering the sanctuary (Ps 118:26), and in conclusion before departure (Lev 9:22–23; 2 Sam 6:18; 1 Kgs 8:14, 55; 2 Chr 30:27). The utterance of blessing is the expressed function of the priest (Num 6:23–29; Deut 10:8; 21:5; 1 Sam 2:20). The priestly blessing contains the necessary elements of an effective performative utterance: there is an accepted conventional procedure having a certain conventional effect; the particular personas and circumstances in a given case are appropriate for the invocation of the particular procedure, the procedure is executed by all participants both correctly and completely; and the person invoking the blessing offers no perfunctory procedure, but truly wishes blessing on the people. In its narrative context, this blessing is intended to equip the community for the journey ahead. It is a beginning, not an end—a prelude rather than a postlude. The Aaronic blessing is expanded in Psalm 121, as the verb "to keep" or "to watch" is found six times in eight verses.

53. Barkay, "The Challenges of Ketef Hinnom."

> I lift up my eyes to the mountains—
>   where does my help come from?
> My help comes from the LORD,
>   the Maker of heaven and earth.
>
> He will not let your foot slip—
>   he who *watches* over you will not slumber;
> indeed, he who *watches* over Israel
>   will neither slumber nor sleep.
>
> The LORD *watches* over you—
>   the LORD is your shade at your right hand;
> the sun will not harm you by day,
>   nor the moon by night.
>
> The LORD will *keep* you from all harm—
>   he will *watch* over your life;
> the LORD will *watch* over your coming and going
>   both now and forevermore. (Ps 121:1–8)

Other places in the Old Testament take up the priestly blessing.[54] The Songs of Ascent use regularly the words *bless, watch, grace,* and *peace* as expansions of the priestly blessing. Psalm 67 revisits this blessing, particularly the presence of God through his people among the foreign kingdoms: "May God be gracious to us and make his face shine on us—that your ways may be known on earth, your salvation among al nations" (Ps 67:1–2). Malachi deconstructs this blessing as he sarcastically wonders whether God will be gracious when sacrifices are so distained and offered so heartlessly (Mal 1:8—2:9).

---

54. Levine traces the use of this blessing in Second Temple and later Judaism; *Numbers 1–20*, 242–44.

11

"Curse God and Die"

Rhetorical Brinkmanship in Job

WHEN IS A CURSE A BLESSING AND A BLESSING A CURSE? THE PROSE PROLOGUE

"SILENCE IS A SIGN of death, but the curse is a sign of life which has no rest."[1] In the book of Job, the prose frame (Job 1:1—2:13; 42:7-17) does more than merely surround the poetic center, and the poetic center is part of the ongoing plot of the book initiated by the prose prologue.[2] Prose and poetry work in tandem to present a poignant question, "Will Job really curse God?" The blessing/cursing motif is not only dominant in the prose prologue but is also a key element in the poetic center of the book. As a result, blessing and curse are pivotal thematic elements in the plot and theology of the entire book.[3]

Because no one wants to blatantly entertain the idea that a righteous figure like Job might actually curse God, the performative language of blessing and cursing is characterized by circumlocution. A game, which really is no game at all, of rhetorical brinkmanship puts Job on the very cusp of cursing his maker. One does not have to use specific curse

1. Beuken, "Job's Imprecation as the Cradle of a New Religious Discourse," 78.

2. Clines, *Job 1-20*, xxxvii; and Habel, *The Book of Job*, 26.

3. Gordis translates the speeches of the prologue in poetic style; *The Book of Job*, 1–12.

terminology to express a curse. Freely composed curses have the same illocutionary force. This dangerous potential that Job might indeed curse God plays an important role in several pivotal texts in Job, which form linchpins between major sections of the book. The prologue (1:1—2:13), the beginning and end of Job's dialogue with his friends (3:1-10, 27:1-2), and Job's formal legal appeal to God by means of a self-curse (31:1-40) all contain curses or oaths. The possibility presented in the prologue that Job might curse God sets the stage for the remainder of the book. The curses of the poetic center beginning in chapter 3, in part, address this possibility, provoking their respective reactions from Job's friends as well as from Yahweh. Thus, between the opening curse of Job 3 and the closing oath of Job 31 two conflicts emerge: one is between Job and his friends and the other is between Job and his God.

The Hebrew root "to bless," *brk*, is a key *lietwort* throughout the entire prologue. There are five scenes, each with alternating settings moving back and forth between earth and heaven (Job 1:1–5; 1:6–12, 1:13–22; 2:1–7a, 2:7b–10), with the word *brk* in each scene.[4] In four of the five scenes, *brk* is actually a circumlocution for "curse" (Job 1:5, 11; 2:5, 9) and in two instances it is translated literally as "bless" (Job 1:10, 21).[5] Whether English translators render the word as "blessing" or "curse" depends entirely on the context. The avoidance of traditional curse words creates innuendo and suspense. The structure of each of the five scenes is marked off by the recurring phrase, "one day . . ." *wayĕhi hayôm*. Only in the final scene is this phrase not present, for a reason that will be explained below. Additionally, the root *brk* connects the prologue with the epilogue (Job 42:12), bringing the tension of blessing and curse to completion.[6]

In four instances, *brk* is a euphemism for *qll*.[7] This circumlocution may have been employed because of the religious concerns of a later

4. Clines (*Job 1-20*, 6) and Janzen (*Job,* 32) include a sixth scene (2:11-13). I am following Habel, who views 2:11-13 as an introduction to the poetic material that begins in chapter 3 for the following reasons: First the pattern of the alternating settings of heaven and earth is not continued in 2:11-13. Second, there is no occurrence of the *brk* lietwort. Third, 2:10b brings a clear completion to the unit of 1:1—2:10. Last, 2:11-13 introduces the characters of the following dialogue (Habel, *The Book of Job,* 26).

5. Contra Linafelt, "The Undecidability of *brk* in the Prologue of Job and Beyond."

6. Weiss, *The Story of Job's Beginning,* 81.

7. Sheldon H. Blank, "The Curse, the Blasphemy, the Spell, and the Oath," 83, argues that *brk* is actually a euphemism for *'rr*. Brichto, *The Problem of Curse in the Hebrew Bible,* 171; Mitchell, *The Meaning of BRK, "to Bless" in the Old Testament,* 62; and others argue that Blank is mistaken because the Piel stem of *qll* is understood as

redactor or even the original author.[8] Regardless, this euphemism is part of the larger rhetoric of the book, where curses against God, whether real or potential, are characterized by circumlocutions. The first scene takes place on earth,

> In the land of Uz there lived a man whose name was Job. This man was blameless and upright; he feared God and shunned evil. He had seven sons and three daughters, and he owned seven thousand sheep, three thousand camels, five hundred yoke of oxen and five hundred donkeys, and had a large number of servants. He was the greatest man among all the people of the East. His sons used to take turns holding feasts in their homes, and they would invite their three sisters to eat and drink with them. When a period of feasting had run its course, Job would send and have them purified. Early in the morning he would sacrifice a burnt offering for each of them, thinking, "Perhaps my children have sinned and cursed (*ûbērakû*) God in their hearts." This was Job's regular custom. (Job 1:1–5)

The curse is first mentioned in Job 1:5, where blameless Job is concerned that his children might at some point have *blessed* God in their hearts. Here the possibility exists that an imprecation need not formally be a verbal speech act to be a curse. Job's children need only to curse God in their hearts to need their father's mediation. Job is a fitting mediator, as he is blameless and upright, fearing God and shunning evil.

The recurring phrase *wayĕhi hayôm* introduces the second scene (Job 1:6–12), which shifts to heaven.

> One day the angels came to present themselves before the LORD, and Satan also came with them. The LORD said to Satan, "Where have you come from?" Satan answered the LORD, "From roaming through the earth and going back and forth in it." Then the Lord said to Satan, "Have you considered my servant Job? There is no one on earth like him; he is blameless and upright, a man who fears God and shuns evil." "Does Job fear God for nothing?" Satan replied. "Have you not put a hedge around him and his household and everything he has? You have blessed (*brk*) the work of his hands, so that his flocks and herds are spread throughout the land. But stretch out your hand and strike everything he has, and he will surely curse (*brk*) you to your face." The

---

blasphemy in Ezek 22:27; 1 Sam 3:13; and Isa 8:21. The Syriac of Job reads *qll*, and other prohibitions against blasphemy in the Old Testament ordinarily use the term *qll*.

8. Gordis, *The Book of Job*, 13.

> Lord said to Satan, "Very well, then, everything he has is in your
> hands, but on the man himself do not lay a finger." Then Satan
> went out from the presence of the LORD. (Job 1:6–12)

In this scene *brk* is translated in opposite ways: as blessing in Job 1:10, and
as curse in 1:11. The Satan argues that Job is righteous only because of a
blessing hedge that God has placed around him. If that hedge is removed,
Job will certainly *bless* (*brk*) God. Job is righteous because he is blessed,
not blessed because he is righteous. A number of authorities have rightly
viewed the Satan's wager as a self-curse, "I'll be damned if he doesn't curse
you to your face," or, "May a nameless catastrophe swallow me up if he
doesn't curse you."[9] This self-curse essentially provokes God to prove that
the Satan is wrong. Similarly, in Job 31:1–40, it is Job's self-curse that provokes a response from the deity to his demand for a divine audience.

The recurring phrase, *wayĕhi hayôm* introduces the third scene (Job
1:13–22), which shifts once again to the earth.

> One day when Job's sons and daughters were feasting and drink-
> ing wine at the oldest brother's house, a messenger came to Job
> and said, "The oxen were plowing and the donkeys were grazing
> nearby, and the Sabeans attacked and carried them off. They
> put the servants to the sword, and I am the only one who has
> escaped to tell you!" While he was still speaking, another mes-
> senger came and said, "The fire of God fell from the sky and
> burned up the sheep and the servants, and I am the only one
> who has escaped to tell you!" While he was still speaking, an-
> other messenger came and said, "The Chaldeans formed three
> raiding parties and swept down on your camels and carried
> them off. They put the servants to the sword, and I am the only
> one who has escaped to tell you!" While he was still speaking,
> yet another messenger came and said, "Your sons and daughters
> were feasting and drinking wine at the oldest brother's house,
> when suddenly a mighty wind swept in from the desert and
> struck the four corners of the house. It collapsed on them and
> they are dead, and I am the only one who has escaped to tell
> you!" At this, Job got up and tore his robe and shaved his head.
> Then he fell to the ground in worship and said:
>
> "Naked I came from my mother's womb,
>   and naked I will depart.

9. Good, "Job and the Literary Task," 475; Clines, *Job 1–20*, 26. The claims of Good
and Clines are shared by Rowley, *The Book of Job*, 31, and Robertson, *The Old Testament and the Literary Critic*, 45.

The LORD gave and the LORD has taken away;
   may the name of the LORD be praised (*brk*)."
In all this, Job did not sin by charging God with wrongdoing
   (*nātan tiplâ*). (Job 1:13–22)

After Job is confronted with a series of horribly unfortunate personal catastrophes, the Satan is ironically proven right . . . yet wrong. Job does indeed *brk* God, but not with the euphemistic meaning presented in Job 1:11. Righteous Job states, "the LORD gave and the LORD has taken away, blessed be the name of the LORD" (Job 1:21, ESV). In a literal translation the narrator concludes, "in all this, Job did not *sin with his lips.*" The meaning of *tiplâ*, which is used only in Job, is unclear here. There are several possibilities. The first is to translate *nātan tiplâ* as "to spit" or "reproach"; or even "unsavoriness" or "unseemliness."[10] M. Dahood offers the possibility that like the root *brk*, so *tiplâ* can have opposite meanings.[11] If it is pointed slightly differently the word could carry, again by means of circumlocution, the meaning "curse." Thus it would be read, "in all this Job did not sin and uttered no (prayer of) curse against God."

Not to be prematurely defeated, the Satan repeats a broader challenge in the fourth scene (Job 2:1–7), set in heaven, which uses the same self-cursing formula,

> On another day the angels came to present themselves before the LORD, and Satan also came with them to present himself before him. And the LORD said to Satan, "Where have you come from?" Satan answered the LORD, "From roaming through the earth and going back and forth in it." Then the LORD said to Satan, "Have you considered my servant Job? There is no one on earth like him; he is blameless and upright, a man who fears God and shuns evil. And he still maintains his integrity, though you incited me against him to ruin him without any reason." "Skin for skin!" Satan replied. "A man will give all he has for his own life. But stretch out your hand and strike his flesh and bones, and he will surely curse (*yĕbārakekā*) you to your face." The LORD said to Satan, "Very well, then, he is in your hands; but you must spare his life." So Satan went out from the presence of the LORD and afflicted Job with painful sores from the soles of his feet to the top of his head. (Job 2:1–7)

---

10. Michal, *Job in Light of Northwest Semitic*, 25.

11. Dahood, "Hebrew-Ugaritic Lexicography XII," 390.

The fourth scene closes exactly as the second, as the Satan leaves the presence of God.

The phrase that separated the first four scenes is not present prior to scene 5, which is set again on earth.

> Then Job took a piece of broken pottery and scraped himself with it as he sat among the ashes. His wife said to him, "Are you still holding on to your integrity? Curse (*brk*) God and die!" He replied, "You are talking like a foolish woman. Shall we accept good from God, and not trouble?" In all this, Job did not sin *in what he said*. (Job 2:8–10)

Habel calls this omission, "a brilliant deviation in structure."[12] This scene transfers the events of the plot permanently to the earthly realm. The root *brk* is strikingly put in the lips of Job's wife, *bārēk 'ĕlōhîm wāmut*, "curse God and die." In a play on words, she spurns Job (Job 2:9), "why do you hold to your integrity (*twm*), curse God and die (*mwt*)." Job's response is in keeping with his piety as portrayed in the prologue. In spite of all the evil that has befallen him, Job does not "sin with his lips," although the Qumran Targum not so subtly anticipates the poetic center: "but in his thoughts he already cherished sinful words."[13] Job's friends come to visit him to bring comfort but are so appalled that they say nothing. This brings an end to the prose prologue.

The prologue is preoccupied with speech acts, and acts of pronouncement in particular. Job 2:11–13 sets the stage for Job's curse and lament in Job 3. The closing words of the fifth scene ("Job did not sin with his lips") anticipates the opening of the poetic center: "Job opened his mouth," and utters a curse. This shocking string of incantations in Job 3:1–10 is so strong that it effectively stirs the rebuke of his friends who up to this point have been silent. Thus, the speech cycles of Job and his three friends begin (3:1–10) and end (31:1–40) with a curse.[14]

"Cursed Be the Day I Was Born": The Poetic Center

> After this, Job opened his mouth and cursed (*qll*) the day of his birth. He said:

12. Habel, *The Book of Job*, 80.
13. Mangan, "Blessing and Cursing in the Prologue of Targum Job."
14. Crenshaw, *Old Testament Wisdom*, 105–6.

May the day of my birth perish (*yōʾbad yôm*),
    and the night it was said, 'A boy is conceived!'
That day—may it turn to darkness;
    may God above not care about it;
    may no light shine upon it.

May gloom and utter darkness
    claim it once more;
    may a cloud settle over it;
    may blackness overwhelm it.
That night—may thick darkness seize it
    may it not be included among the days of the year
    nor be entered in any of the months.

May that night be barren
    may no shout of joy be heard in it.
May those who curse (*yiqqĕbuhû*) days curse (*ōrrē yôm*) that day,
    those who are ready to rouse Leviathan.

May its morning stars become dark;
    may it wait for daylight in vain
    and not see the first rays of dawn,
    for it did not shut the doors of the womb on me
    to hide trouble from my eyes. (Job 3:1–10)

Job 3 includes a curse (vv. 1–10) and a lament (vv. 11–26). Job's curse on the day of his birth has remarkable parallels to Jeremiah's twofold curse in Jeremiah 20:14–18.[15] The weightiest question of this pivotal unit is its relation to the question set up by the prologue: will Job curse God? Authorities vary as to exactly what Job's caustic words entail. Clines suggests that the words may not be a curse at all, since it is impossible to curse the past. Alter observes that the phrase is not an explicative and does not imply damnation, so renders the verb *annul*.[16] Clines argues, instead, that Job's words are a parody on a curse, or a curse with no teeth.[17] If so, the curse is a wholly literary phenomenon. It is more likely, however, Job does indeed utter a curse, but in a backhanded, safe sort of way, and not uttered directly against God. Blank suggests that v. 3 is an ancient circumlocution designed to prevent gross impiety.[18] Job's statements here and elsewhere in the body

15. Lundbom, "The Double Curse in Jeremiah 20:14–18."
16. Alter, *The Wisdom Books*, 8.
17. Clines, *Job 1–20*, 79.
18. Blank, "Perish the Day!: A Misdirected Curse (Job 3:3)," 63.

of the book border on curses, but fall just short of actual imprecation. Good states, "Job comes within an ace of cursing God, if he doesn't," and Rick Moore argues that the curse is a piece of rhetorical brinkmanship.[19] He observes no irreconcilable difference between the Job of the prologue and the Job of the poetic sections of the book. Job falls short of cursing God by cursing his own life. J. L. Austin discusses three categories of fallacies that render speech acts impotent: misinvocations, misapplications, and misexecutions. From a perspective of speech-act theory, it is possible that Job's curse fails at any of these three points.[20]

It may be, however, that Job's speech proves the Satan correct; Job indeed curses God. Michael Fishbane argues that a curse against the day is the same as a curse against the Creator who made the day.[21] He contends that in the ancient Near East, cosmologies were often used as models for magical incantations that adapted the archetypal pattern. The magician priest would, in essence, participate in the power and efficacy of the primordial event in order to reach the particular goals of the incantation. Job's curse literally amounts to a countercosmic incantation, which, by reversal of the created order, is an indirect attack on the Creator. In chapter 3 Job adopts the same verbal pattern used in the first creation account in Genesis 1 but in a way that is a parody against the divine order. No less than sixteen jussives fuel his incantations against God's created order, a pattern that will be repeated in his oath of innocence in Job 31. David Penchansky echoes this affirmation, providing additional examples from the poetic materials of Job's accusatory characterization of God.[22] Polzin states that Job's words are among the most anti-Yahwistic statements in the Hebrew Bible.[23]

Job's caustic characterization of the deity flirts with blasphemy. Job portrays Yahweh as the source of his evil afflictions (Job 6:4; 7:14–15), as a whimsical tyrant (Job 9:18–19), as a crooked judge (Job 9:20–29), as a persecutor of the innocent (Job 10:6–7), and as a ruthless warrior (Job 16:12–14). God is oblivious to guilt or innocence, makes the innocent guilty, and actually favors the wicked. If blasphemy is defined as the

19. Good, "Job and the Literary Task," 476; Moore, "The Integrity of Job," 24.

20. Austin, *How to Do Things with Words*, 14–15.

21. Fishbane, "Jeremiah IV 23–26 and Job III 3:13"; see also Fishbane, "Studies in Biblical Magic."

22. Penchansky, *The Betrayal of God*, 47–48.

23. Polzin, "The Framework of the Book of Job," 184. See also Wilcox, *The Bitterness of Job*, 55–70.

deliberate and perverse repudiation of God's work, then Job's utterances certainly qualify. Both the propositional content and the illocutionary force of Job's words in the dialogues constitute a curse equivalent to blasphemy. This may be an answer to a fact that has troubled interpreters of Job for generations. But it that is the case, why does God not respond to the question of theodicy revealed by Job's curses? Why is the doctrine of divine retribution for sin not even mentioned in Yahweh's answer to Job? While the doctrine of retribution is never addressed in God's response from the whirlwind, the unknowable nature of this created order is. Could it be that Yahweh's tirade in Job 38–41 is responding in part to Job's curse on the created order of Job 3?

Another pivotal curse text is Job 27:1–12. This response of Job, in effect, closes the cycles of dialogue with his three friends and anticipates Job's formal testimony of chapters 29–31.

> And Job continued his discourse:

> As surely as God lives, who has denied me justice,
>   the Almighty, who has made my life bitter,
> as long as I have life within me,
>   the breath of God in my nostrils,
> my lips will not say anything wicked,
>   and my tongue will utter no lies.

> I will never admit you are in the right;
>   till I die, I will not deny my integrity.

> I will maintain my innocence and never let go of it;
>   my conscience will not reproach me as long as I live.

> May my enemies be like the wicked,
>   my adversaries like the unjust!
> For what hope have the godless when they are cut off,
>   when God takes away my life?
> Does God listen to their cry
>   when distress comes upon them?
> Will they find delight in the Almighty?
>   Will they call upon God at all times?
> "I will teach you about the power of God;
>   the ways of the Almighty I will not conceal.

> You have all seen this yourselves.
>   Why then this meaningless talk? (Job 27:1–12)

The text includes a freely composed self-curse (vv. 2–4) followed by a curse on Job's adversaries/enemies (v. 7). His oath, which begins, "as Yahweh lives," concludes by reflecting on the prologue, as Job again affirms his integrity: "till I die (*mwt*) I will not put away my integrity (*twm*) from me." This is the same play on words uttered by Job's wife in chapter 2. Job 2:7 can be read as a freely composed curse against his enemy. This enemy, elsewhere identified as God (Job 16:9; 19:11), is, as one might expect, not clearly identified here.

Job 29–31 contains an elaborate articulation of Job's integrity. This unit concludes in chapter 31, another pivotal text with a long series of oaths, expressed in the formula of a self-curse:[24]

> If I have walked with falsehood
>> and my foot has hastened to deceit;
> (Let me be weighed in a just balance,
>> and let God know my integrity!)
> if my step has turned aside from the way
>> and my heart has gone after my eyes,
>> and if any spot has stuck to my hands,
> then let me sow, and another eat,
>> and let what grows for me be rooted out.
>
> If my heart has been enticed toward a woman,
>> and I have lain in wait at my neighbor's door,
> then let my wife grind for another,
>> and let others bow down on her.
> For that would be a heinous crime;
>> that would be an iniquity to be punished by the judges;
> for that would be a fire that consumes as far as Abaddon,
>> and it would burn to the root all my increase.
> If I have rejected the cause of my manservant or my maidservant,
>> when they brought a complaint against me,
> what then shall I do when God rises up?
>> When he makes inquiry, what shall I answer him?
> Did not he who made me in the womb make him?
>> And did not one fashion us in the womb?
> If I have withheld anything that the poor desired,
>> or have caused the eyes of the widow to fail,
> or have eaten my morsel alone,
>> and the fatherless has not eaten of it

24. Dick, "Job 31, The Oath of Innocence, and the Sage."

(for from my youth the fatherless grew up with me
as with a father,
and from my mother's womb I guided the widow),
if I have seen anyone perish for lack of clothing,
or the needy without covering,
if his body has not blessed me,
and if he was not warmed with the fleece of my sheep,
if I have raised my hand against the fatherless,
because I saw my help in the gate,
then let my shoulder blade fall from my shoulder,
and let my arm be broken from its socket.
For I was in terror of calamity from God,
and I could not have faced his majesty.
If I have made gold my trust
or called fine gold my confidence,
if I have rejoiced because my wealth was abundant
or because my hand had found much,
if I have looked at the sun when it shone,
or the moon moving in splendor,
and my heart has been secretly enticed,
and my mouth has kissed my hand,
this also would be an iniquity to be punished by the judges,
for I would have been false to God above.
If I have rejoiced at the ruin of him who hated me,
or exulted when evil overtook him
(I have not let my mouth sin
by asking for his life with a curse),
if the men of my tent have not said,

'Who is there that has not been filled with his meat?'
(the sojourner has not lodged in the street;
I have opened my doors to the traveler),
if I have concealed my transgressions as others do
by hiding my iniquity in my bosom,
because I stood in great fear of the multitude,
and the contempt of families terrified me,
so that I kept silence, and did not go out of doors—
Oh, that I had one to hear me!
(Here is my signature! Let the Almighty answer me!)
Oh, that I had the indictment written by my adversary!
Surely I would carry it on my shoulder;
I would bind it on me as a crown;
I would give him an account of all my steps;
like a prince I would approach him.

> If my land has cried out against me
>> and its furrows have wept together,
> if I have eaten its yield without payment
>> and made its owners breathe their last,
> let thorns grow instead of wheat,
>> and foul weeds instead of barley."
> The words of Job are ended. (Job 31:5–40, ESV)

This lengthy series of oaths is remarkably similar to curses in Deuteronomy 27, and has parallels to two other oaths uttered by Job, (Job 13:1–17; 27:2–6). Valerie Pettys has observed sixteen conditionals that are intended to exonerate Job from judgment, which balance the sixteen jussives employed in Job's curse in chapter 3.[25] The irony of these self-curses is evidenced by the fact that they are uttered by an individual who has already had nearly every catastrophic event imaginable happen to him. It is like a destitute person saying, "if I have done anything wrong, may all my riches be taken away from me." Nevertheless, this ludicrous irony adds to the force of these self-curses. Even in the midst of this adversity, Job affirms repeatedly his integrity.[26] Good has pointed out the force of the curse in chapters 29–31.These curses, like the self-curse uttered by the Satan in the prologue, force God out into the open, and Yahweh responds.[27] The failure of these curses to come upon Job's head would be tantamount to acquittal. At the same time, complete restoration of Job leaves his blasphemous pronouncements unaddressed. Yahweh's appearance functions in two ways: as a vindication for Job as well as an opportunity for self-vindication.

After the self-curse of Job 31, there are no more curse formulas. The anticlimactic appearance of Elihu (chaps. 32–37) serves only to heighten the anticipation of the divine response. Poor Elihu! He doesn't even know enough to know that he doesn't know. His youthfully confident, brash repetitions of stale arguments do not even merit the dignity of a response from Yahweh. A divine response to Job, however, is entirely another matter. Yahweh appears to Job and speaks from the whirlwind. The drastic

25. Pettys, "Let There Be Darkness," 101.

26. Note the telling comment by Blank: "Job boldly defies all conventions and without restraint puts into words what is hardly ever spoken. Nothing could more forcibly produce in his hearers the conviction of Job's innocence than these curses pronounced by Job on himself, this audacious breach or word-taboo" (Blank, "The Curse, Blasphemy, the Spell, and the Oath," 92).

27. Good, "Job and the Literary Task," 474–75. Contra Pelham, "Job's Crisis of Language," 33–54, who argues that Job's call for God's response in chapter 31 is a ruse, based on his experience of God's silence and absence.

nature of Job's self-imprecation forces God's hand. While Yahweh might very well be compelled to respond to Job's oath of innocence to maintain a sense of divine integrity, Yahweh is not forced to respond in a way Job wants. But Job's self-curse creates a cradle of a new religious discourse.[28] Yahweh answers Job . . . with a vengeance. Yahweh's speech shifts the issue from retribution and Job's innocence to the unexplainable natural order of the universe—not coincidently that very order reversed by Job's curse in chapter 3. The implications of the divine speech are that the moral and natural orders are analogous. The natural order is often unexplainable; so also the moral order is not simply based on a naïve doctrine of retribution. The divine speech does not address the issue of retribution even once. This, in effect, neither affirms nor denies retribution theology, but it marginalizes it, and marginalizes it absolutely.[29]

Job's answer shows that he is reduced to silence: "I am unworthy (*qlty*)—how can I reply to you? I put my hand over my mouth. I spoke once, but I have no answer—twice, but I will say no more" (Job 40:4–5). Using the root *qll*, often translated "curse," Job makes light of himself: "I am cursed—how can I respond to you?"

Yahweh's tirade from the whirlwind helps explain Job's repentance in chapter 42:

> Then Job replied to the LORD:
> "I know that you can do all things;
>   no plan of yours can be thwarted.
> You asked, 'Who is this that obscures my plans without knowledge?'
>   Surely I spoke of things I did not understand,
>   things too wonderful for me to know.
>
> "You said, 'Listen now, and I will speak;
>   I will question you,
>   and you shall answer me.'
> My ears had heard of you
>   but now my eyes have seen you.
> Therefore I despise myself
>   and repent in dust and ashes." (Job 42:1–6)

Job repents, not because he is unrighteous (Terrien), or insincere (Robertson), but because he spoke rashly in ignorance of the moral order of

---

28. This is Beuken's language ("Job's Imprecation as the Cradle of a New Religious Discourse").

29. Clines, *Job 1–20*, xlvi.

things (Good). Job's brash words of the poetic center begin with his curse in chapter. 3. His closing comments reveal this ignorance: "I have *uttered* what I did not understand" (Job 42:3, ESV). From beginning to end the story of Job is a story of the intended and unintended consequences of speech acts (particularly of malevolent speech directed against God), yet God is never intimidated by the illocutions of humans.

"The Lord Blessed the Latter Days of Job More than the Beginning": The Epilogue

The epilogue resumes the retribution theology of the prologue, but with an ironic twist. In essence Job states, "I was wrong" (Job 42:3), to which Yahweh might as well have replied, "No, actually you were right" (Job 42:7–17). Job, in the end, is the one who is blessed while his friends are rebuked. It is specifically the impropriety of their speech that is condemned, while Job's restored relationship with God is reaffirmed.[30] "And the LORD blessed the latter days of Job more than the beginning" (Job 42:12). This new blessing of the prose epilogue demonstrates that Job has been rewarded for his righteousness, twice as much as he had before. Yet, the poetic center of the book has modified this viewpoint significantly. Ironically, Job is the only mediator Yahweh will accept. Retributional elements have been completely marginalized.[31] Admittedly, God's wager with the Satan throws doubt on God's ability to be just. This casts a dark shadow on the nature and character of God. The relation of prologue and epilogue to the poetic center creates a double structure to the curse, each with its own conflict and resolution. The conflict introduced in the prologue questions, will Job curse Yahweh? That question is not so much addressed in the epilogue as it is in the closing words of the poetic center, where Job confesses, "I uttered what I did not understand." The conflict introduced in the poetic center has Job cursing the day of this birth, his enemy, and even himself. This demands a resolution in the divine address where Yahweh responds against Job's countercosmic incantation of chapter 3. If the prose narrative were to be considered alone, there would be no curse pronouncement. Job blesses Yahweh (Job 1:21), and in the end of the epilogue (Job 42:12) Yahweh

30. Timmer, "God's Speeches," 303.

31. Walter Brueggemann has argued that while deeds do bear consequences, Yahweh is not a prisoner of the system and can act in freedom. He draws a parallel between the freedom of God in the curse of David and Shimei and the issue in the debate between Job and his friends (Brueggemann, "On Coping with Curse," 183–84).

blesses Job. The poetic center of the book, however, begs for another perspective. Job's curse on his day, his cosmos, his enemy, and himself draws a response from Yahweh that not only affirms the integrity of Job but also reveals God's paradoxical sovereignty.

JOB IN THE BROADER CONTEXT OF WISDOM THEOLOGY

What lessons does the theology of Job reveal that are relevant for the broader world of the Wisdom traditions of the Old Testament? First, in the book of Job, as in other Wisdom books of the Old Testament, wisdom is grounded in creation rather than covenant. Job has no mention of torah, exodus, the monarchy, or the ancestors of Israel. This is similar to the books of Proverbs and Ecclesiastes as well. Where Proverbs affirms Torah, it does not refer to a divinely inspired text but in a generic sense to wise instruction or teaching. This dispassionate interest in Israel's traditions is shared by Ecclesiastes. Instead of the narrower Israelite themes common in Old Testament theology, the book of Job exploits creation themes. Yet, creation in biblical wisdom is not limited to cosmology alone, but is a much broader topic that relates to anthropology, community ethics, and epistemology.[32] Job refutes traditional wisdom's answers of his friends based on observation (experience teaches that sin leads to suffering), tradition (everyone else knows that sin leads to suffering), and special revelation (God told us in a vision that sin leads to suffering). This triad of easy answers is weighed and discarded by means of Job's rebuttals to his friends. Personally, Job epitomizes the isolation typically associated with suffering. The curse in Job 3 arises from the person who has nothing left . . . except words. But Job's words are potent words. These words amount to a negation of the creation blessing in Genesis 1. The blessing metaphor of fertility is turned on its head. The curse negates reproduction and brings on sterility.[33] His opening salvo of the poetic center in chapter 3 is nothing less than a frontal assault on creation. Seven malevolent incantations contrast with the seven benevolent days of creation. Yahweh, however, is not one to be intimidated. Yahweh's answer from the whirlwind throws the argument right back in Job's face. The intense cross-examination with the staccato-like questions, "Where were you when . . . ," accentuates God's defiant refusal to defend the moral ambiguity often present in the world. And Yahweh uses creation theology as a stick. God's wisdom

---

32. Perdue, *Wisdom & Creation*, 35.

33. Perdue, *Wisdom in Revolt*, 74.

and justice will always transcend human comprehension. God upholds his own sovereignty. Anything less than absolute sovereignty limits God's actions to predictable results, making God a hapless puppet who responds automatically in predetermined ways.[34] These ways, incidentally, all too conveniently have been predetermined by humans. Although chaos resides in the world, God acts with freedom to sustain justice and harmony. The forces of chaos are kept at bay (Job 38:11). The message of the book of Job is also an attack on the mechanical application of the dogma of double retribution. Much of the Old Testament's message implies a direct correlation between on the one hand obedience and blessing, and on the other hand disobedience and curse. Wisdom theology provides a powerful answer to Deuteronomic theology's law of succession (curse follows sin) and law of proportion (punishment fits crime). Job's defense against his critics is simultaneously a defense against a reading of the Old Testament that distills all of life's ambiguity into a nice, neat, doctrine of retribution.

The book of Proverbs also grounds wisdom in creation in a very different way in that it exhibits a profound confidence in a rational moral order. Therefore Proverbs is the most optimistic of biblical Wisdom literature. Such dependability provides stability and assurance for all of life's variable circumstances. Proverbs offers that the creation of wisdom is the first and best of God's creative acts (see also Prov 3:19–20):

> The LORD brought me forth as the first of his works,
>   before his deeds of old;
>
> I was appointed from eternity,
>   from the beginning, before the world began.
> When there were no oceans, I was given birth,
>   when there were no springs abounding with water;
> before the mountains were settled in place,
>   before the hills, I was given birth,
> before he made the earth or its fields
>   or any of the dust of the world.
>
> I was there when he set the heavens in place,
>   when he marked out the horizon on the face of the deep,
> when he established the clouds above
>   and fixed securely the fountains of the deep,
> when he gave the sea its boundary
>   so the waters would not overstep his command,

---

34. On Job as a necessary corrective to a cause-and-effect understanding of divine operations in the world, see Dumbrell, "The Purpose of the Book of Job."

and when he marked out the foundations of the earth.
Then I was the craftsman at his side.

I was filled with delight day after day,
    rejoicing always in his presence,
rejoicing in his whole world
    and delighting in mankind. (Prov 8:22–31)

Harmut Gese's classic study on wisdom in Egypt investigated the idea
that *Maʾat*, the undergirding principle that galvanized truth, justice, and
order, was the organizing principle for wisdom tradition in Egypt.[35] He
argued that this principle was then assimilated and transformed by Israel's
sages. Cosmic order and social structure gave a kind of regularity in the
world. Creation, as a theological category, is a logical basis for that order and regularity in the world.[36] In the book of Proverbs, predictability
provides stability in that it leads to a confident assurance that the ways
of the world are consistent, providing practical habits to order one's life.
The basic truths observed by experience are a reliable guide for ordering a
person's daily life. The book of Proverbs employs two basic literary forms
to convey this live-and-learn ethic: the proverb (*mašal*) and the wisdom
poem (*musar*). A proverb is a brief, colorful, assertive saying that connects
a deed and a result.[37] The following example is typical of the picturesque
speech used in Old Testament proverbs: "The tongue of the wise makes
knowledge acceptable, but the mouth of fools sprouts folly" (Prov 15:2, my
translation). Such imagery is designed to make a lasting impression. Who
can forget the sluggard creaking in his bed (Prov 26:14) or the beautiful
woman without discretion portrayed as a pig with a ring in its snout (Prov
11:22)? These images stay with the reader, providing easy recall of the
practical advice so common in Proverbs. The *mashal* in the book of Proverbs is not a truth; it is a truism, something that is ordinarily, consistently,
and regularly true. This sense of regularity is found through boilerplate
language in Proverbs where particular proverbs are often repeated in the
book's disparate anthologies. For example, it is generally true that if one
works hard, a person will be rewarded for her labors. It is also generally
true that people are better off if they are careful about the words that come

35. Gese, *Lehre und Wirklichkeit in der alten Weisheit*.

36. Murphy argues that the concept of order has been pushed too far in Wisdom
theology. He states that accepted regularities are not the same as order, if order is
envisioned as operative in the reality of everyday experience and the goal of wisdom;
The Tree of Life, 116–17.

37. Perdue, *Wisdom & Creation*, 67.

out of their mouths. But people's experiences often run counter to these two examples. Thus, we have the genius of the proverb. Something that is generally true does not have to be true all the time. For example,

> Do not answer a fool according to his folly,
>> or you will be like him yourself.

> Answer a fool according to his folly,
>> or he will be wise in his own eyes. (Prov 26:4–5)

Which of these two *mashalim* are true? They both are, but in different circumstances. Yet even this seeming inconsistency does not deny the basic order of things. Divine providence continues to sustain the cosmic and social orders, which are intrinsically connected.[38]

Ecclesiastes, however, tells a different story. One must be comfortable with ambiguity when it comes to Wisdom literature of the Old Testament. Not only does the wisdom tradition often counter traditional covenant theology, but there are also tensions in wisdom itself. Ecclesiastes takes this theme of regularity and turns it on its head. Using the language of creation, *contemptus mundi* might be a good theme for Ecclesiastes. Qoheleth observes plenty of regularity all right, but it leads him in entirely different directions theologically:

> "Meaningless! Meaningless!"
>> says the Teacher.
> "Utterly meaningless!
>> Everything is meaningless."

> What do people gain from all their labor
>> at which they toil under the sun?
> Generations come and generations go,
>> but the earth remains forever.
> The sun rises and the sun sets,
>> and hurries back to where it rises.
> The wind blows to the south
>> and turns to the north;
> round and round it goes,
>> ever returning on its course.
> All streams flow into the sea,
>> yet the sea is never full.
> To the place the streams come from,
>> there they return again.

38. Perdue, *The Sword and the Stylus*, 113.

All things are wearisome,
    more than one can say.
The eye never has enough of seeing,
    nor the ear its fill of hearing.
What has been will be again,
    what has been done will be done again;
there is nothing new under the sun.
Is there anything of which one can say,
    "Look! This is something new"?
It was here already, long ago;
    it was here before our time.
No one remembers the former generations,
    and even those who are yet to come
will not be remembered
    by those who follow. (Eccl 1:2–11)

Regularity? Of course! But regularity is a source of frustration, not a source of comfort. The author introduces his cosmological observations with the question, "What do people gain from all their work which they toil under the sun?" The answer? Futility, nothing but futility. Ecclesiastes takes up three storied examples of regularity: the created order, work, and time.

First, the regularity in God's created order, which might be a source of confidence for some, promotes madness for the author of Ecclesiastes. Circular movement, like the regularity of the rising and setting of the sun is a sign of endless, agonizingly repetitive futility. The wind blows in all directions only to return again to repeat its futility. The fact that rivers flow into the sea, yet that the sea is never full is no comfort either. It is a sign that there is nothing really new under the sun. The truth that the earth lasts forever, even as generations come and go, is simply a painful reminder of one's temporality. So wind, river, sun, and generations all point to futility.

Likewise, the regularity of work might be interpreted positively as that human effort to fulfill God's command to master the world. But, the sense of accomplishment and purpose that comes from one's own daily work yields nothing but a sense of frustration for the author of Ecclesiastes.

> So I hated life, because what is done under the sun was grievous to me, for all is vanity and a striving after wind. I hated all my toil in which I toil under the sun, seeing that I must leave it to the man who will come after me, and who knows whether he will be wise or a fool? Yet he will be master of all for which I toiled and used my wisdom under the sun. This also is vanity. So I turned about and gave my heart up to despair over all the

> toil of my labors under the sun, because sometimes a person who has toiled with wisdom and knowledge and skill must leave everything to be enjoyed by someone who did not toil for it. This also is vanity and a great evil. What has a man from all the toil and striving of heart with which he toils beneath the sun? For all his days are full of sorrow, and his work is a vexation. Even in the night his heart does not rest. This also is vanity. (Ecc 2:17–23 ESV)

One works day after day only to give the results of hard labor to one who never had to work for it, and who cannot be counted on to take care of it. Work provides no gain, no rest—just plenty of envy and rivalry (Eccl 4:4). It is better to just eke out some kind of satisfaction and enjoyment with your work while you can. This theme of the enjoyment of life does provide a glimmer of hope. Ecclesiastes does have much to say about enjoying life (Ecc 2:24; 3:12–13, 22; 5:18; 8:15; 9:7–10; 11:8–10). William Brown sees this as the interpretive crux of Ecclesiastes.[39] Sadly, however, there is profound sense of inconsequentiality to the joy one experiences in this life. It is fine to enjoy life, but that enjoyment won't make a dime's worth of difference in the end.

Third, Ecclesiastes takes on the theme of the regularity of time to demonstrate life's futility (3:11–14; 7:14ff.):

> He has made everything beautiful in its time. Also, he has put eternity into man's heart, yet so that he cannot find out what God has done from the beginning to the end. I perceived that there is nothing better for them than to be joyful and to do good as long as they live; also that everyone should eat and drink and take pleasure in all his toil—this is God's gift to man. I perceived that whatever God does endures forever; nothing can be added to it, nor anything taken from it. God has done it, so that people fear before him. (Eccl 3:11–14, ESV)

For this author, time is frustrating for the very reason that some may see as a positive sign of purposeful life. God has placed eternity in the human heart. But that yearning for eternity is matched by the ephemerality of life. While humans long for eternity, death comes all too quickly to each soul. Life is dreadfully short. Skepticism because of the brevity of life permeates the message of Ecclesiastes. There is a pathetic irony in the truth that humans long for the eternal but will end up not one bit different than the animals. The conclusion? *Carpe Diem!* Seize the day; enjoy life while you

39. Brown, "Whatever Your Hand Finds to Do," 279.

can (Ecc 2:24–26; 3:12–13, 22; 5:17–19; 8:15; 9:7–10; 11:7–10). Certainly there is a God, and that God rules over creation, but God rules the world in secrecy. No one really knows whether the fate of humans is any different than the fate of animals. So the injunction in Ecclesiastes is to enjoy one's youth while there is still time,

> Remember your Creator
> in the days of your youth,
> before the days of trouble come
> and the years approach when you will say,
> "I find no pleasure in them"—
> before the sun and the light
> and the moon and the stars grow dark,
> and the clouds return after the rain;
> when the keepers of the house tremble,
> and the strong men stoop,
> when the grinders cease because they are few,
> and those looking through the windows grow dim;
> when the doors to the street are closed
> and the sound of grinding fades;
> when men rise up at the sound of birds,
> but all their songs grow faint;
> when men are afraid of heights
> and of dangers in the streets;
> when the almond tree blossoms
> and the grasshopper drags himself along
> and desire no longer is stirred.
> Then man goes to his eternal home
> and mourners go about the streets. (Eccl 12:1–5)

BLESSINGS AND CURSES AND WISDOM'S TWO-WAY INSTRUCTION

The book of Proverbs takes up a subject that has implications for the theme of blessings and curses mentioned elsewhere in the Old Testament. It is the theme of *the two ways* found prominently in the first nine chapters of the book.[40] The author of Proverbs regularly employs language of walking divergent paths that lead to opposite outcomes. Human choice is everything. The wise individual, who chooses the path of righteousness and justice, is contrasted with the one who might choose a different path—one of

---

40. In particular, Prov 1:15–19, 2:7–20, 4:11–19, 7:25–27, 8:1–11, 8:32–36, 9:1–18.

darkness and evil. The wise person is the one who makes good judgments at crucial places where paths diverge. The human decision to choose one path over another can have benevolent or malevolent outcomes. Note the two-way instruction in the selected passage below and the application of that instruction to the theme of sexual immorality:

> Then you will understand what is right and just
>   and fair—every good path.
> For wisdom will enter your heart,
>   and knowledge will be pleasant to your soul.
> Discretion will protect you,
>   and understanding will guard you.
>
> Wisdom will save you from the ways of wicked men,
>   from men whose words are perverse,
> who leave the straight paths
>   to walk in dark ways,
> who delight in doing wrong
>   and rejoice in the perverseness of evil,
> whose paths are crooked
>   and who are devious in their ways.
>
> It will save you also from the adulteress,
>   from the wayward wife with her seductive words,
> who has left the partner of her youth
>   and ignored the covenant she made before God.
> For her house leads down to death
>   and her paths to the spirits of the dead.
> None who go to her return
>   or attain the paths of life.
>
> Thus you will walk in the ways of good men
>   and keep to the paths of the righteous.
> For the upright will live in the land,
>   and the blameless will remain in it;
> but the wicked will be cut off from the land,
>   and the unfaithful will be torn from it. (Prov 2:9–22)

Scholars have long been interested in the relationship between the two-way instruction of the wisdom tradition and the blessings and curses in the Mosaic law. [41] The binary nature of the two-ways formulation in proverbial wisdom connects with Deut 30:19 and the blessings and curses

---

41. Nickelsburg, "Seeking the Origins of the Two-Ways Tradition"; J. S. Anderson "Two-Way Instruction and Covenantal Theology"; Kraft, "Barnabas and the Didache." See also Kraft, "Early Development of the Two-Way(s) Traditions."

of covenant theology. The imagery of the two ways may or may not have originated with Deuteronomy, but this image was a common metaphor already present in early Wisdom literature. There is really no way to know which came first in Israelite tradition. The two-way theology of biblical wisdom portrays an ordered ethical dualism.[42] Likewise, Deut 30:15–19 places before the people a choice of life and prosperity or death and adversity, blessing or curse. Klaus Baltzer and Lars Hartman both have demonstrated links of this two-way thinking to blessings-and-curses covenantal theology.[43] Baltzer's classic work on the covenant formulary pointed out the Hebrew Bible's reuse of an ancient form preserved over the centuries through public use in worship. Early Jewish writers also borrowed the form (particularly the blessings and curses) as a two-way schema that would eventually be fulfilled in the eschaton.[44] Both the strong dualism of life and death in the two-way imagery and the blessings and curses of the covenant serve the same metaphorical intent. For Deuteronomy, walking in God's ways and observing the commandments represent identical ethical behaviors. Arguably, as the Torah assumed a central role in Israelite religion, this imagery was incorporated into the Torah consciousness of Israel, particularly later in Israel's history.[45] The Torah is the touchstone for defining good and evil conduct while the two-way metaphor envisions alternative ethical behaviors. Some have argued that the imagery of the two ways may or may not have necessarily originated in the wisdom tradition, but its use there undoubtedly preceded its adoption by the Mosaic Torah.[46] Jack Sanders has observed a number of Second Temple Jewish works that demonstrate evidence of an internal struggle as the Mosaic Torah emerged as the dominant force in Jewish religion.[47]

Look at one example of how two-way theology was given specific ethical context in the book of Proverbs. There is, perhaps, no better example than the contrast between Woman Wisdom and Woman Folly. (Woman Folly is given a handful of colorful names: adulteress, forbidden

---

42. For pioneering work on ethical dualism, see Gammie, "Spatial and Ethical Dualism."

43 Hartman, *Asking for a Meaning*, 96–104; Baltzer, *The Covenant Formulary*, 165.

44. Baltzer, *The Covenant Formulary*, 166.

45. Blenkinsopp, *Wisdom and Law in the Old Testament*, 77.

46. At least this is the argument by Blenkinsopp. Robert Kraft has suggested that the binary, two-way approach is so obvious and commonplace in human experience that it might have arisen at various times and places in human history, rather than simply tracing the theme back to a single origin; Kraft, "Early Development," 143.

47. Sanders, "When Sacred Canopies Collide."

woman, prostitute, married woman, evil woman, and so forth.) The women serve as vibrant paradigms, of, respectively, wisdom (Prov 1:20–33; 3:12–18; 4:5–13; 8:1–36; 9:1–12) and folly (Prov 2:16–19; 5:3–23; 6:24–35; 7:1–27; 9:13–18). Proverbs take up themes of a woman's beauty and of seduction to personify these two opposite ideals. Remarkable parallels and contrasts arise between Woman Wisdom and Woman Folly: where these two commonly live, what they say, how they say it, who they typically attract, and what becomes of those who are drawn to them. They both station themselves at important crossroads of life: where two paths or noisy streets meet, in the bustling marketplaces, where beautifully adorned gates provide access to two different avenues, near doors that open two very different lifestyle choices, and on the highest hills of the city (Prov 8:2–3; 9:3, 14). Both, to be frank, are loud. They cry out with strong voices and beckon those who would come to them. Woman Wisdom calls out and raises her voice (Prov 1:20; 8:1), and Woman Folly is equally brash, crying out to any fool who might be passing by, "going straight along the way," or in the modern vernacular, "minding his own business (Prov 7:11; 9:13). She uses smooth, seductive words to entice foolish young men (Prov 2:16; 5:3; 6:24; 7:5). While the tone of these two women is the same, the content of what they say is entirely different. The wise woman invites, "Come, eat my food and drink the wine that I have mixed, leave your simple ways and you will live; walk in the way of understanding (Prov 9:6). And Woman Folly? "Let all who are simple come in here," she says, to those who lack judgment (Prov 9:16). The life consequences for those who choose wisely and for those who choose foolishly could not be any more different. The guests who visit Woman Folly do not even know that the dead are there, that they will end up in the depths of Sheol (Prov 2:18, 7:22–27; 9:18). Those who choose the path of Woman Wisdom find riches, honor, and righteousness. Those who pursue her have an inheritance filled with treasures (Prov 8:18–21). One of the reasons that scholars have been attracted to parallels between covenant blessings and curses and the two-way theology of Wisdom literature is that both traditions include warnings. The covenant curses and the writings of prophets feature the language of calamity. Likewise, Proverbs ominously warns of calamity for those who do not heed the instruction of Wisdom,

> I in turn will laugh at your disaster;
>> I will mock when calamity overtakes you—
> when calamity overtakes you like a storm,
>> when disaster sweeps over you like a whirlwind,
>> when distress and trouble overwhelm you. (Prov 1:26–27)

For the person who chooses wisely, however, life if the reward. Note the parallels to several of the keywords of Deuteronomic theology: *hear, watch, keep,* and *love.*

> Now then, my children, listen (*šim'û*) to me;
>> blessed are those who keep (*yišmōrû*) my ways.
> Listen (*šim'û*) to my instruction and be wise;
>> do not ignore it.
> Blessed are those who listen (*šōmē'a*) to me,
>> watching (*lišmōr*) daily at my doors,
>> waiting at my doorway.
> For those who find me find life
>> and receive favor from the LORD.
> But those who fail to find me harms themselves;
>> all who hate me love (*'āhabû*) death. (Prov 8:32–36)

12

"A Curse Devours the Earth"

Old Testament Apocalyptic Theology

APOCALYPTICISM IN THE OLD TESTAMENT

SCHOLARS HAVE MADE A great deal of progress in the study of apocalyptic literature in the last fifty years, not only in the Bible but also in the important Jewish texts of the Second Temple period. No small advancement has been the clarification of terminology.[1] An apocalypse is defined as a narrative literary genre normally characterized by the disclosure of divine mysteries to humans by a divine intermediary. This disclosure can take place by means of the recipient's journey to an otherworldly location where sacred knowledge is imparted, or in cases where no otherworldly journey takes place, the recipient receives visions of current and impending actions of God. The term *apocalyptic* is an adjective describing not only this literary genre but also the broader ideas, theology, and worldview of the parties behind these revelations of divine mystery. The use of the term *apocalyptic* as a noun, once quite common, is now passé in academic circles. *Apocalypticism* is the preferred descriptive noun for the movements and thinking behind the apocalyptic genre. After searching for the origins of apocalyptic literature in either prophetic or wisdom traditions in Israel, scholars are now convinced that the origins and development of this genre

1. Collins, *The Apocalyptic Imagination*, 2–8; Cohn, *Cosmos, Chaos, and the World to Come*; Cook, *Prophecy & Apocalypticism*, 20–34.

are widespread and diverse in Second Temple Judaism. Broad variation in content, form, and historical setting of this genre is evident. Daniel and Revelation make excellent examples of apocalypses in the Bible, and outside biblical literature, most prominent are the books of *Enoch*, *4 Ezra*, and *2 Baruch*, to name just a few. While the term *proto-apocalyptic* perhaps carries a more excessively evolutionary content than is actually the case, Isaiah 24–27 and Zechariah 9–14 both display strong apocalyptic elements, such as the description of the universal world judgment and widespread use of symbolic language. As they are in other Jewish apocalypses, the universal judgments in Isaiah and Zechariah are firmly anchored in history, anticipating the physical return of God's people from exile.

Apocalypses are resistance literature.[2] The literature emerged from no single group or movement in Second Temple Judaism.[3] Apocalypticism flourished in Second Temple Jewish religious thought—including in Christianity, which began as a movement within Judaism. In addition to those apocalypses mentioned above, the *Testament of Moses*, the *Apocalypse of Zephaniah*, and the *Apocalypse of Abraham* are other examples of this diverse genre. Most of these works share general characteristics. *Dualism* is perhaps an overused word when applied to apocalypticism, but it is one that I think still accurately portrays many parts of apocalyptic thought. *Temporal dualism* is a term that describes the tension between this present, evil age and a coming age of glory.[4] These works display a hope for a better world and a final struggle and victory against all the injustices of this life. *Spatial dualism* names the distinction between this visible, physical world and the spiritual world of the heavens, or even between various levels in heaven itself. Because of the huge distance, both qualitative and quantitative, between the visible cosmos and this unseen world, mediation is necessary through contact with angelic beings or through heavenly dreams and visions. *Cosmic dualism* or *ethical dualism* is a term that describes the fight between forces of good and evil. The transformation of this sinful age to an age of justice and uprightness is a rallying point of this literature. Apocalyptic works are often pseudonymous, as prominent figures such as Daniel, Ezra, Moses, and Enoch are adopted by the authors to convey a greater authority for the visions described in the apocalypses.

2. Portier-Young, *Apocalypse against Empire*, 3–45.

3. See the series of essays in Wright and Wills, *Conflicted Boundaries in Wisdom and Apocalypticism*.

4. Wright downplays temporal dualism in apocalyptic thought; *Jesus and the Victory of God*, 512.

In this chapter we will examine three apocalyptic or proto-apocalyptic texts: the Little Apocalypse in Isaiah 24–27, Daniel's prayer of confession and subsequent reinterpretation of Jeremiah's seventy weeks in Daniel 9, and Zechariah's prophecy about the Day of the Lord and the impending battle between Jerusalem and foreign kingdoms in Zechariah 14. All these examples take up the theme of blessings and curses.

The Little Apocalypse: Isaiah 24–27

Isaiah 24–27 is traditionally called the Little Apocalypse. Recent resurgence of interest in apocalyptic thought has given this unit a pivotal position in the development of apocalypticism.[5] There is almost unanimous agreement for treating these chapters as some sort of unity, but the consensus quickly evaporates at that point. The Little Apocalypse is composed of a number of separate literary elements, primarily including eschatological prophecies and songs, and it is often difficult to determine where one prophecy ends and a song begins. This unit lacks many of the qualities of full-blown apocalypses but expresses a significant stage in the transition to the apocalyptic genre.[6] Richly evocative apocalyptic elements abound in Isaiah 24–27. Themes of universal judgment (Isa 24:1) and punishment of the host of heaven (Isa 24:21), signs in the sun and moon (Isa 24:22–23), the end of death (Isa 25:8) and the possibility of resurrection (Isa 26:19), and the final defeat of two primordial chaos monsters, Leviathan and the Dragon (Isa 27:1), reveal strong apocalyptic undertones, yet in the end the message of this Isaiah 24–27 is firmly anchored in history. This is consistent with the nature of apocalyptic literature: such literature uses wildly symbolic cosmic language to depict historical events. To put it another way, apocalyptic literature often uses otherworldly language to describe this-worldly realities.[7]

To summarize the message of the Little Apocalypse in brief, after a calamitous universal judgment in which a curse devours the earth, Israel will return to the land and receive God's blessing. That blessing is bestowed in vineyard language similar to what we explored in our discussion of prophetic literature. Ultimately the peoples of the world will worship Yahweh

---

5. For disparate perspectives, see P. D. Hanson, *The Dawn of Apocalyptic*. See also Millar, *Isaiah 24–27 and the Origin of Apocalyptic*; Johnson, *From Chaos to Restoration*.

6. Collins states that Isaiah 24–27 comes closer to apocalyptic thought than other prophecies of the postexilic period; *The Apocalyptic Imagination*, 24.

7. Wright, *The New Testament and the People of God*, 282–88.

on the holy mountain in Jerusalem. Isaiah 24–27 concludes, not with a cosmic upheaval, but with the return of the people from the four corners of the earth to worship God in the holy temple of Jerusalem. The Little Apocalypse begins with a lament:

> See the LORD is going to lay waste the earth
> and devastate it;
> He will ruin its face
> and scatter its inhabitants—
> It will be the same
> for priest as for people,
> for master as for servant
> for seller as for buyer
> for borrower as for lender
> for debtor as for creditor
> The earth will be completely laid waste
> and totally plundered.
> The LORD has spoken this word
> The earth dries up and withers,
> the world languishes and withers,
> the exalted of the earth languish.
> The earth is defiled by its people;
> they have disobeyed the laws,
> violated the statutes
> and broken the everlasting covenant
> *Therefore a curse ('ālâ 'āklâ) consumes the earth* (italics added)
> its people must bear their guilt.
> Therefore the earth's inhabitants are burned up,
> and very few are left. (Isa 24:1–6)

Isaiah 24–27 is remarkably universal in scope when compared with the group of against foreign kingdoms that precede it (Isaiah 13–23), and the announcements of judgment afterwards (Isaiah 28–33). In the larger context of the book of Isaiah, the chapters before and after this unit describe specific historical circumstances. Consequently, Isaiah 24–27 introduce one way of reading the sections immediately before and after this unit—in light of apocalypticism.[8] God does not merely react to what the peoples do on the stage of history. God is sovereign in both time and space. In spite of the way things may appear, history is headed in a divinely ordered direction. Isaiah 24:1–6 describes the travail visited on creation itself. The only way for a new age to dawn is for the evil system that

---

8. Oswalt, "Isaiah 24–27: Songs in the Night," 79.

currently exists to be completely destroyed. The Hebrew is emphatic in
24:3 as this very literal translation shows: "emptied there will be emptying
of the earth, and spoiled there will be spoiling of the earth." Using six pairs
of opposites, the prophet shows that all social and economic classes will be
under this universal judgment. No one will escape. The oppressive social
structures of this present, evil age will be reversed by an impending catastrophe in which the earth will be reduced to a wasteland.[9] The language
of un-creation is liberally employed, and the devastation will be complete.
Such destruction of the created order is universal. Paul House argues that
this describes the literal end of human history, but metaphorical language
like this more likely relates to some catastrophic event in history.[10] This
judgment becomes the turning point of the ages and embraces a dualism
of heavenly and earthly worlds as well as of the dead and the living (Isa
24:21).

It is in this context that the writer takes up curse language. The word
"therefore" in Isa 24:6 points back to the refusal of God's people to keep
the everlasting covenant (*bĕrît 'ôlām*). Much has been written about which
of the many Old Testament covenants Isaiah refers to here. The expression
"everlasting covenant" (or perhaps "ancient covenant") is found a dozen
times in the Old Testament.[11] Steven Mason summarizes four possible
covenant backdrops to Isa 24:5: the creation covenant, the Noachic covenant, the Mosaic covenant, or a combination of these covenants.[12] The
imagery of Isaiah 24 speaks of a cataclysmic judgment against all creation
in language reminiscent of that used in the Genesis story of the primeval
deluge. The heavens and earth are laid waste and desolate; a curse lurks,
devouring the earth; the windows of heaven are open; Yahweh has punished the heavens and the earth; and only a remnant is left. Creation has
given way to un-creation. The broken covenant to which vv. 5–6 allude is
quite possibly the Mosaic covenant, with its laws and statutes. But Mason
argues that the eternal covenant mentioned here is the Noachic covenant
from Gen 9:16, and the primary abuse of the human community that is
condemned is indiscriminate violence. This also makes sense in light of
the motif of un-creation. The double "therefore" in Isa 24:6 is the interpretive crux of chapter 24. A curse has been unleashed and it devours

9. B. W. Anderson, *Contours of Old Testament Theology*, 306–7.

10. House, *Old Testament Theology*, 284.

11. This expression is found in Gen 9:16; Exod 31:16; Lev 24:8; 2 Sam 23:5; 1 Chr
16:17; Ps 105:10; Isa 24:5, 55:3; Jer 32:30, 50:5; Ezek 16:60; 37:26.

12. Mason, "Another Flood?," 178.

the earth. The judgment of God affects the entire cosmos. The language is similar to Isa 33:7–9:

> Look, their brave men cry aloud in the streets;
> > the envoys of peace weep bitterly.
> The highways are deserted,
> > no travelers are on the roads.
> The treaty is broken,
> > its witnesses are despised,
> > no one is respected.
> The land mourns and wastes away,
> > Lebanon is ashamed and withers;
> Sharon is like the Arabah,
> > and Bashan and Carmel drop their leaves.

Many interpreters have failed to fully explore the significance of this curse in attempts to identify the eternal covenant. Some hardly mention it at all. Hardly any study of covenant in the ancient Near East or in the Bible can escape the prolific references to blessing and curse in covenantal contexts, including in the context of the eternal covenant mentioned here. The Hebrew *'lh* denotes the curse that is the operating force behind and motivator of the oath: the spoken or written words behind nearly every covenant. At a basic level, every oath is a conditional self-curse.[13] The consequences of such a curse are self-evident: plants fade, towns collapse, inhabitants wail and disappear from the surface of the earth. Similar to uses of *'lh* in Jer 23:10, the whole of the country decays, all its pastures wither (Jer 29:18; 42:18; 44:12; and Dan 9:11). Jon Levenson has observed that in the flood story the basis for security in a postdeluge world is not creation itself but God's mysterious oath not to destroy the world: "Only that oath, only that universal covenant sworn to Noah and nothing more, keeps human life safe from total annihilation."[14]

Two very different cities are described in Isaiah 24–27. Isaiah 24:12 mentions a desolate city. In vivid ancient Near Eastern curse rhetoric, this city is in chaos; its gates are smashed and every home vacant. This city languishes in desolation, and the only sound that can be heard is the sound of mourning. The city is broken, inaccessible, empty, and stricken by famine. Only the fewest of survivors remain (Isa 24:10–12). Such language reflects the consequences of the covenant curse. Terror and pit and snare afflict every inhabitant of the earth. Isaiah 25 continues with the theme of this

---

13. Brichto, *The Problem of "Curse" in the Hebrew Bible*, 40.

14. Levenson, *Creation and the Persistence of Evil*, 48.

first city: it wastes away as a heap of ruins (Isa 25:2–5). It is a city that will never be rebuilt. The interpretation of this city lies at the heart of the understanding of Isaiah 24–27. A city is mentioned on four occasions in the unit (24:10–12, 25:1–5, 26:5–6, and 27:10–11). The identification of the city will always be a matter of strong debate, since there are very few historical allusions here. Among literal capital cities of the time that might be the city in question within the unit, the most popular suggestions are Jerusalem, Samaria, or some foreign capital such as Tyre, Sidon, Susa, Babylon, or Nineveh. This city, however, is unnamed, perhaps intentionally.[15] As a symbol of power, the city is identified as one that abuses the poor and the lowly. Yahweh is avenged by the destruction of this city, which causes the foreign peoples to fear God.

Yet, another city is portrayed positively in the Little Apocalypse of Isaiah (Isa 26:1–6): this is a city where Yahweh is worshiped. Instead of being full of corruption and without understanding of God, it is a holy city, set apart, where no corruption and idolatry can be found. In opposition to the "chaos city," which oppresses the poor and lowly, the "cosmos city" becomes a champion of the poor and lowly, who stream to it from around the world. In this city, the gates are open rather than broken down in heaps of rubble. Unlike the people of the first city, who have broken the everlasting covenant (bĕrît ʿôlām), a righteous people will enter this second city and be faithful to Yahweh, who is the eternal Rock (ṣûr ʿôlāmîm). The theological tension between this chaos city and the cosmos city describes that interplay between curse and blessing. The City of Chaos lies as a heap of ruins while the City of Blessing is a magnet for the peoples who stream to it from around the world. Recalling the language of Genesis, Isaiah promises that all the peoples of the earth will be blessed through it. God's people are to trust in God's ability to establish this strong city:

> You will keep in perfect peace
>> those whose mind is steadfast,
>> because they trust in you.
> Trust in the Lord forever,
>> for the Lord, the Lord himself, is the Rock eternal.
> (Isa 26:3–4)

While the Little Apocalypse does not specifically mention the holiness of Yahweh, one of Isaiah's dominant themes, it does refer to the majesty of Yahweh, who receives universal praise "from one end of the earth to the other" (Isa 24:14–16). All rivals will be struck down and Yahweh will

15. Redditt, "Once Again, the City in Isaiah 24–27."

be enthroned on Mount Zion (Isa 24:23).[16] Isaiah reveals God as king of the universe. Through the annihilation of God's enemies and through the new creation of a new order, God reveals to every human eye a definitive purpose in history.

The formula "in that day" sets the eschatological tone for the Little Apocalypse—particularly eight explicit references in the Little Apocalypse (Isa 24:21; 25:9; 26:1; 27:1, 2, 6, 12–13) mark literary units. In the closing chapter of the Little Apocalypse, the victory of that day will mark the overthrow of Leviathan and the dragon. These two mythical sea monsters were ordinarily portrayed in the primeval battle at the time of the creation of the universe. The Ras Shamra texts depict Leviathan (Job 3:8; Ps 74:4) as locked in a cosmogonic battle with Baal, where Baal vanquishes him. The dragon (Job 7:12; Ps 74:13; Isa 51:9) is portrayed in a similar light. In this case, Isaiah shifts that paradigm from a cosmogonic to an eschatological setting, where Yahweh is victorious over these two creatures. The old combat myth related to the creation of the earth has been refitted and projected onto a future era. The Canaanite and Babylonian myths are taken over and transformed to suit the purposes of the biblical author.[17] Isaiah has transformed these myths into an example of the future unconditional and universal sovereignty of Yahweh over all cosmic powers. Yet, as Jon Levenson notes, these foes are no mere straw men but represent the ongoing persistence of evil.[18] It is also possible that the dragon imagery alludes to Egypt, as in Ezek 29:3, and that the Leviathan imagery refers to Israel's northern Semitic neighbors.[19] This would be consistent with the end of the unit (Isa 27:12–13), which mentions the land of the Euphrates and the Wadi of Egypt as the limits from which the community of Yahweh returns. Yet the imagery in Isaiah 27 goes well beyond Canaanite or Egyptian contexts as God ultimately vanquishes the serpent and the dragon of the deep. Parallels are easily drawn to the New Testament's book of Revelation, where "the great dragon was hurled down, the ancient serpent called the devil or Satan, who leads the whole world astray" (Rev 12:9). As Bernhard Anderson has stated, "the sea—the locus of the powers of chaos—will be no more (Rev 21:1).[20] Indeed, the apex of the book of Revelation, another important apocalypse, also describes a city. The city

16. Roberts, "Isaiah in Old Testament Theology," 65–66.

17. Gordon, "Leviathan, Symbol of Evil," 2.

18. Levenson, *Creation and the Persistence of Evil*, 27.

19. Widyapranawa, *The Lord Is Savior*, 159.

20. B. W. Anderson, *Contours of Old Testament Theology*, 301.

metaphor of Revelation harkens back to Edenic life in the early chapters of Genesis. In this city a river flows containing the water of life, and on each side of the river grows the tree of life. In this new Eden, there will be "no more curse" (Rev 22:3). We will see below that identical imagery is also present in Zechariah 14 and Revelation 22.

Again, the formula "in that day" opens the allegory of the restored vineyard of Isa 27:2–6. Most commentators agree that this allegory is set contextually in clear contrast with the original vineyard allegory of Isaiah 5.[21] Isaiah 27:8–9 make explicit that Israel's punishment has been exile, and that exile is a means of atonement. While we have already demonstrated that there are elements of continuity and discontinuity in the vineyard tradition, the punishment of the exile has rendered the meaning of the first song, in Isaiah 5, obsolete. It must be reinterpreted for a new generation. Now Jacob will take root, and Israel will blossom and bud. Yahweh will care for the vineyard, forgive the sin of Jacob, and call the exiles home, where they will once again worship at the holy mountain. This blessing imagery using the metaphor of the vineyard conveys a blessing, all that entails a life of fullness.

The language of the mountain of Yahweh ends the Little Apocalypse. People from all over the world will come to Jerusalem to worship. This brings full circle the feast for all peoples served at the mountain of Yahweh in Isaiah 25. Yahweh will swallow up death forever and wipe away tears from each face (Isa 25:8). Death-of-death language returns to the destruction of death forever, mentioned in Isa 25:8.

> On this mountain the LORD Almighty will prepare
>   a feast of rich food for all peoples,
> a banquet of aged wine—
>   the best of meats and the finest of wines.
> On this mountain he will destroy
>   the shroud that enfolds all peoples,
> the sheet that covers all nations;
>   he will swallow up death forever.
> The Sovereign LORD will wipe away the tears
>   from all faces;
> he will remove the disgrace of his people
>   from all the earth. (Isa 25:6–8)

---

21. Johnson points to numerous points of contact between the two allegories; *From Chaos to Restoration*, 11.

The Hebrew root *hmwt* recalls Ugaritic mythology, where Baal's enemy, Mot, swallows up Baal, who is ultimately resurrected with the assistance of his sister, Anat. Likewise, resurrection is a key motif in the Little Apocalypse,

> But your dead will live, LORD;
>> Their bodies will rise.
> You who dwell in the dust,
>> Wake up and shout for joy.
> Your dew is like the dew of the morning;
>> The earth will give birth to her dead. (Isa 26:19)

This is no full-blown doctrine of resurrection like one finds in the New Testament. Yet, it is clearly depicted here that Yahweh is victorious over death, and that he provides a lavish feast for all peoples in celebration of his triumph. Isaiah's Little Apocalypse takes these ancient myths, transforming them into tools that display Yahweh's majestic power in spite of the visible world in which his audience lived, a world where God's power might often be questioned, a world probably lived in exile. Isaiah 24–27 shares a literary mission with Psalms 74 and 89, and even with Job's encountering Yahweh in Job 38–41. Curse has given way to blessing and the Little Apocalypse closes with this promise of restoration: "In that day the LORD will thresh from the flowing Euphrates to the Wadi of Egypt, and you, O Israelites, will be gathered up one by one. And in that day a great trumpet will sound. Those who were perishing in Assyria and those who were exiled in Egypt will come and worship the Lord on the holy mountain in Jerusalem" (Isa 27:12–13).

A KINGDOM MADE WITHOUT HANDS: DANIEL 2:31–45

People have long noted that the abrupt switch from Hebrew to Aramaic in Dan 2:4, and back to Hebrew in Daniel 8:1 appears to be arbitrary. Yet the Aramaic section of Daniel expresses a theme repeatedly that also provides a thematic covering for the entire book. The earthly transient kingdoms of this world will be replaced by the spiritual eternal kingdom of God (Dan 2:44; 4:3, 25b, 34; 6:26; 7:13–14, 27). Note this in a few important texts:

- And in the days of those kings the God of heaven will set up a kingdom that shall never be destroyed, nor shall this kingdom be left to another people. It shall crush all these kingdoms and bring them to an end, and it shall stand forever. (Dan 2:44, NRSV)

- His kingdom is an everlasting kingdom, and his sovereignty is from generation to generation. (Dan 4:3, NRSV)

- For he is the living God, enduring forever. His kingdom shall never be destroyed, and his dominion has no end. (Dan 6:26b, NRSV)

- I saw one like a human being coming with the clouds of heaven. And he came to the Ancient One and was presented before him. To him was given dominion and glory and kingship that all peoples, nations, and languages should serve him. His dominion is an everlasting dominion that shall not pass away, and his kingship is one that shall never be destroyed. (Dan 7:13–14, NRSV)

The theme of an impending eternal kingdom of God is no arbitrary co-incidence in Daniel. The entire book, including the six court stories in chapters 1–6 and the four night visions in chapters 7–12, are all compatible with this theme. Daniel himself serves as a model for how to live with integrity and faithfulness as a religious minority in an unbelieving culture. Along with Abraham, Esther, Joseph, Tobit, and Judith, Daniel never rejects his role as a member of the religious minority; he never asks God to remove him from such a setting, and his faithfulness in seemingly minor issues serves as a platform for faithfulness in weightier matters that would eventually threaten his very life. Yet Daniel holds on to the groundbreaking vision that this new kingdom will replace the repressive kingdoms of this world.

Crucial to this theme is King Nebuchadnezzar's dream followed by Daniel's interpretation in Dan 2:31–45. Here the Babylonian king is troubled by a night vision about a huge figure, with a head of gold, chest of silver, belly and thigh of bronze, legs of iron, and feet of iron and baked clay. Daniel's interpretation of the dream is that these symbols represent mighty earthly kingdoms, which will all fade away, ultimately leading to God's eternal kingdom. These diminishing earthly kingdoms are listed in decreasing value. Each kingdom will first give way to another earthly power, then the last to an eternal kingdom.

> As you looked on, a stone was cut out, not by human hands, and it struck the statue on its feet of iron and clay and broke them in pieces. Then the iron, the clay, the bronze, the silver and the gold, were all broken in pieces and became like the chaff of the summer threshing floors; and the wind carried them away, so that not a trace of them could be found. But the stone that struck

the statue became a great mountain and filled the whole earth.
(Dan 2:34–35, NRSV)

Daniel's interpretation of the night vision describes this eternal kingdom in three ways. First, it is a kingdom not made with human hands (v. 34). It is a spiritual, not an earthly, kingdom. This point is emphasized by the fact that the plot and interpretation of the dream are not given to the earthly wisemen of Babylon but are revealed to Daniel by God alone (Dan 2:27–28).

The Greek version of Daniel includes a humorous story, "Bel and the Dragon," which illustrates this point. It also describes Daniel's existence as a religious minority, though in this case he is under Babylonian instead of Persian dominion. Day after day the Babylonians provide lavish flour, sheep, and wine for their god Bel to consume. When challenged as to why Daniel does not participate providing for this god, Daniel charges that Bel consists merely of clay and bronze. Unconvinced, Nebuchadnezzar has the door to Bel's temple sealed after food provisions are left so that no human can sneak in and consume them. Nebuchadnezzar naively has no inkling that the seventy priests of Bel and their families are entering through another, hidden entrance at night, consuming all the food. Daniel, however, is suspicious. Daniel secretly scatters ashes over the floor of the temple while in the king's presence, but away from the observation of the priests. The next morning all the food has vanished. The king is convinced that Daniel had been mistaken when he observes that no food remains. Yet, Daniel asks the king to look on the floor. There the king sees the footprints of men, women, and children belonging to the priests of Bel, damning Bel's authority. This story highlights that both the Hebrew and Greek versions of Daniel ridicule the earthly nature of Babylonian worship and contrast that with God's divine kingdom and power.

It is well known that the New Testament draws heavily on eternal-kingdom imagery from Daniel. From the beginning of the Gospels to their end, they uniformly portray John the Baptizer and Jesus as both preoccupied with the kingdom of God (Matt 3:2; 4:17). Note Luke's account of the promise to Mary and note the eternal nature of that promise: "He will be great, and will be called the Son of the Most High, and the Lord God will give to him the throne of his ancestor David. He will reign over the house of Jacob forever, and of his kingdom there will be no end" (Luke 1:32–33). There is no doubt that the imagery of the rock not made with human hands provides the background for the gospels, particularly the

Gospel of Luke.[22] "The stone that the builders rejected will become the capstone. Everyone who falls on that stone will be broken to pieces, but he on whom it falls will be crushed" (Luke 20:18).

Not only is the eternal kingdom Daniel describes, first, not made by human hands. Second, this kingdom crushes earthly kingdoms (Dan 2:34–35, 44–45). What does this promise mean in a context of living as a minority faith community in an unbelieving culture? Believers of all faiths typically get sidetracked by becoming preoccupied with events in earthly kingdoms, yet God has a purpose beyond one's own or any other people's. For Christians, this promise does not necessarily mean that any particular people will eventually be transformed into a Christian majority. If history is any record, that is usually naïve wishful thinking among believers. One can hardly think of any example in the Bible where believers make up the dominant culture. Instead, there are multiple biblical models as to how to live faithfully as a religious minority. Instead of the destruction of a secular government or power, the promise of crushing earthly kingdoms has to do with a spiritual, not an earthly domain. Jesus himself said, "My kingdom is not of this world" (John 18:36).

Third, according to Dan 2:35, this stone becomes a great mountain that fills the whole earth. This new kingdom will grow and thrive. The metaphor of the growth of this mountain is similar to Jesus's kingdom parable of the mustard seed which filled the entire earth. As cited above, Dan 7:13–14 affirms that this kingdom will include peoples from all kingdoms and speakers of all languages. The book of Revelation also affirms such kingdom growth: "You are worthy to take the scroll and to open its seals, for you were slaughtered and by your blood you ransomed for God saints from every tribe and language and people and nation; you have made them to be a kingdom and priests serving our God and they will reign on earth" (Rev 5:9–10).

Does the proposition that the kingdom of God is an eternal kingdom not made with human hands necessarily mean God has no plan for the peoples of the earth? Certainly not. God uses earthly powers, godly and ungodly, to fulfill his purposes for his kingdom. Jeremiah, for example, commanded the exiles to seek the welfare of the physical kingdom where they lived. Yet one should want to ask, if only one kingdom is ultimately going to last forever, which is most important to be given priority?

The theme of the eternal kingdom in Daniel issues an invitation to be part of something eternal. God calls humans to be a part of his spiritual

22. Hillyer, "Rock-Stone Imagery in 1 Peter."

kingdom, "pleading that you lead a life worthy of God, who calls you into his own kingdom and glory" (1 Thess 2:12). However, one can only be born into this divine kingdom (John 3:3). There is no other way to become a citizen. An eternal kingdom means investing one's life in eternal things: the Word of God, the nature of God, the kingdom of God. This means other things must take second place. Sadly, the spiritual all too often gives way to the tangible. There is another way of restating the application of this text. Where you are going determines everything along the way. If you are headed in the wrong direction, you may see all kinds of wonderful things, but you are still going in the wrong direction. Ironically, these wonderful things may be a distraction from God's divine kingdom, the believer's ultimate goal. Alternatively, if you are headed in the right direction, even those difficulties along the way confirm that you are going where you need to go.

THE CURSE AND EXILE: DANIEL 9

Claus Baltzer argued that the early literature of the Old Testament portrayed the ancient context as a time of blessing while the curses skulked as a threat for the future. After the fall of Jerusalem, the tables were turned, and the curse became a present humiliation and the blessing was something to look forward to in the future.[23] Daniel 9 shares this line of reasoning in Daniel's prayer of confession. Daniel's prayer in chapter 9 has much in common with similar postexilic prayers in Ezra 9:6–15; Neh 9:5–38; Baruch 1:15–3:8; 1QS 1:2; 2:1; 4Q504; and Solomon's prayer in 1 Kings 8. These prayers are all highly stylized.[24] In addition to a clear admission of collective guilt there is the realization that all the curses of the covenant have come upon the inhabitants of Jerusalem.[25] Adopting language from Deut 29:20–21, Daniel describes the status quo in one word used three times: "disaster" (*r'h*). This disaster is inevitable since God has decreed it so through the conditional covenant curse (Deut 29:20–21). The prayer repeatedly admits Israel's guilt:

> O Lord, the great and awesome God, who keeps his covenant
> of love with all who love him and obey his commands, we have
> sinned and done wrong and acted wickedly and rebelled, turn-
> ing aside from your commandments and rules. We have not

23. Baltzer, *The Covenant Formulary*, 116–18, 129–30, 153–60.

24. Smith-Christopher, *The Book of Daniel*, 127.

25. Redditt, "Daniel 9," 244–45.

listened to your servants the prophets, who spoke in your name to our kings, our princes and our fathers, and to all the people of the land. To you, O Lord, belongs righteousness, but to us open shame, as at this day, to the men of Judah, to the inhabitants of Jerusalem, and to all Israel, those who are near and those who are far away, in all the lands to which you have driven them, because of the treachery that they have committed against you. To us, O Lord, belongs open shame, to our kings, to our princes, and to our fathers, because we have sinned against you. To the Lord our God belong mercy and forgiveness, for we have rebelled against him. and have not obeyed the voice of the Lord our God by walking in his laws, which he set before us by his servants the prophets. All Israel has transgressed your law and turned aside, refusing to obey your voice. And the curse and oath (*hāʾālâ wĕhaššĕbʿâ*) that are written in the Law of Moses the servant of God have been poured out upon us, because we have sinned against him. He has confirmed his words, which he spoke against us and against our rulers who ruled us, by bringing upon us a great calamity (*rāʿâ gĕdōlâ*). For under the whole heaven there has not been done anything like what has been done against Jerusalem. As it is written in the Law of Moses, all this calamity (*kol hārāʿâ*) has come upon us; yet we have not entreated the favor of the Lord our God, turning from our iniquities and gaining insight by your truth. Therefore the Lord has kept ready the calamity (*rāʿâ*) and has brought it upon us, for the Lord our God is righteous in all the works that he has done, and we have not obeyed his voice. And now, O Lord our God, who brought your people out of the land of Egypt with a mighty hand, and have made a name for yourself, as at this day, we have sinned, we have done wickedly.

O Lord, according to all your righteous acts, let your anger and your wrath turn away from your city Jerusalem, your holy hill, because for our sins, and for the iniquities of our fathers, Jerusalem and your people have become a byword (*lĕherippâ*) among all who are around us. Now therefore, O our God, listen to the prayer of your servant and to his pleas for mercy, and for your own sake, O Lord, make your face to shine upon your sanctuary, which is desolate (*haššāmēm*). O my God, incline your ear and hear. Open your eyes and see our desolations (*šōmĕmōtênû*), and the city that is called by your name. For we do not present our pleas before you because of our righteousness, but because of your great mercy. O Lord, hear; O Lord, forgive. O Lord, pay attention and act. Delay not, for your own sake, O my God, because your city and your people are called by your name. (Dan 9:4b–19, ESV)

Daniel's prayer begins with an ascription of praise that recurs throughout (vv. 4, 7, 9, 15), followed by an honest admission of guilt (vv. 5–10). Daniel confesses numerous sins including rebellion against the law, wickedness, and failure to abide by the words of the prophets. Daniel's bottom line is blindingly obvious: Israel's absolute refusal to obey Yahweh has led to open shame (Jer 7:19; Ezra 9:7; 2 Chr 32:21). Dan 9:11b–14 describe the painful consequences of exile. God's people are now living in the time of the curse (Deut 29:20, 27). The result is disaster, and the curse has overwhelmed Israel. The parallels between what Daniel describes and Deuteronomy 31 are striking,

> On that day I will become angry with them and forsake them; I will hide my face from them, and they will be destroyed. Many disasters and difficulties will come upon them, and on that day they will ask, "Have not these disasters come upon us because our God is not with us?" And I will certainly hide my face on that day because of all their wickedness in turning to other gods. (Deut 31:17–18)

The final element of the prayer involves taking responsibility for sin and offering a plea for forgiveness (Dan 9:15–19). Daniel's appeal in v. 17 that Yahweh listen to their prayers adopts blessing language from Num 6:25: "make your face shine on your desolate sanctuary." Such language is similar to other prayers in the book of Psalms (Pss 31:17; 67:2; 80:4, 8, 20; 119:135). One could only wonder exactly how long such an ordeal will last. The book of Baruch describes a similar line of reasoning. God's people are now living under the curse, and the prophetic catchword, *calamity*, characterizes the community in exile,

> So to this day there have clung to us the calamities and the curse that the Lord declared through his servant Moses at the time when he brought our ancestors out of the land of Egypt to give to us a land flowing with milk and honey. We did not listen to the voice of the Lord our God in all the words of the prophets whom he sent to us, but all of us followed the intent of our own wicked hearts by serving other gods and doing what is evil in the sight of the Lord our God. (Bar 1:20–22, NRSV)

> He made them subject to all the kingdoms around us, to be an object of scorn and a desolation among all the surrounding peoples, where the Lord has scattered them. (Bar 2:4 NRSV)

One of the larger issues related to Daniel 9 is the relation of prayer in Daniel 9 to the chapter as a whole.[26] August von Gall called the prayer in Daniel 9 "a shoot on foreign soil."[27] The covenantal theology and Deuteronomic language is not evident in the chapters preceding the prayer. The prayer contains no Aramaisms as the rest of the book does, and the flow of the book appears to be interrupted by the prayer. The divine name, Yahweh, used six times in vv. 4–14 is found nowhere else in the book of Daniel. Some have argued that the Deuteronomistic view of history is at odds with the generally deterministic view of history portrayed elsewhere in Daniel, and thus that chapter 9 is a secondary insertion.[28] Yet there are good reasons to argue that the prayer is an integral part of Daniel 9, even if it is a preexisting prayer that has been incorporated into the prophetic narrative. This prayer links artfully with the prophecy that follows in Dan 9:24–27. The chapter begins with, and returns to, the famous seventy-week prophecy of Jeremiah 25:8–14.

In some respects Daniel 9 is a midrash concerned with the application of this prophecy to the author's present day. Daniel consults certain books to see just how long this devastation and shame will last. Contextually, it is the prayer (vv. 4b–19) that leads directly to the response by Gabriel (Dan 9:25–27).

> Know and understand this: From the issuing of the decree to restore and rebuild Jerusalem until the Anointed One, the ruler, comes, there will be seven 'sevens,' and sixty-two 'sevens.' It will be rebuilt with streets and a trench, but in times of trouble. After the sixty-two 'sevens,' the Anointed One will be cut off and will have nothing. The people of the ruler who will come will destroy the city and the sanctuary. The end will come like a flood: War will continue until the end, and desolations (*šōmēmôt*) have been decreed. He will confirm a covenant with many for one 'seven.' In the middle of the 'seven' he will put an end to sacrifice and offering. And on a wing [of the temple] he will set up an abomination that causes desolation (*šiqqûṣîm mešōmēm*), until the end that is decreed is poured out on him.

---

26. Meadowcroft, "Exploring the Dismal Swamp," 434–35.

27. Von Gall, *Die Einheitlichkeit des Buches Daniel*, cited in Portier-Young, *Apocalypse against Empire*, 247.

28. Wilson, "The Prayer of Daniel 9," 91–92, argues that this prayer is motivated not by the delay in the promised restoration, but by the desire to fulfill the conditions for restoration set out in Jer 29:12–14.

The connection between the prayer and the prophecy is made explicit in vv. 20–21. It is repeated twice with emphasis: "While I was still in speaking and praying," and "While I was still in prayer, Gabriel came to me." This explicit connection is reaffirmed for the third time in v. 23: "as soon as you began to pray, an answer was given." The appearance of Gabriel also answers Daniel's question in Dan 8:13: "How long will it take for the vision to be fulfilled?" Some artful literary connections arise between the prayer and the prophecy as well. The curse-oath (*šbʿh*) that is poured out (*ttk*) on Jerusalem (v. 11) is comparable to the weeks (*šbʿym*) that must be poured out (*ttk*) before the end (vv. 24, 27).[29] In both cases the oath, or weeks, respectively, are "decreed" or "engraved." The high point of the prayer in v. 19 asks for mercy on "your city and your people." Then in v. 24 Gabriel's message is directed at "your city and your people." There is, however, no connection between the prayer and the reference to the anointed prince, perhaps the most sought after but elusive interpretive cipher in the text.

Gabriel decrees seventy weeks (or sevens), a reinterpretation of Jeremiah's seventy years, with six infinitives: "to finish," "to put to an end," "to atone," "to bring in," "to seal up," and "to anoint."[30] Seven weeks are followed by sixty-two weeks, leading to the final climactic week. These seventy weeks of years, or 490 years, indicates that Israel is paying sevenfold for its sins. This extended length of time is not only seventy sabbatical years but also ten Jubilees. Daniel is not alone in this schematized view of history. The *Book of Jubilees*, 11QMelch 6–8, and *1 Enoch* take a similar approach.[31] Just because these numbers are symbolic does not mean that they are arbitrary. The desolations of living under the curse roughly correspond to the length of the monarchy. The seventy years of Jeremiah 25 are interpreted in the context of the covenant curses and the Jubilee theology of Leviticus 26.[32] The seventy sabbatical years owed but never paid have been exacted sevenfold.[33] Lev 26:34–35 applies the concept of Sabbath rest to the exile as does 2 Chr 36:21. "Then the land will enjoy its Sabbath years all the time that it lies desolate and you are in the country of your

29. Jones, "The Prayer in Daniel IX," 491; Portier-Young, *Apocalypse against Empire*, 250–51.

30. For a review of this prophecy's interpretation in early Christianity, see Adler, "The Apocalyptic Survey of History."

31. Beckwith, *Calendar and Chronology, Jewish and Christian*, 219–33, 261; Dimant, "The Seventy Weeks Chronology"; Meadowcroft, "Exploring the Dismal Swamp," 433.

32. Collins, *Daniel*, 352–54

33. Goldingay, *Daniel*, 232. See McComiskey, "The Seventy Weeks of Daniel."

enemies; then the land will rest and enjoy its Sabbaths. All the time that it lies desolate, the land will have the rest it did not have during the Sabbaths you lived in it." Both Daniel and 2 Chronicles imply that throughout the monarchy, the land was farmed continually and is long overdue for its Sabbath rest. Second Chronicles 36:21 sets the precedent for interpreting the seventy years of Jeremiah as Sabbaths. The closing verses of Leviticus 26 show that these years of desolation and ruin need not be permanent. If the people of God acknowledge their sin and turn to God, things can certainly change. This brings us back to the reason for the prayer of confession in Daniel 9. Even though Israel's faithfulness has fundamentally disrupted the relationship of blessing between Yahweh and Israel, God may restore them if they return (Lev 26:39–45; Deut 30:1–10; Jer 29:10–14). Daniel 9 takes the seventy weeks and makes from them an ultrajubilee. The messiah figure will bear the brunt of Gentile fury but will be ultimately vindicated. Then will come the real end of exile, final atonement for sin, anointing of a most holy place, arrival of anointed prince, cutting off of an anointed one, cessation of sacrifices and setting up of the abomination.[34]

Tectonic Shifts and the Changing Eschatological Landscape: Zechariah 14

There are plenty of enigmas to go around in the book of Zechariah. Consensus dissipates at most points, but there are a few foundational observations impossible to miss. First, the setting, themes, and tone of Zechariah 1–8 vary widely from those in chapters 9–14. The first eight chapters contain dated material that overlaps directly with the book of Haggai. There is a sense of optimism in the air. Yahweh is laying the foundations for new beginnings in the aftermath of a long horrible exile. The construction of the temple is underway, new leadership is emerging, and hopes for the future are high. Haggai had drawn a line in the sand. From this very day forward, Yahweh would bless his people (Hag 2:19). Zechariah 1–8 is characterized by a series of eight vision reports that convey God's impending restoration of Israel. These visions are full of vibrant colors and vivid movement. The restoration is not Israel's alone, but spans the whole earth. In Zechariah 9–14, a noticeable shift occurs as optimism gives way a sense of malaise. The tone here is more akin to Malachi than Haggai. Textually, this unit is "a chaotic collection of texts that cannot be pinned down to

---

34. Wright, *Jesus and the Victory of God*, 515.

convey a clear image or a unifying vision."[35] The language of threat replaces the language of hope. The Day of Yahweh is coming and Jerusalem will face some of its most perilous times ever. Yet, in the end, this city, or part of it, and its people, or some of them, will be spared.

Zechariah 14 closes out the book by imagining a changing eschatological landscape. Three main themes are taken up: a coming day of Yahweh, Jerusalem's ultimate battle with foreign kingdoms, and the restoration of Jerusalem as the attractive centerpiece for all the peoples of the earth. Just as it was found liberally in Isaiah's Little Apocalypse, so the expression "on that day" is found seven times in the Zechariah 14. This second account of a future battle between Jerusalem and the foreign peoples has much in common with a battle account in Zechariah 12, where all the peoples of the earth will gather against Jerusalem. There is no "easy believism." The Day of the Lord will unleash turmoil of epic proportions. The city will initially be captured, houses plundered, and women raped. Virtually half the city will be taken away into exile. After these calamities, Yahweh will fight against those peoples that oppose Israel. His feet will stand on the Mount of Olives and the mountain will be split from west to east by a wide valley. This new topography allows a way of escape for the city's inhabitants. As people flee, Yahweh, the deliverer, will appear and all the holy ones with him. This final deliverance ushers in a time of peace and Yahweh will reign over the entire earth.

Zechariah 14 takes up the language of fertility and blessing as well a promise that the curse will be removed:

> On that day living water will flow out from Jerusalem, half to the eastern sea and half to the western sea, in summer and in winter. The LORD will be king over the whole earth. On that day there will be one LORD, and his name the only name. The whole land, from Geba to Rimmon, south of Jerusalem, will become like the Arabah. But Jerusalem will be raised up and remain in its place, from the Benjamin Gate to the site of the First Gate, to the Corner Gate, and from the Tower of Hananel to the royal winepresses. It will be inhabited; never again will it be destroyed (*wĕḥērem lōʾ yihyeh ʿôd*). Jerusalem will be secure. (Zech 14:8–11)

Zech 14:6–11 describes the eschatological re-creation of the land as consequence of a grand epic battle. The changes are cosmic in scope, and include four radical tectonic shifts that occur on the Day of Yahweh:

35. Nogalski, *The Book of the Twelve*, 817.

climate, luminescence, water source, and topography.[36] Amid these changes Yahweh will establish his reign as king, without rival, over the entire earth. The first change has to do with climate: dangers posed by cold and frost will be negated. The highlands of Canaan are notorious for perilous frosts and relatively cold winters. Therefore they are often a threat to productivity and produce: all that the blessing of fertility entails. In the new, changing eschatological landscape, these environmental dangers become a thing of the past. Note the similarity of language in Zechariah 14 to language about re-creation and the removal of the curse in Genesis:

> The LORD smelled the pleasing aroma and said in his heart: "Never again will I curse the ground because of man, even though every inclination of his heart is evil from childhood. And never again will I destroy all living creatures, as I have done.
>
> As long as the earth endures,
>   seedtime and harvest,
>   cold and heat,
>   summer and winter,
>   day and night
>   will never cease. (Gen 8:21–22)

This language connotes a renewed assurance based on the regularity of nature.[37] Zechariah, like Amos, portrays an uninterrupted time of planting and harvest.

The second tectonic shift relates to luminescence. This reordering of cosmology conveys unending light plus the elimination of darkness. In the ancient world light had much more to do with mobility and security than it does today.[38] There are several allusions to Genesis 1:5. Even in the evening, there will be plenty of light. Eschatological language commonly employs the theme of the elimination of darkness (Rev 21:23–24; 22:5) and conveys the opposite of Amos's promise that the Day of Yahweh will be darkness (Amos 5:20).

The third major shift happens when living water flows from Jerusalem in two directions: to the east and to the west (Joel 4:18; Ezek 47:12; Rev 22:1–2). The language here is similar to language in Jer 17:13, which likens Yahweh to a fountain of living water, and to language in Ezek 47:12, which depicts water flowing from the mountain of God. This imagery, like

36. Meyers and Meyers, *Zechariah 9–14*, 432–42.

37. Smith, *Micah–Malachi*, 288.

38. Nogalski, *The Book of the Twelve*, 975.

that in Isaiah 24–27, constitutes a homecoming to Eden, a return to the fertility of the garden. A reading of Zechariah 14 recalls paradise motifs of Gen 2:10–14. In some ways Zech 14:9 interrupts the theme of the reordered geography, but in others it demonstrates exactly who is behind that cosmic redesign. "The LORD will be king over the whole earth, on that day there will be one LORD and his name the only name" (Zech 14:9). This is a grand announcement that Yahweh is king, echoing Daniel's promised transition that the transient kingdoms of this world will be replaced by the eternal kingdom of God. There is now a new unity to the cosmos. The Hebrew root for "one" (*'ḥd*) is found in v. 7 and once in v. 9. Unlike Zech 9:9, 12:7, and 13:1, this is no vision of a new earthly king. Like Daniel 2 it portrays Yahweh's reign as supreme Lord of the universe. Verse 9 is an allusion to Deut 6:4: "Yahweh is our God, Yahweh is one" (my translation). The last tectonic shift in Zechariah's eschatological landscape is topography. Jerusalem will become the navel of the earth. It will be the dominant force in the universe. The text painstakingly and specifically lays out the four corners of the city. Just as it does in Isaiah 40, Isaiah's call for the exiles to return to their homeland, here in the book of Zechariah too the ground becomes level and the land becomes a plain. "The rugged contours of the Judean hills, long an anathema to highland plow agriculture (hence the extensive terracing around Jerusalem), would at last be accommodating to the use of the animal-traction plow."[39] In the midst of this flat plain stands Jerusalem, impressively elevated above all around. She becomes the cosmic mountain to which all the peoples return (Ps 48:2; Isa 2:2; Mic 4:1).[40]

Zechariah 14:11 promises that Jerusalem will never again be devoted to destruction (*ḥrm*). This word is notoriously dicey to translate. It is curse-like but not a curse, although the Septuagint translates *ḥrm* as "anathema" some thirty-five times. It connotes the idea of taking a military oath to exterminate the populace of a city. Childs draws a contrast between Zech 5:3, where the *'lh* curse goes over the land, and Zech 14:11, where the *ḥrm* ban has been removed.[41] In the Old Testament, *ḥrm* is used most frequently in Deuteronomic texts. In postexilic prophecy it is most often employed in various prophecies against foreign kingdoms, with the twist that unlike in earlier cases in the Bible, in these writings Yahweh alone carries out the destruction (Isa 11:15; 34:2, 5; Jer 50:21, 26; 51:3; Dan 11:44; Mic 4:3). The root *ḥrm* also appears in passages

---

39. Meyers and Meyers, *Zechariah 9–14*, 442.

40. Clifford, *The Cosmic Mountain*.

41. Childs, *Introduction to the Old Testament as Scripture*, 482.

describing Yahweh's actions toward Israel (Isa 43:28; Zech 14:11; Mal 3:24).[42] In spite of the semantic ambiguity of *ḥrm*, the promise is inescapable. Jerusalem will never again be destroyed—but not before it is almost completely destroyed. Now the shoe is on the other foot. The foreign peoples, not Jerusalem, will face a devastating plague, and those who survive will go up to Jerusalem to worship Yahweh, lest no rain come upon their lands.

What theological conclusions can we draw from the examination of these three apocalyptic texts? Admittedly Isaiah 24–27 deploys a barrage of disparate metaphors, even in the same unit, so we have to be cautious about drawing conclusions about the historical progression of any events mentioned in the Little Apocalypse. But some clear parallels do emerge with important theological implications. The language that is used. The phrase "in that day" refers to future activities of God and intends to give hope for the future. On that day there will be cosmic upheaval: the earth will be emptied and the entire created order turned upside down. These texts describe nothing less than cosmogonic overthrow, but in metaphoric, not literal language. And out of the ashes a new order emerges. The curse has been a voracious, consuming devourer, so only a remnant is left. But there is a remnant. In the final battle most of Jerusalem will be destroyed. The besieged city gives way to the blessed city. As the common expression goes, "what doesn't kill you will cure you." Daniel 2 is one interpretive key, not just for Daniel 9, but for all these apocalyptic texts. Exile and curse unite in Old Testament theology. But exile and curse give way to restoration and renewal. The kingdoms of this earth will be replaced by the kingdom of God. This new eschatological landscape reduces the importance of empire. God's people will stream to Jerusalem from the four corners of the earth. These devastations will never happen again,

> In an age of foreign domination, war, and terror, early Jewish apocalypses prompted their readers to look through and beyond visible, familiar phenomena to apprehend God's providential ordering of space, time, and created life. While exposing the violence and deceit of empire and its collaborators, they revealed powerful angelic, semi-divine, and divine actors at work in and beyond human experience and history. Shared memory, interpretation of past and present, and a new vision of the cosmos shaped hope for a transformed future. The apocalypses asserted

42. Lohfink, "*ḥrm*," 198.

a threatened identity and covenant and empowered their readers for resistance.[43]

KIDRON AND THE MOUNT OF OLIVES IN TRADITION
AND THEOLOGY

In apocalyptic literature, the seer receives revelations and proclaims the
content of those revelations in ways that often transcend space and time.[44]
While spatial transcendence dominates apocalypses that emphasize a
heavenly journey, and temporal transcendence crosses historical boundaries, many apocalypses also place their revelations in specific geographic
locations. In short, the proper person receives and imparts revelations
from precise places at exact times. In speech-act theory, the bringing together of the specific person, time, and space provides the proper force to
the illocutionary speech act. Spatial demarcations use space to construct
legitimacy for the message. Social practices are mediated through spatial
frameworks, and social boundaries are associated with spatial demarcations. The merging of geography and message is common in the Bible and
in Second Temple Jewish literature. Balaam, for example, shuttles from
mountain to mountain to find that exact spot that would make a curse or
blessing more potent. In Deuteronomy the priests utter the blessings and
curses from strategic rhetorical locations of Mounts Gerizim and Ebal,
a fact not lost on Jotham, who utters his own malediction from Mount
Gerizim (Judges 9). Moses and Jesus both ascend mountains to receive or
reinterpret the law of God, and in *4 Ezra*, Ezra moves back and forth to
and from a field to receive his revelations.

Kidron is a place of ambiguity. In the Hebrew Bible, Kidron is a
consistent geographical marker; but it is a theological marker as well. The
word *Kidron* means "dark" or "unclear." To cross the Kidron was to cross
a geographical boundary, to leave the city of David. For example, David
crosses the Kidron to escape Absalom (2 Sam 15:23), and Solomon warns
Shimei not to cross the Kidron to leave the city (1 Kgs 2:37).[45] The expression "from the temple to the Kidron" in 2 Kgs 23:6 denotes such geographical boundaries. This language is geographical and metaphorical, a

43. Portier-Young, *Apocalypse against Empire*, 382.

44. L. L. Thompson, "Mapping an Apocalyptic World."

45. T. L. Thompson explores the connection between David's ascent up to the
Mount of Olives and Absalom's subsequent death and Jesus's ascent and subsequent
crucifixion; T. L. Thompson, "If David Had Not Climbed the Mount of Olives".

spatial framework that denotes social boundaries as well. Thus, the Kidron was the consummate exit boundary. The Kidron Valley and the Mount of Olives east of the valley were also infamous burial places with a long history of association with ancient tombs.[46] A short ten-minute walk from east from the Mount of Olives placed one squarely in the Judean desert.

There is a theological boundary as well. To cross the Kidron also meant to cross a metaphorical line. Solomon established a vibrant center of foreign cult worship on the eastern slope of the Kidron, associating the site with idolatry and apostasy. The fact that the Tomb of Pharaoh's daughter, even if an anachronism, exists on the lower slopes of the Kidron today, attests to this connection of foreign cult worship and the western slopes of the Kidron Valley. The Old Testament conveys the tradition of three good kings (Asa, Hezekiah, and Josiah) who carry the unclean vessels from the temple to the Kidron (a metaphorical boundary line), burn the Asherah there, and cast the dust of these idols on the graves of the common people (1 Kgs 15:13; 2 Kgs 23:4–12; 2 Chr 29:16; 30:14). The two good kings mentioned in a later apocalypse—2 *Baruch's* vision of the black and bright waters—are, perhaps not coincidentally, Hezekiah and Josiah. Later in Jewish, Christian, and Muslim tradition, the upper valley became called the Valley of Jehoshaphat as the place of the final judgment. It is no stretch to say that across the boundary of Kidron existed a spiritual wilderness, a dump of illicit cult objects—a literal and metaphorical graveyard. Today thousands of Jewish, Christian, and Muslim graves cover the western slopes of the Mount of Olives, as well as the valley floor and the eastern slopes of the Kidron all the way up to the eastern wall of the Old City of Jerusalem.

In Ezekiel's painful account of the temple's demise (Ezek 11:23), the glory of the Lord rises up from the city of Jerusalem, leaves it, and stands over the mountain east of the city (the Mount of Olives). This geographical depiction denotes the departure of God's presence from the temple. In a later reversal (Ezek 43:2), the glory of the Lord returns from the east, entering the temple by the gate that faces east, and the glory of the Lord once again fills the temple (Ezek 44:4). Zech 14:4 describes a battle between all the foreign kingdoms and Jerusalem. In spite of heavy losses, Yahweh takes up the fight against the kingdoms:

> On that day his feet shall stand on the Mount of Olives that lies
> before Jerusalem on the east, and the Mount of Olives shall be
> split in two from east to west by a very wide valley, so that one

---

46. Ussishkin, *The Village of Silwan*, 1–2.

half of the Mount shall move northward, and the other half
southward. And you shall flee to the valley of my mountains, for
the valley of the mountains shall reach to Azal. And you shall
flee as you fled from the earthquake in the days of Uzziah king
of Judah. Then the LORD my God will come, and all the holy
ones with him. (Zech 14:4–5, ESV)

First Enoch graphically depicts the Kidron and surrounding area as
the *cursed valley* (1 *Enoch* 26:1—27:5), a place where the cursed would
gather at the last times. Enoch proceeds from the center of the earth (*Jub*
8:12, 19), a blessed place, full of healthy trees.[47] The *Book of Enoch* describes the geographical terrain in unambiguous detail. At that *axis mundi*
is a mountain, presumably the temple mount. Beneath it (from Ophel or
Gihon) water came from the east flowing south. To the east of the mountain Enoch describes another mountain, higher than the first (the Mount
of Olives). Between these mountains lies a deep valley with water (the
Kidron Valley). West of the mountain is another mountain, lower than it
(the Hill of Evil Counsel), with a deep and dry valley between (Hinnom).
No tree is planted in these accursed valleys. Enoch contrasts this desolate
valley with the blessed land filled with trees. The cursed valley (Kidron)
exists for those who are cursed forever. Here the cursed will gather at the
last times. Significant for this present study, their sin is a sin of speech, uttering words against God. Yet here the godless will bless the Lord of Glory,
King of eternity. This text in *1 Enoch* probably derives from Isaiah 65:

You will leave your name
    for my chosen ones to use in their curses;
the Sovereign LORD will put you to death,
    but to his servants he will give another name.
Whoever invokes a blessing in the land
    will do so by the God of truth;
he who takes an oath in the land
    will swear by the God of truth.
For the past troubles will be forgotten
    and hidden from my eyes. (Isa 65:15–16)

Liv Lied's *The Other Lands of Israel* explores the ambiguities of Kidron
with *2 Baruch's* message in his remnant's death-like situation.[48] In stark
contrast with Mount Zion, Kidron is not only outside the city but also
much lower in elevation than Mount Zion. Here, Baruch sits in a cave, the

47. Nickelsburg, *1 Enoch 1*, 317–19.
48. Lied, *The Other Lands of Israel*, 122–46.

lowliest part of the topographical continuum. Yet Kidron and its nearby wilderness is a place of revelation and instruction. Moses, Isaiah, John the Baptizer, and Jesus all sought the wilderness as a place of new revelation. Just as the depiction of Zion in 2 *Baruch* is as a wilderness, so the picture of Kidron is also as uninhabitable, chaotic, and connoting death. In spite of these negative images, Kidron is the geographical context where the past can be repaired and the future recreated.

Jesus purposefully chooses the Mount of Olives as his setting to describe the horrible time when the temple will be destroyed (Mark 13:2–3). In a setting that obviously carries connotations of a re-created future, Jesus combines traditions from Daniel 7 and 9, Ezekiel 46, Zechariah 7 and 14, and 1 Maccabees 1–3 to describe a military conflict and desolation of the temple—not unlike the earlier desolation at the hands of Antiochus IV in the Maccabean period. Mark 13 reenacts the Maccabean crisis. In Mark 13, the epic battle recounted in Zechariah 7 and 14 is recast in the temple's downfall. There will be a time of tribulation that the disciples will barely make it through; they are not to fight but to escape Jerusalem, and the great deliverance and vindication that the prophets predicted will ultimately come to pass.

13

The Other Side of Covenant Failure

The Destination of Abraham's Blessing

A BRIEF REVIEW

PAUL'S LETTER TO THE Galatians boldly claims that God announced the gospel in advance when he uttered the blessing promise that all the peoples on earth would be blessed through Abraham. If that is the case, then both the Old Testament *and* the New Testament affirm that there is a destination to Abraham's blessing, a direction to this long and winding theme of blessing and curse. In this study we have tried to demonstrate that the blessing and the curse entail a dominant theme, particularly along important seams in the narrative of the Old Testament. The goal of following the trajectories of this theme has been to provide a fresh way of looking at several important aspects of Old Testament theology often neglected in traditional theological dichotomies of promise/fulfillment, law/grace, old/new. After a review of the status of the discipline of Old Testament theology, we began with a few definitions and a brief exploration of blessing-and-curse language. A blessing is a potent way to invoke, distribute, or celebrate the well-being that comes from divine favor. To bless is to convey some kind of benefit, but the focus is less on the benefit itself and more on the life or relationship enhanced by the blessing. Conversely, curses are expressions or wishes of misfortune, calamity, and evil. But blessings and curses are not mere wishes; they are performative utterances that either enhance or oppose to a life of fullness. Just as the focus of the blessing is the relationship enhanced by it, so the focus of the curse is more on the relationship that is in this case severed, and less on the actual curse itself. While the blessing effects a strengthening of solidarity with the community, the curse effects a separation from that community, including exclusion or banning. Functional models from social anthropology and parallels of blessings and curses in the ancient Near East illustrate that blessings and curses are widely distributed in many cultures, ancient and modern. God is the subject of both blessing and curse in the Old Testament, a thorny dilemma that many theologians have tended to evade. (Blessings and curses are therefore both divine prerogatives.) In addition to traditional insights from historical-critical research, new understandings from speech-act theory allow the interpreter a fresh methodology to reflect on ways that God enhances or opposes a life of fullness without viewing blessings and curses as some primitive, magical notion that has no place in a twenty-first-century reflection about God. The words of blessing and curse are not magically self-fulfilling, yet they are nevertheless incredibly potent, given both formal and informal social conventions. Speech-act theory brings a convincing challenge to the traditional view about the dynamic power of the word or the older idea of the power of the soul. Words produce effects because of the societal understanding of the function of speech acts, not because of some magical power of the spoken word alone. Speech-act theory allows for genuinely potent power in uttered speech without resorting to inflexible distinctions between magic and religion.

Before we move further, offering a recap of the trajectories of this theme might be helpful. First, the Old Testament begins with a threefold blessing, but humans shirk their responsibility to forward that divine purpose for the cosmos. Second, scholars have long noted the recurring pattern of sin, exile, and grace in the primeval history of Genesis 1–11. Third, they have pointed to a definite descending progression of curses along with a return to the language of creation, un-creation, and re-creation. All three of these trajectories demonstrate the curse's power and the need for the blessing. God's blessing to Abraham in Genesis 12 introduces something new, which from day one was broadly promised to all humanity. It is ironic that the only piece of real estate that Abraham ever owns is his grave. It is what he leaves to posterity that matters most. The narrowing of the promise of blessing-after-Babel to Abraham's family leads to an expansion of that same promise to the entire world. This blessing is an open-ended dynamic, which is unaltered, undiminished, and available. God's plan in Abraham's blessing is for nothing less than complete recovery of divine purpose for the cosmos. Yet the curse lurks insidiously around nearly every corner. The responsibility of blessing is no afterthought subsequent to the failure of Israel to faithfully execute that responsibility, but provides the very foundation to the biblical language of promise. In spite of numerous obstacles to that blessing (not the least of which is the exile of the entire family into Egypt), God delivers his people from the hand of the Egyptians and brings them to Sinai where they receive and learn Torah: divine instruction for being God's covenant people. But Israel violates the Torah while it is still being uttered; and Israel is forgiven even before they are confronted with their sin. That is the nature of covenant. Israel's unbelief and resulting exile in the wilderness leads to the death of an entire generation. The next generation begins with a hopeful blessing through an unlikely seer named Balaam, but like their predecessors, turn that blessing into curse at Baal Peor. When this new generation finally enters Moab, Moses recounts the law, and verbally utters the promise of blessing and threat of curse, not at all convinced that the people will have much hope of being faithful.

The Deuteronomistic History recounts stories of tribes, priests, and kings who follow this same pattern of sin, exile, and restoration. The three kings of the united monarchy serve as paradigms of blessing and curse: the ends of each of their reigns show that curse, not blessing, has characterized their final days. The prophetic irony made so scathing is that Israel, the source of blessing to all peoples, is now by metonymy a reproach, a byword, a taunt, and a curse—a curse incarnate. Thus, Israel is doomed to exile for its sins. The prophetic and apocalyptic literature both convey the divine working out of that curse. The curse comes to its sharpest focus in exile, where even after the historical return to Jerusalem, the authors of Daniel 9 and numerous other Second Temple Jewish texts are convinced that Israel still languishes in exile. Israel's cult incorporates blessings and curses into communal worship and sacred ritual. The wisdom tradition in ancient Israel daringly considers that a blameless man might indeed curse God, and presents the two-way instruction: an alternative outside covenantal theology to present the power of life's choices.

MALACHI AND THE CLOSE OF THE OLD TESTAMENT CANON

The Old Testament begins with a hopeful blessing. The end of the Old Testament, however, does not share that optimism, at least for the most part. Pervasive apathy and dark disillusionment rule the day—not excitement, promise, or hopeful expectation. Malachi's prophetic messages almost certainly arose from this period of empty malaise roughly a century after the second temple was completed. All the wonderful blessings that the prophet Haggai promises after the temple's completion (and he really did promise the moon) never really come to fruition. When there is no accountability, people get lazy. God calls Malachi the prophet to confront the people and jar them out of their lethargy. His method of startling people into realizing how far they have fallen is forceful, point-blank, and controversial. Using a question-and-answer, disputation format, he targets four fatal flaws to survival of the nation: disrespect for temple service by priests and laity, cessation of tithing, questionable marriages accompanied by heightened divorce rates, and the oppression of the poor. Malachi's message is couched in the first person. God is speaking through the prophet. Malachi distills the dilemma of sagging temple worship down to one issue: disrespect. Priests have become disillusioned by the seeming emptiness of earlier prophetic promises, so they show outright contempt and indifference to their priestly functions. Instead of following sacrificial rituals prescribed in the law, they unapologetically offer inferior sacrifices clearly disallowed by the Law.

> "But you profane it by saying, 'The Lord's table is defiled,' and, 'Its food is contemptible.' And you say, 'What a burden!' and you sniff at it contemptuously," says the Lord Almighty. "When you bring injured, lame or diseased animals and offer them as sacrifices, should I accept them from your hands?" says the Lord. "Cursed (*û'ārûr*) is the cheat who has an acceptable male in his flock and vows to give it, but then sacrifices a blemished animal to the Lord. For I am a great king," says the Lord Almighty, "and my name is to be feared among the nations." (Mal 1:12–14)

Given this malaise that breeds disrespect, Malachi's message to the priests is that Yahweh will turn what little blessing they have into curse. "'And now this admonition is for you, O priests. If you do not listen, and if you do not set your heart to honor my name,' says the Lord Almighty, 'I will send a curse upon you, and I will curse your blessings. Yes, I have already cursed them, because you have not set your heart to honor me'" (Mal 2:1–2). Malachi's direct question-and-answer format delineates all the shortcomings of Israel's religious leadership. The curse is explicit, yet not necessarily ultimate. Malachi picks up the prophetic metaphor of fruitful vineyards to retain the promise of blessing:

You are cursed with a curse, for you are robbing me, the whole
nation of you. Bring the full tithes into the storehouse, that there
may be food in my house. And thereby put me to the test, says
the LORD of hosts, if I will not open the windows of heaven for
you and pour down for you a blessing until there is no more
need. I will rebuke the devourer for you, so that it will not destroy the fruits of your soil, and your vine in the field shall not
fail to bear, says the LORD of hosts. Then all nations will call you
blessed, for you will be a land of delight, says the LORD of hosts.
(Mal 3:9–12, ESV)

The Old Testament closes with a handful of themes that would
later be raised in the early pages of the four New Testament Gospels: the
coming messenger, the Elijah figure, the Day of Yahweh, the law and the
prophets, and the promise of blessing and curse. But the very last words of
the Protestant Old Testament are a threat. This threat brings together all
five of these themes,

Remember the law of my servant Moses, the decrees and laws I
gave him at Horeb for all Israel. See, I will send you the prophet
Elijah before that great and dreadful day of the LORD comes.
He will turn the hearts of the fathers to their children, and the
hearts of the children to their fathers; or else I will come and
strike the land with a curse (ḥrm). (Mal 4:4–6)

Childs contends that the canonical form of Malachi demonstrates
Israel's conviction that law and prophets constituted an essential unity
within the divine purpose.[1] This closing threat of curse (ḥrm) sadly employs the same malediction that Zechariah promised would never happen
again. Is threat of curse really the last word of the Old Testament? If so,
what does this mean, not only for the message of the Old Testament, but
also for the New Testament and the Christian canon?

This Elijah figure is prominent in all four of the New Testament gospel accounts of the life and ministry of Jesus. Even though the four gospels
vary widely in their chronological approach to the life of Jesus, each gospel
opens with a remarkable parallel: an account of John the Baptizer, a messenger who prepares the way for the Messiah, Jesus. John brings together
both themes of promised messenger and promised Elijah figure. In John's
gospel, John the Baptizer explicitly denies that he is the fulfillment of
Malachi's Elijah prophecy (John 1:21). Indeed, he even denies that he is
a prophet. But Jesus, when asked about John, emphatically confirms the

1. Childs, *Introduction to the Old Testament as Scripture.*

ation of John with the closing prophecy of the Old Testament (Matt 11:10), affirms that not only was John a prophet but he fulfilled the Elijah prophecy.

NEW TESTAMENT CONNECTIONS WITH OLD TESTAMENT BLESSINGS AND CURSES

While much could be said about blessings and curses in the New Testament, I would like to stick to my promise in the opening chapter to let the Old Testament speak for itself, and only consider New Testament parallels when the New Testament specifically interprets Old Testament texts of blessing and cursing. As tempting as it might be to go into Jesus's cursing of the fig tree in Mark 11 or Paul's contention that no one can say "Jesus is accursed" by the Holy Spirit (1 Cor 12:3) or the Beatitudes in the Sermon on the Mount, or other intriguing texts, I will leave those for New Testament scholars more able to do them justice.[2] The New Testament does, however, directly interpret several key texts related to crucial Old Testament trajectories of blessings and curses. The most prominent among these are the blessings and curses of Deuteronomic law in Deuteronomy 27–30, and the blessing promise to Abraham in Genesis 12, 15, and 17. Revelation's concluding blessings and curses parallel the closing promises and threats of the book of Malachi. Thus, four key New Testament texts are Gal 3:6–14, Rom 10:1–13, Rom 4:1–25, and Rev 22:1–21.

The Curse in Galatians 3:6–13

In rapid succession, Paul strings together no less than six Old Testament texts in Galatians 3:6–14.

> Consider Abraham: "He believed God, and it was credited to him as righteousness." Understand, then, that those who believe are children of Abraham. The Scripture foresaw that God would justify the Gentiles by faith, and announced the gospel in advance to Abraham: "All nations will be blessed (*eulogia*) through you." So those who have faith are blessed along with Abraham, the man of faith. All who rely on observing the law are under a curse (*kataron*), for it is written: "Cursed (*epikataratos*) is

2. Other intriguing possibilities include the angry Paul bringing blindness on Bar Jesus (Acts 13:9–11) and Jesus's refusal to call fire down from heaven to destroy a Samaritan village (Luke 9:51–56).

everyone who does not continue to do everything written in the Book of the Law." Clearly no one is justified before God by the law, because, "The righteous will live by faith." The law is not based on faith; on the contrary, "The man who does these things will live by them." Christ redeemed us from the curse (*kataros*) of the law by becoming a curse (*katara*) for us, for it is written: "Cursed (*epikataratos*) is everyone who is hung on a tree." He redeemed us in order that the blessing (*eulogia*) given to Abraham might come to the Gentiles through Christ Jesus, so that by faith we might receive the promise of the Spirit. (Gal 3:6–14)

Paul begins by citing Gen 15:6. In spite of all Abraham's personal and external circumstances that at the time indicated otherwise, Abraham believes God's promise that one day he will have numerous descendants. Paul argues in Galatians 3 and elsewhere that it is Abraham's faith, not the law, that is now the new paradigm for Christian belief (the new paradigm for, in other words, what it means to be in God's family). Next, Paul cites the promise to Abraham in Genesis 12 as an assurance whereby the Gentiles would eventually also enter that spiritual family. Through this blessing promise, God preaches the gospel beforehand to Abraham. Paul would add to this argument in Romans 4 that this blessing promise was uttered before Abraham's circumcision, one of the three covenant signs mentioned earlier in this study. While baptism also plays a very important part in Paul's thinking, the covenant sign for New Testament believers is faith, not circumcision. It is those who have faith who are blessed along with Abraham, the model of faith (Gal 3:9). Gal 3:12 illustrates the opposition of law and faith. Each represents a completely different way of establishing one's standing before God. Paul also contrasts the "works of the law" with faith elsewhere (in Gal 2:16; 3:2; and 3:5). The most profound citation of an Old Testament text in Galatians 3 is the third citation, an explicit reinterpretation of the curse of Deut 27:26: "Cursed is anyone who does not uphold the words of this law by carrying them out. Then all the people shall say, 'Amen!'" This reference to the covenant ceremony at Shechem has been completely reinterpreted. But, as we shall see, that reinterpretation has puzzled students of the Bible for a long time. A quote from Habakkuk 2:4, Paul's fourth citation in Galatians 3, enhances this interpretive contrast: "but the righteous will live by his faith" (Rom 3:11). Paul's final citation, and the interpretive crux of the passage, can now be stated: "Christ redeemed us from the curse of the law by becoming a curse for us" (Gal 3:13). This last Old Testament citation is another curse, although one that is mentioned quite casually, a loose citation of Deut

21:22–23: "If someone guilty of a capital offense is put to death and their body is hung on a tree, you must not leave the body on the tree overnight. Be sure to bury him that same day, because anyone who is hung on a tree is under God's curse. You must not desecrate the land the LORD your God is giving you as an inheritance" (Deut 21:22–23). The result of the Messiah's redemptive work is that in Jesus the blessing of Abraham comes upon the Gentiles.

William Dumbrell contends that when Paul uses the phrase "those who rely on the works of the law," he is thinking of Jewish covenant relationships.[3] This expression does not necessarily refer to performance of the law but refers to a broader, more foundational communal relationship to the Mosaic covenant. Following the exclusionary understanding of the meaning of curse, to be cursed is to be cut off and outside the covenant grace of God. Paul's curse on law keepers simply follows the law keepers' own logic, which is that full obedience to the Mosaic law is a compulsory prerequisite for covenant membership.[4] For some in the early Jewish-Christian community, the Messiah did not come to abrogate the Mosaic covenant but only interpret it. So members of this community still required circumcision as a covenant sign, even for believers in the Messiah. Dumbrell suggests that Gal 3:10 applies to the *now* of a new covenant age. The day of the Sinai covenant and of Israel's exclusive role as carrier of Abraham's covenant and national association of righteousness is over. Now there is no accompanying means of forgiveness for those in Mosaic covenant. How one enters this new covenant has already been addressed by Paul in Gal 2:14–17. People are now justified by faith in Jesus the Messiah. The law's role, therefore, was for covenant maintenance, not covenant entrance. The selfless act of Christ's death and subsequent resurrection did not destroy merely the curse of the law, but ultimately, the curse of God who is the lawgiver.[5] The cross of Christ placed those in Christ firmly in the Abrahamic circle.

Perhaps the most formidable New Testament scholar to take up the theme of the curse in Galatians 3 in recent years is N. T. Wright. Wright's "Curse and Covenant," a chapter in *The Climax of the Covenant: Christ and the Law in Pauline Theology,* is well worth a close look here.[6] In this chapter, which features his exegesis of Gal 3:10–14, Wright begins by

3. Dumbrell, "Abraham and the Abrahamic Covenant."
4. Ibid., 22.
5. Ibid., 26.
6. Particularly in Wright, *The Climax of the Covenant,* 137–56.

pointing out the obvious: Gal 3:10–14 is one of the most complicated and controverted passages in Paul.[7] There are basically two interpretive sides. One is that Paul is combating legalism that espouses a works theology. The other—the case Wright makes—is that Paul is making the salvation-history point that justification by faith is now open to Gentiles.[8] Wright admits that the exegesis of this passage is complicated by several factors. First, the use of the first-person plural in vv. 13–14 is problematic. Does this use of the plural refer to Jewish Christians or to all Christians; or, as some have argued, is Paul simply confused? Second, Paul's use of Old Testament passages here is highly idiosyncratic and sometimes differs from his treatment of the same passages in Romans. Finally, there is a problem over what exactly Paul means by the death of Jesus, its significance, and its relation to the Torah. Traditionally this passage has been taken as a broad reflection of the theological core of Paul's atonement theology, but most now agree that such a broad, universal interpretation distorts the passage. Instead, this section of Paul's Letter to the Galatians deploys a particular argument, not an abstract doctrinal statement.

As for Jesus and the curse, Wright rejects the idea that the law somehow cursed Jesus and that the resurrection proved the law all wrong. This ill-advised theory posits that Deut 27:26 is the quintessential anti-Christian proof text. A crucified Messiah is cursed by God and is, therefore, no Messiah. Wright also rejects the contention of some who think Paul was simply confused, while he partially agrees with those who suggest that Jesus's vindication means that Gentiles, formerly cursed, are now welcome into God's family. Wright's contribution is to introduce a fresh reason as to *why* the Gentiles are now welcome into God's family. Wright's thesis builds on Paul's use of covenantal themes from Deuteronomy and Genesis. Galatians 3 is actually an extended discussion of covenant theology in Genesis 15. That is, Genesis 15 juxtaposes righteousness and faith in the same way that Galatians does. Paul's use of curse terminology in Galatians 3 draws on language from Deuteronomy 27–28. These blessings and curses are not take-it-or-leave-it options. Instead, Moses is convinced that Israel will eventually pull the wrong handle, make the wrong choice, experience exile, and yet also live see the other side of covenant failure (Deuteronomy 30). Deuteronomy 27–30 is all about exile and restoration;

---

7. Bonneau, "The Logic of Paul's Argument"; Braswell, "'The Blessing of Abraham' versus 'the Curse of the Law'"; O'Brien, "The Curse of the Law (Galatians 3.13)"; Young, "Who's Cursed—and Why?"

8. Wright, *Paul*, 29.

covenant judgment and covenant renewal. This is the Old Testament covenant context of Galatians 3: "It is the sharp expression of a theme which occupies Paul throughout the chapter: the fact that in the cross of Jesus, the Messiah, the curse of exile itself reached its height, and was dealt with once and for all, so that the blessing of covenant renewal might flow out the other side, as God always intended."[9]

No doubt Paul is thinking of Deuteronomy 27–30 because he quotes directly from Deut 27:26: "Cursed is anyone who does not uphold all the words of this law by carrying them out." In Galatians 3, there is no general abstract curse hanging over the human race. In context, this letter is not simply concerned with the matter of individual transgression anyway but with a much larger issue related to the life of the people as a whole. God entrusted the covenant promises to Israel, and these promises were to be lived under the law. But how could these promises reach their intended destination if the Torah itself renders them null and void due to Israel's willful and deliberate disobedience? The promises of Genesis 12, 15, and 17 were not just to Israel but to the worldwide human family.

Abraham's promises of blessing remain the very core of Paul's argument, but the Torah has veto power on those promises. The death of Christ means that the blessing of Abraham can come upon the Gentiles. God promised to Abraham a blessing for the whole world; but the Torah looked like it would prevent the blessing from getting to its destination. The death of Christ has broken through this logjam, and now the blessing can reach its destination securely. Again, Paul's point is not general or abstract but specifically relates to the people of Israel and the covenant promise.[10]

N. T. Wright offers three syllogisms, each with a suppressed minor premise, to explain various ways that the expression "by the works of the law" has been understood in scholarship. First, all who fail to do the whole Torah are cursed; no individual in fact does the whole Torah; therefore all who are live "by the works of the law" are cursed. Second, all who fail to do the whole Torah are *subject to* a curse; therefore all who live "by the works of the law" are *under the threat of* the curse. Third, living "by the works of the law" means being committed to earning one's own salvation. Such a process is an arrogant attempt to establish a claim upon God. Therefore all who are living by the works of the law are under a curse.[11] Wright

---

9. Wright, *The Climax of the Covenant*, 141.

10. Wright, *Paul*, 139.

11. Wright, *The Climax of the Covenant*, 144–45.

rejects all three syllogisms. Deuteronomic covenant theology provides the answer here.

> In Deuteronomy 27–30 Israel is warned about the blessing and the curse, and is warned, moreover, that she is likely to incur the curse through her hard-heartedness and willful disobedience. The remedy for this held out in this passage in Deuteronomy itself is not the usual Rabbinic scheme of repentance, sacrifice and atonement; it is the scheme which so many books of the Old Testament see worked out in Israel's history of exile and restoration; of judgment followed by mercy. And the pattern of judgment and mercy ends (Deut 30) with the renewal of the covenant by God's circumcising the hearts of his people so that they love him and keep his Torah from the heart.[12]

Again, this is not a question of individual sin but sins of the people. The king of the Jews took the brunt of the exile on himself. Wright's own fourth syllogism can now be stated: all who embrace Torah are thereby embracing Israel's way of life; Israel as a people has suffered, historically, the curse which the Torah held out if Israel did not keep it; therefore all who embrace Torah now are under the curse. (Wright admits that his thinking rests on syllogism 1 above). Consequently, Paul is not thinking of some future post-mortem damnation but Israel's historical exile.

The problem then is what happens to the covenant promises to Abraham in light of Torah. Ironically, the Torah stands between promise and fulfillment of those promises. The law brings a curse, not a blessing. God's solution comes by means of the strangest irony: the death of the Messiah. The crucifixion of the Messiah is the embodiment of the curse of exile, and its climactic act. That is why the context of Galatians 3 demands the use of the first-person plural here in v. 13: "Christ redeemed us from the curse of the law."

> Christ as the representative Messiah, has achieved a specific task, that of taking on himself the curse which hung over Israel and which on the one hand prevented her from enjoying full membership in Abraham's family and thereby on the other hand prevented the blessing of Abraham from flowing out to the Gentiles. The Messiah has come where Israel is, under the Torah's curse in order to be not only Israel's representative but Israel's redeeming representative. That which in the scheme of Deuteronomy, Israel needed if she incurred the curse of the law,

12. Ibid., 146.

is provided in Christ; the pattern of exile and restoration is acted out in his death the resurrection. He *is* Israel, going down to death under the curse of the law, and going through that curse to the new covenant life beyond.[13]

Paul does not say the law cursed Jesus and that then the resurrection showed the law to be in the wrong. The death of Jesus is instead understood in covenant-renewing terms. The death of Jesus brings blessing to the Gentiles. Thus the Gentiles can inherit the blessing as promised in Genesis 12, 15, and 18. Here is the watershed theological implication of Galatians 3. The Torah cannot demarcate the covenant family. Only faith can. The Messiah brings Israel's destiny on himself, and his death functions theologically as the fulfillment of the whole story of Israel. The death of Jesus *exhausts* the curse. Wright's argument is similar to that of James Dunn, who understands all too well that if the Old Testament curse means anything, it implies rejection and expulsion: "The point is, however, that the covenant-breaking Israelite thus cursed and expelled from the covenant land has in effect been expelled from the covenant. That is to say, he is placed in the same position as the one already outside the covenant, the Gentile. The cursed Israelite is like the uncovenanted Gentile."[14] In his death, Christ identifies with Jew and Gentile alike, and provides a way for both to enter into covenant relationship with God.

David Brondos has noted that Wright's argument fails to make enough of the fact that Galatians 3 quotes two different curses: one in Deut 27:26 and another in Deut 21:23.[15] They are two separate curses for several reasons—not the least of which is that the first has a definite article while the second does not. Even though same law is behind both curses, these two curses are to be distinguished from one another. The curse that Jesus underwent is the same curse deserved by humans. Brondos contends that the redemption underlying Gal 3:13 is the same as the story told in the Jesus tradition and in the primitive kerygma of the gospel, not some external reflection on atonement substitution or representation.[16] Jesus gave up his life seeking the redemption of others, and resurrection made God's promises a reality.

Craig Evans agrees, for the most part, with Wright's thesis that Israel was still in exile at the time of Jesus. He attempts to demonstrate that many

13. Ibid., 151–52.

14. Dunn, *The Theology of Paul the Apostle*, 225.

15. Brondos, "The Cross and the Curse," 25.

16. Ibid.," 23.

Jews in the first century saw themselves as in bondage, thus in exile.[17] Given the perception of exile, they sensed their own need for redemption. Evans cites Josephus's descriptions of two first-century Jewish revolutionary leaders: Theudas and the Egyptian Jew, who saw themselves as the successor of Moses to lead Israel out of exile. Evans points to a host of texts in Second Temple Jewish literature that also demonstrate this self-perception of present exile (Ben Sira 36:15–16; 48:10, Tobit 13:3; Baruch 2:7–10; 2 Macc 2:18, 4Q504 2:7–17, 3:7–12, 5:7–21; *1 Enoch* 89:73–75; *2 Baruch* 68:5–7). (Michael Knibb has made the same argument about the Qumran community's perception that the exile had not yet ended.[18]) Then, Evans raises six additional examples from Jesus's ministry that present the theme of the new Israel's restoration from exile:[19] Jesus's appointment of twelve as a reconstitution of Israel; Jesus's response to multiple requests for a sign; Jesus's appeal to Isa 56:7 as rationale for cleansing the temple; Jesus's allusion to themes of escape in Zech 2:6; Jesus's prophetic threats against Israel's rulers, which threaten their imposed, status-quo exile; and traces of exilic theology elsewhere in the New Testament and early Christian writings. Evans's work confirms our own supposition that the Old Testament linking of curse and exile is no mere geographic displacement alone but the cessation of life's possibilities, a withdrawal of fruitfulness.[20]

Abraham's Blessing-Promise in Galatians 3 and Romans 10

> Is the law then contrary to the promises of God? Certainly not! For if a law had been given that could give life, then righteousness would indeed be by the law. But the Scripture imprisoned everything under sin, so that the promise by faith in Jesus Christ might be given to those who believe. Now before faith came, we were held captive under the law, imprisoned until the coming faith would be revealed. So then, the law was our guardian until Christ came, in order that we might be justified by faith. But now that faith has come, we are no longer under a guardian, for in Christ Jesus you are all sons of God, through faith. For as many of you as were baptized into Christ have put on Christ. There is neither Jew nor Greek, there is neither slave nor free,

---

17. Evans, "Jesus & the Continuing Exile of Israel."
18. Knibb, "Exile in the Damascus Document."
19. Evans, "Jesus & the Continuing Exile of Israel," 91.
20. Balentine, "The Prose and Poetry of Exile."

> there is neither male nor female, for you are all one in Christ
> Jesus. And if you are Christ's, then you are Abraham's offspring,
> heirs according to promise. (Gal 3:21-29, ESV)

In this section of Galatians, the law, in principle, does not oppose the promise; yet the law does stand squarely between promise and fulfillment. The Torah simply does not have the power to impart righteousness; it only has the power to illuminate sin. If it had been able to illuminate righteousness, righteousness could have come by the law. From the beginning, the promise substantiates faith. God gave that promise to those who believe. Paul takes up the analogy of a guardian responsible for the heir: The law was the guardian for the Israelites until the Messiah came (Gal 3:24). Once the Messiah appeared, was crucified, and was raised again, the Jews have come of age and no longer need this guardian.[21] Their justification now derives from faith; and baptism, not circumcision is the covenant sign of the adoption as Abraham's offspring. Unlike circumcision, baptism conveys no differences in gender, social status, or ethnic status (Gal 3:28). Whoever belongs to Christ is an heir according to the promise. The cross brings to a halt any hint of Jewish privilege.

This reining in of privilege applies to Christians as well as to Jews. As I complete this project, I am on sabbatical in Jerusalem. It has always perplexed me how the blessing promise to Abraham in Gen 12:3 has become in many Christian camps *the* biblical basis for Christian Zionism, particularly for those who see things from a premillennial, dispensational theological perspective. What is most peculiar is that Gen 12:3 is interpreted by Christians, of *all* people, to refer to ethnic Jews, particularly when John the Baptist, Jesus, and Paul plainly taught otherwise (Matt 3:8-9; Luke 3:8; John 8:39-40; Rom 4:1-25; Gal 3:6-9). This nationalistic reading of Gen 12:3 romanticizes Jewish culture and mandates political support for Israel that is almost carte blanche. This reading underwrites theft of Palestinian land and violates biblical warnings about injustice. It carelessly assumes that the modern state of Israel is the fulfillment of the divine promise to the Jewish people. Timothy Weber has traced the historical trajectories of this idea in some Christian circles and has articulated its many flaws.[22] Moberly has also rightly questioned the hard-nosed distinction between unconditional and conditional covenants that permeates such theology (See also 1 Sam 2:30; Jer 7).[23]

21. Thielman, *Paul & the Law*, 132-33.

22. Weber, *On the Road to Armageddon.* Also see the helpful survey by Burge, *Whose Land? Whose Promise?*

23. Moberly, *The Theology of the Book of Genesis*, 163-75.

> If at any time I declare concerning a nation or a kingdom, that I
> will pluck up and break down and destroy it, and if that nation,
> concerning which I have spoken, turns from its evil, I will relent
> of the disaster that I intended to do to it. And if at any time I
> declare concerning a nation or a kingdom that I will build and
> plant it, and if it does evil in my sight, not listening to my voice,
> then I will relent of the good that I had intended to do to it. (Jer
> 18:7–10 ESV)

Moberly also warns that it is unwise to appeal to Israel's record as nullifying God's promises when the Christian record is equally dismal.

Paul understands that the redefinition of Abraham's descendants places the Gentiles in God's worldwide family. Elsewhere in Galatians, Paul refers to Abraham, Isaac, Sarah, and Hagar—all in context of the blessing promise of God. In Romans 4, Paul cites both covenant stories—Genesis 17 and Genesis 15—and quotes a blessing from Ps 32:1–2.

> Blessed is the one
>   whose transgressions are forgiven,
>   whose sins are covered.
> Blessed is the one
>   whose sin the LORD does not count against them
>   and in whose spirit is no deceit. (Ps 32:1–2)

When David speaks this blessing, he speaks it to the one who God counts righteous apart from works. Is this blessing only for the circumcised? No. Abraham received this blessing long before he was circumcised (circumcision being the sign of the covenant) in Genesis 17. Abraham's sign of circumcision was a seal of righteousness that came while he was still uncircumcised. The promise comes by faith and not through the law, and rests on grace, not only to all his offspring, but to all who walk in the footsteps of faith (Rom 4:12),

> No distrust made him waver concerning the promise of God,
> but he grew strong in his faith as he gave glory to God, fully
> convinced that God was able to do what he had promised. That
> is why his faith was "counted to him as righteousness." But the
> words "it was counted to him" were not written for his sake
> alone, but for ours also. It will be counted to us who believe in
> him who raised from the dead Jesus our Lord, who was deliv-
> ered up for our trespasses and raised for our justification. (Rom
> 4:20–25, ESV)

The next text under consideration, Romans 10, directly and un-equivocally interprets Deuteronomy 30. Deuteronomy 30 speaks of the restoration and return from exile.[24] Romans 10 interprets the work of Jesus as a finished work of return from exile. Deuteronomy 30 portrays the other side of covenant failure. God will restore the fortunes of Israel, have compassion, gather them from the peoples, and bring God's people back into the land, prosperous and numerous. In Deut 30:6 the language of circumcision is changed from describing physical circumcision to describing spiritual circumcision of the heart. God's people will love the Lord. As far as the curse, the curse will be on their enemies (Deut 30:7), not on the people of God. Yet the message of Deuteronomy 30 is self-defeating. When will all these things happen? When will Israel return from exile? When will the curse be over? When Israel obeys the Lord . . . something they simply and clearly cannot do (Deut 30:10). What is the solution? It is in Paul's other side of covenant failure, as he directly quotes Deut 30:12–13 in Rom 10:6, and Deut 30:14 in Rom 10:8:

> Now what I am commanding you today is not too difficult for you or beyond your reach. It is not up in heaven, so that you have to ask, "Who will ascend into heaven to get it and proclaim it to us so we may obey it?" Nor is it beyond the sea, so that you have to ask, "Who will cross the sea to get it and proclaim it to us so we may obey it?" No, the word is very near you; it is in your mouth and in your heart so you may obey it. (Deut 30:11–14)

> But the righteousness (*dikaiosunē*) that is by faith says: "Do not say in your heart, 'Who will ascend into heaven?'" (that is, to bring Christ down) "or 'Who will descend into the deep?'" (that is, to bring Christ up from the dead). But what does it say? "The word is near you; it is in your mouth and in your heart," that is, the word of faith we are proclaiming. (Rom 10:6–8)

Romans 10 is perhaps Paul's premier chapter on the nature of Christianity. One cannot find a clearer statement in the Bible about the essence of saving faith. Paul suggests (based on direct citation of Deuteronomy 30) that the word of faith is not something that is too hard to grasp or receive. This word of faith is actually quite near: it is in the mouth and in the heart. These two bodily metaphors encompass saving faith. There is an outward, confessional dimension and an inward, existential dimension.

---

24. On a similar theme in 4QMMT, which also interprets Deut 30:1–3 in light of return from exile, see Fraade, "Rhetoric and Hermeneutics in Miqsat Ma'ase Ha-Torah (4QMMT)."

Christianity, to put it simply, is both belief and confession. Both the inward and the outward are necessary for right relationship (*dikaiosunē*) with God. Note that Rom 10:8, cited from Deuteronomy 30:14: "The word is near you. It is in your mouth and in your heart, that is, the word of faith that we are proclaiming." This order is reversed in vv. 9–10, so that readers can be sure that it is not a matter of whether confession or faith comes first: "if you confess with your mouth, 'Jesus is Lord,' and believe in your heart that God raised him from the dead, you will be saved. For it is with your heart that you believe and are justified, and it is with your mouth that you confess and are saved" (Rom 10:9–10). Both belief and confession are necessary for righteousness. Confession with the mouth without belief in the heart is hypocrisy. Belief in the heart without any outward confession is an aborted faith that never experiences a healthy birth. This is consistent with what the Bible says elsewhere about the inward. Human belief comes from the heart, but actions do too. Both spring from the heart,

> For out of the abundance of the heart the mouth speaks. The good person out of his good treasure brings forth good, and the evil person out of his evil treasure brings forth evil. I tell you, on the day of judgment people will give account for every careless word they speak, for by your words you will be justified, and by your words you will be condemned." (Matt 12:34b–37, ESV)

Proverbs 4:23 echoes, "Above all else guard your heart, for it is the wellspring of life." Today it is common to use the expression "his heart just wasn't in it." The New Covenant speaks directly to Deuteronomy 30's idea of getting a new heart. Ezek 36:26 says, "I will give you a new heart. I will remove your heart of stone and give you a heart of flesh." Heb 8:8 echoes, "I will put my laws into their minds and I will write them on their hearts." Paul's argument from Deuteronomy 30 in Romans 10 is that righteousness begins in the heart. Nevertheless, one cannot exclude the outward either (v. 10): "For it is with your heart that you believe and are justified and with your mouth that you confess and are saved." What does one believe? That God raised Jesus the Messiah from the dead (v. 9). What does one confess? That Jesus is Lord (v. 13). Confession drives the inward focus outward. Faith is more than something private and personal. The test of a person's inward convictions is outward expression of faith through a life lived righteously (Matt 6:19-21). This groundbreaking section of Romans 10 ends with a promise: "Anyone who trusts in him will never be put to shame" (v. 11).

There Shall Be No More Curse: Revelation 22 in Context

It is well known that there are remarkable thematic parallels in the Christian canon between Genesis and Revelation. Ironically a handful of the common themes and theological concepts originally introduced in Genesis are for the most part virtually ignored in the rest of the Old Testament, not to be taken up again until in the book of Revelation. From a canonical perspective, these common themes bring the Bible's message full circle. The tree of life, the serpent, and the fall are examples of images from the primeval history that are virtually ignored until the final book of the Bible. Other important themes that fitfully occur elsewhere in the Bible but are particularly dominant in Genesis and Revelation include the following pairs: the first death (Genesis) and the death of death (Revelation), the first curse (Genesis) and the elimination of the curse (Revelation), the creation of the sun and moon (Genesis) and the new creation with no sun or moon (Revelation), the creation of the sea (Genesis) and the elimination of the sea (Revelation), the river that flows from the middle of the garden (Genesis) and the river that flows from the middle of the city (Revelation), the first blood sacrifice (Genesis) and the final blood sacrifice (Revelation), the image of God (Genesis) and the image of the beast (Revelation), and the motif of the city of Babel (Genesis) and the motif of the New Jerusalem (Revelation). In a new twist in Revelation on the creation, un-creation, and re-creation theme of Genesis 1–11, God forms a new creation patterned after the first one. The apocalyptic theme of Daniel 2 is taken up in the seventh trumpet of Rev 11:15: "The kingdom of the world has become the kingdom of our Lord and of his Christ, and he will reign for ever and ever." We argued earlier that this interpretive paradigm (that the kingdom of God will overtake the kingdom of the world) overshadows much of Daniel and is also a dominant theme in Revelation as well.

Paul Minear contends that the curses of Gen 3:15–20 dominate all of Revelation 12.[25] The enmity of curse between humans and the serpent is the backdrop of this pivotal chapter. Revelation 12 describes the release from the curses of Genesis 3 and 4. The pain in childbirth parallels the birth pangs of the woman in Rev 12:2: "She was pregnant and cried out in pain as she was about to give birth." The perpetual enmity between the woman's offspring and the serpent's is depicted in Rev 12:4, "The dragon stood in front of the woman who was about to give birth so that he might devour her child the moment it was born." The promise that one of Eve's

---

25. Minear, "Far as the Curse Is Found," 72.

offspring will bruise the serpent's head fulfills the curse on the serpent as Michael's heavenly forces defeat the great dragon and ancient serpent and heave him down to earth. Minear notes that the murder of Abel is the first illustration of the fulfillment of God's primordial curse, an example of enmity between the Eve's seed and the serpent's. He traces several other more subtle allusions in Revelation 12 to Genesis 4. Minear argues that the other seed of the woman, as well as the brothers of Rev 12:10, have overcome Satan by the blood of the Lamb, by the word of their testimony, and by their willingness to die as martyrs.

The book of Genesis opens the canon with a threefold blessing in Genesis 1. The book of Revelation concludes the canon with a sevenfold blessing (Rev 1:3 [2x]; 14:13; 16:15; 19:9; 20:6; 22:7, 14). Two of these blessings are in Revelation 22. Revelation 22 takes the prophetic theme of a fruitful vineyard to exponential extremes. The Edenic Tree of Life yields twelve kinds of fruit, a different fruit each month. The leaves of the Tree of Life are for the healing of the peoples, a significant adjustment from Ezek 47:12, which merely states, "their fruit will serve for food and their leaves for healing." John also takes up other themes common to the Little Apocalypse, the book of Daniel and Zechariah 14. The themes of the city, continuous light, plentiful water, attraction of the peoples, removal of the curse, and replacement of the temporal by the eternal are common tectonic and temporal shifts shared in these books. The Little Apocalypse (Isa 25:8) and Revelation 20–21 also share the theme of the death of death.

Eden imagery illustrates the enhancement of a life of fullness. It depicts the realization of God's presence in the midst of the human community. This depiction of God's dwelling in the midst of the city is a direct reflection of the covenant blessing mentioned in Lev 26:11 as well as the similar blessing in Zech 8:3. The city imagery takes up themes seen earlier in the Little Apocalypse and Zechariah 14. In this city, God's sovereignty, God's presence, and God's people's faithful service become a reality: "No longer will there be any curse. The throne of God and of the Lamb will be in the city, and his servants will serve him" (Rev 22:3). The symbolism of the throne of God in the midst of the city indicates that the kingdom of God now stands, and a river flowing through the middle of the city symbolizes a life of fullness. If there were any doubt whether the Bible teaches a general abstract curse hanging over the human race, this should by now be settled. The removal of the curse guarantees the abiding presence of God: "They will see his face, and his name will be on their foreheads" (Rev 22:4, ESV). Instead of the mark of Cain they will bear the name of the

Messiah. The allusion to Balaam's blessing ("the bright and morning star") in v. 16 solidifies the blessed state of this city. Revelation links Balaam's prophecy with the lineage of David. The New Testament gospels, particularly the Gospel of Matthew, exploit the Son of David theme. Luke depicts Jesus's birth in David's town. Revelation contributes three crucial Davidic metaphors: the key of David (Rev 3:7), the root of David (Rev 5:5), and the offspring of David (Rev 22:6).

The book of Revelation concludes with a twofold blessing, a fourfold invitation, one final threat, and one final promise. Those who keep the words of the prophecy (v. 7) and wash their robes (v. 14) are blessed. The fourfold invitation (v. 17) parallels the invitation in Deuteronomy 30 for humans to make fresh decisions, but in the context of Revelation that decision is to come to the Messiah, the Alpha and the Omega, the first and the last, the beginning and the end: cyphers for the very name of Yahweh.[26] With some poignant similarities to Malachi, Revelation's penultimate conclusion contains an ancient copyright curse similar to one in the *Letter of Aristeas*: a threat against the one who would add or take away from the words of this specific prophecy. The final promise affirms that the Messiah is coming. The New Testament ends just as the Old Testament begins: with a speech act. "Come, Lord Jesus!"

THREE THEOLOGICAL NOTIONS TOO TRIVIAL TO BE TRUE

The privileging of biblical blessings at the expense of their corresponding curses tends to trivialize several important biblical doctrines. Inherent in an Old Testament theology of blessings and curses is an absolute *refusal to trivialize life*. Life's decisions matter. That is why it is unfortunate that so many projects in Old Testament theology undercut or ignore the biblical concept of the curse. As Childs warned, one should not be too quick to move from threat to promise. Taking the curse seriously means that a person's decisions in this life really bear enduring consequences. The Old Testament corroborates time and time again the human penchant for turning God's blessing into curse. Here is where the two-way theology of Wisdom literature and the covenant blessing-and-curse language of Deuteronomy come together. Both affirm that wrong choices end in death just as surely as wise choices lead to life and fulfillment. In one sense, the promise of blessing and the threat of curse entail an ultimatum to carefully weigh one's choices in life. However, as Wright argues, the blessing

26. Mangina, *Revelation*, 249.

and the curse signify not simply a take-it-or-leave-it proposition. There is also a word of caution in this refusal to trivialize life. Two principles in Deuteronomic thought simply do not stand up theologically to the test of the rest of the canon of Scripture or to human common sense. These two principles are the law of succession and the law of proportion. The first law—the law of succession—is the idea that one deed necessarily leads a commensurate outcome. The law of succession is a theological quid pro quo. Any honest reading of the Old Testament admits that a high percentage of its literature upholds the law of succession. Yet the book of Job challenges the simplistic notion that if someone just follows Torah, everything will be all right, and life will be wonderful. The Old Testament stories about the ancestors also demonstrate repeatedly that often it is the possessor of the blessing who has to endure all manner of challenging hardship. Blessing does not mean a life free of turmoil. The second law—the law of proportion—is the idea that the punishment always fits the crime. Yahweh patently rejects this notion outright in the response from the whirlwind. The Psalms are full of complaints against Yahweh because the wicked lead charmed lives and their immoral lifestyles go unpunished for inordinately long periods of time. Israel's countertestimony, to adopt Brueggemann's language, was a summons to call God out on this injustice, to challenge God to take notice, and to do something about it. This thinking was especially pronounced because curses progressively intensified over Israel's history, and in the minds of the writers, the punishment was much more severe than the crime.

A second notion inherent in a theology of blessings and curses in the Old Testament is the absolute *refusal to trivialize election*. The message of the Old Testament is clear that from the beginning: God's plan was directed toward all humankind, all the peoples of the earth. In carrying out that plan, however, there was a certain narrowing of God's design through the election of one family. A handful of character pairings illustrate the theology of election in Genesis. While many other ethnic groups were a part of God's story, there was only one elect family. In the New Testament, that narrowing extended even further to one individual (to use the language of Barth, the elect one). The theological irony behind this is that the move toward an ever-expanding universality came through an ever-deepening particularism. Yet Paul's interpretation of the curse enhances the original intention of God's blessing to Abraham, which is for all the peoples of the earth to be in God's story, not just as participants, but as the chosen ones. This interpretation moves the non-elect and even the anti-elect to the top tier of God's decreed elect ones. The blessing and the curse provide a theology of history from Abraham, through the metanarrative of the Bible, to Jesus. We cannot, however, take this second notion at the expense of the first. God's foreordination does not preclude human freedom.

This discussion of Galatians 3 and its background in Deuteronomic covenant theology takes us back fifty years to Karl Barth's controversial doctrine of election. God's absolute decree, if one may speak of such a thing, is a decree of God's yes. This yes is God's gracious and intentional choice to be *for* humanity *in* Jesus Christ. Jesus is both the subject and object of divine election. Through the cross, Jesus redeemed humankind from the curse of the law by becoming a curse himself. To put it crassly, Jesus played both sides. Jesus embodied, through the incarnation, death, and resurrection, not only God's election and blessing of humanity but also God's denunciation and curse of human sin. Because of the incarnation, Jesus is both the electing God and the elect human. Revelation 5 makes this clear, as Jesus is the Lamb with seven horns (omnipotence), seven eyes (omniscience), and seven spirits (omnipresence), yet is the Lion of Judah, the Root of David. This concept of election allowed Barth to subscribe to traditional Reformed double predestination, albeit by coming through the back door. Since Jesus, the incarnate one, is the electing God, Jesus elects all humanity . . . in himself. Everyone who is in Christ is elect in him. Another way of saying this is that Jesus the Messiah completed that for which Israel was originally chosen, not because Israel fumbled the ball, but because Jesus the descendent of David represented faithful Israel. The promise of blessing is not Abraham's alone. By metonymy he is a blessing to all the peoples of the earth. This expressed linking of peoplehood and international blessing begins in Genesis 12 but extends throughout the entire Christian canon of both testaments. How will the elect community bless all peoples? It has already been done through the work of Jesus the Messiah. Because of this finished work, the broadening, missional purpose for the church can be seen throughout the pages of the Bible.

A final notion inherent in the theology of Old Testament blessings and curses is the absolute *refusal to trivialize divine providence*, particularly the uncomfortable side of divine providence whereby God stands in opposition to a life of fullness. Jeremiah 45:27—"I am watching over you for evil—is probably not one of those verses that people in the community of Christian faith keep in their Bible promise prayer books. The doctrine of providence affirms that God upholds and governs heaven and earth. Providence is a way of talking about God's directing creativity in relation to the course of events. But God does so in surprising ways. God disposes of creation in any way that God sees fit. Christianity does not affirm a deist god who simply stirs up the pot every so often and then walks away to attend to other matters. In 1963 Langdon Gilkey lamented the widespread neglect of the doctrine of providence, due in large part to the ways World War II and its horrors had shattered social optimism. Perhaps. Regardless, Charles Wood contends that the situation has not changed markedly since Gilkey wrote these words.[27] The doctrine of providence is often an unexamined element in Christian piety. And that doctrine has both positive and negative dimensions. Like Abraham, people experience God's blessings. Like Pharaoh, people can and do experience God's opposition to a life of fullness.

Every fisherman knows to fish the confluences of creeks and rivers. The confluence is where two or more autonomous currents mix, creating eddies that swirl together unpredictably, often in counterintuitive ways. The successful fisherman knows that the confluence is where the fish are. Along with the food for the fish, debris also drifts down from currents above, swirls about, and settles on the bottom. Along with the fish comes a certain amount of annoying debris. Thus it is with the doctrine of providence and its subsidiary doctrine called the doctrine of confluence or concurrence. The doctrine of confluence refers to the mysterious way that autonomous human choices mix with God's uncontested and sovereign will to accomplish God's purpose. In the Old Testament God often used human free will to accomplish ultimate divine will. God's purposes were often realized through Israel's own free choices, the choices of Israel's friends, and even the choice of Israel's enemies. The result of this confluence of human and divine sovereignty is often maddeningly counter intuitive, and annoying debris presents obstacles to easy intellectual solutions. Yet, that is where the fish are. In the case of blessings and curses, an adequate recognition of the theological implications of this theme forces the interpreter to deny exhaustive determinism that robs human life of its significance and recognize the cooperation of secondary human agents in divine providence.[28] The mix of human and divine agency is impossible to explain, but is nevertheless present in the texts of the Old Testament.

I have argued in this study that there have been three typical contemporary solutions to the theological problem of the curse. One is to ignore texts that associate God with curse. This is a simple solution but not a very

27. Wood, "Providence."

28. Olson, *Arminian Theology*, 116–20.

elegant one. Frankly, this solution relies much too heavily on traditional notions of the optimistic God of Christian theology (to use David Gunn's language), where evil is always something of an embarrassment to the tradition. It relies far less on the consistent yet discomforting witness of the Bible.

A second solution is Westermann's longitudinal one. Blessings and curses developed separately. The blessing developed along a diachronic path that eventually encompassed God's providential and benevolent care of creation. Curses, on the other hand, did not develop in any such way, retaining their magical quality. This gauzy solution to the annoying presence of curse texts in the Bible presents curses as merely old, outdated remnants of a primitive, tired folk religion. In this reading, the curse is something that for modern and postmodern society will simply have to go.

A third solution, one argued in this study, is to admit that the biblical materials support the contention that God stands to enhance *or* oppose a life of fullness, depending on decisions made by humans. Blessings and curses stand as a monumental challenge to those who take a Reformed position to extremes. There is a persistent reticence in curse language when such language is applied to God—a reticence that must be carefully considered, to be sure. God does not place curses on people like some magical, self-fulfilling improvised explosive device that sticks to the soul and waits for detonation at just the right time. At the same time, both Old and New Testaments affirm that God does oppose a life of unrepentant sin, and like the doctrine of God's wrath, this opposition is no emotional response. It is drawn from the very nature of God. Opposition to evil is a fundamental characteristic of God's character. From time to time, God may use secondary agents to bless or curse. The double agency, where God uses pagan peoples or the created order to bless or curse bears a consistent witness in the Scriptures. The Old Testament texts flatly warn that God's curse can put the entire creation in jeopardy. Consequently, Rom 8:22 speaks of the whole of creation groaning in anticipation of final redemption. Yet, note that nowhere in this study have I argued that blessing is equivalent to eternal salvation or that curse is tantamount to eternal damnation. To do so is to entirely miss the point that both blessing and curse are present realities for the community of faith. Our discussion of Galatians 3 and Deuteronomy 27–30 has revealed that the Messiah became a curse for us; Jesus's death completely did away with the curse of the law. This does not mean that for Christian believers there should only be talk of divine blessing. Nor does this mean that we ignore a collection of texts that testify to the reality of both blessings and curses. Again, this is wishful thinking to disregard an entire the vibrant biblical witness of curse texts that demonstrate God's displeasure with sin. I am not proposing a more sophisticated variation of the first option, which chooses to ignore the evidence from both testaments. I am simply advocating a recognition that redemption came when Jesus the Messiah assumed the curse on behalf of humanity. In addition to Paul's writings, the book of Revelation also takes up the theme of blessing and curses in the context of several Old Testament texts. The New Testament ends with an elimination of the curse, and the message of the gospel is that Jesus the Messiah has become a curse for us. As a result, Paul can claim in his Letter to the Ephesians,"Blessed be the God and Father of our Lord Jesus Christ, who has blessed us in Christ with every spiritual blessing in the heavenly places (Eph 1:3–4, ESV).

Works Cited

Achtemeier, Elizabeth. *The Old Testament and the Proclamation of the Gospel*. Philadelphia: Westminster, 1973.

Adams, Jim W. *The Performative Nature and Function of Isaiah 40–55*. Library of Hebrew Bible/Old Testament Studies 448. London: T. & T. Clark, 2006.

Adler, William. "The Apocalyptic Survey of History Adapted by Christians: Daniel's Prophecy of the 70 Weeks." In *The Jewish Apocalyptic Heritage in Early Christianity*, edited by James C. VanderKam and William Adler, 201–38. Minneapolis: Fortress, 1996.

Albertz, Rainer. *A History of Israelite Religion in the Old Testament Period*. 2 vols. Translated by John Bowden. OTL. Louisville: Westminster, 1995.

—————. "Religionsgeschichte Israels statt Theologie des Alten Testaments! Plädoyer für eine forschungsgeschichtliche Umorientierung." In *Religionsgeschichte Israels oder Theologie des Alten Testament?*, 3–24. Jahrbuch für Biblische Theologie 10. Neukirchen-Vluyn: Neukirchener, 1995.

Albertz, Rainer, and Rüdiger Schmitt. *Family and Household Religion in Ancient Israel and the Levant*. Winona Lake, IN: Eisenbrauns, 2012.

Alexander, T. Desmond. *From Paradise to the Promised Land: An Introduction to the Pentateuch*. 3rd ed. Grand Rapids: Baker, 2012.

—————. "Royal Expectations in Genesis to Kings." *TynBul* 49 (1998) 191–212.

Allison, Dale C., Jr. "Jesus and the Victory of Apocalyptic." In *Jesus and the Restoration of Israel*, edited by Carey C. Newman, 126–41. Downers Grove, IL: InterVarsity, 1999.

Alter, Robert. *The David Story: A Translation and Commentary of 1 and 2 Samuel*. New York: Norton, 1999.

—————. *The Wisdom Books: Job, Proverbs, and Ecclesiastes*. New York: Norton, 2010.

Anderson, Bernhard W. *Contours of Old Testament Theology*. Minneapolis: Fortress, 1999.

—————. *Out of the Depths: The Psalms Speak for Us Today*. Rev. ed. Philadelphia: Westminster, 1983.

Anderson, Jeff S. "Curses and Blessings: Social Control and Self Definition and the Dead Sea Scrolls." In *The Dead Sea Scrolls in Context: Integrating the Dead Sea Scrolls in the Study of Ancient Texts, Languages, and Cultures*, edited by Armin Lange et al., 47–60. VTSup 140. Leiden: Brill, 2010.

—————. "The Metonymical Curse as Propaganda in the Book of Jeremiah." *BBR* 8 (1998) 1–14.

—————. "The Social Function of Curses in the Hebrew Bible." *ZAW* 110 (1998) 11–15.

Works Cited

————"Two-Way Instruction and Covenantal Theology in the Epistle of Enoch." *Henoch* 28 (2006) 161–76.

Anderson, John E. *Jacob and the Divine Trickster: A Theology of Deception and YHWH's Fidelity to the Ancestral Promise in the Jacob Cycle.* Siphrut 5: Literature and Theology of the Hebrew Scriptures. Winona Lake, IN: Eisenbrauns, 2011.

Arnold, Bill T. "The Love-Fear Antinomy in Deuteronomy 5–11." *VT* 61 (2011) 551–69.

Austin, J. L. *How to Do Things with Words.* The William James Lectures 1955. Cambridge: Harvard University Press, 1962.

Baden, Joel S. "The Tower of Babel: A Case Study in the Competing Methods of Historical and Modern Literary Criticism." *JBL* 128 (2009) 209–24.

Balentine, Samuel E. "The Prose and Poetry of Exile." In *Interpreting Exile: Displacement and Deportation in Biblical and Modern Contexts,* edited by Brad E. Kelle et al., 345–63. SBL: Ancient Israel and Its Literature 10. Atlanta: SBL, 2011.

Baltzer, Klaus. *The Covenant Formulary: In Old Testament, Jewish, and Early Christian Writings.* Translated by David E. Green. Philadelphia: Fortress, 1971.

Barker, Kit. "Divine Illocutions in Psalm 137: A Critique of Nicholas Wolterstorff's 'Second Hermeneutic.'" *TynBul* 60 (2009) 1–14.

Barker, Paul A. "The Theology of Deuteronomy 27." *TynBul* 49 (1998) 277–303.

Barkay, Gabriel. "The Challenges of Ketef Hinnom: Using Advanced Technologies to Reclaim the Earliest Biblical Texts and Their Context." *NEA* 66 (2003) 162–71.

Barr, James. *The Concept of Biblical Theology: An Old Testament Perspective.* Minneapolis: Fortress, 1999.

————. *The Garden of Eden and the Hope of Immortality.* 1992. Reprinted, Eugene, OR: Wipf & Stock, 2003.

————. "The Literal, the Allegorical and Modern Biblical Scholarship." *JSOT* 46 (1990) 3–17.

————. *The Semantics of Biblical Language.* 1961. Reprinted, Eugene, OR: Wipf & Stock, 2004.

————. "Story and History in Biblical Theology." *JR* 56 (1976) 1–17.

Barth, Karl. *Church Dogmatics,* II/2: *The Doctrine of God, Part 2.* Edited by G. W. Bromiley and T. F. Torrance. Translated by G. W. Bromiley et al. Edinburgh: T. & T. Clark, 1957.

Baskin, Judith R. *Pharaoh's Counsellors: Job, Jethro, and Balaam in Rabbinic and Patristic Tradition.* BJS 47. Chico, CA: Scholars, 1983.

Beckwith, Roger T. *Calendar and Chronology, Jewish and Christian: Biblical, Intertestamental, and Patristic Studies.* AGJU 33. Leiden: Brill 1996.

Bell, Catherine. *Ritual Theory, Ritual Practice.* New York: Oxford University Press, 1992.

Beuken, W. A. M. "Job's Imprecation as the Cradle of a New Religious Discourse." In *The Book of Job,* edited by W. A. M. Beuken, 41–78. BETL 114. Leuven: Leuven University Press, 1994.

Biddle, Mark. *Deuteronomy.* Smyth & Helwys Bible Commentary. Macon, GA: Smyth & Helwys, 2003.

————. "The 'Endangered Ancestress' and the Blessing for the Nations." *JBL* 109 (1990) 599–611.

Birch, Bruce C. et al. *A Theological Introduction to the Old Testament.* 2nd ed. Nashville: Abingdon, 2005.

Blank, Sheldon H. "The Curse, Blasphemy, the Spell, and the Oath." *HUCA* 23 (1950–1951) 73–95.

————."Perish the Day!: A Misdirected Curse (Job 3:3)." In *Prophetic Thought: Essays and Addresses*, 61–64. Jewish Perspectives 2. Cincinnati: Hebrew Union College Press, 1977.

Blenkinsopp, Joseph. *Creation, Un-creation, Re-creation: A Discursive Commentary on Genesis 1–11*. London: T. & T. Clark, 2011.

————. *Wisdom and Law in the Old Testament: The Ordering of Life in Israel and Early Judaism*. Oxford Bible Series. Oxford: Oxford University Press, 1983.

Bohak, Gideon. *Ancient Jewish Magic: A History*. Cambridge: Cambridge University Press, 2008.

Bonneau, Normand. "The Logic of Paul's Argument on the Curse of the Law in Galatians 3:10–14." *NovT* 39 (1997) 60–80.

Bosman, H. L. "The Absence and Presence of God in the Book of Exodus as Theological Synthesis." *Scriptura* 85 (2004) 1–13.

Botha, J. Eugene. *Jesus and the Samaritan Woman: A Speech-Act Reading of John 4:1–42*. NovTSup 65. Leiden: Brill, 1991.

Braswell, Joseph P. "'The Blessing of Abraham' versus 'the Curse of the Law': Another Look at Gal 3:10 13." *WTJ* 53 (1991) 73–91.

Brettler, Mark. "Biblical History and Jewish Biblical Thought." *JR* (1997) 563–83.

Brichto, Herbert. *The Problem of "Curse" in the Hebrew Bible*. SBLMS 13. Atlanta: Society of Biblical Literature, 1963.

Briggs, Richard S. "Speech-Act Theory." In *Words & the Word: Explorations in Biblical Interpretation & Literary Theory*, edited by David G. Firth and Jamie A. Grant, 75–110. Downers Grove, IL: IVP Academic, 2008.

Bright, John. *A History of Israel*. 4th ed. Westminster Aids to the Study of the Scriptures. Louisville: Westminster John Knox, 2000.

————. *Jeremiah*. AB 21. New York: Doubleday, 1965.

Britt, Brian M. "Curses Left and Right: Hate Speech in Biblical Tradition." *JAAR* 78 (2010) 633–61.

Brondos, David. "The Cross and the Curse: Galatians 3.13 and Paul's Doctrine of Redemption." *JSOT* 81 (2001) 3–32.

Brown, William P. "Whatever Your Hand Finds to Do: Qohelet's Work Ethic." *Int* 55 (2001) 271–84.

Brueggemann, Walter. *Israel's Praise: Doxology against Idolatry and Ideology*. Philadelphia: Fortress, 1988.

————. "The Kerygma of the Deuteronomistic Historian." *Int* 22 (1968) 387–402.

————. "The Kerygma of the Priestly Writers." In *The Vitality of Old Testament Traditions*, edited by Walter Brueggemann and Hans Walter Wolff, 101–13. 2nd ed. Atlanta: John Knox, 1982.

————. *The Message of the Psalms: A Theological Commentary*. Minneapolis: Augsburg, 1984.

————. *Old Testament Theology: An Introduction*. Library of Biblical Theology. Nashville: Abingdon, 2008.

————. "On Coping with Curse: A Study of 2 Sam 16:5–14." *CBQ* (1974) 175–92. Reprinted in Brueggemann, *David and His Theologian: Literary, Social, and Theological Investigations of the Early Monarchy*, edited by K. C. Hanson, 137–56. Eugene, OR: Cascade Books, 2011.

————. *The Prophetic Imagination*. 2nd ed. Philadelphia: Fortress, 2001.

————. *Theology of the Old Testament: Testimony, Dispute, Advocacy*. Minneapolis: Fortress, 1997.

————. "Theology of the Old Testament: Testimony, Dispute, Advocacy Revisited." *CBQ* 74 (2012) 28–38.

Brueggemann, Walter, and Hans W. Wolff. *The Vitality of Old Testament Traditions*. 2nd ed. Atlanta: John Knox, 1982.

Brun, Lyder. *Segen und Fluch im Urchristentum*. Oslo: Dybwad, 1932.

Brunner, Emil. *Revelation and Reason: The Christian Doctrine of Faith and Knowledge*. Translated by Olive Wyan. Philadelphia: Westminster, 1946.

Burge, Gary M. *Whose Land? Whose Promise?: What Christians Are not Being Told about Israel and the Palestinians*. Cleveland: Pilgrim, 2003.

Burkert, Walter. *Structure and History in Greek Mythology and Ritual*. Sather Classical Lectures 47. Berkeley: University of California Press, 1979.

Campbell, Antony F., and Mark A. O'Brien. *Sources of the Pentateuch: Texts, Introductions, Annotations*. Minneapolis: Fortress, 1993.

————. Campbell "The Yahwist Revisited," Australian Biblical Review 27 (1979) 2–14.

Carlson, R. A. *David, the Chosen King: A Traditio-Historical Approach to the Book of Second Samuel*. Translated by Eric J. Sharpe. Stockholm: Almqvist & Wiksell, 1964.

Carr, David M. *Writing on the Tablet of the Heart: Origins of Scripture and Literature*. Oxford: Oxford University Press, 2005.

Carroll, Robert P. *Jeremiah: A Commentary*. OTL. Philadelphia: Westminister, 1986.

Cartlege, Tony W. *Vows in the Hebrew Bible and in the Ancient Near East*. JSOTSup 147. Sheffield: Sheffield Academic, 1992.

Cazelles, Henri. "*šry*." In *TDOT* 1:445–48. 1974.

Chaney, Marvin L. "Bitter Bounty: The Dynamics of Political Economy Critiqued by the Eighth-Century Prophets." In *The Bible and Liberation: Politics and Social Hermeneutics*, edited by Norman K. Gottwald and Richard Horsley, 250–63. The Bible & Liberation Series. Maryknoll, NY: Orbis 1993.

Chester, Tim, and Steve Timms. *Total Church: A Radical Reshaping around Gospel and Community*. Wheaton, IL: Crossway, 2008.

Childs, Brevard S. *Biblical Theology in Crisis*. Philadelphia: Westminster, 1974.

————. *The Book of Exodus*. OTL. Philadelphia: Westminster, 1974.

————. *Introduction to the Old Testament as Scripture*. Philadelphia: Fortress, 1979.

————. *Old Testament Theology in a Canonical Context*. Minneapolis: Fortress, 1985.

Christensen, Duane L. "Form and Structure in Deuteronomy 1–11." In *Das Deuteronomium: Enstehung, Gestalt, und Botschaft,* edited by Norbert Lohfink, 135–44. BETL 68. Leuven: Leuven University Press, 1985.

Church, F. Forrester, ed. *The Essential Tillich: An Anthology of the Writings of Paul Tillich*. New York: Macmillan, 1987.

Clements, R. E. *Jeremiah*. IBC. Atlanta: John Knox, 1988.

Clifford, Richard J. *The Cosmic Mountain in Canaan and the Old Testament*. HSM 4. Cambridge: Harvard University Press, 1972.

————. "The Exodus in the Christian Bible: The Case for 'Figural' Reading." *TS* 63 (2002) 345–61.

Clines, David J. A. "Biblical Interpretation in an International Perspective." *BibInt* 1 (1993) 84–86.

————. *Job 1–20*. WBC 17. Dallas: Word, 1989.

————. *The Theme of the Pentateuch*. JSOTSup 10. Sheffield: Department of Biblical Studies, University of Sheffield, 1978.

Coats, George W. "The Curse in God's Blessing: Genesis 12:1–4a in the Structure and Theology of the Yahwist." In *Die Botschaft und die Boten: Festschrift für Hans Walter Wolff,* edited by Jörg Jeremias and Lothar Perlitt, 31–41. Neukirchen-Vluyn: Neukirchener, 1981.

Cohn, Norman. *Cosmos, Chaos, and the World to Come: The Ancient Roots of Apocalyptic Faith.* 2nd ed. Yale Note Bene. New Haven: Yale University Press, 2001.

Collins John J. *The Apocalyptic Imagination.* Grand Rapids: Eerdmans, 1998.

———. *The Bible after Babel: Historical Criticism in a Postmodern Age.* Grand Rapids: Eerdmans, 2005.

———. *Daniel: A Commentary on the book of Daniel.* Hermeneia. Minneapolis: Fortress, 1993.

Cook, Stephen L. *Prophecy & Apocalypticism: The Postexilic Social Setting.* Minneapolis: Fortress, 1995.

Craigie, Peter. C. *The Book of Deuteronomy.* NICOT. Grand Rapids: Eerdmans, 1996.

Crenshaw, James L. *Old Testament Wisdom: An Introdocution.* Atlanta: John Knox, 1981.

Dafni, Amots. "The Supernatural Characters and Powers of Sacred Trees in the Holy Land." *Journal of Ethnobiology and Ethnomedicine* 3/10 (2007) 1–16.

Dahood, Mitchell. "Hebrew-Ugaritic Lexicography XII." *Bib* 55 (1974) 381–93.

Darr, Katheryn Pfisterer. *The Book of Ezekiel.* NIB 6. Nashville: Abingdon, 2001.

Dempster, Stephen. "Exodus and Biblical Theology: On Moving into the Neighborhood with a New Name." *Southern Baptist Journal of Theology* 12 (2008) 4–23.

deClaissé-Walford, Nancy L. *Reading from the Beginning: The Shaping of the Hebrew Psalter.* Macon, GA: Mercer University Press, 1997.

Dever, William H. "Social Structure in Palestine in the Iron II Period on the Eve of Destruction." In *Archaeology of Society in the Holy Land,* edited by Thomas Levy, 416–31. London: Leicester University Press, 1995.

Dick, Michael Brennan. "Job 31, The Oath of Innocence, and the Sage." *ZAW* 95 (1983) 31–53.

Dietrich, M. et al., eds. *Keilalphabetischen Texte aus Ugarit.* Vol 1. AOAT 24. Kevelaer: Butzon & Bercker, 1976.

Dimant, Devora. "The Seventy Weeks Chronology (Daniel 9:24–27) in the Light of New Qumranic Texts." In *The Book of Daniel,* edited by A. S. van der Woude, 57–76. BETL 106. Leuven: University Press, 1993.

Dirksen, Peter. "Israelite Religion and Old Testament Theology." *SJOT* 2 (1990) 96–100.

Dothan, Trude, and Moshe Dothan. *People of the Sea: The Search for the Philistines.* New York: Macmillan, 1992.

Dozeman,Thomas B., and Konrad Schmid, eds. *A Farewell to the Yahwist? The Composition of the Pentateuch in Recent European Interpretation* SBLSymS 34. Atlanta: Society of Biblical Literature, 2006.

Dumbrell, William J. "Abraham and the Abrahamic Covenant in Galatians 3:1–14." In *The Gospel to the Nations: Perspectives on Paul's Mission,* edited by Peter Bolt and Mark Thompson, 19–31. Downers Grove, IL: InterVarsity, 2000.

———. *Covenant and Creation: A Theology of Old Testament Covenants.* Nashville: Nelson, 2009.

———. "The Purpose of the Book of Job." In *The Way of Wisdom: Essays in Honor of Bruce K. Waltke,* edited by J. I. Packer and Sven K. Soderlund, 91–105. Grand Rapids: Zondervan, 2001.

Dunn, James D. G. *The Theology of Paul the Apostle*. Grand Rapids: Eerdmans, 1998.

Eaton, J. H. *Kingship and the Psalms*. 2nd ed. Biblical Seminar 3. Sheffield: JSOT Press, 1986.

Edelman, Diana V. *King Saul in the Historiography of Judah*. JSOTSup 121. Sheffield: Sheffield Academic, 1991.

Eichrodt, Walther. *Ezekiel*. Translated by Cosslett Quin. OTL. Philadelphia: Westminster, 1970.

———. *Theology of the Old Testament*. 2 vols. Translated by J. A. Baker. OTL. London: SCM, 1961

Emerton, John. "The Priestly Writer in Genesis." *JTS* 39 (1988) 396–400.

Enns, Peter. Review of *Old Testament Theology,* by Paul House, and *Theology of the Old Testament,* by Walter Brueggemann. *Beginning with Moses* blog. Online: http://beginningwithmoses.org/books/100/old-testament-theology/review.

Evans, Carl D., William W. Hallo, and John B. White, eds. *Scripture in Context: Essays on the Comparative Method*. Pittsburgh Theological Monograph Series. Pittsburgh: Pickwick Publications, 1980.

Evans, Craig A. "Jesus & the Continuing Exile of Israel." In *Jesus & the Restoration of Israel: A Critical Assessment of N. T. Wright's "Jesus and the Victory of God,"* edited by Carey C. Newman, 77–100. Downers Grove, IL: InterVarsity, 1999.

Evans, Donald D. *The Logic of Self-Involvement*. Library of Philosophy and Theology. London: SCM, 1963.

Faraone, Christopher A. "Molten Wax, Spilt Wine, and Mutilated Animals: Sympathetic Magic in Near Eastern and Early Greek Oath Ceremonies." *Journal of Hellenic Studies* 113 (1993) 60–80.

Faust, Avraham. "Socioeconomic Stratification in an Israelite City: Hazor VI as a Test Case." *Levant* 31 (1999) 179–90.

Feinstein, Eve Levavi. "The 'Bitter Waters' of Numbers 5:11–31." *VT* 62 (2012) 300–306.

Fensham, F. Charles. "Common Trends in Curses of the Near Eastern Treaties and the Kudurru Inscriptions Compared with Maledictions of Amos and Isaiah." *ZAW* 75 (1963) 155–75.

———. "Malediction and Benediction in Ancient Near Eastern Vassal Treaties and the Old Testament." *ZAW* 74 (1962) 1–9.

Finnegan, Ruth. "How to Do Things with Words: Performative Utterances among the Limba of Sierra Leone." *Man* 4 (1969) 537–52.

Fishbane, Michael. "Jeremiah IV 23–26 and Job III 3–13: A Recovered Use of the Creation Pattern." *VT* 21 (1971) 151–67.

———. "Studies in Biblical Magic: Origins, Uses, and Transformations of Terminology and Literary Form." PhD diss., Brandeis University, 1971.

Fleming, Daniel E. *The Legacy of Israel in Judah's Bible: History, Politics, and Reinscribing of Tradition*. New York: Cambridge University Press, 2012.

Fokkelman, J. P., *Narrative Art and Poetry in the Books of Samuel: King David* (vol 1). Van Gorcum, Amsterdam, 1981.

Fraade, Steven D. "Rhetoric and Hermeneutics in Miqsat Ma'ase Ha-Torah (4QMMT)." *Dead Sea Discoveries* 10 (2003) 150–61.

Frazier, James. *The Golden Bough: A Study in Magic and Religion*. London: Macmillan, 1890.

Fretheim, Terence E. *The Book of Genesis*. NIB 1. Nashville: Abingdon, 1994.

————. "Which Blessing Does Isaac Give Jacob?" In *Jews, Christians, and the Theology of the Hebrew Scriptures*, edited by Alice Ogden Bellis and Joel S. Kaminsky, 279–91. SBLSymS 8. Atlanta: Society of Biblical Literature, 2000.

————. "Word of God." In *ABD* 6:961–68.

Friedman, Richard Elliott. *The Disappearance of God: A Divine Mystery*. Boston: Little, Brown. 1995.

Gabler, J. P. "About the Correct Distinction between Biblical and Dogmatic Theology and the Right Definition of Their Goals." In *Kleine theologische Schriften: Opuscula academica 2*, edited by Th. A. Gabler and J. G. Gabler, 179–98. Ulm: Stettin, 1831.

Gall, August Freiherr von. *Die Einheitlichkeit des Buches Daniel*. Giessen: Ricker, 1895.

Gammie, John G. "Spatial and Ethical Dualism in Jewish Wisdom and Apocalyptic Literature." *JBL* 93 (1974) 356–85.

Gehman, Henry Snyder. "The Oath in the Old Testament." In *Grace upon Grace*, edited by James I. Cook, 51–63. Grand Rapids: Eerdmans, 1975.

Gerstenberger, Erhard S. "Life Situations and Theological Concepts of Old Testament Psalms." *OTE* 18 (2005) 82–92.

————. *Theologies in the Old Testament*. Translated by John Bowden. Minneapolis: Fortress, 2001.

Gese, Harmut. *Essays on Biblical Theology*. Translated by Keith Crim. Minneapolis: Augsburg, 1981.

————. *Lehre und Wirklichkeit in der alten Weisheit: Studien zu den Sprüchen Salomos und zu dem Buche Hiob*. Tübingen: Mohr/Siebeck, 1958.

————. "Tradition and Biblical Theology." In *Tradition and Theology in the Old Testament*, edited by Douglas A. Knight, 301–26. Philadelphia: Fortress, 1977.

Gilkey, Langdon B. "The Concept of Providence in Contemporary Theology." *JR* 41 (1963) 194–205.

————. *Reaping the Whirlwind: A Christian Interpretation of History*. New York: Seabury, 1976.

Goldingay, John. *Daniel*. WBC 30. Waco: Word, 1989.

————. *Old Testament Theology*. 3 vols. Downers Grove, IL: InterVarsity, 2003–2009.

————. "Old Testament Theology and the Canon." *TynBul* 59 (2008) 1–26.

————. *Psalms*. Vol 1, *Psalms 1–41*. 3 vols. Baker Commentary on the Old Testament Wisdom and Psalms. Grand Rapids: Baker Academic, 2006.

Good, Edwin M. "Job and the Literary Task: A Response." *Soundings* 56 (1973) 470–84.

Gordis, Robert. *The Book of Job: Commentary, New Translation, and Special Studies*. Moreshet Series 2. New York: Jewish Theological Seminary, 1978.

Gordon, Cyrus H. "Leviathan, Symbol of Evil." In *Biblical Motifs: Origins and Transformations*, edited by Alexander Altmann, 1–9. Philip W. Lown Institute of Advanced Judaic Studies, Brandeis University. Studies and Texts 3. Cambridge: Harvard University Press, 1966.

Gottwald, Norman K. "Domain Assumptions and Societal Models in the Study of Premonarchic Israel." In *Community, Identity, and Ideology: Social Science Approaches to the Hebrew Bible*, edited by Charles E. Carter and Carol L. Meyers, 170–81. Sources for Biblical and Theological Study 6. Winona Lake, IN: Eisenbrauns, 1996.

Gowan, Donald E. *Theology in Exodus: Biblical Theology in the Form of a Commentary*. Louisville: Westminster John Knox, 1994.

Gnuse, Robert K. "Redefining the Elohist." *JBL* 119 (2000) 201–20.

Greenburg Moshe. *Ezekiel 21–37*. AB 22A. New York: Doubleday, 1997.

Grüneberg, Keith N. *Abraham, Blessing, and the Nations: A Philological and Exegetical Study of Genesis* 12:3 *in Its Narrative Context.* BZAW 332. Berlin: de Gruyter, 2003.

Gunn, David M. *The Fate of King Saul: An Interpretation of a Biblical Story.* JSOTSup 14. Sheffield: JSOT Press, 1980.

Habel, Norman C. *The Book of Job.* OTL. Philadelphia: Westminster, 1985.

———. "The Form and Significance of the Call Narratives." *ZAW* 77 (1965) 297–323.

Hall, Kevin. "The Theology of Genesis 1–11." *SwJT* 44/1 (2001) 56–74.

Hallo, William, James C. Moyer, and Leo Perdue, eds. *More Essays on the Comparative Method.* Scripture in Context 2. Winona Lake, IN: Eisenbrauns, 1983.

Halpern, Baruch. *David's Secret Demons: Messiah, Murderer, Traitor, King.* The Bible in Its World. Grand Rapids: Eerdmans, 2001.

Hamilton, Victor P. *Exodus: An Exegetical Commentary.* Grand Rapids: Baker Academic, 2011.

Handy, Lowel D., ed. *The Age of Solomon: Scholarship at the Turn of the Millennium.* Studies in the History and Culture of the Ancient Near East 11. Leiden: Brill, 1997.

Hanson, K. C. "'How Honorable!' 'How Shameful!': A Cultural Analysis of Matthew's Makarisms and Reproaches." *Semeia* 68 (1996) 83–114. Online: www.kchanson. com/ARTICLES/mak.html.

Hanson, Paul D. *The Dawn of Apocalyptic.* Philadelphia: Fortress, 1975.

Hartman, Lars. *Asking for a Meaning: A Study of* 1 *Enoch* 1–5. Coniectanea Biblica. New Testament Series 12. Uppsala: Almqvist & Wiksell, 1979.

Hasel, Gerhard. *Old Testament Theology: Basic Issues in the Current Debate.* 4th ed. Grand Rapids: Eerdmans, 1991.

Hauge, Martin. "The Struggles of the Blessed in Estrangement I." *ST* 29 (1975) 1–30.

Hawkins, Ralph K. *The Iron Age I Structure on Mt. Ebal: Excavation and Interpretation.* BBRSup 6. Winona Lake, IN: Eisenbrauns, 2012.

Head, Peter M. "The Curse of Covenant Reversal: Deuteronomy 28:58–68 and Israel's Exile." *Churchman* 111 (1997) 218–26.

Hempel, Johannes. "Die israelitischen Anschauungen von Segen und Fluch im Lichte altorientalischer Parallelen." In *Apoxysmata: Vorarbeiten zu einer Religionsgeschichte und Theologie des Alten Testaments: Festgabe zum 30. Juli 1961,* 58–61. BZAW 81. Berlin: Töpelman, 1961. (Orig. pub. 1925.)

Hendricks, William L. *A Theology for Children.* Nashville: Broadman, 1980.

Heyler, Larry. "The Separation of Abraham and Lot: Its Significance in the Patriarchal Narratives." *JSOT* 26 (1983) 77–88.

Hill, A. E. "The Ebal Ceremony as Hebrew Land Grant." *JETS* 31 (1988) 399–406.

Hillers, Delbert R. *Covenant: The History of a Biblical Idea.* Seminars in the History of Ideas. Baltimore: Johns Hopkins University Press, 1969.

———. "Some Performative Utterances in the Bible." In *Pomegranates and Golden Bells: Studies in Biblical, Jewish, and Near Eastern Ritual, Law, and Literature in Honor of Jacob Milgrom,* edited by David P. Wright et al., 757–66. Winona Lake, IN: Eisenbrauns, 1995.

———. *Treaty-Curses and the Old Testament Prophets.* Biblica et orientalia; Sacra Scriptura antiquitatibus orientalibus illustrata 16. Rome: Pontifical Biblical Institute, 1964.

Hillyer, Norman. "Rock-Stone Imagery in 1 Peter." *TynBul* 22 (1971) 58–91.

Hoffmeier, James K. *Ancient Israel in Sinai: The Evidence for the Authenticity of the Wilderness Tradition.* Oxford: Oxford University Press, 2005.

Holladay, William L. *Jeremiah 2.* Hermeneia. Minneapolis: Fortress, 1989.

————. *The Psalms through Three Thousand Years: Prayerbook of a Cloud of Witnesses*. Minneapolis: Fortress, 1993.

House, Paul R. *Old Testament Theology*. Downers Grove, IL: InterVarsity, 1998.

Humphreys, W. Lee. *The Tragic Vision and the Hebrew Tradition*. OBT. Philadelphia: Fortress, 1985. Reprinted, Eugene, OR: Wipf & Stock, 2003.

Janzen, David. "An Ambiguous Ending: Dynastic Punishment in Kings and the Fate of the Davidites in 2 Kings 25.27–30." *JSOT* 33 (2008) 39–58.

Janzen, J. Gerald. *Job*. IBC. Atlanta: John Knox, 1985.

Jeremias, Jörg. "Worship and Theology in the Psalms." In *Psalms and Liturgy*, edited by Dirk J. Human and Cas J. A. Vos, 89–101. JSOTSup 410. London: T. & T. Clark, 2004.

Jewett, Paul K. *Man as Male and Female*. Grand Rapids: Eerdmans, 1975.

Joffee, Alexander. "The Rise of Secondary States in the Iron Age Levant." *Journal of the Economic and Social History of the Orient* 45 (2003) 425–67.

Johnson, Dan. G. *From Chaos to Restoration: An Integrative Reading of Isaiah 24–27*. JSOTSup 61. Sheffield: JSOT Press, 1988.

Jones, Bruce William. "The Prayer in Daniel IX." *VT* 18 (1968) 488–93.

Kaiser, Walter C., Jr. *Toward an Old Testament Theology*. Grand Rapids: Zondervan, 1979.

Kaminsky, Joel S. *Yet I Loved Jacob: Reclaiming the Biblical Concept of Election*. Nashville: Abingdon, 2007.

Keck, Leander E., ed. *The New Interpreter's Bible*. 12 vols. Nashville: Abingdon, 1999.

Kelle, Brad. "Dealing with the Trauma of Defeat: The Rhetoric of the Devastation and Rejuvenation of Nature in Ezekiel." *JBL* 128 (2009) 469–90.

Keller, C. A. "*qll*." In *Theologisches Hanwörterbuch zum Alten Testamen*, edited by Ernst Jenni with assistance from Claus Westermann, 2:641–47. 2 vols. Munich: Kaiser, 1971.

Kidner, Derek. *Genesis: An Introduction and Commentary*. TOTC. Downers Grove, IL: InterVarsity, 1967.

Kitz, Anne Marie. "Curses and Cursing in the Ancient Near East." *Religion Compass* 1/6 (2007) 615–27.

Kletter, Raz. "Between Archaeology and Theology: The Pillar Figurines from Judah and the Asherah." In *Studies in the Archaeology of the Iron Age in Israel and Jordan*, edited by A. Mazar, 179–216. JSOTSup 331. Sheffield: Sheffield Academic, 2001.

Knibb, Michael A. "Exile in the Damascus Document." *JSOT* 25 (1983) 99–117.

Knierim, Rolf. *The Task of Old Testament Theology: Method and Cases*. Grand Rapids: Eerdmans, 1995.

Knight, Douglas A. *Law, Power, and Justice in Ancient Israel*. Library of Ancient Israel. Louisville: Westminster John Knox, 2011.

————, ed. *Tradition and Theology in the Old Testament*. Philadelphia: Fortress, 1977.

Knoppers, Gary N. "Solomon's Fall and Deuteronomy." In *The Age of Solomon: Scholarship at the Turn of the Millennium*, edited by Lowell K Handy, 392–410. Studies in the History and Culture of the Ancient Near East 11. Leiden: Brill, 1997.

Korošec, Victor. *Hethitische Staatsverträge: Ein Beitrag zu ihre juristischen Wertung*. Leipziger Rechtswissenschaftlische Studien 60. Leipzig: Weicher, 1931.

Kraft, Robert A. "Barnabas and the Didache." In *The Apostolic Fathers: A New Translation and Commentary*, edited by Robert A. Grant, 134–62. New York: Nelson, 1965.

Works Cited

──────."Early Development of the Two-Way(s) Traditions, in Retrospect." In *For a Later Generation: The Transmission of the Traditions of Israel, Early Judaism, and Early Christianity*, edited by Randy Argall et al., 136–43 Harrisburg, PA: Trinity, 2000.

Kratz, Corinne A. "Genres of Power: A Comparative Analysis of Okiek Blessings, Curses, and Oaths." *Man* 24 (1989) 636–56.

Lamb, David T. "The Eternal Curse." In *For and Against David: Story in History in the Books of Samuel*, edited by A. Auld and Erik Eynikel, 315–24. BETL 232. Leuven: Peeters, 2010.

Lehmann, Manfred. "Biblical Oaths." *ZAW* 81 (1969) 74 –92.

Lemche, Niels Peter. *The Old Testament between Theology and History: A Critical Survey.* Louisville: Westminster John Knox, 2008.

Lemke, Werner. "Circumcision of the Heart: The Journey of a Biblical Metaphor." In *A God So Near: Essays on Old Testament Theology in Honor of Patrick D. Miller*, edited by Brent A. Strawn and Nancy R. Bowen, 299–319. Winona Lake, IN: Eisenbrauns, 2003.

Leuenberger, Martin. *Segen und Segenstheologien im alten Israel: Untersuchungen zu ihren religions- und theologiegeschichtlichen Konstellationen und Transformationen.* ATANT 90. Zurich: TVZ, 2008.

Levenson, Jon. *Creation and the Persistence of Evil.* San Francisco: Harper & Row, 1988.

──────. "The Davidic Covenant and Its Modern Interpreters." *CBQ* 41 (1979) 205–19.

──────. *Sinai and Zion: An Entry into the Jewish Bible.* San Francisco: Harper & Row, 1985.

Levine, Baruch. *Numbers 1–20.* AB 4. New York: Doubleday, 1993.

Levine, Herbert J. *Sing unto God a New Song: A Contemporary Reading of the Psalms.* Indiana Studies in Biblical Literature. Bloomington: Indiana University Press, 1995.

Lewis, Theodore J. "How Far Can Text Take Us: Evaluating Textual Sources for Reconstructing Ancient Israelite Beliefs about the Dead." In *Sacred Time, Sacred Place: Archaeology and the Religion of Israel*, edited by Barry M. Gittlen, 169–217. Winona Lake, IN: Eisenbrauns, 2002.

Lied, Liv Ingeborg. *The Other Lands of Israel: Imaginations of the Land in 2 Baruch.* Supplements to the Journal for the Study of Judaism 129. Leiden: Brill, 2008.

Linafelt, Tod. "The Undecidability of *brk* in the Prologue of Job and Beyond." *BibInt* 4 (1996) 154–72.

Linafelt, Tod et al., eds. *The Fate of King David: The Past and Present of a Biblical Icon.* Library of Hebrew Bible/Old Testament Studies 500. New York: T. & T. Clark, 2010.

Lohfink, Norbert "ḥrm." In *TDOT* 5:180–99. 1986.

Luc, Alex. "Interpreting the Curses in the Psalms." *JETS* 42 (1999) 395–410.

Lundbom, Jack R. "The Double Curse in Jeremiah 20:14–18." *JBL* 104 (1985) 589–99.

Mangan, Celine. "Blessing and Cursing in the Prologue of Targum Job." In *Targum and Scripture: Studies in Aramaic Translation and Interpretation in Memory of Ernest G. Clarke*, edited by Paul V. M. Flesher, 225–29. Studies in the Aramaic Interpretation of Scripture 2. Leiden: Brill, 2002.

Mangina, Joseph L. *Revelation.* Brazos Theological Commentary on the Bile. Grand Rapids: Brazos, 2010.

Mann, Thomas W. *The Book of the Torah: The Narrative Integrity of the Pentateuch.* 2nd ed. Eugene, OR: Cascade Books, 2013.

Martens, Elmer A. *God's Design: A Focus on Old Testament Theology.* 2nd. ed. Grand Rapids: Baker, 1994.

———. "Old Testament Theology since Walter C. Kaiser, Jr." *JETS* 50 (2007) 673–91.

Mason, Steven D. "Another Flood?: Genesis 9 and Isaiah's Broken Eternal Covenant." *JSOT* 32 (2007) 177–98.

Mauss, Marcel. *A General Theory of Magic.* London: Routledge & Kegan Paul, 1972.

Mays, James Luther. "The Place of the Torah-Psalms in the Psalter." *JBL* 106 (1987) 3–12.

———. *Psalms.* IBC. Louisville: Westminster John Knox, 1994.

McCabe, David R. *How to Kill Things with Words: Ananias and Sapphira under the Prophetic Speech-Act of Divine Judgment (Acts 4:32—5:11).* Library of New Testament Studies 454. New York: T. & T. Clark. 2011.

McCann, J. Clinton, Jr. *The Book of Psalms.* NIB. Nashville: Abingdon, 1996.

———. *The Shape and Shaping of the Psalter.* JSOTSup 159. Sheffield: Sheffield Academic, 1993.

McCarter, P. Kyle, Jr. *II Samuel.* AB 9. New York: Doubleday, 1984.

McCarthy, Dennis J. "Notes on the Love of God in Deuteronomy and the Father–Son Relationship between Israel and Yahweh." *CBQ* 27 (1965) 144–47.

———. *Treaty and Covenant.* Analecta Biblica 21. Rome: Biblical Institute Press, 1978.

McComiskey, Thomas E. "The Seventy Weeks of Daniel against the Background of Ancient Near Eastern Literature." *WTJ* 47 (1985) 19–25.

McConville, J. G. "The Shadow of a Curse: A 'Key' to Old Testament Theology." *Evangel* 3 (1985) 2–6.

McKane, W. "Poison, Trial by Ordeal, and the Cup of Wrath." *VT* 30 (1980) 474–92.

McKenzie, Steven L. *King David: A Biography.* Oxford: Oxford University Press, 2000.

———. "Saul in the Deuteronomistic History." In *Saul in Story and Tradition*, edited by Carl S. Ehrlich, 59–70. FAT 47. Tübingen: Mohr/Siebeck, 2006.

McKeown, James. *Genesis.* Two Horizons Old Testament Commentary. Grand Rapids: Eerdmans, 2008.

———. "A Theological Approach." In *Make the Old Testament Live: From Curriculum to Classroom*, edited by Richard S. Hess and Gordon Wenham, 48–60. Grand Rapids: Eerdmans, 1998.

Meadowcroft, Tim. "Exploring the Dismal Swamp: The Identity of the Anointed One in Daniel 9:24–27." *JBL* 120 (2001) 429–49.

Mendenhall, George E. *Law and Covenant in Israel and the Ancient Near East.* Pittsburgh: The Biblical Colloquium, 1955.

———. *The Tenth Generation: The Origin of Biblical Tradition.* Baltimore: Johns Hopkins University Press, 1973.

Meshel, Ze'ev. *Kuntillet 'Ajrud: An Iron Age II Religious Site on the Judah-Sinai Border.* Jerusalem: Israel Exploration Society, 2012.

Meyers Carol L., and Eric M. Meyers. *Haggai, Zechariah 1–8.* AB 25B. New Haven: Yale University Press, 1987.

———. *Zechariah 9–14.* AB 25C; New York: Doubleday, 1993.

Michal, Walter L. *Job in Light of Northwest Semitic.* Biblica et orientalia 42. Rome: Biblical Institute Press, 1987.

Milgrom, Jacob. *Numbers*. JPS Torah Commentary. Philadelphia: Jewish Publication Society, 1989.

Millar, William R. *Isaiah 24–27 and the Origin of Apocalyptic*. HSM 11. Missoula: Scholars, 1976.

Miller, Patrick D. *Interpreting the Psalms*. Philadelphia: Fortress, 1986.

―――. *They Cried to the Lord: The Form and Theology of Biblical Prayer*. Minneapolis: Fortress, 1994.

Miller, Robert D. *Covenant and Grace in the Old Testament: Assyrian Propaganda and Israelite Faith*. Perspectives on Hebrew Scriptures and Its Contexts. Piscataway, NJ: Gorgias, 2012.

Minear, Paul S. "Far as the Curse Is Found: The Point of Revelation 12:15–16." *NovT* 33 (1991) 71–77.

Mitchell, Christopher Wright. *The Meaning of BRK 'to Bless' in the Old Testament*. SBLDS 95. Atlanta: SBL, 1987.

Moberly, R. W. L. *The Bible, Theology, and Faith: A Study of Abraham and Jesus*. Cambridge Companions in Christian Doctrine 5. Cambridge: Cambridge University Press, 2000.

―――. *The Theology of the Book of Genesis*. Old Testament Theology. Cambridge: Cambridge University Press, 2009.

Mobley, Greg. "Glimpses of the Heroic Saul." In *Saul in Story and Tradition*, edited by Carl S. Ehrlich, 80–87. FAT 47. Tübingen: Mohr/Siebeck, 2006.

Moore, Michael S. "Ruth the Moabite and the Blessing of Foreigners." *CBQ* 60 (1998) 203–17.

Moore, R. D. "The Integrity of Job." *CBQ* 45 (1983) 17–31.

Mowinckel, Sigmund. *Psalmenstudien*. 6 vols. in 2. 1921–24. Reprinted, Amsterdam: Schippers, 1961.

―――. *The Psalms in Israel's Worship*. Vol. 2. Translated by D. R. Ap-Thomas. 1962. Reprinted, Biblical Resource Series. Grand Rapids: Eerdmans, 2004.

―――. "The Spirit and the Word in the Prophets." In *The Spirit and the Word: Prophecy and Tradition in Ancient Israel*, 83–99. Fortress Classics in Biblical Studies. Minneapolis: Fortress, 2002.

Muilenburg, James. "Abraham and the Nations: Blessing and World History." *Int* 19 (1965) 387–98.

Murphy, Roland E. *The Tree of Life: An Exploration of Biblical Wisdom Literature*. 2nd ed. Grand Rapids: Eerdmans, 1996.

Myers, David N. "Remembering Zakhor: A Super-Commentary." *History and Memory* 4 (1992) 129–46.

Nelson, Richard D. *Deuteronomy*. OTL. Louisville: Westminster John Knox, 2002.

Nicholson, Ernest W. *God and His People: Covenant and Theology in the Old Testament*. Oxford: Clarendon, 1986.

―――. "P as an Originally Independent Source in the Pentateuch." *IBS* 10 (1988) 192–206.

―――. *Preaching to the Exiles: A Study of the Prose Tradition in the Book of Jeremiah*. Oxford: Blackwell, 1970.

―――. "Story and History in the Old Testament." In *Language, Theology, and the Bible: Essays in Honor of James Barr*, edited by Samuel E. Balentine and John Barton, 135–50. Oxford: Clarendon, 1994.

Nickelsburg, George W. E. *1 Enoch 1*. Hermeneia. Minneapolis: Fortress, 2001.

————. "Seeking the Origins of the Two-Ways Tradition in Jewish and Christian Ethical Texts." In *A Multiform Heritage: Studies on Early Judaism and Christianity in Honor of Robert A. Kraft,* edited by Benjamin G. Wright, 95–108. Scholars Homage Series 24. Atlanta: Scholars, 1999.

Niehaus, Jeffrey J. *God at Sinai: Covenant and Theophany in the Bible and Ancient Near East.* Studies in Old Testament Biblical Theology. Grand Rapids: Zondervan, 1995.

Nitzan, Bilhah. *Qumran Prayer and Religious Poetry.* STDJ 12. Leiden: Brill, 1994.

Nogalski, James D. *The Book of the Twelve: Micah–Malachi.* Smyth & Helwys Bible Commentary 18B. Macon: Smyth & Helwys, 2011.

Noth, Martin. *The Deuteronomistic History.* JSOTSup 15. 2nd ed. Sheffield: JSOT Press, 1991.

————. *A History of Pentateuchal Traditions.* Translated by Bernhard W. Anderson. 1972. Reprinted, Chico, CA: Scholars, 1981.

O'Brien, Kelli S. "The Curse of the Law (Galatians 3.13): Crucifixion, Persecution, and Deuteronomy 21.22–23." *JSOT* 29 (2006) 55–76.

Ollenburger, Ben C., ed. *Old Testament Theology: Flowering and Future Sources for the Bible and Theological Study.* Sources for Biblical and Theological Study 1. Winona Lake, IN: Eisenbrauns, 2004.

————. *The Book of Zechariah.* NIB 7. Nashville: Abingdon, 1996.

Olson, Dennis T. *The Death of the Old and the Birth of the New: The Framework of the Book of Numbers and the Pentateuch.* BJS 71. Chico, CA: Scholars, 1985.

————. "How Does Deuteronomy Do Theology?" In *A God So Near: Essays on Old Testament Theology in Honor of Patrick D. Miller,* edited by Brent A. Strawn and Nancy R. Bowen, 201–13. Winona Lake, IN: Eisenbrauns, 2003.

————. *Numbers.* IBC. Louisville: John Knox, 1996.

Olson, Roger. *Arminian Theology: Myths and Realities.* Downers Grove, IL: IVP Academic, 2006.

Onibere, S. G. A. "Potent Utterance: An Essay on the Bini View of a Curse." *EAJT* 4 (1986) 161–69.

Oswalt, John H. "Isaiah 24–27: Songs in the Night." *CTJ* 40 (2005) 76–84.

Overholt, Thomas W. "Prophecy: The Problem of Cross-Cultural Comparison." In *Community, Identity, and Ideology: Social Science Approaches to the Hebrew Bible,* edited by Charles E. Carter and Carol L. Meyers, 404–22. Sources for Biblical and Theological Study 6. Winona Lake, IN: Eisenbrauns, 1996.

Parker, Simon B. "The Vow in Ugaritic and Israelite Narrative Literature." *UF* 11 (1979) 693–700.

Parpola, Simo, and Kazuko Watanabe, eds. *Neo-Assyrian Treaties and Loyalty Oaths.* State Archives of Assyria 2. Helsinki: Helsinki University Press, 1988.

Patrick, Dale. *The Rhetoric of Revelation in the Hebrew Bible.* OBT. Minneapolis: Fortress, 1999.

Paul, M. J. "King Josiah's Renewal of the Covenant (2 Kgs 22–23)." In *Pentateuchal and Deuteronomistic Studies,* edited by C. Brekelsmans and J. Lust, 269–76. BETL 94. Leuven: Leuven University Press, 1990.

Pedersen, Johannes. *Der Eid bei den Semiten: In seinem Verhältnis zu verwandten Erscheinungen sowie die Stellung des Eides im Islam.* Studien zur Geschichte und Kultur des islamischen Orients 3. Strassburg: Trübner, 1914.

————. *Israel, Its Life and Culture.* 2 vols. London: Oxford University Press, 1926.

Pelham, Abigail. "Job's Crisis of Language: Power and Powerlessness in Job's Oaths." *JSOT* 36 (2012) 33–54.

Works Cited

Penchansky, David. *The Betrayal of God: Ideological Conflict in Job.* Literary Currents in Biblical Interpretation. Louisville: Westminster John Knox, 1990.

Perdue, Leo G. *The Collapse of History: Reconstructing Old Testament Theology.* 2nd ed. OBT. Minneapolis: Fortress, 2005.

———. "Old Testament Theology since Barth's *Epistle to the Romans.*" In *Biblical Theology: Introducing the Conversation,* edited by Leo G. Perdue et al., 55–136. Library of Biblical Theology. Nashville: Abingdon, 2009.

———. *The Sword and the Stylus: An Introduction to Wisdom in the Age of Empires.* Grand Rapids: Eerdmans, 2008.

———. *Wisdom & Creation: The Theology of the Wisdom Literature.* 1994. Reprinted, Eugene, OR: Wipf & Stock, 2009.

———. *Wisdom in Revolt: Metaphorical Theology in the Book of Job.* JSOTSup 112. Sheffield: Sheffield Academic, 2009.

Perry, T. A. *God's Twilight Zone: Wisdom in the Hebrew Bible.* Peabody, MA: Hendrickson, 2008.

Pettys, Valerie Forstman. "Let There Be Darkness: Continuity and Discontinuity in the Curse of Job 3." *JSOT* 98 (2002) 89–104.

Polzin, Robert. "Curses and Kings: a Reading of 2 Samuel 15–16." In *The New Literary Criticism and the Hebrew Bible,* edited by J. Cheryl Exum and David J. A. Clines, 201–26. 1994. Reprinted, Valley Forge, PA: Trinity, 1994.

———. "The Framework of the Book of Job." *Int* 28 (1974) 182–200.

Porter, J. R. "Biblical Classics III. Johannes Pedersen: *Israel.*" *ExpTim* 90 (1978–79) 36–40.

Portier-Young, Anathea E. *Apocalypse against Empire: Theologies of Resistance in Early Judaism.* Grand Rapids: Eerdmans, 2011.

Preuss, Horst Dietrich. *Old Testament Theology.* Translated by Leo G. Perdue. 2 vols. OTL. Louisville: Westminster John Knox, 1995–96.

Prichard, James B., ed. *Ancient Near Eastern Texts Relating to the Old Testament.* 3rd ed. Princeton: Princeton University Press, 1969.

Rad, Gerhard von. *Genesis: A Commentary.* Rev. ed. OTL. Translated by John H. Marks. Philadelphia: Westminster, 1972.

———. *Old Testament Theology.* Translated by D. M. G. Stalker. 2 vols. New York: Harper & Row, 1962–65.

Ray, Benjamin. "Performative Utterances in African Rituals." *History of Religions* 13 (1973) 16–35.

Redditt, Paul. "Daniel 9: Its Structure and Meaning." *CBQ* 62 (2000) 236–49.

———. "Once Again, the City in Isaiah 24–27." *HAR* 10 (1986) 317–35.

Reid, S. B. *Psalms and Practice: Worship, Virtue, and Authority.* Collegeville, MN: Liturgical, 2001.

Rendtorff, Rolf. *The Canonical Hebrew Bible: A Theology of the Old Testament.* Translated by David E. Orton. Tools for Biblical Study Series 5. Leiden: Deo, 2005.

———. *The Problem of the Process of Transmission in the Pentateuch.* Translated by John J. Scullion. JSOTSup 89. Sheffield: JSOT Press, 1990.

Reventlow, Graf Henning. *Problems of Old Testament Theology in the Twentieth Century.* Philadelphia: Fortress, 1985.

Ringgren, Helmer. "The Impact of the Ancient Near East on Israelite Tradition." In *Tradition and Theology in the Old Testament,* edited by Douglas A. Knight, 31–46. Philadelphia: Fortress, 1977.

Ritner, Robert K. *The Mechanics of Ancient Egyptian Magical Practice*. Studies in Ancient Oriental Civilization 54. Chicago: Oriental Institute of the University of Chicago, 1993.

Robbins, Vernon K., ed. *Semeia 64: The Rhetoric of Pronouncement*. Atlanta: Society of Biblical Literature, 2003.

Roberts, J. J. M. *The Bible and the Ancient Near East: Collected Essays*. Winona Lake, IN: Eisenbrauns, 2002.

———. "Isaiah in Old Testament Theology." In *Interpreting the Prophets*, edited by James Luther Mays and Paul J. Achtemeier, 62–74. Philadelphia: Fortress, 1987.

Robertson, David. *The Old Testament and the Literary Critic*. GBS: Old Testament Series. Philadelphia: Fortress, 1977.

Rofé, Alexander. *Deuteronomy: Issues and Interpretation*. Old Testament Studies. London: T. & T. Clark, 2002.

Rogerson, J. W. *Anthropology and the Old Testament*. Atlanta: John Knox, 1978.

———. "Can a Doctrine of Providence be Based on the Old Testament?" In *Ascribe to the Lord: Biblical & Other Essays in Memory of Peter C. Craigie*, edited by Lyle Eslinger and Glen Taylor, 529–43. JSOTSup 67. Sheffield: JSOT Press, 1988.

Römer, Thomas C. *The So-Called Deuteronomistic History: A Sociological, Historical, and Literary Introduction*. London: T. & T. Clark, 2005.

Rowley, H. H. *The Book of Job*. NCB. Grand Rapids: Eerdmans, 1970.

Sanders, J. T. "When Sacred Canopies Collide: The Reception of the Torah of Moses in the Wisdom Literature of the Second-Temple Period." *JSJ* 32 (2001) 121–36.

Sandmel, Samuel. "Parallelomania." *JBL* 81 (1962) 1–13.

Sarna, Abraham. *Understanding Genesis*. Shocken Paperbacks on Judaica. Heritage of Biblical Israel 1. New York: Schocken, 1978.

Scharbert, Josef. "*'lh*." In *TDOT* 1:262–66. 1974.

———. "*'rr*." In *TDOT* 1:405–18. 1974.

———. "*brk*." In *TDOT* 2:302–8. 1975.

———. "*qll*." In *TDOT* 13:37–44. 2004.

Schley, Donald G. *Shiloh: A Biblical City in Tradition and History*. JSOTSup 63. Sheffield: JSOT Press, 1989.

Schmid, Hans Heinrich. *Der sogennante Jahwist: Beobachtungen und Fragen zur Pentateuchforschung*. Zurich: TVZ, 1976.

Schmidt, Hans. *Das Gebet der Angleklagten im Alten Testament*. BZAW 49. Giessen: Töpelmann, 1928.

Schniedewind, William. *Society and the Promise to David: The Reception History of 2 Samuel 7:1–17*. New York: Oxford University Press, 1999.

Schottroff, Willy. *Der altisraelitische Fluchspruch*. WMANT 30. Neukirchen-Vluyn: Neukirchener, 1969.

Schwartz, Regina M. *The Curse of Cain: The Violent Legacy of Monotheism*. Chicago: Uni-versity of Chicago Press, 1997.

Searle, John. *Speech Acts: An Essay in the Philosophy of Language*. Cambridge: Cambridge University Press, 1970.

Seebass, Horst. "*bḥr*." In *TDOT* 1:83–85. 1974.

———. "Garizim und Ebal als Symbole von Segen und Fluch." *Biblica* 62 (1982) 22–31.

Seitz, Christopher R. *Word without End: The Old Testament as Abiding Theological Witness*. 1998. Waco: Baylor University Press, 2004.

Works Cited

Silva, Moisés. "The New Testament Use of the Old Testament: Text, Form, and Authority." In *Scripture and Truth*, edited by D. A. Carson and John A. Woodbridge, 147–65. 2nd ed. Grand Rapids: Baker, 1992.

Silver, Morris. *Prophets and Markets: The Political Economy of Ancient Israel.* Social Dimensions of Economics. Boston: Kluwer-Nijhoff, 1983.

Simcha, Shalom Brooks. *Saul and the Monarchy: A New Look.* Society for Old Testament Study. Aldershot, UK: Ashgate, 2005.

Skorupsky, John. *Symbol and Theory: A Philosophical Study of Theories of Religion in Social Anthropology.* Cambridge: Cambridge University Press, 1976.

Smith, Mark S. *The Early History of God: Yahweh and Other Deities in Ancient Israel.* 2nd ed. The Biblical Resource Series. Grand Rapids: Eerdmans, 2002.

———. *The Origins of Biblical Monotheism: Israel's Polytheistic Background and the Ugaritic Texts.* New York: Oxford University Press, 2001.

———. "The Psalms as a Book for Pilgrims." *Int* 46 (1992) 156–66.

Smith, Ralph L. *Micah–Malachi.* WBC 32. Waco: Word, 1984.

Smith-Christopher, Daniel L. *The Religion of the Landless: The Social Context of the Babylonian Exile.* Bloomington, IN: Meyer-Stone, 1989.

Smoak, Jeremy D. "Building Houses and Planting Vineyards: The Early Inner-Biblical Discourse on an Ancient Israelite Wartime Curse." *JBL* 127 (2008) 19–35.

Speiser, E. A. "The Angelic Curse: Exodus 14:20." *JAOS* 80 (1960) 198–200.

Spieckermann, Hermann. "YHWH Bless You and Keep You: The Relation of History of Israelite Religion and Old Testament Theology Reconsidered." *SJOT* 23 (2009) 165–82.

Stendahl, Krister. "Biblical Theology, Contemporary." In *IDB*, 1:418–32. Nashville: Abingdon, 1962.

Stendebach, F. J. "ṣlm." In *TDOT* 12:394–95. 2004.

Stern, David. "Recent Trends in Biblical Source Criticism." *JBQ* 36 (2008) 182–86.

Strawn, Brent A. "Keep/Observe/Do—Carefully—Today!" In *A God So Near: Essays on Old Testament Theology in Honor of Patrick D. Miller*, edited by Brent Strawn and Nancy Bowen, 215–40. Winona Lake, IN: Eisenbrauns, 2003.

Stulman, Louis. *The Prose Sermons of the Book of Jeremiah.* SBLDS 83. Atlanta: Scholars, 1986.

Sylva, Dennis. "The Blessing of a Wounded Patriarch: Genesis 27:1–40." *JSOT* 32 (2008) 267–86.

Talmon, Shemaryahu. "The Comparative Method in Biblical Interpretation—Principles and Problems." In *Congress Volume: Göttingen, 1977*, 320–56 . VTSup 29. Leiden: Brill, 1978.

Tambiah, Stanley J. "Form and Meaning of Magical Acts: A Point of View." In *Modes of Thought: Essays on Thinking in Western and Non-Western Societies*, edited by Robin Horton and Ruth Finnegan, 199–229. London: Faber, 1973.

Thiel, Winfred. *Die deuteronomistische Redaktion von Jeremia 26–45.* WMANT 82. Neukirhen-Vluyn: Neukirchener, 1981.

Thielman, Frank. *Paul & the Law: A Contextual Approach.* Downers Grove, IL: Inter-Varsity, 1994.

Thiessen, Matthew. "The Form and Function of the Song of Moses (Deuteronomoy 32: 1–43)." *JBL* 123 (2004) 401–24.

Thiselton, Anthony C. *New Horizons in Hermeneutics: The Theory and Practice of Transforming Biblical Reading.* Grand Rapids: Zondervan, 1992.

———. "The Supposed Power of Words in Biblical Writings." *JTS* 25 (1974) 283–99.

Thomas, Keith. *Religion and the Decline of Magic*. London: Penguin, 1991.

Thompson, Leonard L. "Mapping an Apocalyptic World." In *Sacred Places and Profane Spaces: Essays in the Geographics of Judaism, Christianity, and Islam*, edited by Jamie Scott and Paul Simpson-Housley, 115–17. Contributions to the Study of Religion 30. New York: Greenwood, 1991.

Thompson, J. A. *The Book of Jeremiah*. NICOT. Grand Rapids: Eerdmans, 1980.

Thompson, Thomas L. "If David Had Not Climbed the Mount of Olives." *BibInt* 8 (2000) 42–58.

Tigay, Jeffrey H. *Deuteronomy*. JPS Torah Commentaries. Philadelphia: Jewish Publication Society, 1996.

Timmer, Daniel. "God's Speeches, Job's Responses, and the Problem of Coherence in the Book of Job: Sapiential Pedagogy Revisited." *CBQ* 71 (2009) 286–305.

Toorn, Karol van der. "Theology, Priests, and Worship in Canaan and Ancient Israel." In *Civilizations of the Ancient Near East*, edited by Jack M. Sasson, 3:2043–58. New York: Scribner, 1995.

Upton, Bridget Gilfillan. *Hearing Mark's Endings: Listening to Ancient Popular Texts through Speech-Act Theory*. BibIntSer 79. Leiden: Brill 2006.

Ussishkin, David. *The Village of Silwan: The Necropolis from the Period of the Judean Kingdom*. Jerusalem: Israel Exploration Society, 1993.

Vang, Carston. "God's Love according to Hosea and Deuteronomy." *TynBul* 62/2 (2011) 173–94.

Vanhoozer, Kevin. J. *First Theology: God, Scripture & Hermeneutics*. Downers Grove, IL: InterVarsity Press, 2002.

———. *Is There a Meaning in This Text? The Bible, the Reader, and the Morality of Literary Knowledge*. Grand Rapids: Zondervan, 1998.

———. "The Semantics of Biblical Literature: Truth and Scripture's Diverse Literary Forms." In *Hermeneutics, Authority and Canon*, edited by D. A. Carson and John D. Woodbridge, 53–104. 1986. Reprinted, Eugene, OR: Wipf & Stock, 2005.

Vannoy, J. Robert. *Covenant Renewal at Gilgal: A Study of 1 Samuel 11:14—12:25*. Cherry Hill, NJ: Mack, 1978.

Van Rooy, H. F. "Deuteronomy 28:69—Superscript or Subscript?" *Journal of Northwest Semitic Languages* 14 (1988) 215–22.

Van Seters, John. *Abraham in History and Tradition*. New Haven: Yale University Press, 1975.

———. "David: Messianic King or Mercenary Ruler?" In *Community Identity in Judean Historiography*, edited by Gary N. Knoppers and Kenneth A Ristau, 27–39. Winona Lake, IN: Eisenbrauns, 2009.

Vogt, Peter T. *Deuteronomic Theology and the Significance of Torah: A Reappraisal*. Winona Lake, IN: Eisenbrauns, 2006.

Walsh, Carey Ellen. *The Fruit of the Vine: Viticulture in Ancient Israel*. HSM 60. Winona Lake, IN: Eisenbrauns, 2000.

Waltke, Bruce K., and James M. Houston. *The Psalms as Christian Worship: A Historical Commentary*. Grand Rapids: Eerdmans, 2010.

Walton, John H. *Ancient Near Eastern Thought and the Old Testament: Introducing the Conceptual World of the Hebrew Bible*. Grand Rapids: Eerdmans, 2006.

Watson, Francis. *Text and Truth: Redefining Biblical Theology*. Edinburgh: T. & T. Clark, 1997.

Watson, Wilfred G. E., and Nicolas Wyatt. *Handbook of Ugaritic Studies*. Handbuch der Orientalistik. Erste Abteilung, Nahe und der Mittlere Osten 39. Leiden: Brill, 1999.

Weber, Max. *Ancient Judaism*. Translated and edited by Hans H. Gerth and Don Martindale. New York: Free Press, 1952.

———. *The Sociology of Religion*. London: Methuen, 1965.

Weber, Timothy P. *On the Road to Armageddon: How Evangelicals Became Israel's Best Friend*. Grand Rapids: Baker Academic, 2004.

Wehmeier, Gerhard. *Der Segen im Alten Testament: Eine semasiologische Untersuchung der Wurzel brk*. Theologischen Dissertationen 6. Basel: Reinhardt, 1970.

Weinfeld, Moshe. "Ancient Near Eastern Patterns in Prophetic Literature." *VT* 27 (1977) 178–95.

———. "The Covenant of Grant in the Old Testament and the Ancient Near East." *JAOS* 90 (1970) 184–203.

———. *Deuteronomy and the Deuteronomic School*. 1972. Reprinted, Winona Lake, IN: Eisenbrauns, 1992.

———. "Deuteronomy's Theological Revolution." *BRev* 12 (1996) 38–42.

———. "The Loyalty Oath in the Ancient Near East." *UF* (1976) 379–414.

Weiss, Meir. *The Story of Job's Beginning*. Publications of the Perry Foundation for Biblical Research in the Hebrew University of Jerusalem. Jerusalem: Magnes, 1983.

Weitzman, Steven. *Solomon: The Lure of Wisdom*. Jewish Lives. New Haven: Yale University Press, 2011.

Wenham, Gordon J. "Deuteronomy and the Central Sanctuary." *TynBul* 22 (1971) 109–18.

———. "Reflections on Singing the Ethos of God." *EurJT* 18 (2009) 115–24.

———. "The Symbolism of the Animal Rite in Gen 15: A Response to G. Hasel." *JSOT* 22 (1982) 134–37.

Westermann, Claus. *Blessing in the Bible and the Life of the Church*. Translated by Keith Crim. OBT 3. Philadelphia: Fortress, 1978.

———. *Elements of Old Testament Theology*. Translated by Douglas W. Stott. Atlanta: John Knox 1982.

———. *Genesis 1–11: A Commentary*. Continental Commentaries. Translated by John J. Scullion. Minneapolis: Fortress, 1994.

———. *Genesis 12–36: A Commentary*. Continental Commentaries. Translated by John J. Scullion. Minneapolis: Augsburg, 1981.

Whybray, R. N. *The Making of the Pentateuch: A Methodological Study*. JSOTSup 53. Sheffield: JSOT Press, 1987.

———. "Old Testament Theology, a Non-Existent Beast?" In *Scripture, Meaning, and Method*, edited by Barry P. Thompson, 168–80. Hull: Hull University Press, 1987.

Widyapranawa, S. H. *The Lord Is Savior: Faith in National Crisis; A Commentary on the Book of Isaiah 1–39*. Grand Rapids: Eerdmans, 1990

Wilcox, John T. *The Bitterness of Job: A Philosophical Reading*. Ann Arbor: University of Michigan Press, 1989.

Williamson, Paul R. *Abraham, Israel, and the Nations: The Patriarchal Promise and Its Covenantal Development in Genesis*. JSOTSup 315. Sheffield: Sheffield Academic Press, 2000.

Wilson, Gerald H. *The Editing of the Hebrew Psalter*. SBLDS 76. Chico, CA: Scholars, 1981.

————. "The Prayer of Daniel 9: Reflection on Jeremiah 29." *JSOT* 48 (1990) 91–99.

Wilson, Robert R. "Prophecy and Ecstasy: A Reexamination." In *Community, Identity, and Ideology: Social Science Approaches to the Hebrew Bible*, edited by Charles E. Carter and Carol L. Meyers, 404–22. Sources for Biblical and Theological Study 6. Winona Lake, IN: Eisenbrauns, 1996.

————. *Prophecy and Society in Ancient Israel*. Philadelphia: Fortress, 1980.

Wolff, Hans Walter. "The Kerygma of the Yahwist." In *The Vitality of Old Testament Traditions*, edited by Walter Brueggemann and Hans Walter Wolff, 41–66. 2nd ed. Atlanta: John Knox, 1982.

————. "Prophets from the Eighth through the Fifth Centuries." In *Interpreting the Prophets*, edited by James L. Mays and Paul J. Achtemeier, 14–26. Philadelphia: Fortress, 1987.

Wolterstorff, Nicholas. *Divine Discourse: Philosophical Reflections on the Claim That God Speaks*. Cambridge: Cambridge University Press, 1995

Wood, Charles M. "Providence." In *An Oxford Handbook of Systematic Theology*, edited by John Webster et al., 91–104. Oxford Handbooks. Oxford: Oxford University Press, 2007.

Wright, Benjamin G., III, and Lawrence M. Wills. *Conflicted Boundaries in Wisdom and Apocalypticism*. SBLSymS 35. Atlanta: SBL, 2005.

Wright, Christopher J. H. *The Mission of God: Unlocking the Bible's Grand Narrative*. Downers Grove, IL: IVP Academic, 2006.

Wright, N. T. *The Climax of the Covenant: Christ and the Law in Pauline Theology*. Minneapolis: Fortress, 1991.

————. *Jesus and the Victory of God*. Christian Origins and the Question of God 2. Minneapolis: Fortress, 1996.

————. *The New Testament and the People of God*. Minneapolis: Fortress, 1992.

————. *Paul: In Fresh Perspective*. Minneapolis: Fortress, 1995.

Ya'ari, Ehud, and Ina Friedman. "Curses in Verses." *The Atlantic Magazine* 267 (February 1991) 22–26.

Yamauchi, Edwin M. "Magic in the Biblical World." *TynBul* 34 (1983) 169–200.

Yarchin, William. "Imperative and Promise in Genesis 12:1–3." *Studia Biblica et Theologica* 10 (1980) 164–78.

Yerushalmi, Yosef Hayim. *Zakhor: Jewish History and Jewish Memory*. The Samuel and Althea Stroum Lectures in Jewish Studies. Seattle: University of Washington Press, 1982.

Young, Norman H. "Who's Cursed—and Why? (Galatians 3:10–14)." *JBL* 117 (1998) 79–92.

Zenger, Erich. *A God of Vengeance?: Understanding the Psalms of Divine Wrath*. Translated by Linda M. Maloney. Louisville: Westminster John Knox, 1994.

————. *Der Psalter in Judentum und Christentum*. Herder's Biblical Studies 18. Freiburg: Herder, 1998.

Zevit, Ziony. *The Religions of Ancient Israel: A Synthesis of Paralactic Approaches*. London: Continuum, 2001.

————. "Three Ways to Look at the Ten Plagues." *BRev* 7 (1990) 16–23, 42.

Zimmerli, Walther. "Biblical Theology." In *The Fiery Throne: The Prophets and Old Testament Theology*, edited by K. C. Hanson, 118–37 + 54–58. Fortress Classics in Biblical Studies. Minneapolis: Fortress, 2003.

————. "I Am Yahweh." In *I Am Yahweh*, edited by Walter Brueggemann, 1–28. Translated by Douglas W. Stott. Atlanta: John Knox, 1982.

————. *Old Testament Theology in Outline*. Translated by David E. Green. Atlanta: John Knox, 1978.

————. "Zum Problem der 'Mitte des Alten Testament.'" *Evangelische Theologie* 35 (1975) 97–118.

Index of Subjects

magic, magical word power, 28,
32, 36, 37, 40–44, 46–51,
48n69, 48n70, 48n72, 48n73,
48n74, 56, 87, 116–17, 164,
267, 267n45, 280, 280n21,
326, 348
Melchizedek, 71, 113–14, 123–24,
137
metonymy, metonymical curse, 27,
34–35, 118, 142, 157, 209,
228–230, 229n19, 233, 240,
265, 327, 346
mission, commission, 16, 23, 44, 73,
96n16, 106, 111–13, 111n5,
126, 138, 153, 156, 177, 189,
206, 205, 307, 346
Moab, 22, 36–37, 59, 60, 63, 69, 70,
78–80, 121, 123, 124n21,
137n2, 158–59, 162–63, 166,
166n15, 170, 175, 185, 195,
211, 327
Monotheism, 41, 43n50, 44, 45n57,
179
Moses, 14, 21, 23, 30, 54, 58, 59,
61–62, 64–65, 69, 73–82, 86,
88, 126, 130–130, 136–78,
185, 189–90, 193, 207,
216–17, 244–46, 269–70,
299, 312–13, 321, 324, 327,
329, 333, 337
Mount of Olives, 317, 321–23,
321n45,
music, 198, 242–245, 248, 257
Nathan, 197–205, 208, 213
narrative, 14, 20, 22, 34n22, 43, 54,
57–59, 61–63, 67–77, 80–83,
87, 94–97, 109, 111, 113,
117, 120–24, 127, 130, 132–
34, 135–39, 145–47, 149–50,
153, 157, 159, 162, 166, 171,
183–84, 189, 190–91, 200,
203, 212, 231, 233, 245, 271,
286, 298, 314, 325, 346
new covenant, 7, 33,95, 129, 150,
174, 332, 336, 341
Noah, 66, 70, 95, 99, 101, 105, 121,
125–26, 130, 181, 303

oaths, 22, 30–31, 34–35, 34n22,
34n24, 35n27, 40, 51n81, 73,
114, 124, 128, 141–42, 160,
165n13167, 169, 170, 178,
185–186, 192–93, 218, 229,
263, 267–68, 274, 274n7,
280, 282, 282n24, 284,
284n26, 285, 303, 312, 315,
319, 323
obedience, 46, 56, 63–64, 67–68, 76,
79, 112, 123, 130, 133, 143,
167, 169, 173, 175–76, 182,
288, 332
Old Testament theology
challenges, 1–25
center, 5–6, 23
contested nature, 2
task, 14
ordeal, 31, 31n11, 48, 67, 76, 141,
267–270, 270n50, 270n51,
313
performative utterances, 20, 26–27,
37, 49–50, 50n78, 50n80, 58,
61, 68, 72, 83, 85, 87, 116,
162, 164, 216–17, 244–45,
248, 261–65, 271, 273, 325
Pharaoh, 21, 54, 61, 66, 71–74,
80n26, 91–92, 117, 119, 124,
133, 136–37, 144–51, 166,
170, 322, 347
Philistines, 103, 114–15, 123, 162,
188–90, 192–94, 198, 206,
216
plagues, 25, 58, 61, 74, 136–38,
138n4, 144, 146, 150
priestly source, 58, 65–66, 99, 128,
151
primeval history, 21, 54, 58–60, 65,
68–70, 83, 91, 95–96, 98–99,
102, 109, 111, 113, 121, 132,
326, 342
promise, 5, 7, 21–24, 30, 34n24, 41,
46, 49, 52–56, 59–62, 59n4,
65, 67–69, 71–74, 76, 78–79,
81, 86, 94–101, 107, 109–13,
117, 121–22, 126–33, 138,
141, 143, 146, 149, 151, 156,
158–59, 162, 16–166, 168–70

Index of Authors

Index of Authors

Index of Scripture
and Other Ancient Texts

〜

NEW TESTAMENT

Made in the USA
San Bernardino, CA
17 June 2016